Warfare in the Age of
Gaius Julius Caesar

CAESAR

Warfare in the Age of
Gaius Julius Caesar
VOLUME 2
Brundisium & Massilia to Munda
49 BC to 45 BC

Theodore Dodge

LEONAUR

Warfare in the Age of Gaius Julius Caesar—Volume 2:
Brundisium & Massilia to Munda, 49 BC to 45 BC
by Theodore Dodge

Leonaur is an imprint of Oakpast Ltd

ISBN: 978-1-78282-158-8 (hardcover)
ISBN: 978-1-78282-159-5 (softcover)

http://www.leonaur.com

Publisher's Notes

Contents

CHAPTER 25

Camps, Sieges and Ballistics

In camp the men had tents, which were carried in the column by pack-mules. In winter-quarters the camps were larger and more carefully entrenched, but similar to the daily camps. These latter could be entrenched in a few hours. Little change in fortification and siege work took place from Alexander's era to Caesar's. The walls of the Italian cities were by no means like those of Babylon and Nineveh; but they were high and well built, and much skill was put to defend and take them. The same sheds and screens for approaching walls were used; mounds and towers were built, and the lines of contra and circumvallation were thrown up as of yore. The walls were undermined or battered down by rams. Sorties were made by the garrison to destroy the besieger's works. The ballistic machines of the Romans do not strike us as being as good as those of Alexander, whose field artillery was excellent and easily transported. Still there were small engines used on the walls of camps and sometimes in line of battle. Caesar's sieges were expert; that of Alesia is one of the finest of antiquity.

We do not know exactly how Caesar's camps were laid out. Polybius gives us the plan of the Roman camps in the Second Punic War; Hyginus gives us that of the time of the empire. As Rüstow says, what is common to both was no doubt a constituent of Caesar's camp. Caesar's was presumably much the same as either, the changes relating merely to the differences in organization of troops. Caesar had no definite number of auxiliaries, as was usual in the War against Hannibal, and the camp was calculated accordingly. Its general arrangement was what it had been for centuries. It was pitched on high ground, fronting down a slope, favourably near wood and water, and away from probable opportunity for ambush. A desirable place was the

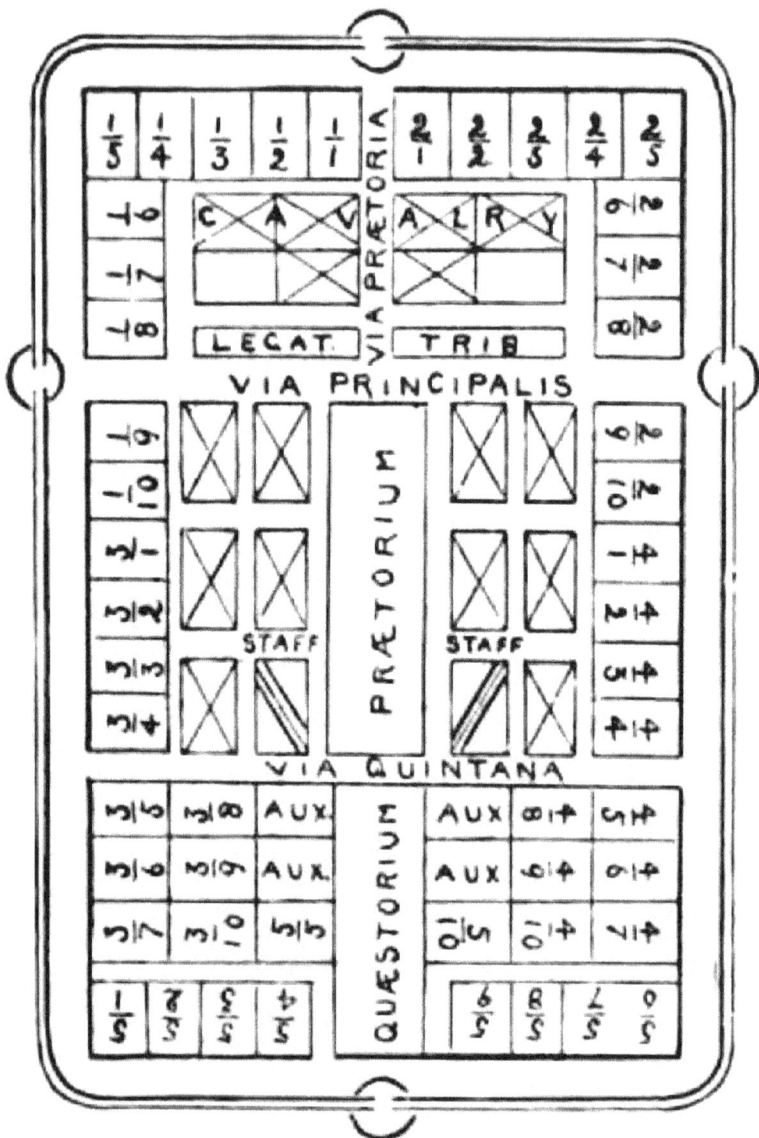

Caesar's camp

slope towards a stream, particularly if the enemy lay beyond. But the Romans camped where they must, if the best site was not at hand, and the shape of the camp was modified by the ground.

A camping party always went ahead to select and stake out camp, and the legionaries pitched and entrenched it in the course of a few hours, while the cavalry served as outposts. Each legion and *cohort* as it arrived was marched into its appointed place, the detail for guard was selected, the baggage was laid down, the weapons, except the sword, put aside. The camp was then fortified, and the tents afterwards put up. If the weather was stormy the tents were put up first. Then the troops took supper, the officers assembled for orders, and much the same routine was gone through which has been described in a previous volume. The fortifications took the place of outpost-duty, which the Romans did not practice in our sense. In the immediate presence of the enemy the work would be done by the third line, the two first being sent out to protect the fatigue party; or by the second line if only two, the first standing in line in front, ready to meet an attack. When the legions marched out to battle, the camp was left in entire order under a guard, usually composed of the younger troops, who were fully able to hold it. The camps were rectangular unless modified by the ground.

The same thing applies to the little camps or redoubts (*castella*) which were built in siege operations or for outpost defences of a general camp. Of these *castella* the smallest were one hundred and twenty feet square, for a garrison of a *cohort*. The corners of all camps were rounded off to prevent the enemy getting a footing on them in the assault. The gates, wide enough for a *maniple* front (forty feet), were protected by half-moons, and materials were on hand for closing them quickly in case of threatened attack. Gates like our modern ones seem to have been unknown, except in permanent fortifications.

The ditch (*fossa*) was nine to twelve feet wide at the top, with a depth of seven to nine feet. It was often deeper and wider, the ratio being preserved. The scarp and counter-scarp had, one or both,

CAMP WALL (SECTION)

9

a slope or not, according to the nature of the soil. The height of the wall (*agger*) was not deemed so important, for the shield of the ancient soldier protected him abundantly. The percentage of darts which took actual effect was, as in the case of bullets, very small. From the wall the soldier could, however, cast his own missiles with better effect upon the enemy below, whom the ditch stopped at a good spear-hurling distance. This, indeed, was the main object of the wall. The height of the wall was supposed to be about two thirds of the surface-width of the ditch. Its thickness was about equal to the height, or a bit greater. The slopes were covered with sods, or inter-laced with branches, fascines or hurdles. There was a banquette of suitable width, and palisades (*vallum*) were planted at the top. The word *vallum* is often used for the entire palisaded wall. Embrasures in the palisades were common and towers were generally built. The inside slope of the wall was cut in steps for easy access, or faced with logs in steps.

It took, as a rule, four or five hours to complete the entrenching of a camp. It could, under favourable conditions, be done in three. The Roman used his spade to good effect. If the troops reached camp by noon, they would have finished their work by sundown of a short day.

The division of the camp was, in nomenclature, much like that of the war against Hannibal. The *cohorts* camped in their regular order. Each *cohort* took up a space one hundred and twenty feet wide, with a depth of one hundred and eighty feet, cut into six parts, thirty feet wide, one for each century. The century tents were pitched back to back and front to front, in streets. A cavalry *turma* took up one hundred and twenty feet by thirty. A regiment of twelve *turmae* took up as much space as two *cohorts*.

The accompanying sketch, added to what has already been given in a previous volume, suffices to show the details of Caesar's camp.

A cavalry picket was usual, which sent out scouts and spies. The gates were specially guarded, the wall was duly lined with sentinels, averaging one every thirty feet. The reliefs, every three hours, were called by the trumpet, and there was blown a sort of tattoo and reveille. The same rounds were made by an officer of the day as of yore.

The winter-quarters were the same as the summer-quarters, but more permanently and comfortably arranged. Huts took the place of tents. It may again be mentioned here that the Roman day was divided into two parts, the day from six a. m. to six p. m., and the night from six p. m. to six a. m. The hours were: the first, from six to seven a. m., the second, seven to eight a. m., and so on. Thus noon was the

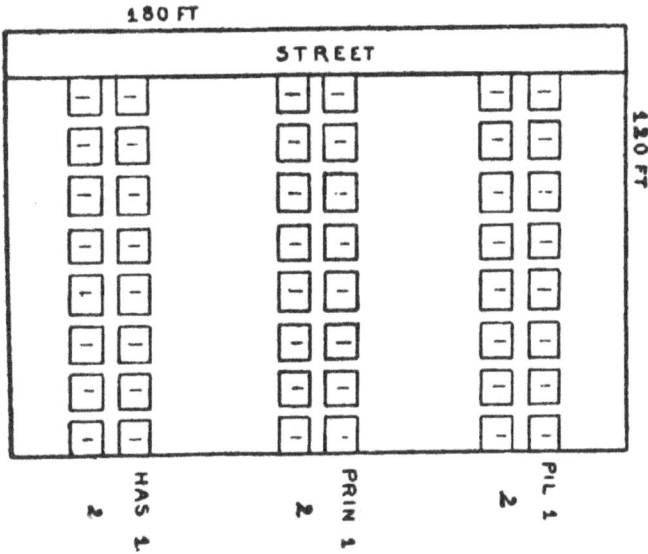

180 FT

STREET

120 FT

HAS 2 4

PRIN 2 1

PIL 2 1

COHORT TENTS (HYGINUS)

sixth hour, and four p. m. the tenth hour of the day, or midnight the sixth hour of the night. The day and night were also divided into four watches of three hours each. Thus six to nine a. m. was the first watch of the day; midnight to three a. m. was the third watch of the night. Occasionally summer hours are spoken of, being the time from sunrise to sunset, divided into twelve hours. This would at times lengthen the hour materially from what it would be if the day had been reckoned as from six a. m. to six p. m.

The art of attacking and defending strong places underwent comparatively little change for more than a thousand years. As far back as there are any records, written or sculptured, the processes of a siege are shown to be substantially the same. The following verses from Ezekiel iv. 1, 2, 3, speak of a siege about 600 B. C.:

"*Thou also, son of man, take thee a tile, and lay it before thee, and portray upon it a city, even Jerusalem.*" This was the plan of the works to be undertaken. "*And lay siege against it, and build forts against it, and cast up a mount (mound) against it; set camps also against it, and plant battering rams against it round about.*"

These are the usual steps of the siege.

"*Moreover take thou unto thee an iron pan, and set it for a wall of iron between thee and the city,*"—this refers to iron mantelets used in preparing the approaches,—"*and set thy face against it, and it shall be besieged, and thou shalt lay siege against it.*"

11

At certain periods, as during the wonderful activity of Alexander's military career, or during the siege of Rhodes by Demetrius Poliorcetes, or the defence of Syracuse by Archimedes, or Sylla's siege of Athens, a marked advance was made, but this again was wont to be lost, and the methods and machines remained almost identical. In fact, from dim antiquity they were so.

The walls of towns were generally of stone, and very high and thick. Those of the Gauls were, as we have seen, sometimes of earth, logs and stone. They were guarded by towers at regular intervals, and were apt to be fronted by a ditch, wet or dry. Immense skill and patience were devoted to the defences of cities and their interior citadels. To capture a town, one must resort to blockade, or siege, or assault. To attack the walls there was no artillery capable of making breaches. The catapults and *ballistas* could throw heavy stones and huge arrows to a remarkable distance, but had not penetration enough to break down walls. To operate a breach, it was essential to approach near to the wall, and either undermine it, or break it down by battering-rams or mural hooks. This approach could not be made except under artificial cover, and hence arose the more or less effective series of tortoises, galleries and mantelets, terraces and towers, added to mining and countermining, which were good or poor according as the skill and energy of the besiegers varied. All this remained unchanged so far as principle was concerned, until the invention of gunpowder reduced the ancient walls to uselessness in the same summary fashion as it unseated the knight in armour.

In sieges either towers were erected to override the wall, or else simple battering was resorted to at its foot. In the former case, so soon as the place had been approached, the army was camped, generally in several suitable locations, having heed to health, sustenance and siege operations. Each camp was fortified by a stockade and ditch, and often much more elaborately. Communications were established between these camps, and a line of investment—or contravallation—was drawn around the city. If there was danger of an enemy's army coming to the relief of the place, another line—of circumvallation—was drawn outside the besieger's camps, facing outward to forestall an attempt to raise the siege. Caesar generally uses the term circumvallation for what was earlier and more properly known as contravallation,—*i. e.*, the works erected against a town.

A terrace or mound (*agger*) was then begun, which should slope up to the bottom of the city wall. In case the city was on a level a terrace was not essential. It might be raised to a point part way up the wall,

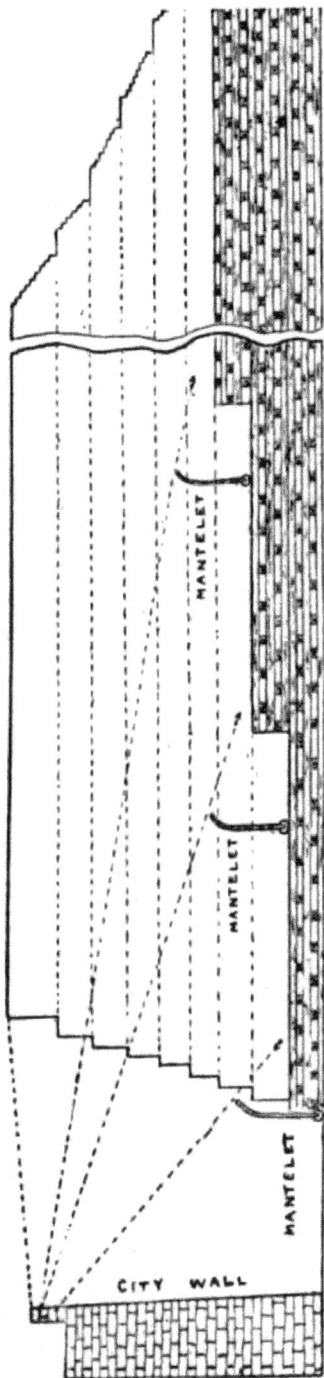

SECTION OF MOUND

MANTELET

MANTELET

MANTELET

CITY WALL

but this was not usual. Its surface was smooth enough to allow the moving of towers along it. The labour was performed by the soldiers and such part of the surrounding population as could be set at it. It was built of any material at hand. As terraces were often set on fire, it is to be presumed that much wood was used in their construction,—logs, hurdles, etc. That it was generally a sort of cob-house work, on the edges at least, filled with loose material .in the middle, is to be inferred from the rapidity with which it was set on fire and burned, a fact which argues a strong draft. The terrace was probably built a story at a time. A line of mantelets (*plutei*) was placed as near the wall as possible, but still out of range. Behind these, galleries made of a succession of small pent-houses (*vineae*), placed end to end, protected the men going to and fro, who brought material through the galleries and began work behind the mantelets. Movable towers with artillery and bowmen kept up a constant fire upon the walls to clear from them the missile-throwers of the enemy who interfered with the work, and sorties. When as much was finished as one set of mantelets were calculated to protect, these were advanced and another section built. Upon this first section or storey a second was constructed, and a third and more, as desirable. The end near the wall was made especially strong so as to bear the weight of heavy towers.

13

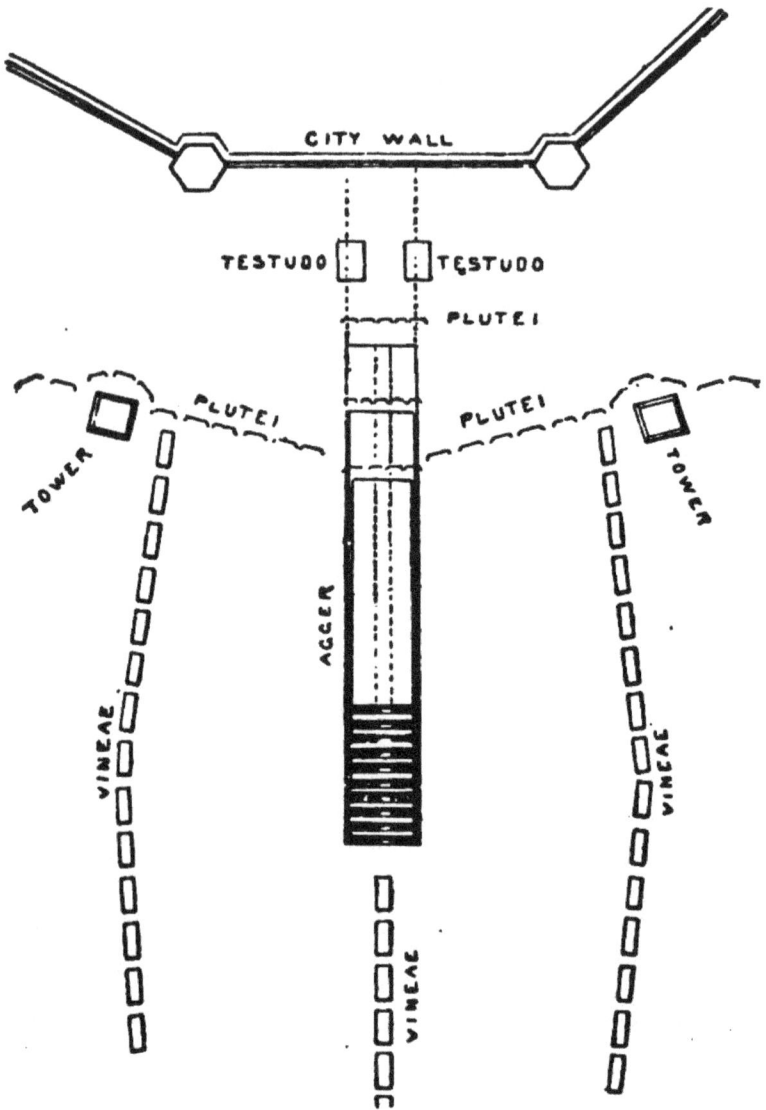

PLAN OF APPROACHES TO A TOWN

The size of some of these terraces excites the same wonder as temporary structures that the Pyramids do as monuments for all time. They are explained by the fact that so many thousands of hands worked at them. The terrace was made as wide as convenient, to contain all the necessary engines—if these were to be used on it—and to allow a storming column to advance along it, say fifty feet. When completed the terrace was crowned by towers which were higher than the city

MUSCULUS, LIGHT

walls, and which were connected by curtains or walls. Such a terrace appears at first blush to be a work more gigantic than called for; but it was made necessary by the fact that so long as the garrison could hold the platform of the wall, they could prevent the approach of the battering-ram or the filling of the ditch, by throwing missiles, inflammables, hot tar and heavy stones from above; or they could interfere by grappling tackle with the free swing of the ram essential to an effective blow, or deaden its effect by cable-aprons hung at its point of impact. But so soon as the besiegers had reached the height of the wall, so as to be able by their greater numbers to drive the garrison from the platform, they could secure free play for the ram, fill up the ditch, and make ready to storm the walls by bridges from the towers, or through a breach after one had been operated.

MUSCULUS, STRONG

15

When the ram was got fairly at work, the capture of the place was deemed secure, and no capitulation was received on any save harsh terms. Sometimes, on a breach being made, a new wall or *demi-lune* was found to have been constructed within, which obliged the besiegers to begin their work all over again.

The pent-house galleries (*vineae, musculi*) took the place of our trenches and parallels. But these latter were not unknown. The galleries were set up obliquely to the wall as trenches are today, but less so. Accidents in the ground were utilized for cover, but so soon as the approaches arrived in the open, they were run with regularity on a most intelligent system. Parallels were not so deep as ours because the missiles were not so destructive. Portable curtains and defences were common for surprises.

Mantelets (*plutei*) were made of skins, cable-mats, mattresses, etc., suspended on masts, and not infrequently iron plates or heavy lumber. They were not unlike huge snow-ploughs mounted on wheels.

The *vineae* were constructed of a roof of plank and wicker-work covered with rawhide, ropes and wet cloth to resist missiles and fire, and were usually sixteen feet long and seven feet wide, resting on posts eight feet high. The sides were also protected by wicker-work. These *vineae* were carried forward by the men. If heavier, they were rolled on wheels. They were then pushed forward obliquely, a number were joined together, and under their cover the terrace foundations were laid close to the ditch. Wet ditches were tapped and drained. The *musculus* was a low triangular hut on rollers for the protection of the men; when working near the walls it was heavier. The *testudo* was much like the *musculus*, but larger.

The building of the terrace was opposed by every contrivance imaginable. Sorties were made at night to destroy the work of the day. Mines were driven underneath the terrace and filled with inflammables which, set on fire, would crumble the earth and drop in its foundation. These were opposed by counter-mines. Mines were run under the walls by the besiegers with a similar object; and they were often run as a means of throwing a force into a town under its walls, which force, once in, would open the gates to the besiegers. Such mines often showed ability to a high degree in design and execution.

The towers with which the terraces were surmounted were often many storeys in height. They were usually structures of wood, but sometimes of earth, stone or brick, so high as to dominate the walls of the town.

The heavy machines of the city were within the walls on the level.

16

VINEA

Only soldiers and light engines occupied the walls and towers. Where a wall was escaladed and the assaulting party had reached the platform, it still had to descend into the inclosure, a work of yet greater danger. On the platform the party had to encounter the cross-fire from the towers, and must get ropes and ladders to descend on the inner side. The operation was difficult. Hence the greater practicability of breaches.

The walls were not usually of solid masonry; one front and one back wall were built of stone, perhaps twenty feet apart; the space between was filled in with the earth taken from the ditch, or with rubble or other available material. Huge earthen ramparts were not uncommon, as at Gaza.

PLUTEI (3 STYLES)

TOWER

The immensity of the towers which surmounted the terraces is perhaps the most astonishing feature of sieges. Vitruvius (who was one of Caesar's engineers in the African war) speaks of two ordinary sizes. The smaller had sixty cubits of height (a cubit is one and a half feet) by seventeen cubits square, and decreased one fifth in going up. The larger was one hundred and twenty cubits high by twenty-seven cubits square. Each had ten storeys. Demetrius at Rhodes made one much larger than even this.

These towers were usually prepared in advance with fitted beams, were brought as close to the walls as could be under cover of mantelets, and there set up. They generally carried a ram in the lower story, and were furnished with drawbridges to drop on the enemy's wall.

The ram could operate under cover of the armed men above, who kept the platform clear by their missiles. These towers were furnished with huge wheels on which they were moved forward. The approach of such a tower to the walls was generally followed by the capture of the town, unless it could be destroyed by fire.

Fire and heavy missiles were the means of combating the approach of these towers. The object of sorties was to fire the towers. The falling drawbridges were kept off by long sharpened beams fastened on the walls of the city.

Rams were either mounted on wheels or suspended by ropes or chains. A huge beam (or one made of several lashed together) was furnished with a heavy cast-iron end, frequently in the form of a ram's

RAM AND TONGS

TELENON

head, fixed to it by iron bands. The beam was reinforced in the centre, the better to withstand the shock. The head was at times furnished with a mural hook as well as a ram. The ram was hung or mounted in a shed, well protected from fire, and was manipulated by soldiers. The size and weight of these rams excite our surprise. Demetrius used a ram one hundred and twenty feet long against Rhodes. Appian speaks of one, at the siege of Carthage, which required six thousand men to mount it. Perhaps this means their labour used in speedily building its emplacement and covering.

To resist the ram, the walls were covered with soft material hung upon them from above, such as bags of feathers and wool, or mattresses, or plaited cordage. Heavy suspended beams were dropped upon it to disable it. Big grappling devices to seize not only rams but other machines, and even to pick up men, were common. Callias, at Rhodes, enjoyed a great reputation for such fishing tackle, until Demetrius constructed such heavy rams and engines that Callias' tackling would no longer work.

The *telenon* was a rude crane by which was raised a cage containing soldiers who could thus reach and attack the platform, or make observations of what was being done inside the walls.

The artillery of the ancients was far from despicable. Caesar calls all the missile-throwers *tormenta*, because they derived their propulsive power from *twisted* ropes, sinews or hair (*torquere*). The catapults and *ballistas* of the Greeks had no doubt survived and been little altered. These have been described in previous volumes. The *ballistas* were able to throw stones weighing five hundred to six hundred pounds. Smaller *ballistas* (*scorpiones*) threw one-hundred pound stones, and were known as *centenaria*. A bundle of arrows placed on the horizontal upper beam at the proper angle and struck by the ballista head could be thrown a great distance. Dead pestilential bodies or other such matter were thrown into the enemy's lines. The average *ballista* could hurl up to twelve hundred feet.

The catapults were on the principle of huge bows, and threw sharpened beams, darts, leaden bullets, fire-pots and fire-darts with great effect. These machines were really, except for size and convenience, almost as powerful as the early artillery. Their aim was good.

The walls of cities and towns were plentifully provided with missile-throwers. Besiegers had to await the bringing up of a siege-train or the construction of fresh machines, which was a long process. There is nothing to show that Caesar had anything like as effective artillery, or artillery as easily transported, as Alexander. But Caesar had missile-throwers with his army, for they are mentioned as being mounted on the walls of his camp.

After a breach was opened, heavy columns assaulted it and were met with the resistance of like bodies. A breach by no means always brought about the capture of a city. A half-moon, or re-entering angle, which the besieged could build in rear of the place where a breach was being made, was all the more difficult to take because the besieged during its attack lay on the besieger's flanks and rear. At Rhodes such a half-moon was faced with a ditch.

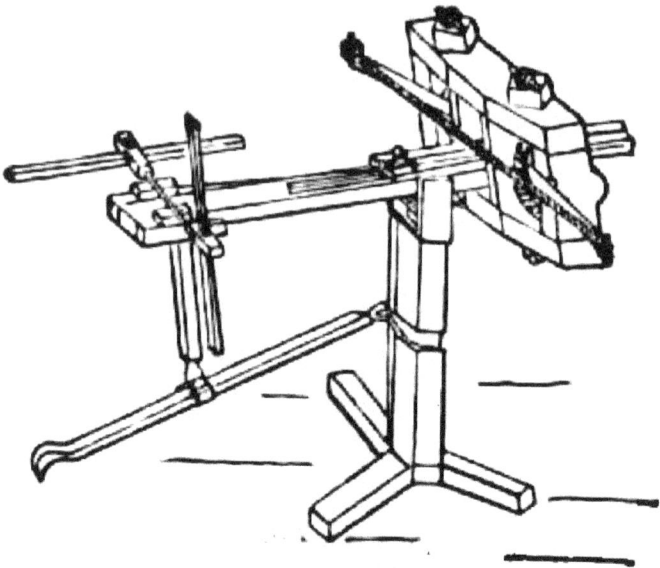

CATAPULT

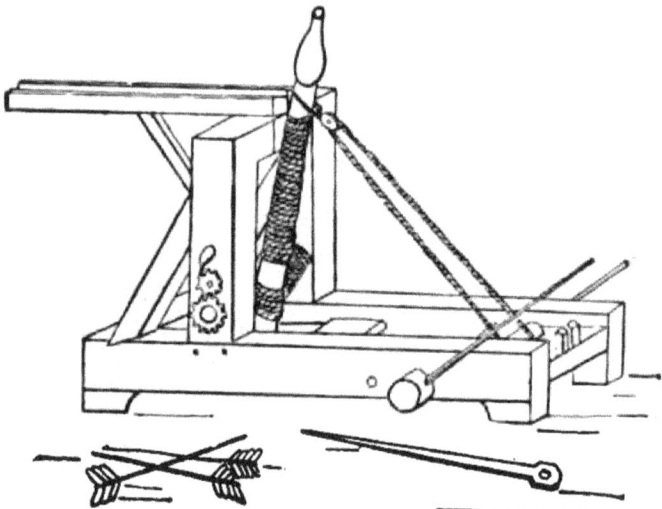

BALLISTA

Ancient sieges were much more obstinately contested than modern ones, and for good reason. The besieged had to face the alternative of victory, or of slavery or death.

The ordinary course of a siege might be stated as:—

1. A reconnoissance of the place.

2. The establishment of camps in suitable positions.

3. The collection of material for the siege.

4. The manufacture of *vineae, plutei, musculi*, etc.

5. The building of redoubts and joining them with line of contra- and perhaps circumvallation.

6. The preparation of covered ways to the town, mines and subterranean passages.

7. The building of a terrace, by *legionaries* within reach of darts, by natives beyond range.

8. The erection of towers on the terrace, or pushing them forward along it.

9. The operation of breaches.

10. Storming the breaches.

This chapter is largely a recapitulation of what has been told in former volumes; but it has been deemed essential to the proper appreciation of Caesar's numerous sieges.

Scorpion

CHAPTER 26

The Opening of the Civil War
December, 50, to May, 49 B. C.

The *triumvirate* had been broken up by the death of Crassus in the Parthian campaign. The friendship of Caesar and Pompey had ended in competition for the sole control. Caesar represented the democratic, Pompey the aristocratic party. War was forced on Caesar. Though he entered into it in self-protection, it was he who took the initiative, when the tribunes of the people fled to him for safety. He marched into Italy with one legion; Pompey had many,—but they were on paper. Great numbers of recruits joined Caesar's standard, while Pompey, from lack of preparation and energy, found his forces dwindle. Caesar's legions were, veterans; Pompey had but fresh levies. Gradually Caesar forced his way down the Adriatic coast to Brundisium, where Pompey with his adherents had taken refuge. On the way, the gates of most of the towns were opened to Caesar; some, especially Corfinium, had to be besieged. Many of Pompey's *cohorts* voluntarily went over to Caesar; others were captured, and then joined his cause. The people were with Caesar; the Senate, the aristocrats and the rich with Pompey. The latter, overwhelmed by Caesar's rapidity and his own lethargy, resolved to transfer the war to Greece instead of fighting in Italy.

When the triumvirs assumed power, Pompey was looked upon as the ruling spirit, Caesar and Crassus much in the light of Pompey's adjutants. To Pompey were opened the treasures and the power of the entire state; to Caesar only those he was given by law. Pompey's term was unlimited; Caesar's was a long but fixed term. Pompey remained at the capital; Caesar was sent to a distant province. But the important work undertaken by Pompey soon developed his weakness. So far from ruling Rome, its rival factions reduced the capital to a state of anarchy which Pompey had not the ability to check. "The rabble of every sort never found a merrier arena." The leaders of the several bands which played fast and loose in the city followed their own sweet will. Never was capital so ungoverned. It is no part of the purpose of this volume to describe political imbroglios; suffice it that Pompey gradually lost his grasp and his standing. He was at times reduced to the condition of a mere puppet. Caesar was gaining laurels in the north, while Pompey's military reputation was in a way to be forgotten. Having lost control of the rabble, Pompey was unable to control the popular assembly; his strength and ability were unequal to the exceptional conditions, and his failure to perform his share in the scheme of joint government necessarily ended by estranging himself and Caesar. This state of things worked against Caesar, who was distant from Rome and with difficulty able to control what friends he had. Power might slip away from him.

The *triumvirs* held a meeting at Luca in the spring of 56 B. C. There were two hundred senators present and numbers of other men of mark. Here a further division of provinces was agreed upon, but it was evident that Pompey had ceded a substantial part of the controlling voice to Caesar.

The aristocrats, meanwhile, were combining against the *triumvirate*. Yet everyone seemed to be his own master. Caesar raised legions without authority; Crassus equally so conducted the Parthian war. The forms of law were observed, but money or violence carried the votes in every election. There was abundant manifestation of the unlicensed spirit of all in the constant armed conflicts in the streets. These finally culminated in the murder of Clodius by Milo, an episode which roused the energy of Pompey to the point of seizing the dictatorship, and to a certain degree bringing the law again into operation.

Crassus had been a make-weight between Caesar and Pompey, but steadily leaned to Caesar's side. In the late division of provinces he was afforded a chance to gain military power and still greater wealth in a Parthian war, which had come about by Pompey's bad faith in failing to respect the line of the Euphrates. Crassus reached Syria instinct with the purpose of another Alexander, resolved to penetrate to India. He had two routes. He could invade Parthia through mountainous and allied Armenia, or through the Mesopotamian desert. He chose the latter route, on the mistaken testimony of a native friendly prince. He had seven full legions, four thousand cavalry and an equal number of archers and slingers,—nearly fifty thousand men. The great Macedonian had made this march nearly three centuries before.

CRASSUS' ROUTES

Careless scouting led Crassus into an ambush of the enemy not far from Carrhae. Surenas, the Parthian *vizier* who commanded the enemy, had recognized the fact that Eastern foot could accomplish nothing against Roman legions; he had utilized his infantry to keep a large body of Armenian horse from joining Crassus, and with a keen tactical appreciation of the conditions had chosen to do his fighting solely with cavalry. Crassus advanced into the desert; soon his marching column of foot was met by a body of mail-clad horsemen, partly heavy lancers, partly lighter archers. The legionary was more than a match for his man when he could get at him, but here the foe could fight or decline to fight as he chose; could cut the Roman communications by his superior activity; could move with twice the Roman's speed. The armies were on a limitless rolling plain, the very arena for a huge body of horse, a very pitfall for foot in those days of short-carry weapons. There was on the sandy soil scarce a chance to entrench a camp; water was at distant intervals; the Roman was out of his bearing, the Oriental in his element. For the first time the legions met a native tactical array with which they could not cope. Close combat weapons were useless. The mounted archer was master of the situation, and the Parthian had made the bow a national weapon.

The Battle of Carrhae is interesting as a defeat of the best of infantry by inferior horse, and yet not by cavalry tactics so called. The

26

Parthians drew up in an extended order affording the greatest scope for their fire. The Romans drew up in their usual dense square. Here we have the deployed line of superior fire—generally assumed to be a modern idea—against a dense mass limited in its ability to hurl missiles. There was but one outcome. The Parthian mounted archers were accompanied by camel-loads of spare arrows. The legions had absolutely no means of attack or defence. Their own archers were of small avail. They were speedily defeated when sent out.

Gradually the thin Oriental line swept by and outflanked the Roman square. Fearing to be surrounded and thus have his progress checked, Crassus sent his son Publius, one of Caesar's young veterans, to attack the enemy with a select body of six thousand mixed troops. This diversion for a moment arrested the Orientals, who summarily retired, pursued by the brave young soldier. But his gallantry had sealed his fate. Luring him to a distance, the Parthians made about face on his column, and, surrounding it, cut the entire force to pieces. They then turned again on the retreating Roman square.

Darkness alone saved the wreck of the Roman army. The Orientals, fearing a night surprise, rode off to camp at a distance, intending to return to their prey next day. But the Romans, by leaving behind some four thousand wounded to be massacred, continued the march and reached Carrhae. Thence, after a brief rest, the mere remnant of the force, some five thousand men, made their way to Sinnaca,

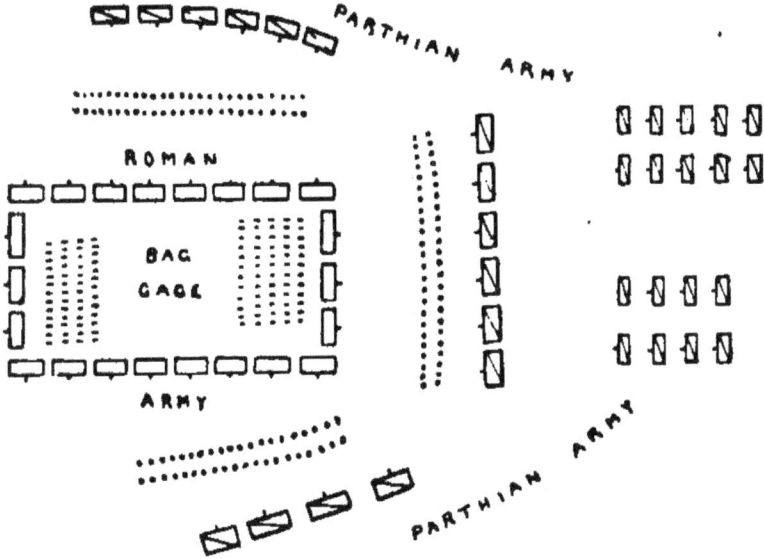

BATTLE OF CARRHAE

a fortress on the foothills of Armenia, only to be followed by the Parthians, and again cut up. The entire army was lost, and Crassus killed. This was in June, B. C. 53.

The end of the *triumvirate* thus came. Caesar and Pompey between them controlled the state, but they had already begun to be politically estranged; socially, the death of Julia, in 54 B. C, severed the last tie. When Pompey had secured for himself the undivided consulship, he was fully prepared to fling his gauntlet at the feet of the man who, he foresaw, would soon outstrip him unless overridden before he acquired more headway. The death of Crassus was a grievous blow to Caesar, who could uniformly rely on his colleague's fidelity. It was in this same year that the insurrection of Vercingetorix occurred; had Pompey taken the vigorous step of having Caesar recalled from Gaul, it would have put a term to Caesar's career. But Pompey was never ready to seize an opportunity; lack of incisiveness was fatally characteristic of the man.

Caesar was strictly and from the beginning a democrat, and was now the leader of the party. Pompey had been playing with democracy and shortly reverted to his old Sullan traditions. He easily effected a reconciliation with the Catonians, and became the head of the aristocratic party. Thus Caesar and he were formally arrayed against each other. Caesar desired no rupture. He had, at Luca, been promised the consulship in B. C. 48, and this he was anxious to obtain peacefully, as a base from which to exert his influence. Through the legal trickery of Pompey and the Catonians this was denied him, and it was sought to disable him by an order to break up his legions. Caesar offered to disarm whenever Pompey was made to do the like. It was during the debate on this matter that Caesar was completing the pacification of Gaul, holding his grand review on the Scheldt, and making his triumphal march through the province of Cisalpine Gaul. Finally, through the management of Curio, Caesar's henchman in Rome, the Senate voted that both Pompey and Caesar, as proconsuls of Spain and Gaul, should lay down their offices. Caesar was willing to do so; Pompey declined. On the assumption that Caesar was disobeying orders, Pompey asked to be instructed by the Senate to march against him. This was refused. But the old consul and the newly elected ones gave Pompey the authority the Senate had denied. On this slender pretence Pompey put himself at the head of the only two legions at hand,—they were the two sent by Caesar to be used in the Parthian war, but wrongfully detained by Pompey, and were far from reliable against their old commander,—and began levies of fresh troops.

Of the prominent Pompeians, Cicero remained in Campania to recruit; Minucius Thermus was sent to Umbria; Lentulus Spinther and Attius Varus to Picenum; Scribonius Libo to Etruria; Domitius Ahenobarbus, whom the Senate, had designated as Caesar's successor in Gaul, went to Corfinium.

This proceeding was substantially a declaration of war. Caesar, if forced to it, was ready to strike the first blow.

Caesar had passed the winter at Ravenna, some two hundred and forty miles from Rome. Here Curio joined hm. The news he brought decided Caesar's action. He ordered his nearest legion to Ravenna,— the Thirteenth from Tergeste (Trieste),—a body which he speedily recruited up to nearly or quite normal strength, five thousand foot and three hundred horse. His other eight legions were far away: four among the Belgae, under Trebonius; four among the Ædui, under Fabius; all in winter-quarters. He had already ordered Fabius to send him the Eighth and Twelfth, and Trebonius to give over one of his own to Fabius, and with the rest to approach the Arar. Fabius, with the three legions thus under his command, was sent to Narbo, lest Pompey's seven legions In the Spanish peninsula should invade Gaul. The strength of Caesar's legions in Gaul varied from three thousand to thirty-five hundred men each.

Caesar, in due course, sent an ultimatum to Rome, couched in a reasonable spirit. Under Pompey's dictation the Senate replied by ordering Caesar to lay down his arms unconditionally, or be deemed a traitor. The *tribunes* of the people, Mark Antony and Q. Cassius, vetoed the resolution, but were forced by Pompey's adherents to flee for their lives. They started north to join Caesar, who was the recognized centre point of the democratic party.

Caesar's mind was soon made up. War was his only resource. He harangued the Thirteenth legion, to explain why he struck the first blow in a civil war. His cause was equalled by his eloquence, and he found a generous response. With these *cohorts* he advanced towards the border of his province, December 16, 50 B. C. The Thirteenth legion crossed the Rubicon on the night of December 16-17. The Civil War had begun.

In Gaul, Caesar had not been noted for foolhardy operations. Bold as Alexander when boldness was demanded, as when he started with seven thousand men to rescue Cicero from sixty thousand Nervii, yet Caesar exhibited as a rule the virtue of caution rather than the error of untimely boldness. We shall, from the outbreak of the Civil War, however, find him in a new role, constantly committing acts of precipitancy which are never altogether admirable, and sometimes much to be condemned. For the present proceeding, even, he has been severely blamed by many critics and historians. It can scarcely be classed as prudent generalship, it is said, however bold, for Caesar to set out with five thousand men against Pompey, an excellent tactician and a man of large experience, who would probably array considerable forces against him. But in this instance it the rather appears that Caesar was both bold and prudent. The temerity was in Caesar's own style. He knew the condition of his enemy's forces: that Pompey had not got his levies made in season; that the two Apulian legions were too far off to be immediately available, even if they were reliable; that the towns on his route were illy garrisoned; that there was a strong sentiment in his own favour if suitably met. Moreover, he could not afford to wait; he believed that a surprise of the enemy before he increased his numbers was his safest course, and that rapid work would secure him control of the northern provinces of Italy. His course, fortunately, was the right as it was the bold one.

Caesar had no difficulty in assuring himself of the personal fidelity of the rest of his legions, of which he ordered some in from Gaul so soon as he learned that the tribunes of the people had fled to him from Rome for protection. This latter fact gave him the required appearance of right. It was in a mood distinctly conciliatory, but determined to give his enemies no unfair advantage, that Caesar set out towards Ariminum. The handful of troops he had with him reflected the feeling of the rest in declaring that they would know how to protect their insulted chief and the tribunes of the people.

Caesar's pause at the Rubicon has pointed many morals. With his quick habit of judgment and action, it was unquestionably of short duration.

From Ravenna were two roads to Rome. One ran from Bononia across the Apennines to Arretium; one down the coast to Fanum, thence southwest. Caesar chose the coast road. His plan was not to move on Rome. He proposed to seize the Adriatic coast, with its many and rich towns, and thus not only rob Pompey of much of his territory, but create a base for himself in Italy.

At Ariminum, taken by surprise December 17, Caesar met the tribunes, and also messengers from Pompey. The latter were Roscius the *praetor*, and young L. Caesar, whose father was one of Caesar's *legates.* They offered in indefinite terms an accommodation. Pompey, no doubt, had been alarmed lest Caesar should take him unawares. Caesar replied by a message agreeing to lay down arms and retire to his province if Pompey would do the like at the same moment and retire to Spain; and requested an interview either in Pompey's camp or his own. To this message, which Roscius and Caesar conveyed to their chief, Pompey, and the Senate, replied by the same messengers that whenever Caesar had disbanded his army and gone to Gaul, he, Pompey, would do the like and go to Spain. It is not improbable that Pompey was desirous of coming to an accommodation; but he did not adopt the proper tone or terms to secure such a result. Caesar was reasonable, but he demanded a crisp understanding. One of our authorities for the tone of these messages is the *Commentaries.* They are presumably accurate as to facts, but they were penned by one of the negotiating parties. Either rival was right in opposing the sole exercise of authority by the other; but we must judge mainly from the facts and from the other authorities, and not from the statements of Caesar, which was least to blame for the war that for years decimated the republic.

The material power of the two chiefs when they should be properly concentrated was very different. Caesar at this time had nine legions; two had been spirited away from him to Pompey, and were now arrayed against him. He had no fleet, and but himself to rely on. Pompey, on the contrary, had the formal power of the Roman state in his own or his friends' hands, and could retain it, if it was not forfeited by some signal error; he practically controlled the entire Italian peninsula except the regions abutting on Caesar's province; he had his Spanish and African legions, and all the forces of Italy, Greece, Egypt and the East. Caesar controlled Gaul—Cisalpine, Narbonese and Transalpine, the latter only just subdued—and Illyricum; Pompey practically controlled the rest of Rome's enormous territory, and especially in the provinces was Pompey's influence still strong. Pompey had the chief officers of the republic, the Senate, the aristocracy, the rich burgesses on his side; Caesar had but his few adherents, the tribunes of the people and the many headed.

But Caesar possessed what Pompey lacked. His authority was undivided within his camp and his party. His lieutenants were truly such. His legions were his, body and soul, and were veterans used to victory. He could do with them what no other captain could do. Their *imperator* was the embodiment of success not only in their eyes, but in

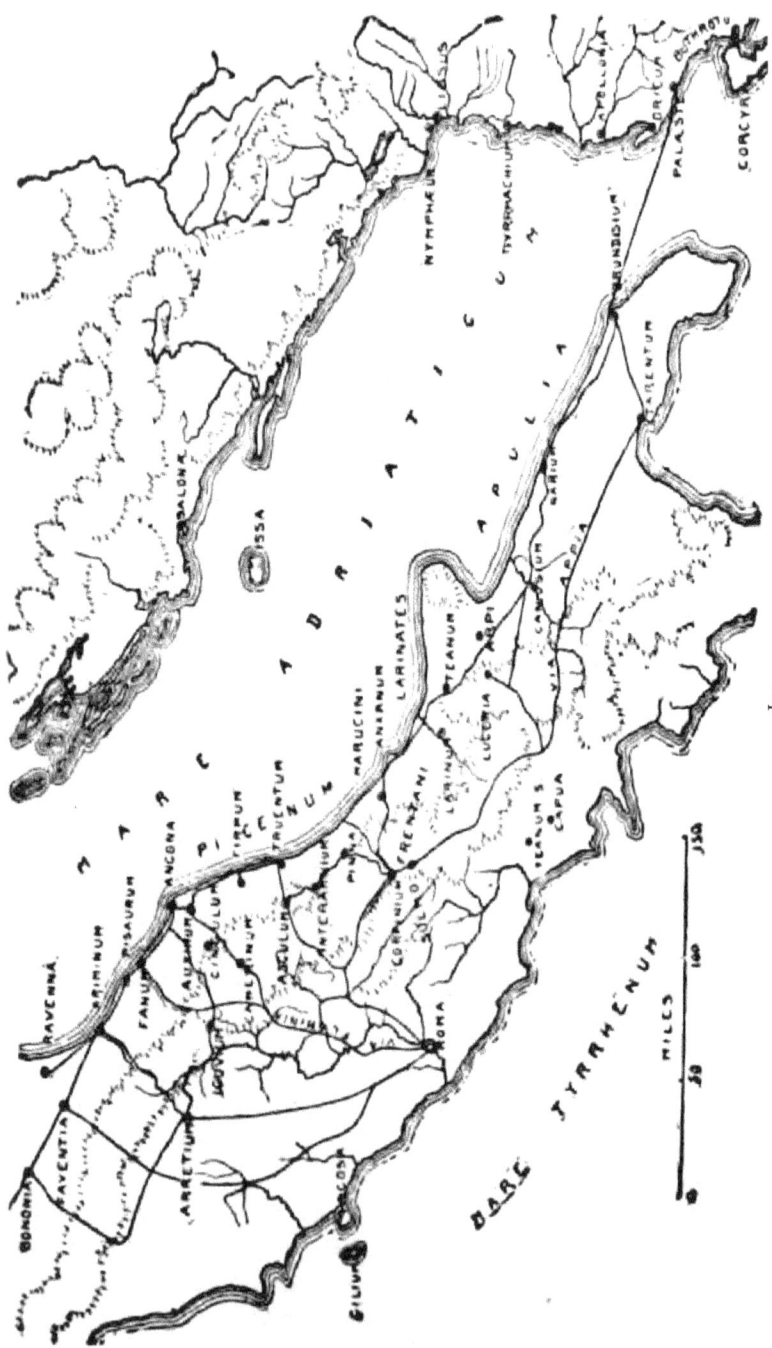

ITALY

the eyes of all soldiers in the service of Rome. Wherever Caesar went, armies would gather from the multitude. Moreover, Caesar was untrammelled and able to act as best to him seemed, while Pompey was really little more than the tool of his party. And above all, deeming the power to be all in their own hands, Pompey's party had taken no immediate measures to defend themselves against Caesar. What they had was scattered at arm's length; what Caesar had he could put to instant use. The material weight was on Pompey's side, the moral weight and the power of initiative on Caesar's. Pompey's reputation was for deeds long gone by; Caesar's was fresh in the minds of all.

Of Caesar's lieutenants every man, save Labienus, who aspired to higher office, had remained faithful. Caesar's plan of keeping his lieutenants in subordinate positions worked well with him, who purposed to do everything himself; but it robbed him sometimes of efficient marshals, who, on occasion, would have served him better.

Pompey's military forces were enormous, but they were scattered. He had seven legions in Spain, and numberless *cohorts* in every part of the empire,—Sicily, Africa, Syria, Asia, Macedonia. In addition to the two legions at Luceria, there were three legions of the levy of 55 B. C, and men already sworn in of the general levy of 52 B. C. in Italy. There was a total of ten legions in the peninsula, not counting the seven in Spain,—not far from one hundred thousand men; but they were not yet under the eagles. It was really no idle boast that "Pompey had but to stamp with his foot to cover the ground with armed men." But time is of the essence in war. Pompey's army was yet a skeleton. As we have seen, he had recognized the fact and had at once sent out eminent nobles to bring in the levies to rendezvous in the various provinces.

The force of Caesar's legions is very hard to gauge. Judging by what they were afterwards at Pharsalus, when they had been reduced by campaigning, Caesar's *cohorts* may at this time have been three hundred to three hundred and fifty men strong. This would have made the average of each legion three thousand to thirty-five hundred men, so that Caesar had under his control a minimum of some thirty-two thousand heavy infantry. No better ever bore arms. Added to this force was a body of auxiliaries and some cavalry. All told, Caesar's army exceeded forty thousand men. Closer calculations are often made, but the data are all founded on estimates. Caesar's manifest advantage lay in the fact that his legions were veteran and at hand; Pompey's weakness was that the legions he might have had ready for the field, though strong on the morning reports, had yet to be assembled.

From Ariminum Caesar sent Mark Antony with five *cohorts* to Arretium. This was for the purpose of anticipating an advance against his line of communications with Gaul by way of that place, and across the Apennines to either Faventia or Bononia. Libo, at Arretium, had taken no measures of defence; Antony seized the place the 20th. Caesar himself remained at Ariminum with two *cohorts*, to raise levies, while he made Pisaurum, Fanum and Ancona secure, with a *cohort* each, on the succeeding two days. If he could get possession of Iguvium, on the Flaminian Way, he would thus gain a base line from Arretium to Ancona, securely protecting Gaul.

Learning that the praetor Thermus, with five *cohorts*, was fortifying Iguvium, whose inhabitants were well disposed towards Caesar, he sent Curio, on the 23rd, to that town, with the three *cohorts* drawn from Ariminum and Pisaurum. On his approach, December 25, Thermus drew out his forces and marched away; but his troops dispersed to their homes, unwilling probably to oppose Caesar. Curio entered the town and later occupied Iguvium. This put an end to any danger to Caesar's rear.

Pompey being nowhere within reach, Caesar then withdrew Antony from Arretium, for by advancing down the coast he would minimize any danger of operations against his communications. Antony drew in Curio at Iguvium and moved to Ancona, where he joined his chief, and Caesar gave the men a day's rest on January 4.

Brief repose was all Caesar could give his troops. In two days he marched on Attius Varus at Auximum, southwest of Ancona, where this *legate* was recruiting for Pompey. His chief, Lentulus Spinther, was at Asculum. The senate of Auximum refused support to Attius. The latter retired from the place. Caesar's van pursued and struck Attius' soldiers. These either dispersed or were for the most part glad to join Caesar, who was welcomed by the inhabitants with loud acclaim. Lucius Pupius, the chief *centurion* of Attius Varus, on being brought to Caesar as a prisoner, was at once released. Caesar had no quarrel with the individuals of his enemy's army. He knew the value of generous treatment. About the same time Hirrus evacuated Camerinum with three thousand men.

At Auximum Caesar was dealt a heavy blow by learning the desertion of Labienus, his hitherto apparently most devoted and able lieutenant. Caesar made no attempt to stop him, but sent his properties and money after him. What was the immediate cause of this sad mishap is not known, but Labienus, after joining the cause of Pompey, exhibited the greatest hatred towards the chief he had for ten years so ably and cordially served.

Though thousands of recruits were willing to leave their homes and cast in their fortunes with Pompey, thus testifying to a strong sentiment for his party, this manifest leaning towards Caesar on the part of the population produced great consternation in Rome, where news of his Umbrian successes arrived the 20th and 21st. It was rumoured that "the monster" was marching on the city. The consuls, Lentulus and Marcellus, followed by most of the magistrates, within two days fled from the protection of its walls. It is curious how infectious the dread of the conqueror of the Gauls could be. It was as if these dreaded barbarians themselves had once more marched on Rome. The enemies of Caesar did not feel secure at any point north of Capua. Here they arrested their flight, and re-established the Roman government. But in their haste they forgot to make the usual sacrifices to the gods, and, worse still, omitted to carry away the public treasure.

Having abandoned Rome, Pompey held a conference with his chief supporters at Teanum Sidicinum on the 27th. The various chances of the campaign were canvassed, Labienus being present, and Pompey decided to take the two legions in Apulia and advance on Picenum, where, by hurrying up the collection of the levies, he might gather a force sufficient to arrest Caesar's farther progress. It was in this province, thirty-five years before, that Pompey had first acquired his reputation by raising troops for Sulla.

Pompey accordingly repaired to Luceria to carry out his plan of campaign. But with his usual listless method he sat down, gave out his work to others to do, and practically accomplished nothing until it was too late.

Caesar moved down Picenum, received with hearty good will and material support by most of the towns, and recruiting with success in each locality. Even Cingulum, a town Labienus had founded,—in fact owned,—offered to join him and sent him soldiers. How great the number of his recruits may have been it is impossible to say. The Twelfth legion now joined him, and with these two, the Twelfth and Thirteenth, Caesar marched, *via* Firmum and Truentum, to Asculum, the chief town of Picenum. Lentulus Spinther here had ten *cohorts*,—five thousand men; but he, too, fled at Caesar's approach, and his soldiers largely deserted to the new chief. Caesar entered the town January 11. Military glory is contagious. All soldiers were anxious to serve under a chief who had accomplished such wonders in Gaul, and in the company of men who had served in so many glorious campaigns.

Vibullius Rufus, an old soldier and a good one, had been sent by

Pompey into Picenum to check the growing sentiment for Caesar. Meeting Lentulus Spinther on his retreat, Vibullius took his few remaining *cohorts* and dismissed him. To these he added those of Hirrus. He then collected as many as possible of the new levies which had been made for Pompey; these with some other retreating Pompeian garrisons made up thirteen *cohorts*, with which he fell back January 11 on Domitius Ahenobarbus, Pompey's lieutenant at Corfinium,—a recruiting rendezvous,—and reported Caesar's advance.

Domitius had about twenty *cohorts*, collected in neighbouring states where recruiting seemed better than elsewhere. With those of Vibullius he made up thirty-three *cohorts*. Had these lieutenants possessed the true soldier's instinct, they would have marched north on Caesar, to seek, by a bold offense, to hold head against him. They might not have succeeded, but it was the thing to do.

Caesar had two legions. He added to their numbers by seeking out the deserters from Lentulus and bringing them under the colours. Having delayed but one day beyond the time needed for the muster of these men to provide corn, he at once marched south to Corfinium, by way of Interamnum and Pinna. In Corfinium were assembled many notables and refugees.

Meanwhile the Senate at Capua was laying the blame of all these losses on Pompey; the new levies did not come in; volunteers were few; and the cause of the aristocrats looked worse and worse. Instead of Pompey's collecting endless *cohorts* to oppose Caesar, it was Caesar whose forces were growing in number and enthusiasm, while Pompey had but two legions rather weak in their allegiance, and a few newly recruited *cohorts*, not yet consolidated into legions.

Caesar found the outposts of Domitius, five *cohorts* strong, breaking down the bridge over the Aternus, three miles north of Corfinium. By an unexpected and impetuous attack his van was able to drive off the party and save the structure. Caesar passed over and sat down before Corfinium on the 18th of January. His position was on the east of Corfinium, cutting Domitius off from communication with Pompey. Domitius, who had thirty *cohorts*, prepared for vigorous defence. He had previously sent hurriedly for aid to Pompey, who was still in Apulia. He told Pompey that Caesar could between them easily be surrounded in the narrow valley in which lay Corfinium, but that without help he himself was apt to be shut up and to lose his army. He promised his men largesses out of his own estate, in the event of success,—to each soldier four acres, with corresponding increase to veterans and centurions. Corfinium was situated on a plain surrounded by high and abrupt mountains,—the bed of an ancient lake. It was a place of much importance and strength. It was protected—by a wall compassing over one hundred acres, and could only be attacked from the south. The plain can alone be entered from the north through the two ravines of the Aternus. Domitius had been wise in selecting Corfinium for his base. Caesar, who was awaiting farther reinforcements from Gaul, pitched two camps before it, on the road to Sulmo.

Caesar shortly received notice that Sulmo, ten miles southeast from Corfinium, was ready to declare for him, but was held in check by a garrison of seven *cohorts* under Lucretius and Attius. Sending Antony thither with five *cohorts* of the Thirteenth legion, the gates were opened to him and the *cohorts* enlisted under Caesar's standards. Caesar cared naught for the leaders. Lucretius escaped; Attius, taken prisoner, was sent away in safety. Antony returned the same day to Caesar's camp, having made a successful campaign in a few hours.

At Corfinium Caesar determined to gather corn, fortify and wait for some of his other troops. In addition to the Eighth legion there shortly arrived twenty-two newly levied *cohorts*, with three hundred Gallic horse from Noricum. He formed a camp in his investment line for these troops, such that it would hold the Via Valeria, and placed Curio in command. He went on with his contravallation, joining the two camps with a line of works crowned by towers. The entire line was nearly five miles long. His three old legions, the Eighth, Twelfth and Thirteenth, and some thirty *cohorts* of new levies made up an army approaching twenty thousand men. Of the new *cohorts* he formed three new legions.

By the time that the works in front of Corfinium were completed, Pompey, after some exchanges of correspondence, had finally replied that he could send no help to Domitius, but that the latter must save his force as best he might and join him. Domitius now changed his conduct; he misled the soldiers by false declarations while personally contemplating flight; and the men, discovering the treachery, mutinied, seized his person, January 23, and sent word to Caesar that they would surrender him. While believing in their intention, Caesar left nothing to chance. He paraded his entire force on his works, exhorted the officers to extra caution, and ordered that no man should sleep that night. Everyone was on the alert. During

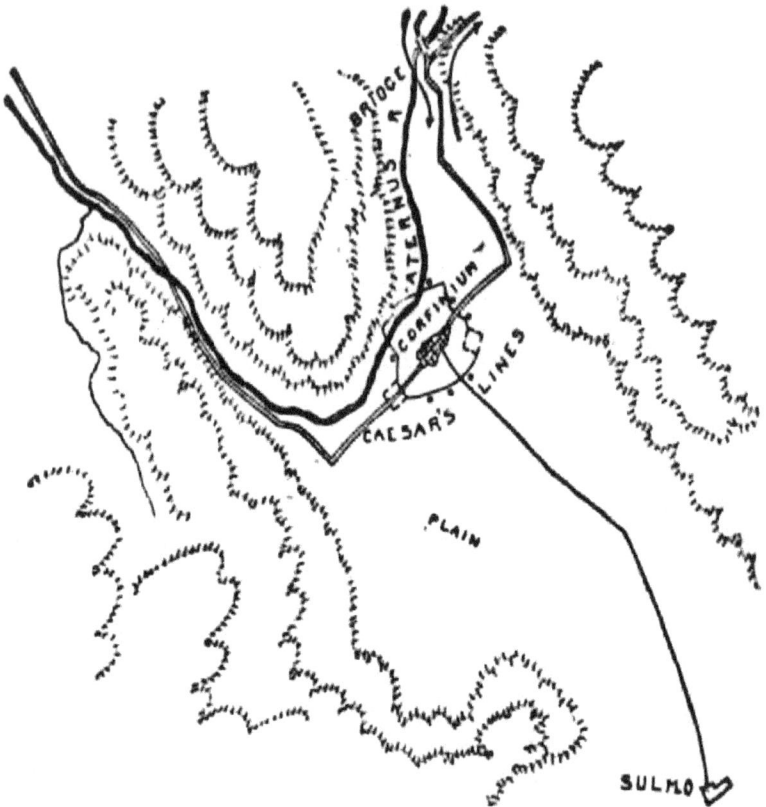

CORFINIUM

the night Lentulus was surrendered, and on being pardoned by Caesar returned to Corfinium, where he reported Caesar's generosity. Next morning, January 24, Domitius, Vibullius, Varus and Rubrius were given up, with many other magnates. Caesar forgave them all for their ingratitude, each one being indebted to him for past favours, protected them from the taunts of the soldiers, and restored to Domitius six millions of *sestertii* which he had brought with him to pay the soldiers, and which had been taken from him. Caesar's clemency at Corfinium was as much a surprise to Rome as his advance had been a terror. He was no longer "the monster." The popular tide began to set in his favour.

Having sworn in the *legionaries* of Domitius under his own eagles, Caesar, after only a week's delay before Corfinium, marched into Apulia, along the coast through the land of the Marrucini, Frentani and Larinates. He guessed that Pompey would seek to leave Italy for Greece. He knew his man as well as the conditions. The port of Brundisium was the most available one for this purpose, in fact all but the only one, and Caesar hoped that he could succeed in anticipating Pompey at this place, and thus confine him to Italy and all the sooner bring him to battle.

This was, indeed, since early in January, Pompey's intention. He saw that almost all the available men in the peninsula were joining the enemy's standard. In all he had lost by defection nearly sixty *cohorts*. He had got together a number of men in the vicinity of Rome, and these had been marched down to Campania. He was certain about no other levies. As matters had eventuated, Pompey could scarcely expect to hold himself in Italy. With a potential army at his command, large enough to crush out Caesar before he fairly reached Picenum, he had allowed all his chances to slip away. His ancient habit of procrastination had grown on him; and it was Caesar's just estimate of this fact which had made his temerity in advancing into Italy safe. Pompey, who now had only the two Luceria legions, the recent recruits from Campania, together with the few remaining faithful *cohorts* in Picenum, was no longer a match for his rapid-thrusting opponent. He deemed it advisable not to come to a general encounter with Caesar in Italy, but to draw him over to Greece, where he could assemble many more troops, and where Caesar would not be so near a friendly population to support him. Every step taken by either of the two men is characteristic. Caesar was positive in what he did. He knew his own intentions well; he was ready and anxious to fight. Pompey was hesitating and uncertain in his purpose; he appeared shy of crossing swords.

Instead of taking the matter personally in hand, he had been lying in and near Luceria, the "key of Apulia," often so valuable to Hannibal. His headquarters were at Larinum. Some *cohorts* had previously moved from Luceria to Canusium; all were now marched to Brundisium, and his levies were instructed to repair thither to join him. He himself reached the place January 28. Not a few, however, of his new *cohorts* deserted and went over to Caesar. Thither he also ordered all available galleys and transports from every nearby port.

Pompey's calculations had from the outset been essentially wrong. He had taken no seasonable means to defend Italy, and he was now leaving it to Caesar as a prize. He was giving up what he ought to have been prepared to hold at all hazards for its mere moral effect. When he had once abandoned Italy, Caesar would have full control of Rome, and would not again afford him a chance to return. Driven from Rome, how long could Pompey maintain his influence over the provinces? His leaving was to all intents and purposes a flight. Unprepared when the struggle came,—though himself had brought it about,—he had now taken such action as to throw a first great advantage over to Caesar's side. His conduct showed a lack of calculation and decision as marked as his apparent dread of Caesar. It is but fair to his colleagues to say that most of them objected strenuously to Pompey's policy.

CAESAR AT OPENING
OF CIVIL WAR

CHAPTER 27

Brundisium and Massilia
February to April, 49 B. C.

Lacking force to meet Caesar in Italy, Pompey retired to Epirus.
Caesar had no fleet and could not at once follow. He sought to pen
Pompey in Brundisium, and there bring him to a decisive conflict, surrounded the place, and built moles to close the harbour
mouth. But Pompey managed his escape with great cleverness, and
took with him to Epirus the Senate, consuls and many notables.
He had rejected all Caesar's overtures of peace. There were seven
Pompeian legions in Spain, under good lieutenants. Caesar feared
that these might invade Gaul and thus strike him at his weakest
point. Relying on Pompey's inertia, he determined to go first to
Spain and neutralize these legions before he followed Pompey to
Greece. He placed affairs in Rome on a basis to uphold his own
interests, and set out for Massilia. This city he found in the hands
of the Pompeians . He laid siege to it, and, placing Trebonius in
command, left for Spain.

Having concluded that he could not hold Italy, and having made
Brundisium his headquarters, Pompey there collected his troops.
He had armed a large number of slaves and had made a corps of
three hundred horse from the Campanian herders,—the cow-boys
of Italy,—a good material for irregular cavalry. A considerable frac-
tion of his levies failed to reach him, the *cohorts* breaking up on the
way. Some further bodies deserted to Caesar while on the march
to Pompey; but there assembled at Brundisium a motley crowd of
politicians and soldiers intermixed, numbering some twenty-five
thousand men. Pompey sent Metellus Scipio to Syria to recruit. He
dispatched the consuls to Dyrrachium in Epirus with a van of thirty
cohorts in January, 49 B. C, promising soon to follow with the balance

41

of the army. But the effect of his mistaken policy was still apparent; desertions continued. His two *praetors*, Manlius and Rutilus, went over to Caesar with nine *cohorts*.

Caesar, in all his communications to Pompey, and repeatedly, had asked for a personal interview, with the feeling that matters could be amicably adjusted. He again made overtures here through Magius, Pompey's chief engineer, whom he had captured. He was wise enough to see that if Pompey escaped to Greece there was a long, tedious and very uncertain war thrust upon him, and was not so blinded by political passion as not to allow this fact to weigh for all it was worth in his calculations. But his efforts were vain; Pompey sedulously avoided a meeting, personal or tactical.

Caesar, having been delayed but seven days before Corfinium, marched on Brundisium *via* Anxanum and Teanum, Arpi, Canusium and Barium. He reached the place February 9, after a march of seventeen days at the rate of nearly seventeen miles a day. He had now six legions, the Eighth, Twelfth and Thirteenth veteran, the rest made up of what he had raised and what had voluntarily joined his ranks, in all, at least twenty-five thousand *legionaries*. Domitius' *cohorts* he had sent to Sicily.

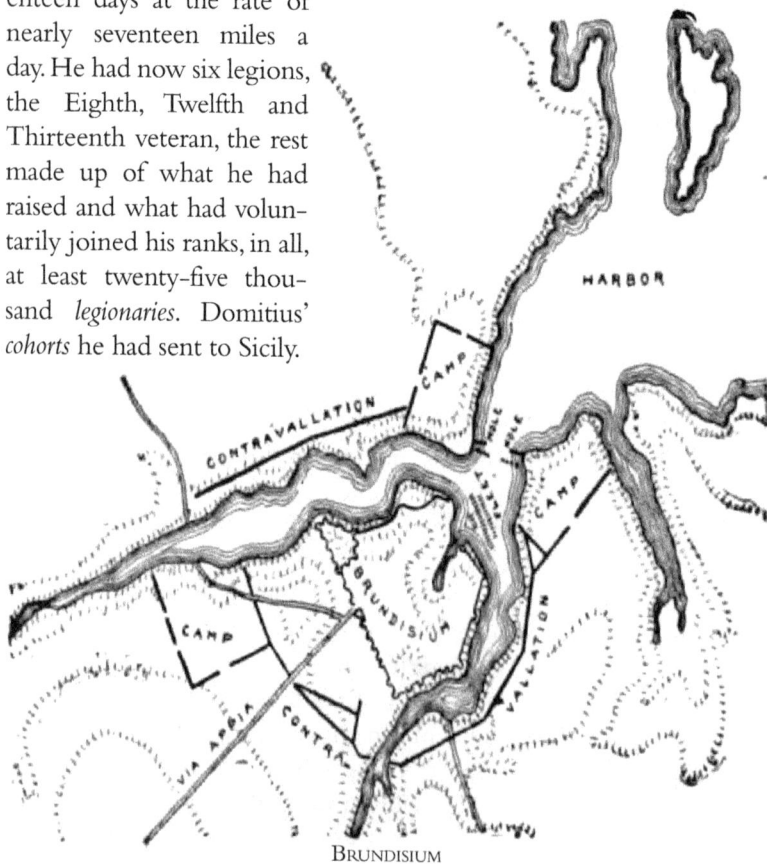

BRUNDISIUM

42

Brundisium was one of the best of the old-world harbours. The town was well defended from the land side by a towered wall. It was a rich city and the principal port on the Adriatic.

Caesar ascertained that the consuls had gone to Dyrrachium with thirty *cohorts*, while Pompey remained at Brundisium with twenty. These fifty *cohorts* numbered some thirty thousand men. Pompey had not had enough vessels to transport all the troops, and non-combatants as well, at one trip. Caesar grasped immediately at the advantage of cutting Pompey off from joining them. This he could do only by depriving Pompey of the use of the harbour of Brundisium, which commanded the Adriatic, and in which Pompey was awaiting the return of his fleet.

Caesar went to work. He blockaded the town from the land side by a circle of works, placing his legions in three camps joined by contravallation walls, and proceeded to build out into the harbour, from opposite sides and near its mouth, where he had located two camps and where it was narrowest and shallow, two moles some twenty feet wide, extending towards each other. These moles were constructed of rough stone, wood or other material near at hand. After building out from each shore a distance of some two hundred and fifty feet, the depth of the water made the work too difficult for speedy completion, and in order to join these moles, yet over five hundred feet apart, Caesar devised a number of floating rafts, thirty feet square, which he joined together, anchored at each corner, covered with earth and protected with a parapet of wicker-work. On every fourth one he built a tower of two storeys, to get an effective cross-fire. To offset this proceeding, Pompey on his side fitted out a number of merchantmen with three-storey towers, and sent them out to interrupt and break through Caesar's works. Skirmishing between these rival naval forces was of daily occurrence, with heavy interchanges of fire from bowmen and slingers.

For the third time Caesar now sought a personal interview, through Scribonius Libo, to whom he sent a messenger. But Pompey evaded it on t he pretext that without the advice and consent of the consuls he could take no action, and they were in Dyrrachium. This subterfuge determined Caesar to push the war with vigour.

When Caesar's works were about half finished,—on the ninth day of the blockade, February 17,—the fleet that had conveyed the forces of the consuls to Dyrrachium returned and made its way into the harbour. Pompey determined at once to leave Brundisium with the balance of his force. He strengthened the city walls and barricaded the streets, lest Caesar should enter the town from the land side while he was embarking. The citizens were distinctly in favour of Caesar, and gave him notice of Pompey's designs. But owing to the defences erected by Pompey, consisting of entanglements of various kinds and excellent entrenchments, and to a rear-guard of chosen men that he left on the walls while he was embarking, which he did at night, Caesar was entirely deceived as to Pompey's actual movements, and was prepared to do nothing to harass his retreat. This, though the citizens, irritated at the high-handedness of Pompey's soldiers, sought to give Caesar notice of what Pompey was doing. The manner in which Pompey managed the retreat was markedly good. He got embarked before Caesar reached the walls with his scaling ladders, and as the notice of the entanglements within had made the latter overcautious, Pompey sailed out of the port before Caesar could get to it. The only mishap which befell Pompey was that two of his ships laden with soldiers became entangled in the harbour chain and at the mole, and were captured.

Pompey thus escaped, despite Caesar's efforts to bring him to battle in Italy; and as he had taken possession of all the ships on the coast, and Caesar could procure none from nearer than Gaul and Spain, the latter was, as he says, compelled to give over all present idea of following his enemy. Had he shut Pompey up in Brundisium, he might have ended the war there, instead of having to spend more than four additional years in pursuing Pompey's partisans all around the Mediterranean basin. It is certain that Caesar began to appreciate the difference between fighting barbarians and Romans. Still he had good cause to be satisfied with what he had accomplished. He had been waging war against Pompey the Great,—the idol of the Roman people. Yet in sixty days from crossing the Rubicon, he had put himself in possession of all Italy. He must have been keenly alive to his own superiority in all that breeds military success. His decision, energy and speed stand out in strange contrast to the weakness, the vacillation of Pompey.

Caesar had unquestionably gained by getting possession of Italy. But his responsibilities and risks had increased in equal measure. A very considerable part of his entire force must now go to garrison the peninsula, which would reduce his military power correspondingly. As he had no fleet, Italy was largely at Pompey's mercy, who could cut it off from its grain supplies in Sicily, Sardinia and Egypt. The revenues of the East would no longer flow into Roman coffers;

they would all be stopped midway by Pompey; and yet Italy had grave need of these contributions, for everything had been organized on a spendthrift scale. Moreover, Caesar was not at first looked on, even by the people whose champion he was, with a feeling of security. Many of his adherents in power were dissolute, irresponsible men, deeply in debt and reckless. People had seriously feared a return of the Marius-Sulla horrors. But it was not long before Caesar succeeded in reassuring people on this head. Italy became tranquil. Though Caesar was practically monarch, everyone saw that the change of masters was for the better.

Caesar now changed his plans to accord with Pompey's escape to Greece. He commanded the coast towns to procure ships from whatever source, and send them to Brundisium. He ordered the construction of two new fleets, one on the Adriatic, one in Etruria, which Dolabella and Hortensius should respectively command. Valerius the *legate* he sent to Sardinia with one legion; Curio the *propraetor* he ordered to Sicily, which was of the highest importance as a granary— with three legions made up of *cohorts* captured at Corfinium and one of new levies, and instructed him, after securing the island, to proceed to Africa, where the government was in dispute by rival Pompeian factions and could perhaps be brought over to his side. On their arrival, these lieutenants found both Sardinia and Sicily hastily abandoned by their respective governors, M. Cotta and M. Cato (who, like the rest, seemed to have taken fright at Caesar's approach), and the population fallen from Pompey's and favourably disposed towards Caesar's cause. The Cavalitans in Sardinia drove out Cotta; Cato, who was energetically equipping vessels and recruiting for Pompey, feeling that he was unable to hold the island for his chief, took ship for Epirus to join him. Here was a large and easily gotten advantage.

The province of Africa had fallen by lot to Tubero; but when he reached his province the new governor found Attius Varus in control. This officer, it will be remembered, had lost his army at Auximum, had fled to Africa, which seemed to be a limitless refuge for all the aristocrats, and finding no governor on hand had assumed the reins, and raised two legions. Having formerly been *praetor* in Africa, he had been able to do this without much opposition. As the days of law and order seemed past, Varus did not propose to give up his power, resisted the attempt of Tubero to land at Utica, and drove him from the coast.

Pompey had been misled by his calculation on the influence of the aristocratic party in Italy. It had proved unequal to facing the democrats headed by Caesar. This was one of the facts which had determined him to leave Italy and to make Greece his battle-ground. He had abandoned the best part of the national prize to Caesar, and it was now Caesar's part to hold it.

There were seven legions of Pompey's in Spain. These were, say the *Commentaries*, a constant and serious threat to Gaul; or they might indeed be brought to Italy. Caesar deemed these legions more immediately dangerous than Pompey. While, therefore, Pompey was flying from Caesar to Hellas, Caesar saw that he might be compelled to turn from Pompey to Iberia.

It is probable that Pompey had formulated a broad strategic plan. We are not told what it was, but an occasional statement in the Commentaries and elsewhere helps us to guess. Not anticipating Caesar's sudden irruption into Italy, Pompey had expected to quietly finish his preparations and then carry the war against Caesar into Gaul, from Spain and Italy at the same moment. With time in his favour he could have thus marched into Gaul with from fifteen to twenty legions, and have utilized Massilia, whose favour he had won, as his base. When this plan was frustrated by Caesar's active campaign, Pompey himself might have done well to go to Spain, where his legions and lieutenants were both efficient, and to make that country his theatre of war, leaving Greece under a *legate*. But Pompey was tied down to his political associates, and his Oriental resources were the greater. He could not look at the matter coolly as a mere military problem. His vacillation persuaded him to ship to Greece and abandon Italy to the democratic party, headed by Caesar.

There is no question that Pompey, with half the mental activity of Caesar, could have held himself in the Italian peninsula instead of decamping from it. But the keystone of war is preparation, and Pompey had not made any. His temperament and actions were always of a *laissez aller* nature. If he had begun his levies, Italian and Eastern, in season; if he had brought half his Spanish legions to Italy, Caesar's task could have been made all but impossible on the lines he had chosen. As it was, Pompey's personal presence in Picenum might have turned the scale. For Pompey, at his best, could exercise an influence few men could equal. If he could not hold Rome, he might have held some point on the coast, every rood of which he controlled with his fleet; and having summoned forces from all the provinces he would have vastly outnumbered Caesar. It stands to reason that to sit still while your opponent is actively pursuing his advantages can result but in

ITALY, SPAIN, EPIRUS

disaster. We shall see that Caesar, in his contests with Roman troops and third-rate generals, was wont to exhibit great caution. Would he not have been less apt to make rapid progress had he known, so soon as he reached Ancona, that Pompey the Great stood personally at the head of even the fresh levies which lay athwart his path? For Caesar had not then as fully gauged his opponent as he later did. Pompey's first great error lay in entering on without preparing for war; this he followed up by a greater one in deserting Italy without a struggle.

As to Caesar, it is by no means clear that he acted wisely in undertaking a campaign to Spain, instead of at once following up Pompey. Every month he gave Pompey enabled the latter to collect more men and material and made him a more dangerous opponent. Though Spain was rich and a valuable acquisition, though Caesar must prevent the Spanish forces from operating on his rear, it would seem that to leave Italy, not to follow Pompey but to go to Spain directly away from Pompey, threatened to lose him a part of the moral strength which he had acquired by his own boldness in pushing into Italy and by Pompey's hebetude in crossing to Greece. Caesar had to march overland to Spain; why not march through Illyricum to Greece, and following up Pompey push him to the wall? It may be said that Caesar counted on Pompey's character, which he well knew, and concluded that Pompey would not attempt to return to Italy. But was this not reckoning without his host? How could Caesar believe that Pompey would behave with such unmilitary laxness? Was he not underrating his opponent? His reasons given in the *Commentaries* are, taken alone, quite insufficient to account for his movement to Spain instead of on Pompey, in Greece. And Caesar's dangerous campaign and narrow escape from disaster in Epirus, after Pompey had raised his Eastern army, show that he was giving his opponent a manifest advantage by not attacking him before he collected his forces.

We may assume that Caesar argued that if he left for Greece, his absence might give rise to partisan movements in Italy, which the presence of the seven Pompeian legions, easily transferred from Spain to Rome, might turn to his disfavour; that Pompey might draw him away from his natural base, which was Italy backed by Gaul; that he hoped that by eliminating the Spanish question he would be more able to attack Pompey to advantage. In other words, he felt that Italy was not his so long as Pompey had seven legions in Spain, and he was unwilling to move on Pompey, with Italy for a base, unless this base was secure beyond a peradventure. This was well enough. But could he not have neutralized the seven Pompeian legions *quoad* Gaul by a lesser force of his veterans at the Pyrenees, and still be strategically stronger by moving on Pompey through Illyricum before the latter had concentrated all his forces, or raised more? The time to strike Pompey was when he most feared to be struck. And was not Pompey in Greece, with his limitless resources, a far graver threat than the seven legions in Spain? How could Caesar safely reckon on Pompey's not returning to Italy so soon as himself had left? It will always remain a question whether Caesar could not have moved on Pompey, through Illyricum,—most of his legions were easily available for such a march,—and have defeated him, or driven him into flight with a hearty dread of his enemy, before any serious danger would happen from the activity of the Spanish legions. And Caesar's Gallic lieutenants were better men than Pompey's Spanish *legates*, and might be fairly relied on to hold the Pyrenean country against them.

All these arguments are based on assumptions. Little is told us by the *Commentaries* about Caesar's reasons for his actions. "I am setting forth to fight an army without a leader," said he, "so as by and by to fight a leader without an army." Aphorisms do not explain. All we are told is that Caesar determined to go to Spain.

After quartering his legions for rest in the chief municipal towns, Caesar went to Rome, had the tribunes call together on the 3rd of March what remained of the Senate and stated his grievances. He claimed that Pompey should be made to obey the law as he himself was willing to do, and demanded that ambassadors should be sent to Pompey to effect a reconciliation between them. But no one was found who cared to act as envoy, for Pompey had declared that those who remained in Rome were as much his enemies as those who were in Caesar's camp.

Caesar was able to accomplish little. His secret enemies were still numerous in Rome. Before he left the city, he appropriated from the treasury the fund deposited there to defend the city against the Gauls, alleging that, as he had conquered them, there was no further use for it. The *tribune* Metellus attempted to prevent him from so doing, but Caesar drew his sword upon him, exclaiming: "Young man, it is as easy to do this as to say it!" The money was soon expended, and Caesar, not long after, was obliged to borrow money from his officers to pay his legions. It must have been a strange spectacle to Roman citizens to see the treasury thus despoiled; but they were powerless. Caesar was sole master.

Caesar had his legions strung out from Gaul to Sicily. He was not well concentrated and had to make many changes to accord with his new plans. His fresh troops he stationed in Apulia and along the Adriatic Sea, garrisoned the coast towns having good harbours, ordered the Eighth, Twelfth and Thirteenth legions back towards Gaul, whence he had already drawn Trebonius with his three legions, and concentrated these and Fabius' three in the Narbonese. Then he placed his Roman interests in the hands of Marcus Lepidus, gave the military command in Italy to Mark Antony, and put Illyricum under Gaius Antonius and Cisalpine Gaul under Licinius Crassus. He released Aristobulus, king of the Jews, who was captive in Rome, hoping he would on his return home oppose the recruiting of Pompey's lieutenant, Scipio, in Syria. After completing these preparations he left Rome March 9, and went to the province of Transalpine Gaul, thence over the Corniche towards Massilia, the vicinity of which he reached in about twelve days.

Meanwhile Vibullius Rufus, whom Caesar set at liberty at Corfinium, had gone to Spain to act for Pompey. Domitius, who, we remember, was Caesar's successor as governor of Gaul, on the appointment of the Senate, had got friends at Igilium and Cosa to fit out seven rowing galleys for him, and had sailed for Massilia. As Cesar marched along the coast he heard that Massilia had collected all the corn from the vicinity and fortified the town, and that Pompey's adherents had roused the citizens in his favour. They had also procured the aid of the Albici, nearby mountain tribes of the Western Alps, between the modern Durance and Verdon Rivers. So soon as he reached the place Caesar invited some of the principal citizens of Massilia to come to him, and endeavoured to talk them over to his cause. But for once his eloquence proved vain. The magistrates claimed that they had received equal favours from Pompey as from Caesar, and could in good faith give allegiance to neither, nor admit the forces of either to their town or harbour. Domitius, during the parley, arrived with his fleet, was admitted to the harbour, and made governor of the place. Caesar, without ships, had no means of stopping him.

Domitius at once set to fitting out a fleet. He seized on all the merchantmen which were in the harbour or in the vicinity, and confiscated their cargoes, mostly corn, which was laid up for a siege. Caesar, incensed that a town in the province should thus turn against him, as well as all but compromised by its treachery—for Massilia, with the aid of the Albici, might cut at Aquae Sextiae the road from Italy to

Spain—began to provide means for besieging the place. He could not leave it in his rear without at least a blockade, for it was one of the most important towns on the Mediterranean, and its example might prove disastrous. He built and equipped twelve vessels in the short space of thirty days, at Arelas nearby, placed these under Decimus Brutus, the skilful victor of the Veneti, and left Trebonius with the three legions he was marching towards Narbo to invest the place. He himself began the construction of a line of contravallation.

Fabius' three legions had, we remember, been wintering in Narbo. Caesar sent word to Antony to hurry up the Eighth, Twelfth and Thirteenth, already on the march, and diverted them from Gaul towards Spain. Meanwhile he dispatched Fabius into Spain, with the three legions at Narbo, to occupy the passes in the Pyrenees, in advance of his own coming. Fabius marched with speed enough to dislodge a small party of Pompey's adherents (part of the forces under L. Afranius) from the passes in the Pyrenees, and descended into Spain. It had been the purpose of Afranius and Petreius to occupy the Pyrenees, but Fabius anticipated them.

POMPEY'S SPANISH LEGIONS

51

Vibullius Rufus had recently arrived with instructions to assume supervisory charge on behalf of Pompey of all Hispania. But the several generals remained in command of their respective armies. The lieutenants who had been there before, L. Afranius, M. Petreius and M. Varro, with seven legions, divided the peninsula between them, each practically independent. Afranius, who had served under Pompey against Sertorius and Mithridates, had three legions in Hither Spain, *i. e.*, Catalonia and the territory south and west; Petreius had two near the River Anas; and Varro had two between the Anas and the west coast. On getting news of the happenings in Italy and at Massilia, Petreius marched towards Afranius, and joined forces near Ilerda (Lerida), on the Sicoris (Segre), early in April, while Varro was left to hold the western part of the peninsula. The five legions of Afranius and Petreius were increased by a large force of auxiliaries and horse recruited by these legates. In all Spain there were the seven legions mentioned, six being old Italian legions and one Spanish; eighty *cohorts* of auxiliaries, those from Hither Spain with shields, those from Farther Spain with round leather targets; and five thousand Spanish horse. It is difficult to estimate these forces. At normal strength they would number eighty-seven thousand men. But if they were of good average field strength alone, say four hundred men to a *cohort*, they would count but sixty-five thousand, with cavalry some seventy thousand men. Caesar counted Fabius with three legions on the ground, the three to arrive by and by from Italy, five thousand Gallic foot-auxiliaries, three thousand horse of old German and Gallic troops, and the same number of new foot and horse recruited of the best material, of whom those of most repute were from the Aquitani and neighbouring mountaineers. The total of these forces is equally hard to estimate. Probably the Caesarian *cohorts* fell below those of Pompey's lieutenants, which had not been ground down by the attrition of war. If his *cohort* numbered three hundred and sixty men, as we formerly called them, the total under the eagles would have been thirty-seven thousand six hundred. It was no doubt under forty thousand men; but the army was veteran and included many of the best of the Gallic chiefs. Stoffel estimates that Fabius had twenty-five thousand men, or with the three legions yet to arrive thirty-six thousand men. These are, as estimates, close enough.

Caesar had used up all his moneys, including the large sum which he took from the Roman treasury, to pay his legions. He now adopted a novel course of conduct to raise more. He borrowed various sums from his tribunes and centurions and distributed the money among the private soldiers. He thus secured the good will of the latter by his gifts and the adherence of the former on account of the loan. This certainly original proceeding was perhaps justifiable in view of the fact that Roman legionaries were now for the first time in this war to meet Romans in hostile array, and a double hold on the fidelity of his men was a further bond to fortune.

CHAPTER 28

Ilerda

April to June, 49 B. C.

Afranius and Petreius held Ilerda. Caesar sent Fabius ahead with his army, leaving the fleet at Massilia. When he himself came up he at once advanced on the Pompeians, who declined battle. Caesar camped nearby and shortly essayed to capture a hill which lay between the Pompeian camp and the city. In this he was checked by his veterans becoming demoralized, but in a fight under the walls of Ilerda got the better of the enemy. For a long while the contention of each army was confined to foraging and seeking to disturb its rival in foraging. Bat shortly a serious storm and flood cut Caesar off from his base, by destroying his bridges over the Sicoris; the enemy kept theirs which was a solid one of stone. In Caesar's camp there was great distress, and a convoy coming to him from Gaul was almost captured by the Pompeians. Caesar contrived a bridge of boats by which he saved the convoy and again victualed his army. The Pompeians began to lose energy.

From the Iberus to the vicinity of Ilerda the country is mountainous and in Caesar's day was in part heavily wooded. North of Ilerda the country was level, and it is well commanded by the city, which stands on a bold, prominent rock on the bank of the Sicoris. While Ilerda was an excellent place for tactical defensive purposes, it was not a strategic point from which central Spain could be controlled or even protected. The River Ebro was the true line of defence, but the Pompeian lieutenants not only did riot hold this, but did not even have secure communications with the river and the interior beyond. Having by delay forfeited the Pyrenees, they were short-sighted in relying solely on Ilerda to protect Spain. They took up the position "on account of the advantages of the situation."

On reaching Ilerda, about April 20, which he had done "by hasty

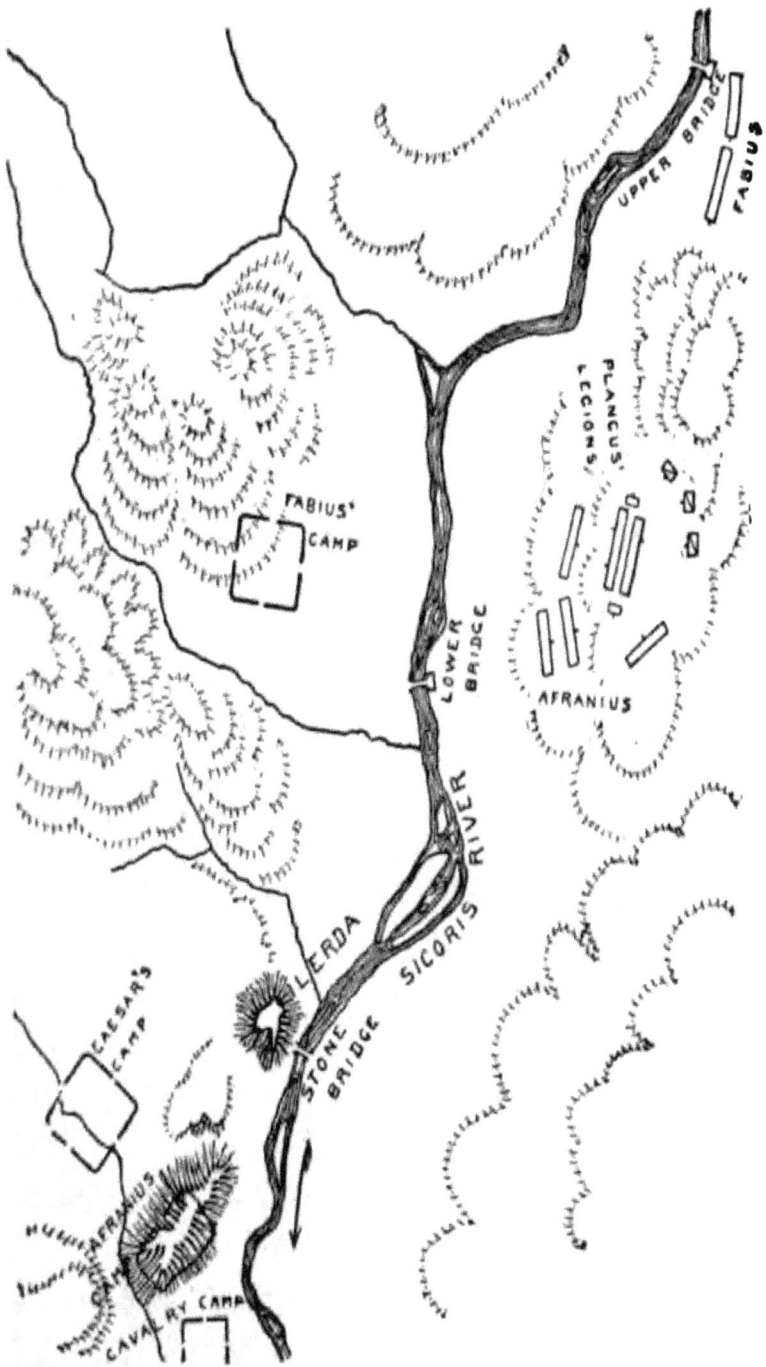

ILERDA AND VICINITY

marches" from the Pyrenees, Fabius found Afranius strongly camped, some eight hundred paces south of the town, on an Isolated hill on the right bank of the River Sicoris. The cavalry lay between this camp and the river, in the plain. The situation of the town made it inexpugnable. Between camp and town lay another piece of slightly elevated ground, the south part of it nearer the camp than the town. In this location Afranius and Petreius had determined to keep on the defensive till Pompey could arrive, for their chief was reported to be on his way through Mauretania to join them. How the rumour originated it is hard to say. There was no foundation whatsoever for it. The Pompeians had accumulated goodly supplies of food in Ilerda, but still not enough to last through a long campaign. They imagined, however, that they could here hold the road into the interior of Spain against Caesar's forces.

Fabius went into camp and entrenched on the right bank of the Sicoris, about three miles upstream from Afranius, on the slope of a hill, between two brooks discharging into the river. Here he "sounded the inclinations of the neighbouring states by letters and messengers." He was joined not far from the middle of May by the three legions from Italy. He had made two bridges over the Sicoris, one near the left flank of his camp, the other four miles upstream. Afranius had control of the stone bridge at the town.

Each army used to send across their own bridges on for-aging expeditions, because the corn supply on the right bank was exhausted, and constant skirmishing resulted. On the 21st of May, when Fabius had sent his foragers, under cover of his cavalry and two legions, across the lower of the bridges, the weight of the train and troops, and the high water, broke it down before the horse could cross, and cut the infantry off from that in camp. The party none the less kept on its way, anticipating no danger. Seeing the debris of the bridge floating down the stream, Afranius guessed the reason and, marching four legions and all his cavalry from Ilerda over his own bridge, attacked the two legions thus left without support. L. Plancus, the *legate* who was in command of the Caesarian party, "took post on a rising ground and drew up his army with two fronts,"—perhaps meaning a square, perhaps that each legion backed on the other with a *cohort* drawn up across the flanks,—so as to resist the enemy's cavalry. This was a formation later used by Caesar at Ruspina, and may have been more or less in use. Here Plancus bravely held head against a furious attack by Afranius. His defence succeeded. Before the enemy had inflicted any serious injury on him, Fabius was seen to be approaching with a reinforcement of two legions. He had made the circuit over the upper bridge by a forced march in light order. This put an end to the combat, as Afranius deemed it wise to withdraw. The broken bridge was speedily repaired.

Two days after this encounter, Caesar arrived with a body-guard of nine hundred horse. After thoroughly reconnoitring the topography of the region, he at once began active operations. He felt that he had no time to waste. Every week was adding to the potential strength of Pompey in Greece. One of the most noticeable features of all Caesar's campaigns is the restless, unceasing activity of the man. He never sits down to await events. He puts his hand to working out the problem so soon as he encounters it. His speed in planning is as remarkable as the rapidity of his execution. He never waits for the enemy to initiate operations. This prerogative he reserves to himself. He now left six *cohorts*—one from each legion—to guard the camp, bridges and baggage, and "with all his forces drawn up in three lines" in battle order, and then faced to the right into column of march, he moved to Ilerda, marshalled his legions opposite the Pompeian camp, and offered Afranius battle on equal terms. But Afranius, though he drew out his forces with a show of resolution, finally declined it. He was well enough off as he was, and wished to wait for Pompey's arrival. Caesar, after remaining in line all day, though barely half a mile from the enemy's camp and at the foot of the hill on which it lay, determined to remain where he was, instead of giving the enemy the moral gain of seeing him retire; kept out his two first lines for protection, and with his third line unobserved began to fortify the front line of a camp with a trench some two thousand feet from the foot of the hill. No rampart was at first added, lest Afranius should attack during the inception of the work which he would be able to see from the greater prominence of the rampart. He could not see the ditch, hidden in rear of the two first lines. An additional reason for omitting the rampart may have been that the legionaries were not provided with palisades; there were none to be obtained close at hand, and it would have been dangerous to send to a distance for them.

This camping in the open plain in the close vicinity of the enemy was a bold thing to do, if it was not a wise one. It reminds one of old Friedrich camping in the very teeth of the Austrians before the Battle of Hochkirch. Caesar does not sufficiently explain what he purposed to accomplish by this proceeding, quite un-Roman and without precedent. The troops lay on their arms all night behind the ditch. Having thus made a beginning, for a day or two Caesar continued to entrench the other fronts of the camp, keeping at all times a large force behind the front ditch for protection, and paid no heed to Afranius and Petreius, who each day drew up as for battle not far off but on their slope .When the ditch was finished, on the third day, Caesar added a rampart to the camp; and after the whole thing was completed, on the same day drew in the baggage and *cohorts* from the first camp up the river. The location of the camp was in every sense un favourable; but it enabled Caesar to cut the Pompeians off from foraging on the right bank of the river.

Afranius and Petreius were, as stated, encamped upon a hill. Between them and Ilerda was a plain some five hundred yards broad, with the slight eminence in the middle, already mentioned, which had abrupt sides about fifty feet high on the south. It occurred to Caesar that he would try to take this eminence, which Afranius had neglected to fortify, because its possession would cut the Pompeian camp off from the town where were the supplies, and from safe access to the bridge by the use of which alone they could contrive to forage on the left bank. This was of itself an admirable diversion, but it was not expertly managed. The hill was nearer the enemy than to Caesar, so that the latter must employ ruse to seize it, as the Pompeians were always on the watch. Instead of sending a party thither by night, which would seem to have been his better plan, Caesar drew up three legions of his army as if again to offer battle, extending them from opposite the Pompeian camp to opposite Ilerda. The Ninth and Fourteenth legions were respectively in the centre and on the left. The duty of the latter was at the proper moment to advance and take the hill. It is probable that only the first two ranks, or the *antesignani*, of the Fourteenth were thrown upon the hill. At all events the attack was not perfectly planned, nor delivered with sufficient vim or speed. Afranius was on the watch. He had no intention of accepting an offer of battle by Caesar, but divining his purpose from some of his movements, he proved too quick for his opponent. He could not permit himself to be thus cut off. He threw forward those of his *cohorts* which happened to be on guard on the north of his camp to anticipate the movement. These *cohorts*, having "a nearer way" to the hill, as Caesar alleges, though this is not borne out by the topography, reached it first and drove back Caesar's men. Even a reinforcement did not suffice to carry the hill. "They were obliged to turn their backs, and retreat to the standard of the legions."

58

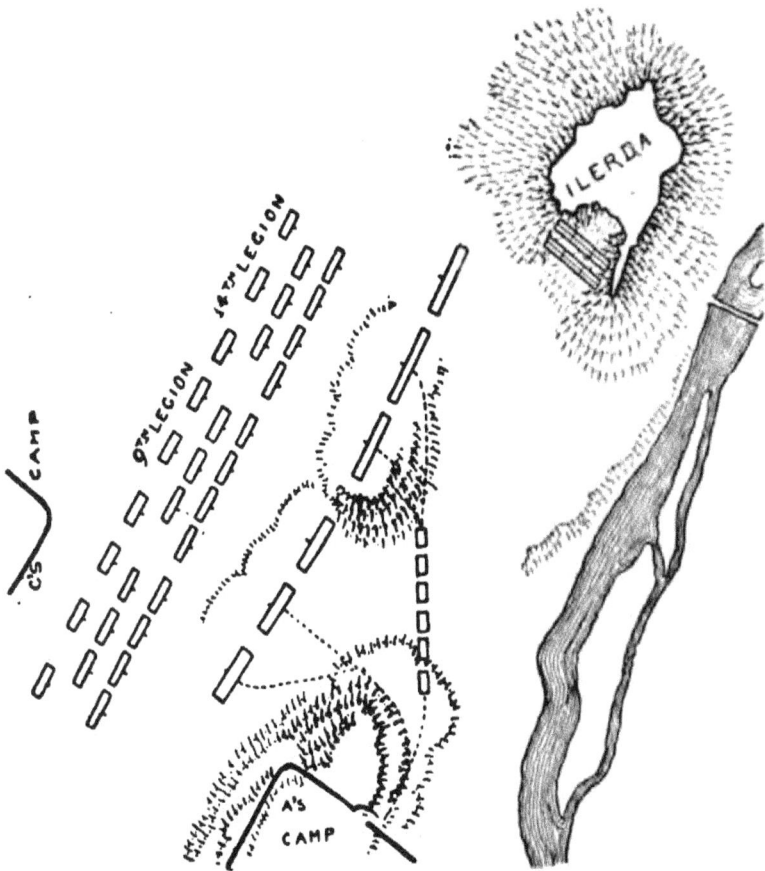

ATTACK ON ILERDA

The method of fighting of Afranius' men, and they were war-hardened veterans, was peculiar. They had learned it in combats with the Lusitanians and other barbarians of Spain . Instead of fighting in close order in the usual legionary manner, they scattered in small parties, and taking advantage of the accidents of the ground advanced or retired, fighting in loose order. "If hard pressed they thought it no disgrace to retire and give up the post ." It seems to have been a sort of loose order in groups, which advanced by short rushes from one cover to another much like the system which has obtained in recent days against the decimation of the arms of precision. Unused to this method and fearing that the rushes of some of these small groups from hiding would jeopardize their exposed (right) flank, Caesar's legionaries were at first considerably unsettled, and when its "advanced guard," i. e., antesignani, fell back from the eminence, the Fourteenth legion also gave way, and retreating to the next hill in its rear, not only weakened the entire line, but imparted a feeling of insecurity to all the *legionaries*.

The effect of this loss of confidence Caesar saw that he must immediately overcome. He seized on and headed the Ninth legion, which was in line on the right of the Fourteenth, and while covering the retirement of his beaten men, by a bold onslaught drove the enemy back in confusion. Part retreated over the hill in dispute, as far as the walls of Ilerda, whore they stopped and drew up; part appear to have retired to their camp.

Ilerda was built on a rock which stands up boldly five hundred feet above the plain, with a plateau of some one hundred and fifty acres on the top. Every side of this rock is practically inaccessible to assault except that on the south. Here, in a sort of ravine, is a slope, up which ran the road to the town, some six hundred yards long from the plain. Near the plain the mouth of the ravine is some three hundred and fifty yards wide; at the town, about a third that width.

It was between the two walls of the ravine that the enemy turned, and backing against the fortifications of the town awaited Caesar's Ninth legion. Emboldened by their success, and advancing too far in their eagerness to efface their comrades' defeat, this legion got engaged on an upslope where it had difficulty in disengaging itself. Its situation was critical. It had advanced well up the rocky hillside, and there met the enemy's line, which it could not destroy; when it essayed to retire the enemy fell upon it from the higher ground. The approach to the town on which they stood was flanked with craggy sides. There was but one way down,— the way they had come. The enemy's men not only stood where they could use their weapons to excellent effect, but

ILERDA FROM THE NORTH-EAST

no aid could be put in on the flanks of the Ninth, nor the cavalry be of the slightest service. Meanwhile the enemy was fighting with his back to the town, and felt confidence accordingly. There was room along the approach for but a front of three *cohorts*, and though Caesar had had no idea of coming to close quarters on such bad ground, he was constrained to send in, from time to time, out of the troops he could not use, fresh forces to relieve the weary. And this the enemy likewise did. "*Cohorts* were frequently sent to their aid by a circuit from the camp through the town," which seems to argue that there was access to the plateau from the river side, at least for friends.

The contest raged on this narrow slope for five hours. Neither line gave way, and Caesar could not well extricate his men without danger of demoralization. He had apparently sent in as many successive *cohorts* as could fight on the narrow front, and kept on putting in fresh ones. This it was which enabled the three *cohorts* front to continue to fight five hours without loss of heart. Finally Caesar's *legionaries* exhausted their javelins. At the sight of this the enemy renewed their efforts, resolved to hold their own. Caesar was threatened with disaster; but under the inspiration of his personal appeals the men persuaded themselves to make one last effort, drew their swords, and charging up the hill on the enemy's *cohorts*, drove them in disorder to the very walls of Ilerda. Under cover of this charge they withdrew down to a point where the cavalry was able to file in on the flanks, "which though stationed on sloping or low ground, yet bravely struggled to the top of the hill and riding between the two armies made our retreat more easy and secure." Cavalry here was enacting one of its chief roles to great advantage. This, added to the smart attack of the foot, prevented the enemy from following.

The combat was drawn. Retiring to camp, Caesar found that he had lost in all one *centurion* and seventy men killed and six hundred wounded. The enemy's loss in killed alone, as the *Commentaries* claim, was two hundred, with five *centurions*. The wounded are not given. Considering that the combat had been hotly contested for five hours, this was not so serious a loss. It shows how safe the Roman legionary was with his excellent armour and broad and skilfully handled shield, so long as he did not break his ranks.

It is to be observed in a general way that while the losses of a thoroughly defeated enemy were often in olden times awful beyond anything we know today, the losses of the victors were usually by no means heavy; and the casualties of ordinary campaign work,—outpost and picket fighting,—such as we are familiar with and which are frequently far more numerous than those of pitched battles, were small compared to those of modern days. The percentage of loss by wounds in one of Caesar's campaigns was as a rule low.

Each party claimed the victory in the fight at Ilerda; Caesar's men because, though they had at first fallen back. they had forced the enemy to his gates and held him there, and had moreover driven him uphill with the sword,—an unusual feat; Afranius' men because they had kept and were able to fortify the eminence in dispute. This they did with strong works and put a garrison in them .

Caesar's operation so far had for result that his cavalry—which was far superior to Afranius'—could hold the surrounding territory, and by watching the bridges could prevent Afranius from foraging at large on the farther side of the Sicoris . He foresaw that want of bread would sooner or later drive Afranius from his position. Still Caesar must have keenly felt the fact that he had in his first combat with Roman troops quite failed to accomplish what he set out to do. His luck had for the moment turned on him, and this in a contest with an officer of minor rank and ability.

No doubt here, too, his persuasive words were employed to advantage in satisfying his soldiers that they had really won the fight. But to construe the *Commentaries* as we often have to do in the Gallic War, this affair at Ilerda looks more like a defeat for Caesar than a drawn battle. Nor can it be said that the attempt to seize the hill in question was brilliantly conceived or executed. Rather is Afranius' defence to be commended.

Two days after the battle a serious disaster happened. A severe storm arose. The melting snows poured down from the mountains in a vast flood, and the waters of the river overflowed their banks— "it was agreed that there had never been seen higher floods in those countries"—and swept away both of Caesar's bridges, which were of but temporary construction. The camp was flooded by the brook which ran through it. Caesar found himself cut off from his communications with Gaul, and shut in between the two rivers Cinga and Sicoris, over the latter of which Afranius still had a bridge, and Caesar now had none. No fords were within thirty miles. Afranius had previously gathered all the corn of the immediate vicinity, so that foraging was difficult, and the light troops attached to the army of Afranius kept up a harassing small-war. His Lusitanians and targeteers of Hither Spain could easily swim the river, "because it is the

62

custom of all those people not to join the army without bladders," and Caesar was no longer able to interfere with the foraging of Afranius on the left bank.

Worse than all, Caesar's convoys could not reach him. A large force of foragers had been prevented from returning to camp. The friendly states could not get to him with corn, and the new crops were not yet ripe. All the cattle had been removed to a great distance. There were no boats to be had, for Afranius had secured these long ago. Caesar's rations grew short. Afranius, on the contrary, was well supplied, and his own bridge was still intact, which enabled him to cross the Sicoris, not only to forage, but to receive supplies from the interior of Spain. The tables were turned. The height of water, the rough banks and the enemy's opposition prevented Caesar from repairing the bridges,—"it was no easy matter at one and the same time to execute a work in a very rapid flood and to avoid the darts,"—and any attempt to cross small parties was headed off by the *cohorts* of the enemy, which lined the banks.

A still more fatal matter was that a large convoy from Gaul—including slaves and freedmen some six thousand souls all told—was near at hand, and Afranius knew the fact, and had set out with three legions and all his cavalry to attack it. In this convoy "there was no order or regular discipline, as everyone followed his own humour, and all travelled without apprehension," knowing nothing of the disaster to Caesar's bridges. Reaching the convoy, Afranius summarily fell upon it, and but for the courage of the Gallic horse—which now as always behaved with consummate gallantry—might have corralled the whole body, in which "there were several young noblemen, sons of senators and of equestrian rank; there were ambassadors from several states; there were lieutenants of Caesar's." But to the aid of the skill and daring of the Gallic horse came the faultiness of Afranius' dispositions, which lacked both vigour and ability. These men held Afranius' forces at a distance by skirmishing about his legions in their own peculiar manner, and thus enabled the convoy to retreat to the uplands. The loss was two hundred bowmen, some horse and non-combatants, and a little baggage.

All these disasters made provisions scarce and high, corn reached fifty *denarii* a bushel. "The want of corn had diminished the strength of the soldiers." Cattle were got, but by great efforts only. Caesar was obliged to forage at a considerable distance. This series of misadventures tended to encourage the enemy, and, reported at Rome, as they were very circumstantially by Afranius, began to lead people to believe that Cesar's fortunes were at an end. Had Pompey actually come to Spain at this moment,—as he should have done,—Caesar might well have been in bad case. But Pompey did not deem it essential to come. He was waiting for Caesar in Greece.

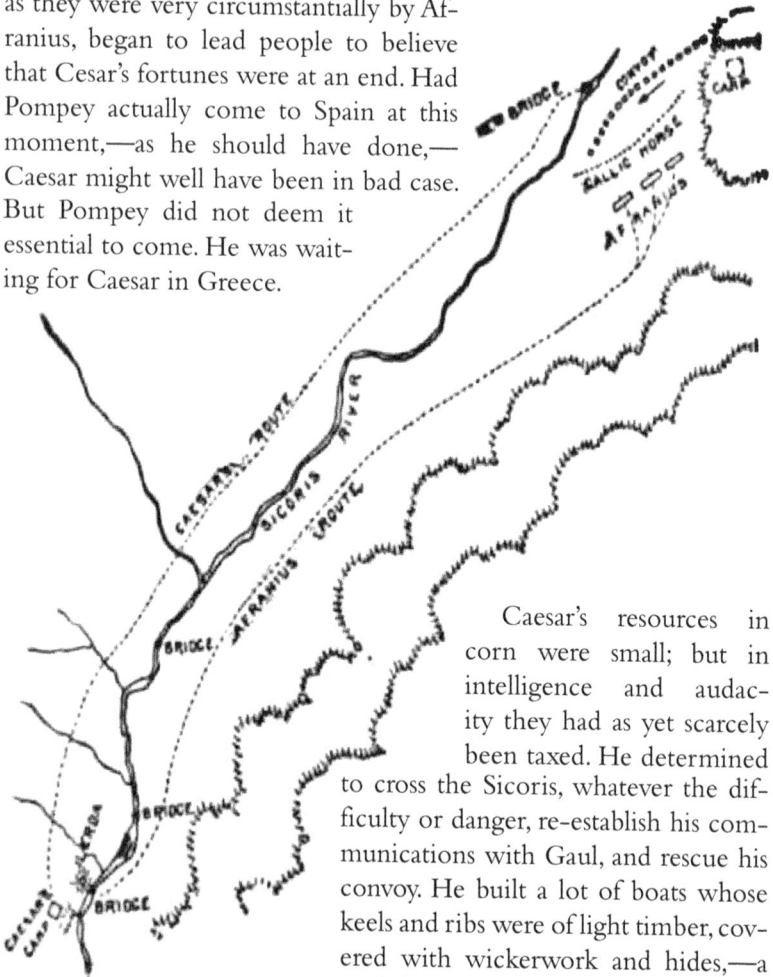

RESCUE OF CONVOY

Caesar's resources in corn were small; but in intelligence and audacity they had as yet scarcely been taxed. He determined to cross the Sicoris, whatever the difficulty or danger, re-establish his communications with Gaul, and rescue his convoy. He built a lot of boats whose keels and ribs were of light timber, covered with wickerwork and hides,—a trick he had learned in Britain. These he now transported on wagons in one night, twenty-two miles from camp, up the river to a place already selected, near the modern village of San Llorens. Here he sent a body of men across, who seized upon and fortified unperceived a hill on the opposite shore; and to this place he soon transported a legion. Then, by beginning a bridge at both ends under cover of this force, he finished it in two days and safely brought his convoy and foragers across to camp (June 11). At the same time he put over a large body of horse, and sending it out at an opportune moment, he surrounded the enemy dispersed as foragers, and captured a great store of men and provisions; and when some Spanish light-armed *cohorts* came to the rescue, a part of the horse protected the plunder, while another advanced against the enemy, cut off one *cohort*, put it to the sword, drove off the rest, in disorder, and returned to camp, across the bridge, with much booty. The question of provisions was thus settled, and the superiority of Afranius and Petreius at once vanished into thin air.

During this time, there was a naval engagement at Massilia between the forces of Domitius and Brutus, near an island (modern Rattonneaux), opposite the town, where Caesar's fleet was stationed. The enemy was largely superior in the number of his vessels. He had seventeen war-galleys, eleven decked and many smaller ones, well manned by archers and the auxiliary Albici, and was the attacking party. Brutus bravely sallied out to meet the enemy. The Romans, though their rowers were new, had aboard *antesignani* and *centurions*, all veterans of stanch courage, who for its honour had requested this service. For a while the skilful manoeuvring of the Massilians threatened disaster. "The Massilians themselves, confiding in the quickness of their ships and the skill of their pilots, eluded ours, and evaded the shock, and as long as they were permitted by clear space, lengthening their line they endeavoured to surround us, or to attack single ships with several of theirs, or to run across our ships and carry away our oars, if possible; but when necessity obliged them to come nearer, they had recourse, from the skill and art of the pilots, to the valour of the mountaineers. But our men, not having such expert seamen, or skilful pilots, for they had been hastily drafted from the merchant ships, and were not jet acquainted even with the names of the rigging, were, moreover, impeded by the heaviness and slowness of our vessels, which having been built in a hurry and of green timber, were not so easily manoeuvred. Therefore, when Caesar's men had an opportunity of a close engagement, they cheerfully opposed two of the enemy's ships with one of theirs. And throwing in the grappling irons, and holding both ships fast, they fought on both sides of the deck, and boarded the enemy's; and having killed numbers of the Albici and shepherds, they sank some of their ships, took others with the men on board, and, drove the rest into the harbour. That day the Massilians lost nine ships, including those that were taken."

The news of this victory tended much to encourage the forces at Ilerda. Caesar purposely exaggerated the success, and as a result a number of towns and native tribes tendered fealty and corn, Osca, Calagurris, Tarraco, the Jacetani at the mouth of the Iberus, the Illurgari south of them, and the Ausitani on the sea near the eastern end of the Pyrenees. Even a *cohort* of Illurgari, in the enemy's camp, deserted to Caesar in a body.

CHAPTER 29

Good Manoeuvring
June, 49 B. C.

Cesar's desire was to capture the Pompeian Army instead of destroying it in battle. His new bridge was many miles upriver. The stream was too full to build one farther down. In order to have a means of crossing near Ilerda, he cut a number of canals in a low island in the middle of the river to divert the stream into many channels, thus lower the water and make an artificial ford. The plan succeeded well. The Pompeians determined to retire to the Ebro. They crossed the Sicoris on their bridge; Caesar followed by way of his ford. The enemy sought to escape to the mountain-passes; Caesar anticipated them and thus cut off their retreat. They then tried to return to Ilerda; Caesar followed, harassed and finally surrounded them. The legions demanded battle; Caesar, anxious to spare Roman lives, refused. Finally, cut off from water, the entire Pompeian Army surrendered, on agreement that they should be discharged. Caesar had thus neutralized Pompey's whole force in Spain without a general engagement. It is one of his finest feats of manoeuvring. The Ilerda campaign had lasted six weeks.

Thus Fortune took a turn. Soon the vigour of Caesar's Gallic horse intimidated Afranius' foragers.

"The enemy, daunted by the courage of our horse, did not scour the country as freely or as boldly as before; but sometimes advancing a small distance from the camp, that they might have a ready retreat, they foraged. within narrower bounds; at other times, they took a longer circuit to avoid our outposts and parties of horse; or having sustained some loss, or descried our horse at a distance, they fled in the midst of their expedition, leaving their baggage behind them; at length they resolved to leave off foraging for several days and, contrary to the practice of all nations, to go out at night."

The neighbouring tribes, too, and many distant ones, so soon as Caesar's success was demonstrated, began to send in their allegiance and desert Afranius; and furnished the army with plenty of corn and cattle. More than this, the rumours of Pompey approaching through Mauretania died away, which still more encouraged the adherents of Caesar.

In order to provide a nearer means of crossing the Sicoris than the bridge lately built, and one less liable to interruption than those which the floods had carried away, Caesar, with his restless ingenuity, devised an artificial ford. Why he did not rebuild the bridges which had been destroyed by the high water, or construct others, it is hard to say. A new flood was improbable. Unless the water was too high and rapid, or unless the enemy was more than usually active in opposing the construction of bridges, the labour involved in building several bridges would have been

ARTIFICIAL FORD

small compared to that he undertook. Wood was not nearby, but it could be floated down from the mountains.

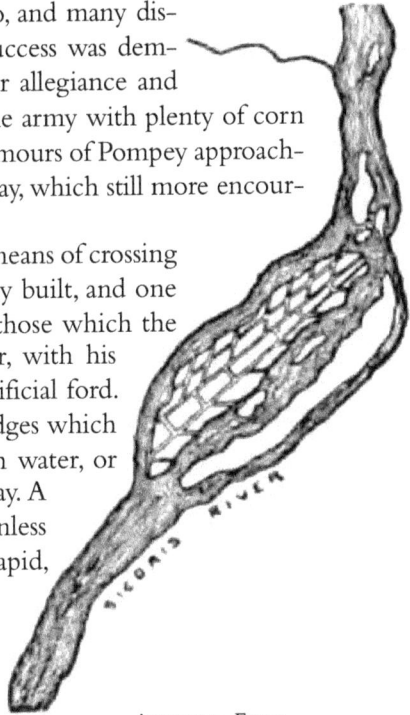

There have been numberless constructions of the passage in the *Commentaries* which narrates this engineering feat; and many clever designs have been made to show how Caesar produced this celebrated ford. What he really did—and there can be no doubt that it was what is now to be explained—is as remarkable by its simplicity as by its ingenuity.

The Sicoris, a mile or more above Ilerda, has a wide bed, in which, in Caesar's day as now, it flowed in three channels, leaving broad, sandy islands between them. The island nearest the right bank is half a mile long. Here, out of dart-throwing distance from the enemy, by sinking a number of drains thirty feet wide, he managed to draw off part of the current of the Sicoris into the beds of these drains, and by thus giving the volume of water more channel room, lowered the depth of the river so as to make it fordable in places. The plan succeeded well. The horse needed no longer to make the long detour by the San Llorens bridge.

This energetic and clever piece of engineering discouraged Afranius and Petreius, as much as the fact that Caesar's horse had proved so much the stronger, and had annoyed them so sorely. Here as in the Gallic campaigns, these gallant fellows were one of his mainstays. The Roman or native cavalry of Afranius and Petreius could by no means cope with them.

With Caesar in possession of the right bank of the Sicoris, and able to scour the country on the left bank, the Pompeians threatened to be in evil case. They must take decided action, and that at once. After long consultation, the *legates* resolved to retire across the Iberus into Celtiberia, where Pompey was well liked by many and feared by others, and where his influence consequently predominated. This was partly because he had been the Roman general who had got the credit of putting down Sertorius. This sentiment led the Pompeians to believe that they could there prolong the war till winter, whose snows in the Pyrenees would weaken Caesar's communication with Gaul; and Caesar, being unknown in that region, could not readily make adherents or victual his army. They therefore collected all the vessels they could in the Iberus at Octogesa (modern Mequinensa), at its confluence with the Sicoris, and ordered a bridge of boats to be there built.

The nearest and easiest road to Octogesa was along the right bank of the Sicoris; but an easy road meant easy pursuit by Caesar's cavalry, and this the Pompeians dreaded. They decided on the more rugged road on the farther bank, which had the advantage of yielding many places of ready defence; but the country had the very objectionable feature of being all but waterless. Only rainwater is there used today, and the inhabitants store this up in reservoirs.

The Pompeians accordingly transported two legions over the Sicoris,—they still retained the stone bridge,—and about June 21 fortified a camp and bridgehead with a rampart twelve feet high on the left bank. All their preparations had been some time completed; but Afranius and Petreius, with the slowness bred of lax purpose, had delayed their retirement too long. What they had done, moreover, had betrayed their intentions. Caesar, by severe toil day and night, had so far completed his ford as to be able—though with some danger—to get his mounted troops across, but the foot had only their shoulders and the upper part of their breast above the water. The enemy recognized the mistake they had made in their delay, and saw that they must speedily move away or forfeit their chance of doing so unmolested.

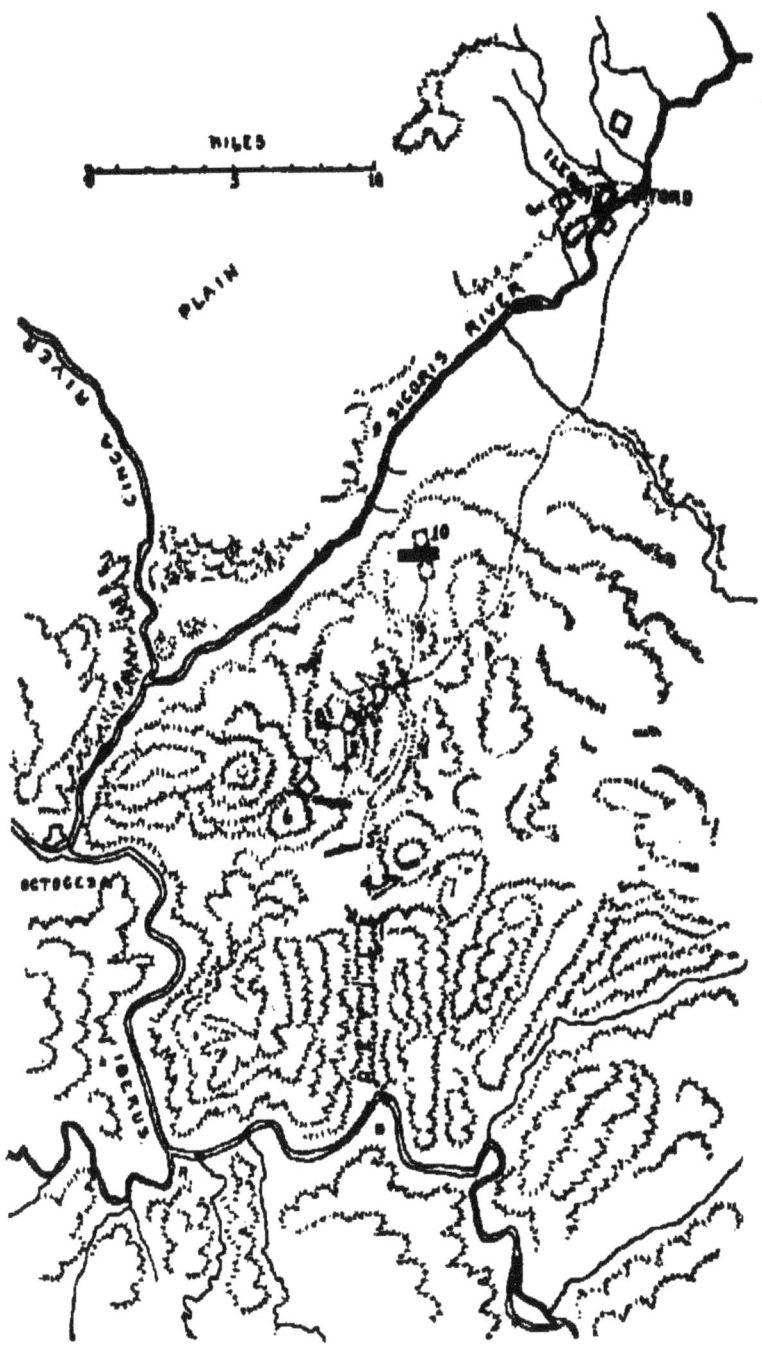

MILES

PLAIN

CINCA RIVER

SICORIS RIVER

ILERDA

OCTOGESA

IBERUS

THEATRE OF OPERATIONS NEAR ILERDA

Afranius and Petreius were growing morally weaker. Though their success had been fair in their general encounters with the Caesarians, they did not care to face Caesar in a pitched battle in the open. This looks as if, though Caesar had not won a success in the late engagement, he had impressed himself strongly on his enemies. At all events, the Pompeians had concluded to abandon his front and retreat to a safer country. Leaving two auxiliary *cohorts* in garrison at Ilerda to cover the withdrawal, they moved their whole army on the night of June 23 to the new camp across the river. "The *legionaries* had been ordered" to carry "sufficient corn to last twenty-two days."

The country from Ilerda to the Iberus, on the left bank of the Sicoris, was at first rolling and fertile, then strongly accentuated, and within five miles or so of the Iberus became much cut up by rocky and mountainous country, difficult to traverse. The march of Afranius and Petreius. if speedy and well conducted, might be free from pursuit. If, they could get beyond the level and into the mountains they were safe.

Caesar saw with regret that his prey was escaping . His only chance now lay in harassing the enemy's rear with a view of bringing them to terms. He sent his cavalry across the Sicoris to do this, and the nimble Gauls performed the duty efficiently.

"When Afranius and Petreius had broken up their camp about the third watch, they suddenly appeared on their rear, and, spreading round them in great numbers, began to retard and impede their march."

Caesar had given up the idea of forcing battle on the Pompeians. He saw that it would be better, if it was possible, to conquer Afranius and Petreius without destroying the Roman legions opposed to him. His hope was to b ring these legions, or at least many of the men, over to his cause. What would have been vacillation in many of his movements may really be ascribed to a sound military motive. He wished to win by manoeuvring rather than by fighting. Let us see how he did it.

On the left bank of the Sicoris, Afranius and Petreius had choice of two routes; one close to the river and through rather flat country, one by a circuit inland over the cut up country. This latter they chose for the same reason as they chose the left rather than the right bank. But it is evident that they had not carefully reconnoitred their ground, for even the latter route was not so cut up as to prevent the cavalry from keeping on their heels.

From the eminences on the right bank of the Sicoris Caesar's army could watch the operations of .the horse, and see how greatly they interfered with the movements of Afranius and Petreius. The squadrons swept around the enemy's flanks and rear, thus demoralizing the *legionaries*, but retired when smartly attacked. The Caesarians were in the forks of the two rivers, Cinga and Sicoris, with their one bridge twenty-two miles upstream. A circuit would be too long to enable them to take part in the action; and the stone bridge being, as we must assume, well held, they could not join their comrades except by the ford, which was up to their necks. But with the eye of veterans they at once perceived that the enemy was about to escape them; and they understood that this meant a long pursuit and a tedious campaign in an unknown territory.

"They applied to their *tribunes* and *centurions*, and entreated them to inform Caesar that he need not spare their labour or consider their danger; that they were ready and able and would venture to ford the river where the horse had crossed."

Caesar took advantage of this enthusiasm, and determined to try the experiment. It is neither stated in the *Commentaries* that Afranius and Petreius had broken down the stone bridge, nor that they had left a garrison to hold it; but one or the other must be the fact, or Caesar would certainly have used it at the present moment to cross. If broken down, he could not do so; unless held by many *cohorts*, it would seem as if Caesar might have brushed away the force at the bridgehead, and have thus frayed himself a passage across the river. The habit of the day, to be sure, was to avoid assaulting breastworks even when held by a handful of men, and anything but an immediate assault would have consumed too much time. But it appears curious, when so much was at stake, and the odds were so greatly in his favour, that Caesar should have hesitated to assault and capture the bridge. Roman legions during the Punic Wars, and at other times, stormed breastworks held by large bodies of regular troops; Caesar's legionaries had before now stormed town walls, and did so later; the defences of the stone bridge could not have been other than the usual ditch and rampart. However it may have been, Caesar preferred the risk of the ford to attacking the bridge, if still standing. The only explanation lies in the probability, either that the ford was easier than assumed by the *Commentaries*, or that the Pompeian generals had left behind, out of their Spanish *cohorts*, a goodly body to hold the bridge defences. In Ilerda, the two *cohorts* were probably enough as a garrison.

Leaving the weaker soldiers and one legion to guard the camp taking no baggage and stationing horse obliquely across, above to break the current and below to catch those who might he swept away, the

71

legions were marched down to the ford and across the river. Though a number were carried off their feet, they were all caught by the horsemen, and not a man was lost.

Caesar ployed his *legionaries* into three columns,—the usual three-line order of battle forward by wings,—and advanced. The good will of the men was such that they speedily gained the rear of the enemy, whose advance had been much retarded by the cavalry. "So great was the ardour of the soldiers that, notwithstanding the addition of a circuit of six miles and a considerable delay in fording the river, before the ninth hour of the day—three p. m.—they came up with those who had set out at the third watch, midnight. The cavalry had so cleverly harassed the march Afranius that his column had been unable to advance any considerable stretch,—not more than six miles.

The appearance of Caesar's legions in his rear constrained Afranius to pause in his retreat and to draw up his army on a rising ground, probably 1 on the chart. The *Commentaries* give certain hints as to time and distances which have helped to locate the operations of the coming days with fair accuracy. Caesar also called a halt and gave his men time to rest and refresh themselves, for they had marched more than twenty miles. He was loath to attack in earnest; but whenever Afranius resumed his retreat, Caesar advanced again upon him. In this manner both armies, in a sort of skirmishing fight, drifted six miles farther to the southwest. Both finally camped, Afranius on some hills which enabled him to avoid Caesar's cavalry (2), and Caesar on an adjoining height(3).

The original purpose of Afranius had been to continue his route nearly west over the hills to Octogesa; but Caesar's proximity led him to fear the effects of further interference by his cavalry. Some five miles to the south was a range too rough for the operations of horse; and through it ran a defile. If, by a sudden march, he could reach the mouth of the defile, he would be safe from pursuit, and could perhaps cross the Iberus farther down than Octogesa, or follow up its bank to that place. At all events the defile, at less than half the distance of Octogesa, was a temporary refuge, and the Pompeian clutched at a straw. It was a vacillating thing to do, and a useless; for Caesar, by marching straight on Octogesa, could head him off from that place; but any port in a storm.

The position of Afranius and Petreius was highly delicate; they had been marching and fending off Caesar's cavalry some sixteen hours. Their men were broken up with fatigue and the leaders were equally unsettled. Out of sheer dread of the cavalry it was determined not to push for Octogesa by the straight road, but to make a dash for the Iberus River by way of the defile; and with a view to this manoeuvre they reconnoitred the ground. Caesar, always active, did the like. Having come to this conclusion, it was the height of folly for the Pompeians not to push for the defile, at all hazards, before Caesar could seriously attack; but, "fatigued by the skirmishes all day and by the labour of their march, they deferred it till the following day." They should have sacrificed part of their army and all their baggage to save the rest. Some generals never know when affairs need a desperate remedy.

After dark it occurred to Afranius that he might steal a march on Caesar. The Gallic cavalry, which continued scouting all night, discovered from some prisoners whom they took at midnight that the enemy was making an effort to retire under cover of the darkness. When this fact was reported to him, Caesar ordered the signal for packing baggage—a certain note on the horns accompanied by a shout—to be given in his own camp. Hearing this signal, and assuming that Caesar was about to break camp,—lest his march should be disturbed by Caesar's *legionaries* as well as his cavalry,—Afranius decided not to move. A night attack with his large train would be apt to be disastrous. Next day (June 26), both generals again reconnoitred the country, and Afranius and Petreius held a council of war. Some advised to move by night, hoping to escape the more easily in the darkness. Others argued that as Caesar's horse was patrolling all night, it would be sure to discover them, and that the soldiers in the dark would not fight by any means as well as under the eye of their commanders. Daylight, said they, raised a strong sense of shame and duty in the soldiers which they lost in the darkness. After weighing the pros and cons, it was decided to move at daylight on the succeeding morning, and to risk whatever losses they must. This they prepared to do; but it was too late.

Caesar had divined the change of plan and decided to make an effort to cut the enemy off from the defile. He set out considerably earlier, "the moment the sky began to grow white," by a long circuit around the enemy's right flank,—to the east of them,—for the mountains. He could not take the main road, for Afranius and Petreius lay across it. He resorted to a clever ruse . He ordered his legions to leave camp by the west gate in the direction opposite to the defile. The movement was perceived by the Pompeians, but it was their opinion that Caesar was retiring. So soon as he could move his legions under cover, Caesar bore to the east and south. The road ahead of him was rough and cut up. "His soldiers were obliged to cross extensive and difficult valleys. In several places craggy cliffs interrupted their march, insomuch that their arms had to be handed to one another, and the soldiers were forced to perform a great part of their march unarmed, and were lifted up the rocks by each other. But not a man murmured at the fatigue, because they imagined that there would be a period to all their toils if they could cut off the enemy from the Ebro and intercept their convoys."

The idea that Caesar was retiring emboldened Afranius and Petreius to take their time. "Afranius' soldiers ran in high spirits from their camp to look at us, and in contumelious language upbraided us, 'that we were forced, for want of necessary subsistence, to run away, and return to Ilerda.' For our route was different from what we proposed, and we appeared to be going a contrary way."

But by and by it was perceived that Caesar's head of column had filed to the right, and that his van had passed the line of their camp. This at once showed the enemy their error, and urged them on to dispatch. If Caesar should cut them off from the defile, their game was lost. Afranius detailed a guard for the camp, and set out at a rapid pace with the bulk of his forces, without baggage, for the defile. The enemy's movements were somewhat hasty and irregular, and Caesar's horse managed seriously to impede their march.

"The affair was necessarily reduced to this point, with respect to Afranius' men, that if they first gained the mountains, which they desired, they would themselves avoid all danger, but could not save the baggage of their whole army, nor the *cohorts* which they had left behind in the camps, to which, being intercepted by Caesar's army, by no means could assistance be given."

As above stated, Afranius and Petreius had decided, because the road was more rugged and they thought would better preserve them from the stinging pursuit of the Gallic horse, to head directly south for the defile of modern Rivaroja. Caesar had divined their purpose and had pushed for the same point.

Though the circuit he was compelled to make lay through a very broken country, where there were no roads, such was the eagerness of his men and the enforced slowness of Afranius' party, that Caesar first reached the point he could hold the mouth of the defile . Here he drew up his army athwart Afranius' path, "in a plain behind large rocks". Afranius was strategically beaten. The men rested, elated with their success and more than ever confident of the ability of their chief.

The horse continued to sweep around Afranius' flanks and rear. It was one of those cases where the problem was plain and every man could see success or failure.

Afranius, seeing the miscarriage of his plan, again changed his mind, and determined to push for the road he had originally chosen, due west over the mountains. He sent out four *cohorts* of Spanish foot to take possession of one of the eminences (6), which seemed from its position to afford a probable opportunity of holding Caesar in check until he could pass in its rear with the main column. But Caesar's horse was on the alert, and smartly attacked these *cohorts*; "nor were they able to withstand the charge of the cavalry even for a moment, but were all surrounded and cut to pieces in the sight of the two armies."

The occasion was now so plainly excellent for an attack in force on the enemy, purposeless and held in place by the horse, that Caesar's *legates, centurions* and *tribunes* crowded round him begging him to engage battle, for the men were most eager for it, especially as all could see that the enemy was demoralized and pressing in irregular groups around their standards as if uncertain what to do. Or if not at the moment battle should be prepared for, as the enemy must soon come down from the hill for lack of water. Caesar plainly saw that a battle at this moment meant fearful slaughter of the enemy, and was not only anxious to spare Roman blood, but to keep these legions intact if possible, for his own use. He had the utmost faith in his ability to bring Afranius and Petreius to a surrender without decimation of either his own legions or the Pompeian. This decision excited great opposition and discontent among the soldiers, many of whom openly declared to each other that if Caesar would not fight when he was so advantageously placed, perhaps they themselves would not fight when Caesar called on them. But Caesar was not the man to change. He paid not the least heed to this exhibition of temper, which he knew really proceeded from soldierly motives. He had other more important things to consider. He allowed the enemy to retire to their camp; and having placed strong outposts on all the avenues to the mountains so as to cut off every road to the Iberus, he fortified his camps close to Afranius and Petreius, the better to observe their movements (7).

There were but two places to which these officers could now retire, Ilerda or Tarraco (Tarragona) on the coast. The latter was too far to attempt to reach it.

Not satisfied with merely observing them, Caesar now made an effort to cut the Pompeians off from water, and sent out his horse to attack the watering parties, which had to go some distance from camp to find reservoirs which were full. This new and serious danger obliged Afranius and Petreius to put out a line of posts to protect the march of the watering parties, and later determined them to throw up a rampart (8) from their camp to the water, a work of some magnitude and one necessitating the absence of both the generals from camp. "Petreius and Afranius divided the task between themselves and went in person to some distance from their camp for the purpose of seeing it accomplished." "The soldiers, having obtained by their absence a free opportunity of conversing with each other," which they eagerly embraced,—for among the soldiers of both armies there were naturally many old friends,—it was soon ascertained by the Caesarians, that there was grave disaffection in the enemy's camp. Many of the *tribunes* and *centurions* came over to see Caesar, and the intercourse between the camps quickly became universal. The Pompeian soldiers openly expressed their regrets that they were not in Caesar's army. The fraternizing even went so far that the *legionaries* deputed some *centurions* of the first rank to visit Caesar and state that they were ready to surrender their generals and join Caesar if the latter would spare the lives of Afranius and Petreius. They keenly felt that Caesar had spared them the day before, when they were so open to attack.

"Every place was filled with mirth and congratulations; in the one army, because they thought they had escaped so impending danger; in the other, because they thought they had completed so important a matter without blows; and Caesar, in every man's judgment, reaped the advantage of his former lenity, and his conduct was applauded by all."

The Pompeian generals soon heard this news. Afranius was disposed not to resist the inclinations of the soldiers, but was ready to accept the situation. Petreius, who had been at a greater distance, on learning of what was going on, either distrustful of Caesar, or from greater native combativeness, decided on action, armed his domestics and a few personal followers, and with the Spanish praetorian *cohort* and a few foreign horse flew to the camp, seized and put to death a number of Caesar's men who were still in his lines, and forced the rest to hide or flee. The latter "wrapped their left arms in their cloaks, drew their swords and defended themselves against the Spaniards and the horse." He then by threats, entreaties and tears brought the legions back to a sense of their duty, and having administered an oath to Afranius and all the officers,—he himself joining in it,—under no circumstances to desert the cause of Pompey, he obliged them to surrender all

Caesarians who could be found, many of whom were still within the camp. These he put publicly to death in the *praetorium*. Many, however, were kept concealed by the men and allowed to depart at night over the ramparts. Caesar was too wise to indulge in such slaughter. After searching out all the enemy's soldiers in his own camp, he allowed them to depart unharmed, with a friendly word to each. A number of officers concluded to remain with him. These he "treated with great respect. The centurions he promoted to higher ranks" (a very unusual step), "and conferred on the Roman knights the honour of *tribunes*." Matters reverted to a war footing; but Caesar had certainly gained ground with his enemy's legions.

Afranius and Petreius had made a series of blunders. Their management was extremely weak. Each error bred a new one. Caesar's energy and skill stand out in contrast. His constant watchfulness made both foraging and watering difficult to the enemy. The Pompeian *legionaries* had some corn, having started with a larger than usual supply; but the Spaniards and auxiliaries had none, being unused to carrying burdens, and many daily deserted to Caesar. Afranius and Petreius finally decided to make an effort to retire to Ilerda,—where they had left much victual,—and by the nearest road, which led north to the river and thence along the left bank. Their old camp there seemed the only harbour of refuge. To do this, they set out at daybreak, took their march along the high ground, to avoid as much as possible Caesar's cavalry, which harassed their rear as sharply as it could. "Not a moment passed in which their rear was not engaged with our horse." Their own cavalry proved to be useless, owing to the demoralization bred of the late combats. They could not be got to face the Gallic squadrons, and to prevent their breaking up had finally to be put in the middle of the legions. On the march the Pompeian foot would turn at every piece of rising ground from which they could cast their darts, and engage Caesar's cavalry to advantage, the *cohorts* which first reached it turning and defending those which followed; but at every descent, where the pursuing horse was on higher ground, they were obliged to make a violent attack to drive it back a distance and enable them to retire at a run to the plain and beyond to the next high ground, where they could again place themselves on a fighting equality with it. These rearguard combats became so dangerous and unsettling to the enemy that they were finally driven to halt and camp on an eminence, having retired but four miles. Caesar also camped (9) and sent out to forage. But the Pompeians had only gone into camp as a ruse and had fortified nothing but the front line. Caesar fell into the trap and allowed his foragers to disperse. The same day at noon, when they saw Caesar's horse was at a distance, the Pompeians endeavoured to escape; but Caesar, on perceiving their withdrawal, leaving a few *cohorts* to guard the camp and pack the baggage, followed them sharply up with his legions in light marching order, instructed the foragers to come in at four o'clock, and the horse to follow as soon as may be. On the return of the troopers they made their way to the front, and again began to harass the march of Afranius and Petreius. Caesar kept on their heels, incessantly edging in on their left and forcing them farther from the Sicoris, whose banks he patrolled with his cavalry. By skilful manoeuvring he finally forced them to camp at a distance from water, and in a highly disadvantageous place (10). He had completed a good day's work.

Caesar did not attack them. He ordered his men to lie on their arms instead of camping, and waited for the still better chance he could see approaching. But he took measures to confine the Pompeians to this place, as well as to protect his own legions from sudden assault, by a wall and trench which he extended about them on all sides. In the course of a day or two, having no fodder; Afranius and Petreius were obliged to kill all their baggage cattle. They perhaps contemplated making a sudden push for freedom. On the third day, July 1, at two p. m., they drew out their army in battle front to interrupt the completion of Caesar's works. Caesar did the like, but awaited their attack. Neither army seemed willing to take the initiative. Caesar did not care to do so; the Pompeians dreaded the conflict. They had lost *morale* since the fight at Ilerda. The camps, say the *Commentaries*, were not distant from each other above two thousand feet,—a space that gave small room for so many men to manoeuvre or to follow up a victory, for each army had five legions. Afranius' five legions were in two lines, and the auxiliary *cohorts* in a third line, in reserve. Caesar had three lines in the following formation: "four *cohorts* out of each of the five legions formed the first line; three more from each legion followed them as reserves, and three others were behind those; the slingers and archers were stationed in the centre of the line, and the cavalry closed the flanks." The battle was not engaged; both parties at sunset retired to camp. The next day, while Caesar was continuing the construction of his works, the Pompeians made a move as if to fray themselves a path and cross the Sicoris by a ford nearby,—if perchance they might reach Ilerda. Caesar headed them off with his cavalry, which he ordered to occupy all the fords and patrol the river banks on the other side.

Beset on all sides, having no fodder, water, wood or corn, seeing no chance of exit, and lacking resolution to cut their way out, Afranius and Petreius asked for a private conference on July 2. This Caesar refused, but granted the Pompeians a public conference to be held in the presence of both armies. The latter took place. Afranius spoke humbly and asked for easy terms; Caesar spoke in his usual persuasive manner, complimenting Afranius and Petreius and their legions for avoiding battle to save Roman life, though reproaching them for massacring his soldiers in their camp; paying a tribute to the high qualities of the troops and promising his good offices to all, but yet with a clear hint that the terms stated were his ultimatum. He knew full well when to be diplomatically generous. As a result of the meeting it was agreed that the legions of the enemy should be discharged from service and sent back to their homes, and that Afranius and Petreius should evacuate Spain and Gaul.

Caesar might have obliged the legions to join his cause, and he was anxious to have them do so. But he was too politic to use force. He accepted only voluntary enlistments. How many of these there were we do not know. He disbanded the legions and furnished corn to all. The Spanish troops were discharged at once, and the Romans were to be discharged at the river Varus on the confines of Italy. Whatever each man had lost, which was found in the possession of Caesar's troops, was returned to him, the soldier having captured it being compensated at a just valuation. The Pompeian soldiers marched to the Varus in charge of four of Caesar's legions, under Calenus, two in the van, two as rearguard, and there they were disbanded. The four escorting legions were subsequently ordered to join the Italian army against Pompey. Thus ended a series of blunders on the part of Afranius and Petreius,—by which Pompey not only lost Spain, but his oldest and best legions,—and a series of brilliant manoeuvres on the part of Caesar. Caesar retained the other two legions, giving command of them to Cassius, for the purpose of completing the conquest of Farther Spain.

The rapidity of these brilliant campaigns has scarce a parallel. Caesar crossed the Rubicon December 17, B. C. 50, by the Julian calendar. In two months he victoriously traversed the length of the Italian peninsula, and Pompey, declining a battle, sailed from Brundisium for Epirus. Caesar then moved his army to Massilia and Spain. On the 23rd of May he reached Ilerda. After a manoeuvring campaign of six weeks, Afranius and Petreius surrendered, July 2. In a period so short as scarcely to afford more time than was needed to make the marches through the countries named, he had reduced Italy and neutralized Pompey's forces in Spain.

Italy had succumbed so soon as Caesar trod her soil. No one had dared fight for her possession against the conqueror of Gaul. While Caesar had turned to Spain, Pompey had lifted no hand against him. Caesar had not counted on his good fortune in vain; but it was as fitting that fortune should attend so able and vigorous a conduct as that it should forsake the weakness and lack of enterprise of Pompey. In this instance, Caesar had made good use of the smiles of Fortune; he had laboured when she was willing to lend her aid; he had avoided her displeasure on the rare occasions when her back was turned.

On the other hand, Pompey's inactivity lay at the root of the forfeiture by his lieutenants in Spain of their seven fine legions and the entire peninsula; and of this weakness and loss of moral courage Caesar made the utmost use. Pompey's weakness was reflected up on his lieutenants. His lack of initiative was such that one can scarcely hold them to blame for not putting to good use Caesar's really grave danger after the flood in Ilerda. Like master, like man.

Caesar's complete accomplishment of his object by manoeuvring, instead. of fighting is one of the best examples of its kind in antiquity' It stands alone as a sample of successful avoidance of battle.

The creation of a ford at the Sicoris has always been considered a noteworthy engineering feat. It certainly was bold and ingenious.

The Italian and Ilerda campaigns have few parallels except in other campaigns by Caesar himself.

SIGNUM

80

CHAPTER 30

Massilia, Gades, Africa

April to September, 49 B. C.

The siege of Massilia, begun by Caesar, had been pushed by Trebonius while his chief was in Spain. The city resisted well, and the garrison made gallant sorties, but its fleet, despite reinforcements, was twice beaten by Caesar's, and the siege works gradually compelled an inevitable surrender. After the Ilerda campaign Caesar had subdued the rest of Spain as far as Gades, and had then returned to Massilia, where he received its surrender and spared it a sack; but heavy penalties were imposed. Pompey's original plan had been to advance on Caesar in Gaul from both Italy and Spain; but Caesar by his speed and ability had anticipated him, driven him out of Italy and captured Spain. Pompey was still engrossed in raising additional forces in Greece. Caesar's luck for once failed him. He sent Curio to reduce Sicily and Africa. In Sicily Curio succeeded in restoring to Rome its usual and necessary grain traffic; in Africa he was defeated by the Pompeians and his army destroyed. This enabled the aristocrats to make their holding in Africa secure. Caesar's means of reaching Greece were limited; Pompey controlled the sea. Pompey's land forces were likewise more than double Caesar's. But the moral force was all on the side of Caesar and his legions. He now prepared to attack his enemy in Greece.

While Caesar was settling matters in northern Spain, Trebonius, with his three legions, had been active in collecting material and building ships for besieging Massilia.

Massilia was founded 600 years B. C, by Phocean refugees, and had grown, owing to its unusual position and advantages, to great prosperity. It had spread Greek civilization in southern Gaul, and taught the barbarians agriculture, learning and art. It had numerous colonies, and an enormous commerce. The port of Massilia was naturally excellent; the town was built to the north of it on a point of land crowned by three hills. Two ravines, each of which ran down to the sea, separated the point from the mainland; the south of the harbour was covered with factories, arsenals and works; the eastern wall was at the edge of the ravines. It was solid, and boasted many towers. Several gates pierced it; the principal one, near the middle, opened on the Via Aurelia, the main road from Gaul to Spain. The town was fortified by nature as well as by art, and was difficult of approach. The habits of the people were honest and simple, and their houses plain; but their public buildings and temples were noteworthy. Trebonius established his camp opposite the centre of the eastern wall, on modern St. Charles Hill, which was somewhat higher than any of the city hills and looked down on the ravines which served as a ditch,—about one third of a mile from the city wall. As the Massilians commanded the sea, Trebonius could only invest the place by

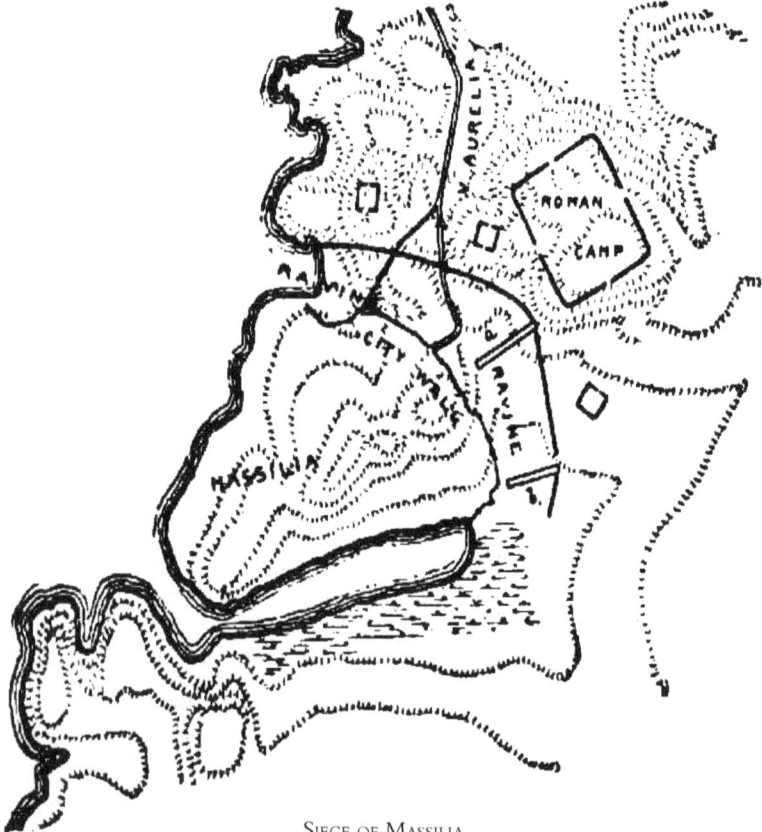

—Siege of Massilia

82

land. The point he chose for his main attack (a) was just south of the junction of the two ravines near the main gate. Deeming one insufficient, Trebonius opened a second point of attack (b), which was nearer the harbour, four hundred yards from the first one.

To reach the wall across the ravine at the main point of attack Trebonius had been forced to build a mound, which in one place was eighty feet high, and sixty feet wide everywhere. There was such abundance of war engines of great strength in the town that the ordinary material for making *vineae* was useless. Some of these engines shot iron-tipped poles twelve feet long, which penetrated even four rows of hurdles and went into the ground some depth. The roofs of the *vineae* had to be constructed of twelve-inch lumber, and in their front was a *testudo* sixty feet long, very stoutly made and covered against fire to protect the men who levelled the ground in front of the approaches. Under such cover alone could the men work with safety. The frequent sallies from the town were uniformly beaten back, but owing to these and the vastness of the works, progress was slow at both points.

Caesar had remained at Massilia, superintending the opening of the siege up to about the 6th of May, when he found it necessary to go to Spain.

Late in the same month there took place the naval battle mentioned in the last chapter; and about a month after this event, L. Nasidius reached Tauroentum, near Massilia, with a fleet of sixteen brass-prowed galleys sent by Pompey. He had passed the straits of Sicily without the knowledge of Curio, Caesar's legate there, had put into Messana and carried off a ship, and had made his way to the vicinity of Massilia. Here he got word to Domitius in the town, advising him to risk another sea-fight against Brutus, in which he, Nasidius, would join, and do his share. The Massiliots had a large supply of seamen and pilots,—the very best of their kind. They had covered some fishing smacks with decks and arranged them to carry archers and engines; had again repaired their war-galleys and built an equal number of other ships. They at once acted on Nasidius' suggestion, and sailed out to join him at one of the forts named Taurois.

"With a fleet thus appointed, encouraged by the entreaties and tears of all the old men, matrons, and virgins to succour the state in this hour of distress, they went on board with no less spirit and confidence than they had fought before."

The Massiliots were to have the right of the line, Nasidius the left. It was the 30th of June.

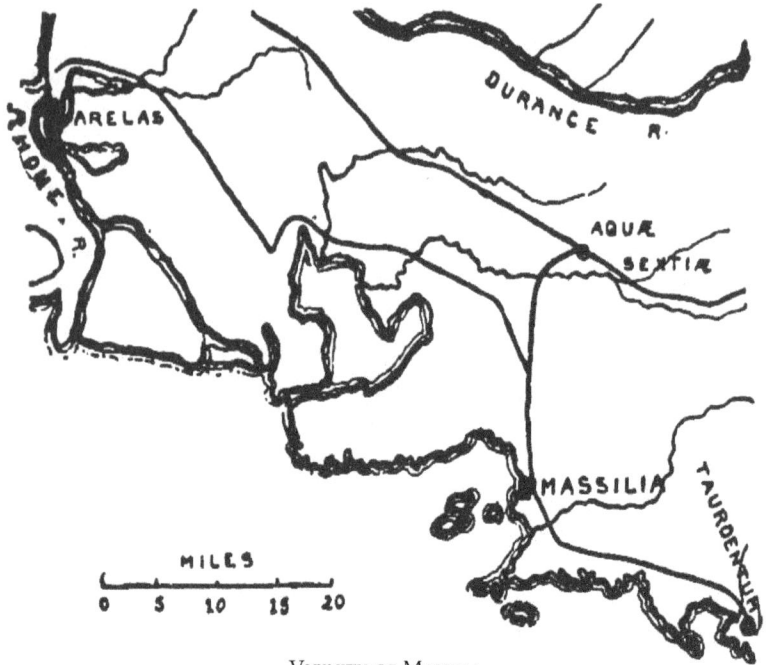

VICINITY OF MASSILIA

Brutus, with courage always uppermost, was not loath to meet them. He had the ships built by Caesar at Arelas (Arles) and six taken from the Massiliots. "Accordingly, having encouraged his men to despise a vanquished people, whom they had conquered when yet unbroken, he advanced against them full of confidence and spirit." Collected on the city walls, all the population of Massilia watched the boats which contained the flower of their youth and manhood; from Trebonius' high pitched camp, the Romans were equally intent. The combat was not lacking in spirit. The Massiliots fought with great courage. Brutus' line was the more open, which allowed better manoeuvring on the part of the Massiliots. The ships came to close quarters and, grappling to each other, boarded and fought with desperation. Brutus' ship was all but run down in the melee, and escaped only by a hair's breadth. But Roman valour again prevailed. The ships of Nasidius, proved to be of little use despite his boasting, soon gave up the fight and fled; of the Massilian ships five were sunk and four captured, one sailed away with Nasidius, and but one got back to the town. Those which escaped made for Hither Spain. This happy victory shut the port and reduced Massilia to a condition of siege.

Taught by the frequent sallies from the main gate that their wooden siege works were insufficient, the Roman *legionaries* built, on the right side of their terrace, near the gate, a thirty-foot square tower of brick or slate, with walls five feet thick, instead of one of wood. Soon this grew in height to six storeys. It had an overhanging roof, and this was gradually raised by screws so as to build the walls of the tower underneath it higher and higher. The outside was protected by heavy rope mats, hanging loose upon the walls. These Trebonius found best resisted the missiles. From this tower the Caesarians built a *musculus* to the enemy's wall. This consisted of a roof sixty feet long but not very wide, and built of much heavier timbers than usual. It was covered with tiles laid in mortar, to save it from fire thrown down by the besieged; the tiles were covered with hides, to protect them against water which the besieged poured down in spouts to dissolve the mortar; and the whole was topped by mattresses, to protect it against heavy stones and the iron-tipped missiles. This *musculus*, when completed, was run on rollers from the brick tower up to the city wall close to the tower selected for breaching, and under cover of the *musculus* the wall began to be undermined. The *musculus* resisted the heaviest stones; fire barrels, rolled off it, and were then pushed away by poles from within. From this tower the soldiers kept up a fire of darts to protect the *musculus*. It was intended to guard the flank of the terrace from sudden sallies from the main gate. As matters eventuated, the terrace never was completed.

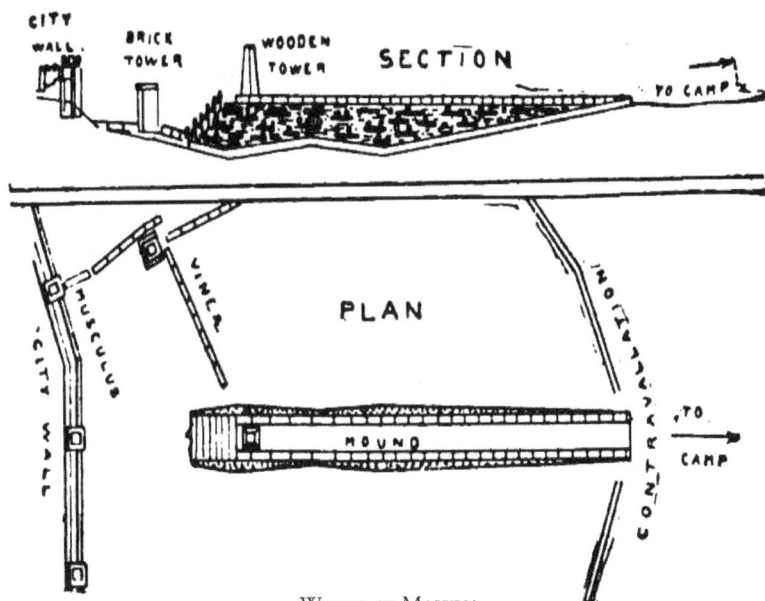

WORKS AT MASSILIA

85

It was not long before the wall of the city, under-mined at more than thirty places, began, to topple, despite the fact that the citizens had flooded the Roman mines by placing reservoirs of water where the mines would tap them; had counter-mined and had resorted to every known method to arrest the approaching crisis. Fearing then the capture and sack of the city, the inhabitants crowded to the gates, and begged the soldiers for a truce till the arrival of Caesar, who, in fact, had ordered Trebonius not to suffer the storming of the city, lest the infuriated soldiers should, as they had threatened to do, put to the sword all the men, which out of policy he desired to avoid. It is evident from many such items,—and the *Commentaries* are full of them,—that Caesar had not the best of control over his *legionaries*; and if he himself could not hold them in hand, his lieutenants could scarcely expect to do so. They were not the old *burgess* soldiers, who obeyed orders because they had, in their intelligent patriotism, the true instinct of discipline; they were professionals, of a far from high grade, who were held down only by the strong hand, and often with difficulty, who broke from restraint whenever a chance occurred. The truce begged by the Massiliots was granted, though the soldiers were hard to restrain from plunder and revenge.

The Massiliots proved treacherous. One day at noon, towards the end of July, when there was a high wind,—the mistral from the northwest,—and the legionaries were off their guard, the inhabitants sallied forth with incendiary utensils, and in an instant set all the works of the Romans on fire. A short hour consumed the labour of months. Next day again the towns-people made a sally, but the Romans were prepared for it, gave them due chastisement, and drove them back within the walls.

The soldiers then set to work, with renewed vigour, to make good the loss occasioned by the sally. The new *agger* was constructed with brick walls floored with timbers, which were shored up at intervals so as to sustain great weight. It was much less liable to be set on fire. In a few days the Caesarians had replaced what had been destroyed, much to the amazement of the citizens, who saw their engines made ineffective by the solidity of the Roman works, their soldiers driven off the walls by the Romans from their equally high towers, and no safety in any course but surrender.

Time-serving Varro, in (Andalusia), had been wavering in his allegiance to Pompey until he heard rumours of Caesar's troubles before Ilerda and at Massilia, when he began to act with more vig-

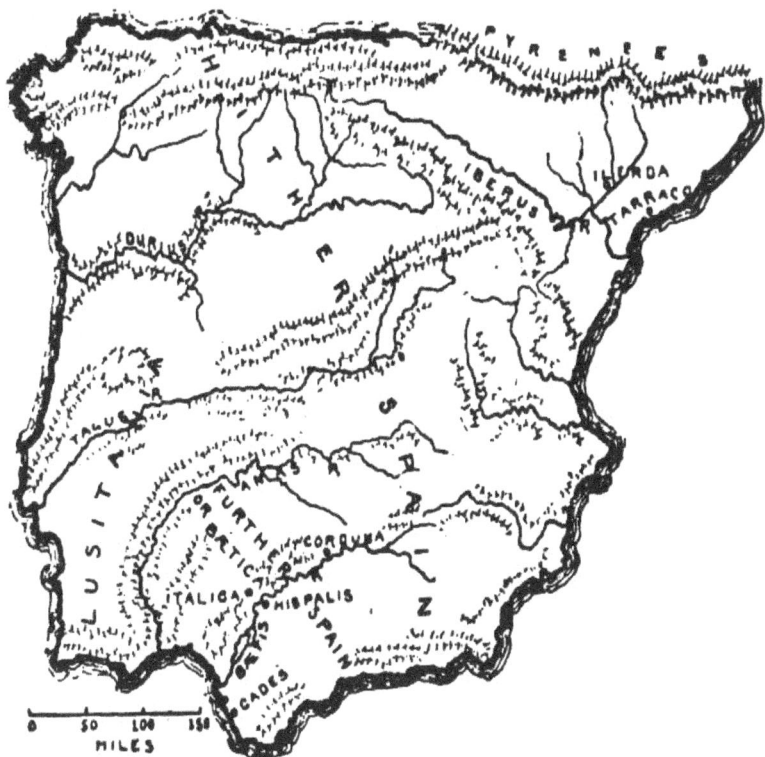

FARTHER SPAIN

our for his chief. Whereas he had theretofore deemed it prudent to praise Caesar, he now loudly denounced him. He was active in raising money, corn and troops,—some of the corn for Ilerda, some for Massilia,—and in preparing for war. He added thirty auxiliary *cohorts* to his force of two legions. As the whole province was somewhat pronounced for Caesar, Varro proposed to carry on the war from Gades (Cadiz), which lay near the coast on an island, and, being a prosperous city with a fine harbour, was most suitable as a base. Here he had built ten ships, and here, too, he accumulated large materials and stores. He constructed a number of vessels in Hispalis, on the Baetis. He despoiled the temple of Hercules, carried the riches into the city of Gades, and sent six *cohorts* there to guard them under C. Gallonius. He laid heavy taxes on the states, and by representing that Caesar was being defeated at Ilerda, got from the Roman citizens of the province eighteen millions of *sestercii*, twenty thousand pounds of silver and one hundred and twenty thousand bushels of wheat to be used in the war. He persecuted Caesar's friends and confiscated much private property. He made himself many enemies and generally blustered about, instead of taking real steps to meet Caesar, who was rapidly approaching, though with only two legions.

Caesar, although, after the surrender of Afranius and Petreius, he felt called to Italy by the pressure of the war and public affairs, yet did not feel as if he ought to leave Spain without finishing its subjection. From Ilerda, therefore, about July 9, he sent Q. Cassius, the *tribune* of the people, with two legions against Varro,—the four others had gone to Italy under Calenus as a guard for the captured Pompeian legions,—and, rather than leave the Iberian question unsettled, preceded them himself. He relied on his knowledge of Pompey's character, believing that he would lie quiet till Spain was finally disposed of. Caesar was lucky in his opponent. At the head of an escort of six hundred horse he marched to Baetica, and notified all the states to send embassies to meet him at Corduba early in August.

The response was unequivocal. Every town and state sent representatives to Corduba, and many towns turned out Varro's *cohorts* or shut their gates on them. Gades, when the citizens had heard of all that had happened, ejected Gallonius, Varro's lieutenant, and declared for Caesar. When this news reached Varro's camp, even one of his Spanish legions mutinied in Caesar's favour and marched to Hispalis. Varro withdrew to Italica, but this, too, declared against him, and he was reduced to surrender with his other legion. He gave up all the military stores, money collected and other booty. Caesar thanked the towns and inhabitants for their fealty, conferred honours on the principal citizens, remitted the taxes Varro had raised, and returned property he had taken. Then about August 20 he visited Gades, where he restored the moneys taken from the temple of Hercules, and left Cassius in command with Varro's two legions, promising him two more of new levies. Thence he sailed with his two old legions, on the ships Varro had constructed, to Tarraco, where he arrived the end of the month, and was received with acclamations. Here, also, he conferred honours on those who had sustained his cause. From Tarraco he marched by land to Massilia, where he received word that, in accordance with his own proposition, he had been created dictator, under a new law, at the nomination of M. Lepidus. From henceforth he was legally acting for the Roman state.

Massilia had surrendered to Trebonius September 6, after a five months' siege, but Domitius managed to escape by sea, and, though pursued, could not be taken. The Massiliots, greatly against the wishes of the enraged soldiery, who desired to sack the town, were spared on account of their ancient reputation; but they were disarmed, their treasure and fleet taken, and a garrison of two legions left in the place. The rest of the troops proceeded to Italy. Caesar himself set out for Rome.

Thus was finally thwarted Pompey's first general plan of advancing on Caesar in his old province of Gaul, from Spain and Italy at once. Originally Pompey had intended to anticipate Caesar in the offensive. When Caesar's remarkable activity resulted in his losing Italy, Pompey had conceived the idea of operating offensively from Macedonia as a diversion to aid his lieutenants in Spain, never doubting that Caesar would consume a year or more in his operations there. But Pompey was never rapid in preparation or action; in comparison with his present opponent he was procrastination itself. Before he had fairly begun the organization of his new levies in Macedonia, Caesar had finished the Spanish campaign and had robbed him of an entire province and seven fine legions. Pompey had been permanently reduced to a defensive strategic role. He took the offensive tactically at Dyrrachium, but he never recovered his strategic initiative.

A misfortune now befell Caesar's arms. His *legate* Curio, after regaining Sicily, had been sent from there into Africa early in July, to reclaim that land from Pompey's cause. Curio, a young but able officer, vigorous and enterprising, was unwise enough to underrate the army of Attius Varus, the Pompeian *legate* in Africa, and took with him but two out of his four legions and five hundred horse. The legions he selected were the ones which had belonged to Pompey, but had come over to Caesar at Corfinium, and were not quite trustworthy. Curio crossed, landed and marched to Utica, where Varus lay. At the inception of his campaign he acted with good judgment, and in a pitched battle with Varus, near Utica, inflicted upon the latter a bitter defeat with loss of six hundred killed and one thousand wounded. The population was largely favourable to Caesar, but shortly after the defeat of Varus, king Juba, who was friendly to Pompey and a personal enemy of Curio's, came to Varus' assistance with an overwhelming force.

Curio retired to the Cornelian camp (Scipio's old and excellent position of the Second Punic War), and should have remained there on the defensive until he had sent for his other legions; for he had supplies, water and timber at hand, and everything could come to him by sea. But being informed that the reinforcing army was only a small one, under command of Sabura, and not Juba's entire force, and elated with his recent successes, Curio was tempted out to risk another battle

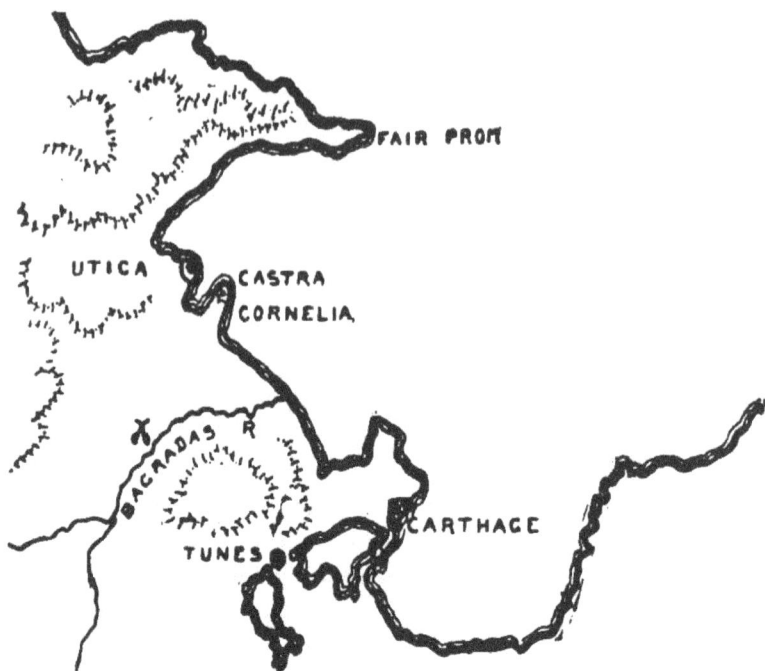

UTICA AND VICINITY

without sufficient reconnoitring. Other-wise intelligent, he was here lacking in discretion. He acted on partial information without testing its accuracy, and Rebilus, whom Caesar had given him as "chief of staff," or adviser, did not hold him back. Sabura did, in fact, command Juba's vanguard, but Juba was not far behind with his whole army.

So soon as Curio put in an appearance, Sabura feigned retreat, but only to lure the Roman into disadvantageous ground where the king's force lay in wait to surround him. And this, indeed, took place. Curio followed up Sabura's retreat to a distance of over twenty miles from his camp, in full confidence of another easy victory. He reached the place in careless order, with tired troops and anticipating no danger, and fell heedlessly into Juba's ambuscade. The king debouched from cover on all hands and took him unawares. His entire army was destroyed. He himself refused to fly, and died in the midst of his men (July 24). The forces left in the Cornelian camp attempted to escape by sea, but, owing to fear and careless loading of the vessels, few got away. King Juba put most of them to the sword.

This disaster, traceable to Curio's errors of judgment and over-eagerness to fight, was a serious blow to Caesar, and enabled the Pompeian party to gain enough ground in Africa to overawe the entire population of the continent. But Curio had previously taken possession of Sicily, and this had relieved the threatened scarcity of corn in Italy. Pompey's plan of starving out the peninsula was frustrated.

Mark Antony had been in command of the army of Italy, as *propraetor*. The ports of Sipus, Brundisium and Tarentum had been held by three legions to forestall a descent by Pompey's fleet. M. Crassus was in charge of Cisalpine Gaul. Two small fleets lay in the Tyrrhenian and Adriatic waters. Gaius Antonius was in northern Illyricum, on the island of Curicta, with two legions. Dolabella, with forty galleys, was in the straits.

To Pompey's admirals the situation at Curicta afforded a good chance of action. Octavius and Scribonius Libo, with a much larger fleet, attacked Dolabella, defeated him, and cooped up Antonius on the island. Despite some reinforcements sent from Italy and the aid of the Tyrrhenian fleet, the superior numbers and skill of Pompey's vessels prevented any rescue. Antonius' legions had to be abandoned to their fate. The *cohorts* were finally captured, taken to Macedonia and incorporated with the Pompeian army. Octavius continued his efforts to reduce Illyricum. Issa joined his cause; but Caesar's adherents held Lissus, and at Salonae severely defeated Octavius, who retired to Dyrrachium.

Caesar found no difficulty in causing himself to be elected consul the next year, B. C. 48. His associate was Publius Servilius. This gave him a power equal to that of dictator and one which sounded more satisfactorily in Roman ears. He resigned the dictatorship, and after eleven days spent in passing some essential laws, celebrating the Feriae Latinae and holding all the elections, began preparations to move on Pompey. Inasmuch as Pompey controlled the sea, Caesar was compelled to look forward to crossing the Adriatic by ruse. Pompey, he knew, would not suppose that he was about to expose his army to the dangers of a winter passage, or to the difficulties of subsisting it in Epirus during this season. His opponent would believe him too busy with affairs of state, and especially the consulship, to leave Italy so soon. For these very reasons, Caesar determined to steal a passage of the Adriatic in midwinter.

Caesar had ordered to Brundisium all his cavalry, several thousand in number, and the twelve legions—nine old, three new—which he now had under the eagles. Of these, four had marched to the Varus under Calenus, escorting Pompey's disbanded legions; two had gone to Baetica under Cassius; three had besieged Massilia under Trebonius.

Calenus' legions had become available in mid-August; those of Cassius towards the end of August; those of Trebonius a month later. All had successively been headed for Brundisium, but they had shown signs of discontent and had been marching slowly.

At Placentia occurred the mutiny of the Ninth legion, which Caesar suppressed by sharp action added to his own personal influence. He ordered the legions decimated; but after a while commuted the punishment to beheading twelve of the ringleaders.

What Caesar's army numbered, it is impossible to say. Two of the new legions no doubt had somewhere near the normal complement; which has been stated at some forty-eight hundred men. The ten old ones, however, had been much depleted, and while no mention is made of recruiting them up to normal standard, probably something of the kind had been done. If they averaged thirty-three hundred men,—as is not improbable,—Caesar's forces, with light troops and cavalry, must still have been under fifty thousand men, all told.

Caesar reached Brundisium the 17th of November. His means of transportation were very limited,—twelve galleys and about one hundred transports. Barely fifteen thousand men and five hundred horse out of his twelve legions and ten thousand cavalry could, according to the *Commentaries*, be embarked on what bottoms he had at command. Why this was so is not very clear. Nearly a year had elapsed since he ordered vessels to be built in the Italian, Sicilian and Gallic ports and collected at Brundisium; and Caesar was wont to look well to the logistics of the future. Some of the ships had been destroyed in Illyricum, but this accounted for but a part of the proposed fleet. Hortensius and Dolabella had carried out their orders, and had built and brought together a goodly number of vessels; but the disaster at Curicta, and the necessity of protecting Sicily and Sardinia, had reduced the quota to this limit.

The size of the seven legions selected by Caesar to be carried over to Epirus—the six old ones of Calenus and Cassius and one new one—must have been much smaller than the above given estimate. The authorities, as well as the *Commentaries* themselves, are contradictory on this point.

"Even these troops embarked very short of their number, because many had fallen in the wars in Gaul, and the long march from Spain had lessened their number very much, and a severe autumn in Apulia and the district about Brundisium, after the very wholesome countries of Spain and Gaul, had impaired the health of the whole army."

The seven legions probably numbered twenty thousand men; and six hundred horse went along.

Pompey had spent a year in inactivity, so far as meeting Caesar was concerned. But he had been industrious in gathering a fleet, "from Asia and the Cyclades, from Corcyra, Athens, Pontus, Bithynia, Syria, Cilicia, Phoenicia and Egypt, and had given directions that a great number should be built in every other place. He had exacted a large sum of money from Asia, Syria and all the kings, *dynasts*, *tetrarchs* and free states of Achaia; and had obliged the corporations of these provinces, of which he himself had the government, to count down to him a large sum."

He had reached Epirus from Italy with five partial legions; he now had nine full ones of Roman citizens from Italy or resident in the provinces; a veteran one from Cilicia (called Gemella, because consolidated out of two others); one from Crete and Macedonia, of veterans settled in that province after their discharge; two from Asia.

"Besides, he had distributed among his legions a considerable number, by way of recruits, from Thessaly, Boeotia, Achaia and Epirus; with his legions he also intermixed the soldiers taken from Gaius Antonius, at Curicta."

He expected two more legions from Syria, making eleven in all. He had a large number of Greek and other auxiliary bowmen and slingers,—probably not less than six thousand, many of distinguished valour,—two thousand volunteers and seven thousand horse, all chosen men. These latter comprised Celts from the Alexandria garrison, Thracians, Cappadocians, Galatians, Armenians, Numidians and mounted archers from Commagene. Some authorities figure Pompey's force as high as ninety thousand men; in fact, it was not more than fifty thousand strong. He had laid in a vast amount of corn from his various tributary provinces, and by holding Dyrrachium, Apollonia and other seaports, imagined that he could prevent Caesar from crossing the Adriatic. His fleet was "stationed along the seacoast."

Whatever the actual force of each, Pompey certainly outnumbered Caesar in land troops, while at sea he was far superior. The number of the vessels he had collected was five hundred, of which one hundred were Roman and the rest furnished by clients. Unwilling to trust M. Cato, he had placed this fleet under the orders of Marcus Bibulus, who with one hundred and ten large ships lay near Corcyra. Under him the younger Pompey commanded the Egyptian contingent; Dec. Laelius and C. Triarius the Asiatic; C. Cassius the Syrian; C. Marcellus and C. Coponius the Rhodian; Scribonius Libo and M. Octavius the Liburnian and Achaian. It would seem that this enormous fleet, used with any kind of energy, must have seriously interfered with Caesar's campaigns in 49 B. C.; have all but starved out Italy, and in many ways have manoeuvred to advantage. But barring the small operation on the Illyrian coast, it had practically accomplished nothing. Under Cato, it would have shown a better record.

At the outset Pompey had lacked nothing with which to carry on the war. All that Caesar wanted Pompey had possessed. But the energy, never splendid to be sure, still such that in former days it had enabled him to triumph over all enemies,—such, says Plutarch, as to have made him conqueror of three continents,—was now on the wane. From youth up, Pompey had been used to a life of self-indulgence. At periods he had been capable of successful exertion, and aided largely by what others had done before him, and unexampled good fortune, had accomplished much; he had no inconsiderable native ability, and had in a measure earned the reputation he possessed. But for the past year he had seemed incapable of exertion. His moral force appeared to have shrunk into nothing before the superior energy and character of his wonderful opponent, and as he had refused to meet Caesar in the cabinet, so now he seemed unwilling to face him in the field. In the case of each man the moral qualities stood in inverse ratio to the material.

Not that Pompey had been absolutely inactive. He had kept busy in drilling and disciplining his troops and in making his forces compact and pliable. Despite his fifty-eight years he had daily taken personal share in the work of organization, and had given his own countenance and example to his troops in their drill and manoeuvring at the camp at Beroea, on the Haliacmon. But this was not war. It was not even preparation for war. While Pompey had been reviewing his legions, Caesar had obtained complete control of Italy and had riven Spain from his dominions. Caesar was working with a perfect army, instinct with a perfect purpose. Pompey was creating a perfect outward military body, but was doing nothing to breathe that soul into it, without which an army is but a well-drilled mob. Caesar had a definite object and was working towards it by direct means. Pompey was taking his time, in the belief that when Caesar finally confronted him, he would be able to demolish him by mere weight of mass. He imagined that in this civil war a simple defensive would enable him to win. This was a thoroughly false conception of the problem. He had as yet not dared to encounter Caesar. He put off the fatal day. This of itself weakened him, as well as his troops and his adherents, more and more.

Caesar on the contrary looked at the matter squarely. He no doubt felt, and he certainly so held out to the world, that he only drew the sword to right the wrongs of the Roman people. And in his course he made no pause, he asked no rest, but carried through his intelligently conceived plan with consummate skill and untiring energy. He had now secured his rear by the subjection of Spain; his base was Italy, with Gaul and Spain, and all their resources behind it, and he was ready to undertake an active offensive against the army under Pompey's personal command. He felt that he was superior to his opponent in all that makes war successful, except numbers, and Caesar was not one of those who believed that the gods were on the side of the heaviest battalions. His faith in his own star was almost blind, and he was willing and anxious to risk his own smaller army in a contest with his bulky but inactive opponent.

Since the opening of the civil war, Pompey had made no offensive movement; Caesar, on the contrary, had operated offensively against Spain, Sardinia, Sicily and Africa. In Spain he had been fully successful; Sardinia had been recovered; in Sicily Curio had succeeded to the extent of effecting a relief in the threatened famine in Italy; in Africa he had failed. Pompey had been checked in all his plans, save only in the success of his ally, Juba, in Africa, and the capture of Antonius' legions in Illyricum. So deliberate had he been in his preparations, that, despite the Spanish interlude, Caesar was still able to take the offensive against him in Greece. These facts are a fair measure of the men.

CHAPTER 31

Epirus

November, 49, to February, 48 B. C.

Caesar had transports enough for but seven small legions and six hundred horse. He set sail, reached Epirus in safety, and landed at an uninhabited roadstead. He ran grave risk in thus moving against Pompey with so small a force. He would have done better to march with his entire army by way of Illyricum, his own province. On reaching Epirus, Caesar renewed his offers of peace to Pompey, but was again refused. He then made a bold demonstration on Dyrrachium, but Pompey returned to this valuable port in season to save it. There was some manoeuvring between the rival armies, but nothing definitive. Caesar had brought over but half his army; the other half was still in Brundisium, watched by Pompey's fleet. Only after many weeks could Mark Antony venture to sea. When finally he reached the Epirotic coast he found himself on the north of Pompey's army, as Caesar was on its south; but by clever marching on their side and want of enemy on Pompey's the Caesarians joined hands. Caesar then made some detachments of troops to various provinces of Greece to secure corn and allies. By a bold manoeuvre shortly after, he cut Pompey off from Dyrrachium, and though he could not capture the town, he established himself south and east of the city, between it and Pompey.

"When Caesar came to Brundisium he made a speech to the soldiers: 'That since they were now almost arrived at the termination of their toils and dangers, they should patiently submit to leave their slaves and baggage in Italy, and to embark without luggage, that a greater number of men might be put on board; that they might expect everything from victory and his liberality.' They cried out with one voice, 'he might give what orders he pleased, that they would cheerfully fulfil them'"

Caesar's small force was largely veteran, tried in the campaigns of Gaul and Spain, hardened by work and accustomed to victory. They believed absolutely in their chief and blindly followed and obeyed him. Caesar could rely on them as on himself. There had been some symptoms of dissatisfaction in the legions, specially exemplified by the mutiny of the Ninth at Placentia, on its way to Brundisium. But Caesar had put this down by his superior moral weight. So far as field work was concerned, the legions left nothing to be desired. Those which had lately mutinied were anxious to rehabilitate themselves.

On the 28th of November, 49 B. C, Caesar, after waiting many days for a north wind, set sail with his seven legions and six hundred horse, but without baggage, on some one hundred transports convoyed by twelve galleys, only four of which had decks. After a lucky passage towards the south-east the army landed next day on the Epirotic coast north of Corcyra, at a place known as Palaeste (Paljassa), in an uninhabited roadway. He had run considerable risk, but had succeeded in avoiding an encounter with any part of Pompey's fleet.

Caesar had no doubt carefully studied his chances of encountering storms and enemy, and had deliberately taken them. But his thus risking his entire cause, by shipping half his army to encounter Pompey's threefold forces on the latter's territory, savours more of foolhardiness than the well-pondered courage of the great captain. It again suggests itself, that to march his entire army through Illyria, and thus base on his ancient province, was preferable to shipping half of it by sea, with a base to create, the chance of capture of his first convoy, and the serious question as to whether the second would ever reach him. Illyria had, to be sure, no great resources; but Caesar's line of communications would have been free from danger.

Still Caesar's venture succeeded, so far as the first convoy went. Such of Pompey's ships as were near at hand—one hundred and ten at Corcyra, thirty-six at Oricum—had not known of the sailing. They had kept to the eastern coast of the Adriatic and had not sought to discover Caesar's movements. They imagined that he was wintering at Brundisium. There was not even a squad of men at any point along the coast, except in the harbours and towns. This argues as much carelessness on the part of Bibulus as Pompey had exhibited listlessness. But it was well in keeping with all which had so far been done, or failed to be done, by all the Pompeian generals. Pompey was confident that Caesar would not seek to open the campaign before spring. When, therefore, his army had been collected, drilled and organized so as to be fit for service, he leisurely broke up his camp of instruction at Beroea and began to move his legions by the Via Egnatia to the Adriatic, where he proposed to put them in winter-quarters, in Dyrrachium, Apollonia and other coast towns, while Caesar was still at Brundisium. He relied so absolutely on the strength of his numbers that, even if he expected it, which is doubtful, he seemed to care little whether or not Caesar advanced against him. He imagined that a single overwhelming victory—which he never doubted he should win—would recover for him all the power, all the influence which for months he had been losing. As Caesar alleges, his arrival was unexpected; no preparation had been made to receive him.

No sooner had he landed than Caesar sent back his ships under Calenus for the rest of his legions. But though for greater security they sailed by night, his fortune no longer attended them; the vessels were delayed by adverse winds, and some thirty, which were driven back, were caught and barbarously burned by Bibulus,—who was watching at Corcyra,—with all the crews on board. The Pompeian admiral hoped "by the severity of the punishment to deter the rest." He also hoped thus to atone for his lack of care in permitting Caesar's fleet to pass him with half the army. Now that Caesar had effected a landing, it occurred to Bibulus that he had better close the ports of Illyricum and Epirus and watch the coast,—which he did, from Salonae to Oricum. It had not been lack of courage on his part, but the fact that no one expected Caesar at this season; for now, "having disposed his guard with great care, he lay on board himself in the depth of winter, declining no fatigue or duty, and not waiting for reinforcements, in hopes that he might come within Caesar's reach."

Pompey had posted his fleet on the coast of Epirus as a curtain behind which to organize and assemble his army. The latter had been strung out from the Haliacmon to Thessalonica, with two legions still in Syria, recently raised by Metellus Scipio. To his headquarters not only came his levies, but his friends and his defeated generals,—Domitius from Massilia, Cato from Sicily, numberless refugees from Rome, men of means and standing. A senate of two hundred members began its sessions at Thessalonica. All this by no means strengthened Pompey's army. Unlike Alexander, he could not control a court and camp in one body. Nor did his presence near Pella, the ancient capital of Macedon, infuse into his conduct aught of the glowing energy of Philip or his splendid son.

Having reached Epirus, where he must absolutely and at once

either make terms with Pompey or fight him, Caesar again sent proposals to his opponent to treat for peace and a disbandment of all forces, agreeing to leave the questions between them to the decision of the Senate and people. He certainly showed every appearance of honestly desiring an accommodation; and as, indeed, the chances were by no means in his favour, he may have been sincere. The bearer of these proposals was Pompey's legate, Vibullius Rufus, whom Caesar had captured, for the second time, in Spain, and had freely forgiven. Vibullius found Pompey in distant Macedonia and gave him the proposals, which, however, met with the same fate as previous ones. Pompey had but just received the first news of Caesar's lauding. Already on the march, so soon as he heard of Caesar's advance, he hurried to the coast towards Apollonia. He had until now been so slow that Caesar, despite the Spanish campaign and the siege of Massilia, could still take the offensive. Startled out of his security, not only by Caesar's landing but by his activity, Pompey now conceived the fear that Caesar might get possession of the whole seaboard, and was spurred on to unusual exertions.

Caesar had, the same day he landed, November 29, marched over the difficult mountain paths from Palaeste, on Oricum, which, after some show of resistance by Pompey's lieutenant, L. Torquatus, the citizens surrendered to him; following which the garrison did the like with the citadel. The fleet there stationed escaped to Corcyra. Thence, notwithstanding the fatigues of the previous night's march, Caesar pushed on to Apollonia, a rich town on a branch of the Via Egnatia, leaving his new legion under Acilius and Marcus in Oricum. He reached Apollonia next day. Straberius, the governor, tried to hold the place for Pompey, watching the citadel and striving to control the citizens. But Apollonia likewise gave Caesar admittance, refusing to do otherwise than as the Roman people and Senate had done in electing Caesar consul. Straberius fled. Caesar headed, December 2, for Dyrrachium. Many distant and more neighbouring states and towns, among them Bullis, Amantia and substantially all Epirus, followed suit.

Pompey, meanwhile, thoroughly frightened at the unexpected turn given to matters by Caesar's arrival, forged ahead by stout marching, day and night, for Apollonia and Dyrrachium. His speed tired, as his evident nervousness demoralized, his men. They were not campaign-seasoned, like the Gallic veterans; they had received but the superficial training of the drill-ground. It is said that the fear of Caesar was such in Pompey's army that many Epirotic soldiers threw down their arms

EPIRUS AND MACEDONIA

and deserted so soon as they learned of his arrival. So strong was this sentiment that Labienus, Caesar's old lieutenant and now Pompey's right-hand man, was obliged, when they reached Dyrrachium, December 3, to subject the men to a new oath not to desert Pompey whatever might happen.

Though Pompey hastened his march with the utmost endeavour, he barely reached Dyrrachium in time to save it from capture. His head of column just anticipated Caesar, who was already on the road towards this to him essential city. Pompey went into an entrenched camp south of Dyrrachium, and, learning that his opponent had secured possession of the town, Caesar, no doubt disappointed, but scarcely expecting uninterrupted success, and in any event too weak to attack his adversary, moved backward and camped in the territory of Apollonia, on the south side of the River Apsus. Pompey, so soon as his army had recovered its tone, thinking to defend the line of this river and thus hold the Dyrrachium territory intact, shortly came and camped opposite Caesar and began to call in all his troops to this place. He made his *cohorts* comfortable, intending, if necessary, to winter here. Each army thus lay somewhat back from the river, facing the other across the Apsus. Caesar was waiting for his other legions. He protected by his position his new allies in the country south of where he lay. He was midway between the two harbours of Dyrrachium and Oricum, where alone Pompey's fleet, his chief danger, could find suitable anchorage.

Pompey had won the rank of a great soldier without the herculean labours usually incident thereto; and at this period, age or luxury had robbed him of whatever moral energy he had once boasted. He had never possessed the mental activity of Napoleon, but like the latter at Waterloo he had lost his old-time bodily activity. Nothing demonstrates the weakness of his present condition more than the fact that he remained in this position in front of Caesar two whole months, vastly Caesar's superior in numbers, and without taking any step to attack him. A bold offensive at this moment might well have been fatal to Caesar. He had but half Pompey's forces. The rest were still at Brundisium, and might indefinitely be kept there by weather and Pompey's fleet; for the latter was well equipped and by good management ought to control the Adriatic. Now was the time, if ever, for Pompey to crush his adversary. A lucky circumstance might any day enable Calenus to bring over Caesar's other legions. Nor were opportunities wanting. Holding as he did the entire coast, Pompey by a simple forward movement of his right, with reasonable precautions, could scarcely have failed to force Caesar into the interior of Epirus, thus dividing his forces beyond a chance of junction, and putting his enemy, if it could be done at all, at his mercy. Moreover, Caesar was placed where his army was already a serious task and might be made all but impossible. For he had no fleet.

Calenus, in the port of Brundisium, having been joined by the Massilia legions, had already put the *cohorts* and cavalry on board the vessels which had returned from Epirus and had actually set sail, when he received notice from Caesar to exercise the greatest caution, as Bibulus commanded the entire coast and was awake to everything that went on. Thus admonished, Calenus recalled the fleet and disembarked, rather than run the risk of capture. It was as well that he did. Bibulus had left Corcyra and come to Oricum, keenly on the watch for him, and seizing one ship which, on starting, had strayed from the rest and been driven out to sea, put the entire crew to death.

In this position in the roadway at Oricum, while Bibulus kept Caesar from the sea, so likewise Caesar's lieutenants kept Bibulus from the land, and cut him off from wood and water, reducing him to great straits. All his supplies and even water had to be brought from Corcyra. On one occasion his men were reduced to the dew which they could collect on wool-hides laid upon the decks. Though Bibulus' men bore their deprivations with fortitude, these hardships were the occasion of a stratagem, taking the form of a request by Bibulus for a truce and conference with Caesar. Caesar had gone with a legion to Buthrotum, opposite Corcyra, to forage and gain allies. But he personally returned on hearing from Acilius and Marcus that Bibulus had asked for a truce. The conference was granted, as Caesar had always been anxious to come to terms with Pompey, but the truce was refused. Caesar saw through the ruse,—that the Pompeian admiral only sought to revictual and water his vessels, Bibulus did not come to the conference, but sent Libo in his stead. This officer, however, offered to bear Caesar's message to Pompey, and renewed the request for a truce meanwhile. This Caesar naturally declined, as he saw that he was harassing the fleet more than the fleet was annoying him, and could not afford to give it the opportunity it was seeking.

About this time Bibulus died from the exposures of a command he would not desert, and the several fleets were permitted by Pompey to remain under their respective commanders without any one head. This was fortunate for Caesar, as Pompey's naval management thus lacked unity of action, which was worse than even a half-competent leader.

Caesar's latest messages to Pompey evoked, it is said, no other reply than that "even life or Rome were not worth holding by the grace of Caesar." Still he persevered in efforts to bring about a conference. The Apsus—which is a narrow river—alone lay between the camps. There was a general understanding among the soldiers that no darts should be hurled across, or arrows shot, whenever either party approached the banks, and they freely conversed at frequent intervals, assembling in groups on the river shore. This suspension of hostilities was similar to what occurred on the Peninsula, at Petersburg, and other places during our civil war. It is not an unusual species of truce, which has always obtained between armies in immediate contact, especially if speaking the same language. To this meeting-place Caesar, who was still sincerely anxious for a personal interview, and who no doubt felt his superiority over Pompey in council as well as in war, sent P. Vatinius to solicit, by a publicly proclaimed request, "the right—granted even to fugitives from justice and to robbers—for Roman citizens to send deputies to Roman citizens to treat for peace." Thus a conference was arranged between Vatinius and Aulus Varro; but when this was being held, and Labienus, who was present, was conversing with Vatinius, it was interrupted by a shower of darts from the Pompeian side, by which many, including three centurions, were wounded. Labienus is said to have exclaimed, "There can be no thought of peace unless we carry back with us Caesar's head!"—apparently seeing in the temper of some of the troops the impossibility of a settlement. Thus again were Cesar's pacific intentions defeated and the heated feelings of Pompey's chief adherents demonstrated. These are the statements of the *Commentaries*. There is no special reason for doubting them, and they are lent colour by other authorities. Caesar was always careful to keep the appearance of right and reason on his side, and even if he did not desire the peace he asked, he would have been likely, knowing that Pompey would decline all his advances, to continue to make them.

Libo, after Bibulus' death, sailed over from Oricum to Brundisium about the middle of January, and blockaded that port, which was the only exit to sea for Caesar's forces still in Italy. He occupied the small island at its mouth. Arriving suddenly, he caught and fired some of Caesar's transports and carried off one laden with corn. Landing, he drove in a party of Antony's men; whereupon he boastingly wrote that Pompey might haul up for repairs the rest of his fleet, for he could with his own force, unaided, keep Caesar's reinforcements from joining him.

Antony was at the time in the town. To oppose Libo, he patrolled the shores and prevented his watering. And in order to come to a combat with him, which he could not well do at sea, he covered with pent-houses a number of the long boats belonging to war-galleys, armed them with veterans, and hid them along the harbour shores. Then sending two three-banked galleys out to the mouth of the port to manoeuvre, he induced Libo to put five four-banked galleys out to intercept them. Antony's galleys retired within the harbour, as if flying, and induced Libo's to follow. So soon as they came within the harbour, the long boats advanced, inclosed the galleys of the enemy, attacked them, captured one and drove the others away. Libo, seeing that he was unable to accomplish anything by lying off the place, and starved for water, which Antony prevented his getting by stationing cavalry posts along the coast, finally gave over the blockade.

Caesar was becoming anxious about his other legions. He had waited nearly three months for them, winter was coming to an end, and he felt that he must run some risk in order to get them. He was, in fact, almost without news of their condition and that of Italy; for he had few ships he could use as couriers. He wrote to his lieutenants at Brundisium that the troops must be sent at all hazards by the first fair wind, even if some vessels were lost. "I need soldiers, not vessels," he wrote. Indeed, he attempted himself to go across on a small twelve-oared boat. It was on this occasion that he is said to have exclaimed to the boatman, who feared to put to sea owing to high running water, "What dreadest thou? Thou carriest Caesar and his fortunes!" But he was unable, for all that, to cross. The voyage was too dangerous, beset by the perils of the sea and the enemy alike.

Antony, Calenus, and especially the rank and file, were all as fretful to join their chief as Caesar was to have them do so. The old soldiers could hardly be held in hand, so anxious were they to be beside their general. On the blowing of the first south wind,—February 15,—they weighed anchor and set sail at nightfall. They were carried past Apollonia and Dyrrachium, were seen by the enemy, and, being caught in a lull of wind, were chased by his fleet, under Q. Coponius, who emerged from the latter place. Just as these war-vessels had all but reached Caesar's transports, the south wind again sprang up and enabled them to make Nymphaeum, above Lissus. This port, with the sailing vessels of that day, could be entered by a south but not a southwest wind, and after Antony's transports had made the roadway, Caesar's luck came in, the wind veered to southwest and not only prevented the enemy from entering, but drove a part of their fleet upon the rocks and lost them sixteen out of twenty ships and many men. Caesar liberated those who were captured. Only one of Caesar's vessels was taken by the enemy, and though the crew of two hundred and twenty recruits, unsuspicious of the enemy's treachery, surrendered on promise of being spared, they were everyone put to death. One other ship went ashore, but the veteran legionaries aboard of her declined terms and happily made their way to shore and joined the army.

On landing, the near-by town of Lissus, which Caesar had fortified while Illyria was one of his provinces, received Antony and his men and gave them all assistance. Otacilius, Pompey's lieutenant, took to flight. From here Antony notified Caesar of his safe arrival by native couriers. He had brought the three veteran Massilia legions and one new one, the Twenty-seventh, about eight hundred horse, and some convalescents belonging to the legions already in Epirus,—something under twenty thousand men. The ships were sent back to Italy for the rest of Caesar's army, save thirty trans-ports, kept on the chance of their being needed.

Caesar and Pompey received the news of Antony's landing about the same time,—perhaps February 18. The ships had been sighted from both Apollonia and Dyrrachium, but had then been lost to view. The immediate duty of each leader was clear. Caesar instantly but openly broke camp February 19, and set out to join Antony, who was at least four days' march away; Pompey had secretly marched the night before, *via* Dyrrachium, on Tirana, to cut him off from moving to-wards Caesar and if possible fall on him from ambush. Pompey had the easier task. He could hold the line of the Apsus against Caesar, as well as move directly upon the newcomers. Caesar was obliged to go some distance up the Apsus to find a ford and perhaps to force a crossing.

Pompey was not rapid in his march, but nevertheless reached the vicinity of Antony one day the sooner,—February 21,—and camped in ambush near the road to which Antony was limited in marching toward Caesar, hoping to catch him unawares. He camped without fires and kept his men close in hiding. News of this proceeding luckily reached Antony through friendly Greeks. He remained in camp, where he was entirely safe, and sent word of his whereabouts to Caesar. This chief, meanwhile, had passed the Apsus, twenty miles above his camp, reached Scampa, and on the 22nd was reconnoitring to ascertain his

CAESAR AND ANTONY JOIN

lieutenant's location. Here he was found by Antony's messengers. On the 23rd he crossed the mountains and marched on Tirana. Pompey had no idea of being caught between the two armies, and decamped, lest he should be forced into immediate battle. That Pompey should have allowed this junction to be made is as much a reproach to him as a credit to Caesar. But it was of a part with his phlegmatic character. The ability or rather the nerve of the two men is well shown in this, as in other minor operations. Pompey's every step was marked by hesitating, not to say timorous, conduct; Caesar's every step by good fortune, to be sure, but good fortune well utilized. All the luck in the world could not have helped Pompey accomplish his ends when he would not put his hand to the work to be done, under even the most favourable conditions.

Up to this moment, Pompey had been acting on a misconception of what was the proper plan of campaign. He had deemed it wise to seek to confine Caesar to a given territory by his largely superior cavalry, and thus starve him out,—a very questionable possibility; whereas when he had outnumbered him three to one, his manifest duty was to attack him. If Pompey had hitherto avoided battle, now that Caesar had been reinforced, he had a double reason for so doing. Though it is clear that Pompey showed distinct lack of enterprise during this period of his great superiority, his plan of starving out Caesar may have been a good one after the latter's junction with Antony.

During this time, Scipio, Pompey's lieutenant in Syria, had, on Caesar's crossing to Epirus, been ordered by Pompey to return to Macedonia and join him there. He apparently did not feel strong enough to cope with Caesar single-handed, however much he might outnumber him.

Caesar held his army well in hand. He had joined Antony and had drawn in most of his garrisons. He had a total of thirty-five thousand men, and circumstances, if not forces, were in his favour. He was entirely ready to come to a decisive struggle with Pompey. Thessaly and Ætolia had sent ambassadors to him, agreeing to support his cause if he would send them troops. Though he could ill afford to make details from his meagre force, Caesar answered these appeals by dispatching a young legion, the Twenty-seventh, and two hundred horse to Thessaly, under L. Cassius Longinus, and five *cohorts* from Oricum and some cavalry into Ætolia, under C. Calvisius Sabinus. Each of these lieutenants had instructions, in addition to protecting and gaining the friendly cooperation of the several provinces, to adopt measures to provide Caesar with corn. Into Macedonia by the Egnatian highway he sent the Eleventh and Twelfth legions and five hundred horse, under Domitius Calvinus, to head off the corps of Scipio, which would soon approach from Thessalonica.

When these detachments were all made, Caesar had but seven legions,—the Sixth, Seventh, Eighth, Ninth, Tenth, Thirteenth and Fourteenth,—say twenty-two thousand men, but his situation was vastly improved. He undertook to try conclusions with Pompey and determined to hold him on the seacoast near Dyrrachium, and thus cut him off from Greece. It was Caesar, though far weaker, who began to force the fighting. He saw through Pompey's intentions, and, like a bold player, met his adversary, though with but half his strength, on his own ground.

Calvisius was well received in Ætolia, "dislodged the enemy from Calydon and Naupactus, and made himself master of the whole country." Cassius found two factions in Thessaly,—Hegasaretus in power and favouring Pompey, Petreius favouring Caesar. This made his work more difficult.

While Domitius was marching on Macedonia from the west, Scipio was moving on the same province from the east. When the latter came within twenty miles of Domitius' army, instead of manoeuvring against it he suddenly filed off southerly towards Longinus in Thessaly, hoping to catch this general napping, and to interfere with his reduction of the country. In order to do this the better, he started in light marching order, having left his baggage with eight *cohorts*, under M. Favonius, south of the Haliacmon, ordering him to strongly fortify himself there. He sent Cotus' cavalry ahead, to fall on Longinus' camp.

Longinus, whose force was fresh and weak, at once retired towards the foothills, intending to cross to Ambracia, and was vigorously followed up by Scipio's cavalry. Domitius, however, was expert enough to make an immediate demonstration against Favonius. The rumour of this danger obliged Scipio to return to his lieutenant and baggage-camp, which he only reached in season to head off Domitius, whose van was already in sight. "The dust raised by Domitius' army and Scipio's advance-guard were observed at the same instant." Domitius was still north of the river. Scipio shortly crossed by a ford above him and camped.

There was a plain six miles wide between the camps. Scipio drew up in front of his camp. Domitius advanced towards him and invited battle. After some skirmishing and an advance and show of battle, Scipio, though he had crossed the Haliacmon to close with his enemy, concluded it to be best to decline the engagement with Domitius' legions, which were very eager for the fray, and to retire across the river to his first camp. In two cavalry combats which supervened in their mutual reconnoitring, Scipio was worsted. Each officer endeavoured to lure the other into some stratagem, but neither succeeded. Domitius apparently had the best of the interchanges. Both remained *in situ*.

Caesar, wishing to concentrate, left but three *cohorts* at Oricum, under Acilius, to protect the shipping which was in the bay, and drew in the rest of his garrisons to the main army. Acilius blocked up the harbour by sinking a merchantman in the mouth and anchoring a war-vessel nearby. But he was not fortunate. Pompey's son, Cnaeus, whom we shall later meet in Spain, and who commanded the Egyptian contingent, anxious to distinguish himself, sailed for the place, captured the man-of-war, raised the sunken ship, and made his way into the harbour. Here he burned the main part of Caesar's fleet, and leaving Decimus Laelius to blockade the port and hinder the entering of corn, he sailed to Nymphaeum and up the river to Lissus, where he also burned the thirty transports Antony had kept there. These losses were highly disadvantageous to Caesar, for they took all the vessels he had on the east of the Adriatic. In landing at Lissus, young Pompey had, however, less fortune, being foiled in his effort to capture the place. But it would appear that Cnaeus possessed the spirit of enterprise, which at this time seemed to have deserted his father.

After the failure of his ambuscade at Tirana, Pompey had retired on Dyrrachium. In pursuance of his plan of avoiding armed conflict, he then determined to defend the line of the Genusus, just south of Dyrrachium, and moved to Asparagium, a town whose location is variously stated, but which, to accord with the operations detailed in the *Commentaries*, must have lain some ten miles up from the mouth of that river and on the south bank. After joining Antony, Caesar had returned to Scampa, had conducted a raid up the Genusus, for the sake of capturing the capital of the Parthenians (a place which cannot be identified at this day) with its Pompeian garrison, and had then followed Pompey to Asparagium. In three days' march he reached a position opposite Pompey and camped. Next day he moved out of camp, drew up in order and offered battle. Pompey declined to accept Caesar's challenge, emerging, to be sure, from camp, but remaining on his heights, where he could not be attacked without much danger.

Caesar, never at a loss for a plan, and determined to leave Pompey no rest, conceived and executed one of those bold operations which

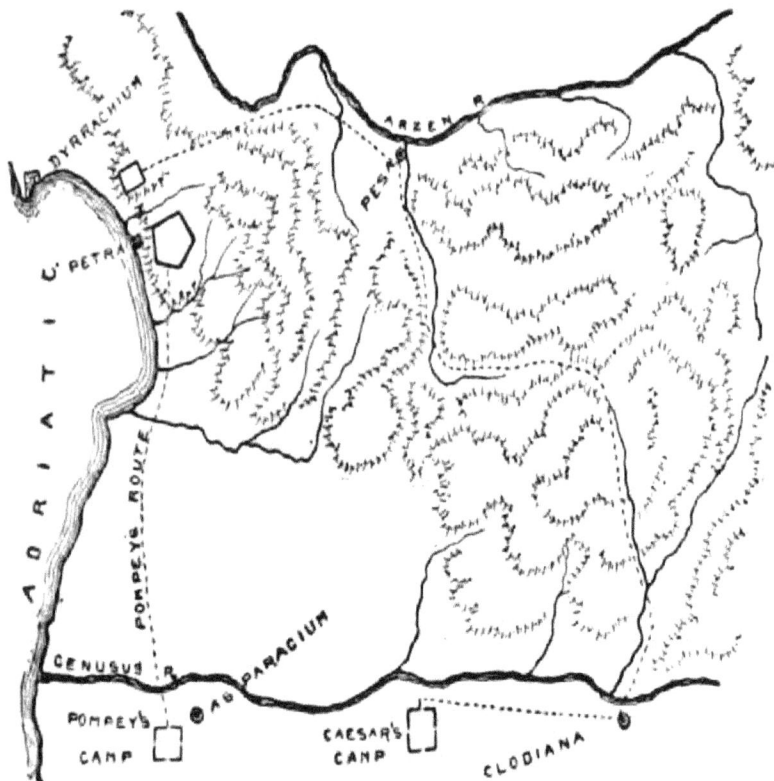

CAESAR'S MARCH TO DYRRACHIUM

show the head and hand of the master. He determined to cut Pompey off from Dyrrachium. By a long and secret circuit over a rugged road, he set out, March 3, to move about Pompey's flank straight on his base of supplies. His route lay over a difficult wooded country, probably with but the barest roads, up the Genusus to Clodiana (modern Pelium), and across the mountains which separated the Genusus from the modern Arzen, whose mouth is north of Dyrrachium, thence down the latter river. From river to river he must ascend and descend the affluents of either, by a circuit of some forty-five miles, which distance, with the route so badly cut up, could not be made at a greater rate than two miles an hour, if that. At the same time, speed was imperative. Success depended on Caesar's keeping Pompey in ignorance of his intentions during a whole day, and on his making the march in not much over twenty-four hours; for Pompey's road to Dyrrachium was straight and easy and less than twenty-five miles long.

Pompey had no idea that Caesar was heading for his communica-

tions; he thought he was moving camp for lack of corn. When, by his
cavalry scouts reporting Caesar's direction, he awoke to the fact, though
he was on a shorter line, which he at once took, it was too late. Caesar,
by vigorous efforts and by stopping but for a short rest at night, reached
the Arzen, followed it down to where it turns northwesterly along the
coast, and thence pushing rapidly towards the sea-shore, seized the adjoining heights, "when the van of Pompey's army was visible at a distance," and shut Pompey off from approach to Dyrrachium, where the
latter had stored all his war material and much provision. Caesar camped
north of the Arzen, on slightly rolling ground. He had conducted an
operation of remarkable boldness and brilliancy.

Cut off from Dyrrachium, though his garrison still held the place,
Pompey, much aggrieved, camped and entrenched on rising ground at
Petra, south of the Arzen, where was a harbour for small ships, by the
use of which he could still victual at Dyrrachium.

THEATRE OF DYRRACHIUM

111

The bay of Dyrrachium describes a bow whose chord runs northwest and southeast. As you approach the coast from the sea you have a perfect *coup d'oeil* of the entire theatre; but the details you must study on the ground. Back of this bow, in an irregular semi-circle, runs the watershed of the streams which feed the Arzen or descend to the sea. This bow is threefold. The outer curve is of lofty hills, which make a rugged frame for the scene of the coming operations; the next inner one consists of irregular chalk-hills, rough and difficult; the inmost curve is one of rolling upland, well covered by verdure and occasional bunches of trees. The entire country is more or less accentuated. The population of Epirus today is smaller than in Caesar's time. This terrain was probably much then as now. The bolder hills of this watershed, from three hundred to twelve hundred feet in height, advance to the sea about the centre of the bow, and form a defile of over one third of a mile in length between the water and the cliffs, which latter are in places almost erect, but are wooded at the summits. At the south of the bow the hills slope down into the plain of modern Cavaia. The ground contained within the bow of the watershed is cut up, rocky, full of ravines and gorges at the back; wooded in parts and with a fair show of cultivation in the centre; rolling and fertile near the sea, with a long, wide beach.

Dyrrachium lies on a point of land at the northwest end of the bow, confined by lagoons to a long triangular stretch of ground, bold and rocky at the seashore on the west. It can be besieged only by sea, for a force attempting to besiege it by land could itself be shut into the triangular foreland by fortifying the narrow land approaches at either end of the lagoons.

Now all the more confirmed in his plan of starving Caesar in Epirus, and not of fighting him, Pompey ordered to Petra new provisions from Asia and other tributary countries. To get these was comparatively easy, as Pompey had plenty of ships. Caesar, on the contrary, experienced difficulty in providing corn for a protracted campaign, for Illyricum was not a grain-bearing country, Epirus had little beyond its scant needs, and Pompey had already used up all there was on hand by foraging or devastation. Nor could Caesar get any supplies from Italy, for Pompey ruled the sea.

In view of all these factors in his problem, it may be said that Pompey was not entirely short-sighted in his present method of gauging the probabilities of the war. It is only in contrasting his slowness and lack of initiative to the restless energy of Caesar, that we feel like denying him his *cognomen* of Great. Still, the Fabian generals of the world are not without their justly earned laurels; nor must we underrate the ability of Pompey. But even if we esteem his present plan of starving out Caesar to be a proper one, it is by no means to be admitted that Pompey was otherwise than lax in not forcing a decisive battle on Caesar when the latter lay opposite him with but a third his force.

CHAPTER 32

Dyrrachium

March to May, 48 B. C.

Caesar lay between Pompey and Dyrrachium; but Pompey could reach the town from his camp by sea. Caesar began to inclose Pompey in siege lines,—a hazardous task, as he was much the weaker. Pompey seized many hills around his camp to inclose as much ground as possible. Many skirmishes resulted. Pompey could victual plentifully from the sea; Caesar had difficulty in gathering corn from the poor country in his rear. But he had good water and better forage for his animals, while able to cut off much of Pompey's water-supply by diverting streams which ran through his lines to the sea. In the fighting during the erection of the siege works, neither side won any marked advantage. Caesar's veterans rather surprise us by not proving superior to Pompey's newer *cohorts*. During an absence of Caesar's, Pompey attacked his lines, but after a long and heavy struggle the Caesarians won a decided advantage. Caesar's left reached the sea, but it was not strong.

If Pompey lacked boldness in his conception and execution, Caesar may be said to have been overbold. No sooner had he succeeded in thus cutting Pompey off from Dyrrachium than he undertook measures for blockading him in the position he had taken up. About Pompey's camp lay the threefold chain of hills already described; but his outlying parties had occupied no part of the watershed proper. As many of the hills of the outer curve as were available, Caesar took, and on them built redoubts,—twenty-six in all were eventually constructed,—and these he began to join by a chain of earthworks more or less elaborate, according as the nature of the ground dictated. In inaccessible places this work was easy; in places less well defended by nature, art was called into play. Each end of the line was intended to lean on the seacoast; the north end at his camp east of Dyrrachium;

the south end at any place he could, in the course of the operations, most conveniently reach. Pompey at once perceived Caesar's intention, but instead of resorting to active measures, he adopted the policy of one already besieged and endeavoured to crowd Caesar outward as much as practicable; and as Pompey still sought to avoid a general engagement, Caesar was able to establish a fairly good line; not one, however, which prevented Pompey from holding, on the surrounding hills, an all but as good interior line.

Caesar's object in this proceeding was to prevent Pompey, who was strong in cavalry, from cutting out his convoys, of corn from Epirus or from devastating the country, for he needed the corn himself; and he desired to reduce Pompey's horse by want of forage. Again, he felt sure he should gain in reputation and Pompey correspondingly lose, if he hemmed him in, and this showed that Pompey had not the vim to fight him. Caesar had for some time prescribed to his legions a set order of battle or encampment; and they now took up position accordingly. The Tenth, Thirteenth and Fourteenth legions formed the right wing; the Sixth and Seventh, the centre; the Eighth and Ninth, the left wing.

The line thus traced by Caesar was nearly sixteen miles long, a vast stretch for twenty-two thousand men to defend. Pompey was anxious enough to regain Dyrrachium, for all his material was there; but he could not bring himself to hazard the battle which was necessary to arrest the completion of Caesar's works. He likewise seized on as many hills as he could, and fortified them in such a way as to oblige Caesar to divide his forces. He thus managed, by his own inner lines facing Caesar's, to inclose a space of about fourteen miles in circuit, in which he was able to get quite an amount of forage for his cavalry. This inclosed line he fortified by twenty-four redoubts and a line of ramparts. Pompey first completed his works, having a greater force and somewhat less extent to fortify. He made no organized sallies, but used his slingers and archers, of whom he had an efficient body, in a very harassing manner; and the Roman soldiers made themselves "coats or coverings of haircloth, tarpaulins and rawhid" to resist the darts. "In seizing the posts, each exerted his utmost power: Caesar, to confine Pompey within as narrow a compass as possible; Pompey, to occupy as many hills as he could in as large a circuit as possible." Pompey had inclosed something like sixteen square miles; Caesar twenty. It was on the terrain thus inclosed that there were constructed the most remark-able fortifications in antiquity.

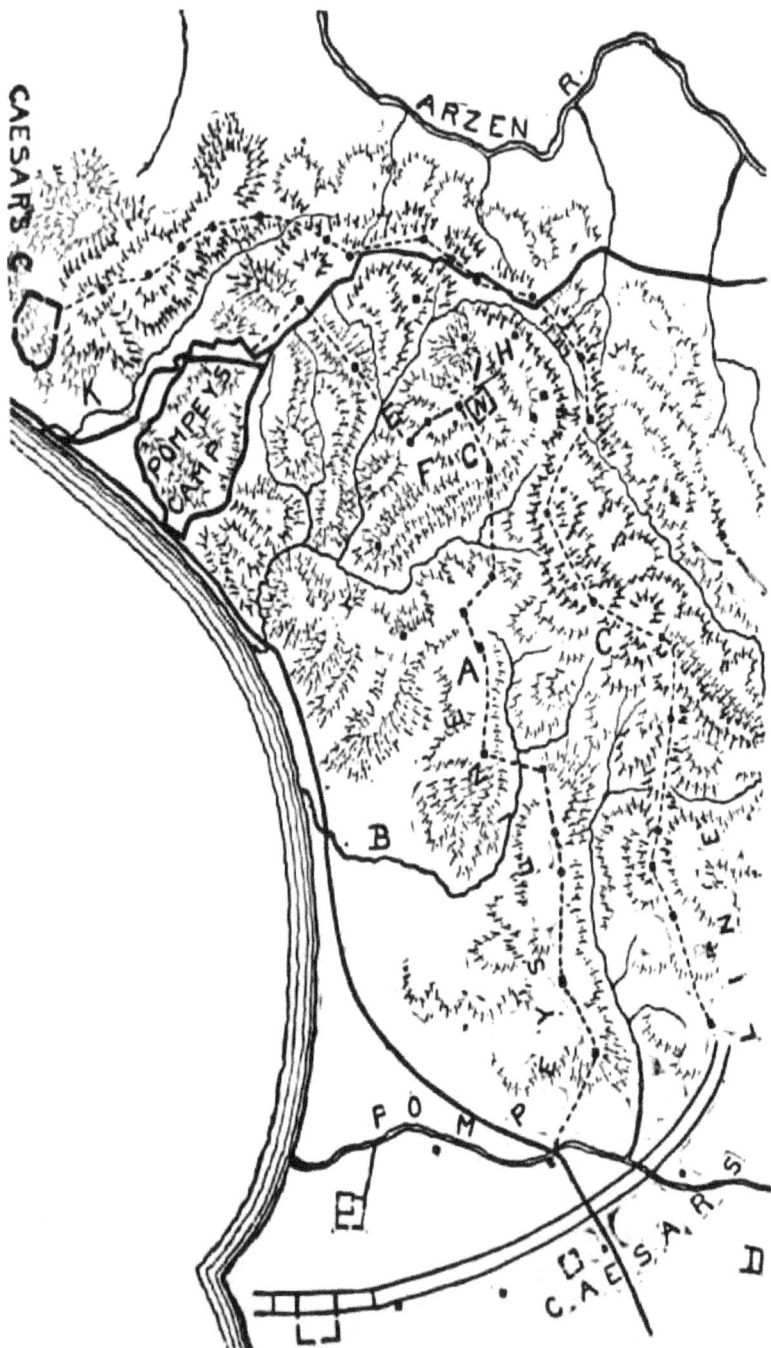

DYRRACHIUM THEATRE OF OPERATIONS

It is not to be supposed that Pompey exhibited want of skill. On the contrary, whenever he put his hand to the work he showed it at every turn. With an ordinary opponent, with even an able one, he might have proved himself the general of old, who had conquered half the world. But Caesar's matchless energy and skill overrode all his efforts; Pompey's morale was so much less than Caesar's that he could not show to advantage. Pompey and Caesar had long known each other, and though he had for many years held the stronger hand, Pompey no doubt recognized his superior, and was cautious accordingly. He simply remained inert.

Pompey's situation was markedly better than Caesar's. He outnumbered him to a dangerous degree. He had much more cavalry. His ships brought him corn and material with ease and regularity from Dyrrachium and elsewhere. His position was central, each flank and all points being easily approached from the others by radial lines. And yet Pompey dared not make a determined attack upon his foe, even while the entrenchments were but half done.

During the erection of Caesar's line of contravallation, skirmishing was constant. The Ninth legion occupied the then left of the works which Caesar was gradually stretching out towards the sea. On one occasion when it had been ordered to take a certain hill that Caesar desired to inclose, and had begun works (A on the chart), Pompey's men seized the adjoining heights to the west, set up a number of engines, and seriously annoyed Caesar's men with their missiles and with archery. Their light troops could advance across the connecting hills to near the position of the Ninth. The reason for disputing Caesar this height was that its possession would afford him a chance of cutting Pompey off from access to one of the streams most essential to his water supply (B), and confine the Pompeians within too narrow bounds. Caesar's manifest purpose was to extend his left to the sea along this stream. He found it necessary to retire the Ninth legion from the place, and Pompey followed up Caesar's legionaries vigorously and inflicted some losses on them. The retreat was down the rugged slope to the east, and gradually became difficult. It is reported that Pompey said that day in triumph to his friends about him, "that he would consent to be accounted a general of no experience, if Caesar's legions effected a retreat without considerable loss from that ground into which they had rashly advanced,"—an utterance which sounds as if Pompey still possessed something of the old spirit.

At this backset Caesar became uneasy, for his veterans were ex-

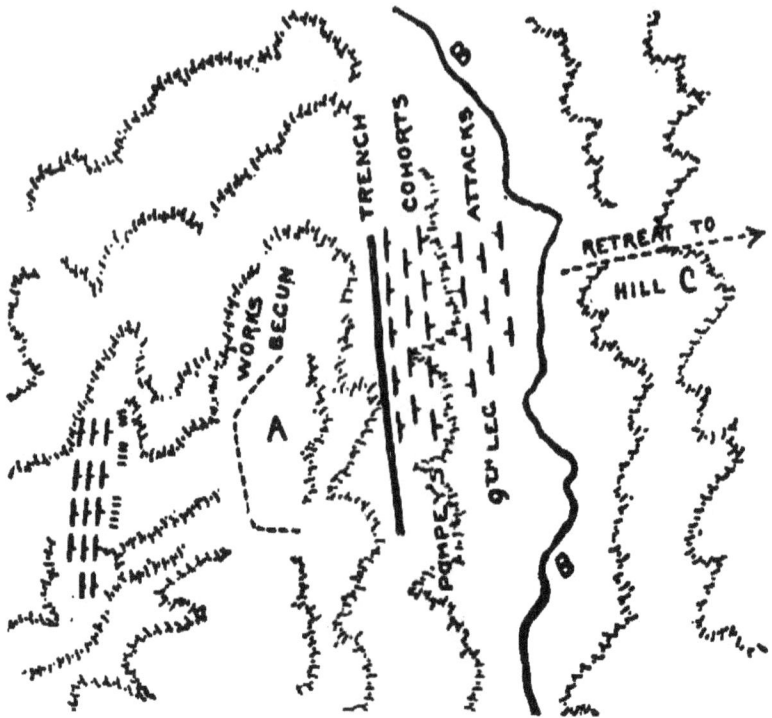

COMBAT OF NINTH LEGION

hibiting unusual lack of nerve. Hurdles were brought, and under their cover a trench was dug and the ends fortified with redoubts. This is one of the earliest recorded examples of field-fortifications made under fire for the purpose of temporarily holding a position, or of covering a retreat. The stand thus made was maintained for a period, and later slingers and archers were thrown out so as to cover a further retreat. The legionary *cohorts* were then ordered to file off, but Pompey's men "boldly and tauntingly pursued and chased" Caesar's, levelling the hurdles and passing the trench. Fearing that this might be the cause of serious demoralization in the army, and that retreat might degenerate into stampede, Caesar ordered Antony, who was in command, when in his withdrawal he reached a given place, to turn and charge. This was gallantly done. At the trumpet signal, the Ninth legion came to a right-about, closed their files,—they were evidently still well in hand,—paused but to cast their javelins, and then rushed upon the enemy with the sword. Though as at Il-erda they were charging up a steep incline, they drove everything before them, and Pompey's men "turned their backs," retired in confusion, and with no little loss, for the hurdles and trench lay in the path of their retreat and tripped up many. Five *legionaries* of Caesar's were killed; of Pompey's, say the *Commentaries*, many more. Another hill (C) was selected and fortified, Pompey retaining the one from which he had driven Caesar. The loss of this hill was the first step in the disaster which was bound to result from Caesar's over-confident undertaking in thus inclosing Pompey in siege lines. It enabled Pompey to occupy a larger extent of ground than Caesar had hoped to confine him to, and obliged Caesar to make his own the greater by nearly a half; and moreover it compelled him to close his left by a long line across an extended plain (D), where later Pompey found his weak spot. Had Caesar been able to close his lines along the brook which has its sources at the hill just lost, there would have been more chance of success. But the operation was, from its inception, doomed to failure. Across the plain, when it was reached, Caesar erected works,—a ditch fifteen feet wide and a parapet ten feet high and wide,—and garrisoned it with the Ninth legion.

The small loss in the late combat does not bespeak a very tenacious fight; but the retreat was as well managed on Caesar's part as the attack had been smart on Pompey's. The number of the light troops killed or wounded is very rarely given. Only the *legionaries* killed are counted; so that a very small figure may sometimes express a material total loss. In this cage the *cohorts* probably lost in killed and wounded fifty men; the light troops perhaps as many, making one hundred casualties in a force of not over four thousand men, say two and a half *per cent*, showing fairly smart fighting.

There was not what we should call picket-fighting between the two camps, but Pompey's men would often go out to a place where they saw camp-fires at night, and suddenly discharge at random a flight of arrows and stones towards it. Caesar's soldiers were obliged to light fires in a place apart from where they mounted guard, to rid themselves of this dangerous annoyance. Petty war was constant.

This entire Dyrrachium proceeding, on Caesar's part, was novel. Blockades are usually for the purpose of cutting off supplies, and are always conducted by larger forces than those inclosed or against an enemy demoralized by defeat. But here was Caesar, with an army one half the size of Pompey's, and himself in need of supplies, blockading by exterior lines Pompey, who had supplies of everything brought to him by sea. The lines were long, and the Caesarians had to work constantly to perform the guard-duty required of them.

They stood their deprivations well. They lived on barley, pulse, and on rare occasions beef, and on a certain root named *chara*, of which they made mush and bread, and remembering the scarcity at Ilerda and Alesia and Avaricum, which had preceded great and important victories, lost not heart. The soldiers said to the Pompeians when they exchanged salutations on picket, that "they would rather live on the bark of the trees than let Pompey escape from their hands." The corn was beginning to ripen, and there was promise soon of plenty. And while the Pompeians had provisions in greater abundance, they were in serious want of water, for Caesar had turned or dammed up all the springs and brooks which he could reach, and had obliged them to sink wells or rely on the brackish water of low, marshy pools. Pompey's men were not used to work, and it told on them. The health of Caesar's men was perfect, owing to the large space they had for camping; that of Pompey's, cooped up in a small area and overworked, was questionable.

So short for forage was Pompey that he was constrained to send his cavalry to Dyrrachium by sea. Here it could be readily fed, and could, moreover, sally out in rear of Caesar's lines and interfere with his foraging parties.

Caesar was now called away from his army for a short time. At this point in the narrative of the *Commentaries* there is a gap, which we are compelled to supply by a hint or two in Appian and Dion Cassius, and by construing what is said in a fashion little short of guess-work. It is more than probable that Caesar was on a diversion against Dyrrachium, to which he was led to believe that he would be given access if he essayed an attack out of hand. At the head of a sufficient body of troops he advanced on the city, crossed the narrows at the south end of the lagoons, left his troops in hiding, and advanced with a small escort towards the walls. But his hopes were not realized. Instead of meeting a friendly reception from the party that had agreed to act with him, the Dyrrachium garrison issued from the gates suddenly and with hostile intent. A party took ship and sailed around to the narrows to cut him off. Another party moved around his right to prevent his making his way up to the north end of the lagoons. A third party attacked him in front. Caesar quickly rallied his men, met these three attacks with three detachments from his forces, and a smart combat began with each body. The combat was without result. Fighting in his rear compelled Caesar to retreat, which he did without meeting any particular difficulty.

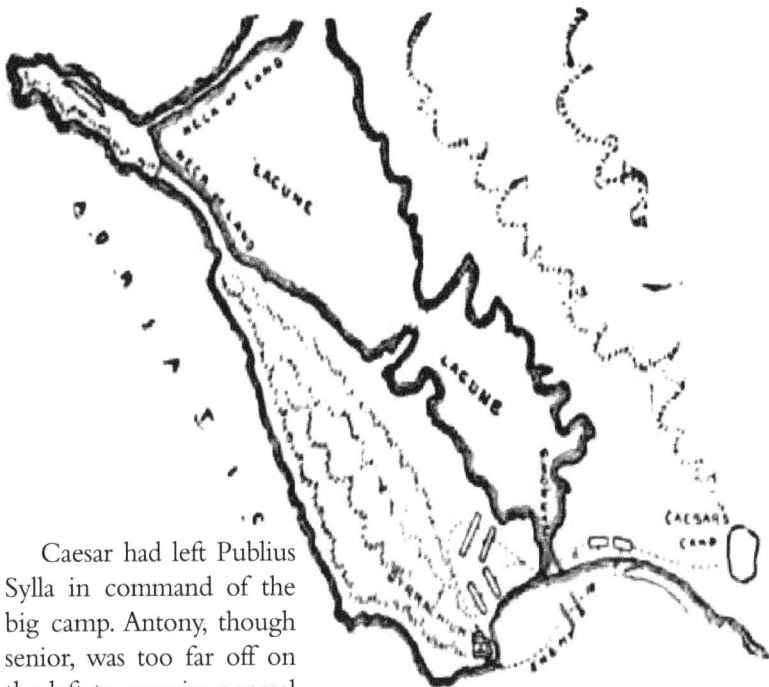

CAESAR BEFORE DYRRACHIUM

Caesar had left Publius Sylla in command of the big camp. Antony, though senior, was too far off on the left to exercise general control. Pompey, apparently soon made aware of the situation, seized the occasion as a good one to break through Caesar's lines, reach Dyrrachium, and perhaps catch Caesar near the city and shut him up with his small force in the Dyrrachium peninsula. Having a much larger army and interior lines, this attack on the legions left under Sylla was a comparatively easy matter. Pompey's plans were well conceived. Whenever he went at a tactical problem he did good work. He organized three attacks on Caesar's siege lines. These were so nearly simultaneous to the ones opposite Dyrrachium that it looks as if Pompey purposely led Caesar into an ambush, by himself dictating the false promise of opening the gates of that city.

The attacks were all against redoubts, and were so managed as to time, numbers and localities, as to make it probable that no reinforcements would be sent from one part of the line to the others. They were at points which lay east of Pompey's camp. There were two columns, of four legions in all. One column advanced up the ravine E, the other up by way of those marked F and G. Arrived on the high ground near H, the legions divided into three columns. By two of these columns attacks were only partially delivered. In one of the assaults, three of Caesar's *cohorts* under Volcatius Tullus easily beat back a legion which

121

formed one column; and in another, the German auxiliaries made a
sally from the lines, defeated another legion with much loss, and retired safely. These were but demonstrations on Pompey's part.

The third or main assault was severe. Pompey's third column of
two legions had attacked in force at one of the forts which was held
by the second *cohort* of the Sixth legion—three hundred men under
the *centurion* Minucius. The *legionaries* resisted the assault with great
stubbornness. Pompey's *cohorts* had scaling ladders, mural hooks and a
ram. They assaulted the towers of the *castellum*, tried to set fire to the
hurdles, filled up the trench, and exhibited the utmost determination
to break down the defences. But the Caesarians held on so stubbornly
and for so long a time that Sylla was enabled to gather from adjoining works and to lead up two legions to drive back the Pompeians.
The latter, exhausted by their efforts, did not stand the charge, but
so soon as the front line was struck yielded ground. Sylla had an excellent chance to bring on a general engagement under auspicious
conditions, and was loudly criticised in the army for not having done

ATTACK ON SYLLA

so. But he deemed that he had no right to deliver battle in Caesar's absence, and was sustained by his chief.

The Pompeians, beaten back, had difficulty in making good their retreat. They were passing over a ridge (I); Pompey halted on the top, not daring to retire down it on the other side, lest he should be overwhelmed on the slope by Caesar's men. He prolonged the combat till nightfall, and then seized an eminence out of engine-range from Minucius' redoubt (N) and fortified it. Caesar's men remained in his front, hoping to have him at a disadvantage when he should retreat. During the night and following days Pompey built turrets and carried the works up fifteen feet, facing the exposed side with mantelets, so as to retire under their protection. On the fifth night, a cloudy one, at the third watch, he stole a march on Caesar's *cohorts* which were in his front, and regained his old camp.

Defences played a great role in those days. A general who wished to avoid battle had only to shut himself up in his camp, where, so long as provisions lasted, he was safe. But if his rival came forward and offered battle by marshalling his legions, it was considered as wanting in the nicest sense of honour to do less than accept it, by emerging from camp and drawing up in line,—unless, indeed, there were preponderating and sufficient reasons for not so doing. If, therefore, a general had camped in a plain, he might have battle forced on him on terms in which his only advantage lay in the proximity to his camp, to which he could retire at will. He was better placed if encamped on a height, with a slope down from the *praetorian* gate, so that when he drew up, the enemy, if he attacked, must do so uphill. The heavy-armed *legionary* did not like to fight uphill, as he got out of breath by the ascent, had to cast his missiles up at his enemy, who, meanwhile, hurled his own down to better effect, and being fresh, could at the proper moment rush in a counter-charge down upon him with perhaps fatal effect.

This action of Pompey's is another proof of the extreme difficulty experienced by the ancients in holding their men in hand when retiring from an enemy pursuing them down a slope. In attacking uphill the *élan* was helpful in over-coming the difficulty; in retiring downhill the equal loss of confidence bred a disastrous condition. To avoid being attacked on a descent was as important then as to avoid being enfiladed by the enemy's batteries is today. The position which afforded the soldier the chance to cast javelins downwards at the enemy was one not to be readily forfeited. The bulk of all fighting was at javelin range. In theory, after casting their javelins the two first ranks fell to with the sword; but practically the lines faced each other and substantially remained in place for hours, with swayings to and fro as one or other side won a temporary advantage, or the rear ranks and lines moved to the front to relieve the weary. Although there were many duels among the more enterprising in each line, it was as a last resort that the sword was drawn by all. A charge with the *gladius* was then much more frequent than charges are today with the bayonet; but it was the last act in the drama. If this failed, it was hard to restore the confidence of the men, and it was not lightly undertaken. If the second or third line was still fresh, they could be called on; but if these, sword in hand, were driven back, the battle was not easily redeemed, and as troops of olden days were quite as much subject to demoralization as our own modern soldiers, if not more so, a retreat down a slope was one of those critical movements which had to be conducted with scrupulous care.

The Caesarians had gained a marked advantage. Pompey had lost nearly two thousand men, many *emeriti* and *centurions*, and six standards, while only twenty Caesarians were missing, if the *Commentaries* are to be believed. But in Minucius' redoubt, not a soldier escaped a wound. In one *cohort* four *centurions* lost their eyes,—a curious coincidence. The *centurion* Scaeva, who had been largely instrumental in saving the fort, produced to Caesar his shield, which had two hundred and thirty holes in it. Caesar presented Scaeva with two hundred thousand pieces of copper money,—about thirty-six hundred dollars,—and promoted him from eighth to first *centurion* (*primipilus*) as a reward for his exceptional gallantry. There were counted thirty thousand arrows thrown into the fort. The soldiers who had defended it were rewarded with double pay, clothing and rations, and with military honours.

Here is a curious discrepancy in the proportion of wounded to killed. Among the Greeks there was something approaching a general ratio—ten or twelve to one; among the Romans there was scarcely any regularity. In a late instance in the *Commentaries*,—Curio's battle in Africa,—the losses were given as six hundred killed and one thousand wounded. In this one we have a loss of only twenty legionaries killed along the whole line, and yet every man wounded in the fort which was most stoutly assailed. Such statistics make it difficult to compare ancient losses with modern. In old times wounds must often have been as slight as missiles lacked in power. In those days of hand weapons and good armour, lines could fight at casting or shooting distance for a long while with but small loss. Had Scaeva's shield been struck by two hundred and thirty bullets he would scarcely have lived to enjoy his munificent reward.

CHAPTER 33

Caesar's Defeat
May, 48 B. C.

Pompey was not abashed by his late defeat. He learned through certain deserters that the left of Caesar's line was not yet completed, and was in any event weak. With excellent skill and by night he prepared an assault at this quarter. He sent a large force of *cohorts* to attack the front of Caesar's lines, and auxiliaries and light troops to attack the rear. The assault was stoutly given, and owing partly to accident, partly to poor preparation, partly to an unexpected demoralization among the legions, Caesar suffered a galling defeat, with loss of one thousand killed. He had rashly ventured on the impossible, and met the necessary consequence. Pompey considered the war at an end. Not so Caesar, whom disaster never abashed; not so his men, who drank in his unconquerable spirit.

During the weeks occupied by these operations at Dyrrachium, Ætolia, Acarnania and Amphilochis had been reduced by Longinus and Sabinus. Caesar, desiring to gain a foothold in the Peloponnesus, sent these officers under the orders of Calenus to take possession of Achaia. To meet this threat Rutilius Rufus, Pompey's lieutenant, began to fortify the Isthmus to prevent Calenus from entering Achaia, for Caesar had no fleet to cross the Corinthian Bay. Calenus recovered Delphi, Thebes and Orchomenus by voluntary submission. A large part of Hellas was under Caesar's control.

In order to leave no part of the responsibility for civil bloodshed upon himself, Caesar had still again made proposals to Pompey for an adjustment through their mutual friend Scipio, when the latter reached Macedonia. He sent Clodius, who was also an intimate of Pompey's, to Scipio. But like the others, this effort at accommodation remained without effect. Whether these approaches were made because Caesar knew they would not be accepted, as has been alleged by his detractors, or from a sincere desire for peace, will never be known. But the fact remains that Caesar did make the proposals and that Pompey refused them. Nothing but the sword was left him.

Every day after the defeat of Pompey's late attack, Caesar drew up his army on the level ground between the camps (K) and offered battle. He even led his lines up almost to the Pompeian ramparts,— at least to the edge of the zone of the engine-missiles. Though Pompey, to save his credit, would lead out his men, he would post them with the third line close against his camp, and under protection of the fire of the light troops from the ramparts. This precluded an attack by Caesar. As above related, the bulk of Pompey's horse had been sent to Dyrrachium.

"Caesar, that he might the more easily keep Pompey's horse inclosed within Dyrrachium and prevent them from foraging, fortified the two narrow passes already mentioned, i. e., the narrows at the ends of the lagoons on the east and the northwest of Dyrrachium (L and M), with strong works and erected forts at them."

This was about May 20. But when fodder thus became particularly hard to get and Pompey derived no advantage from his cavalry, he brought a large part of it back to his camp by sea. While shut off from Dyrrachium by land, his vessels allowed him a free access to it by sea, which Caesar could not prevent. Within his lines, too, where even the young wheat had been eaten by the horses, it was difficult to keep them, and they were fed largely on leaves and plants. Barley and fodder were brought from Corcyra and Acarnania, but not in sufficient quantities. When even this supply gave out, Pompey was left with no resource but a sally. To this he saw that he must sooner or later come.

About this time, though Pompey's men daily deserted to Caesar, the first noteworthy desertions from Caesar's camp to Pompey's occurred. But these were fatal ones. Two Allobrogians, commanders of cavalry, who had been of great service to Caesar in Gaul and were men of birth, intelligence and courage, but, as it happened, had not been careful in their accounts of pay to their men, on being held to task by Caesar, though mildly, for Caesar preferred, he says, to make no scandal of the matter, deserted to Pompey, partly from shame and partly from fear, and conveyed to him detailed information about Caesar's works. Such a desertion being rare (the very first, says Caesar), Pompey made much of these men and took pains to exhibit them in every part of his lines.

Acting on the information obtained from these men, which was exact and thorough, Pompey gathered together a large amount of material for assaulting works, and at night transported his light troops and the material by sea to that part of Caesar's works—on the extreme left—which was nearest the coast and farthest from Caesar's greater camp. On the same night, after the third watch, sixty *cohorts* drafted from the north camp and the lines were marched to the same point, and the war-galleys were sent down the coast to anchor opposite. The foot soldiers were ordered to make osier-shields to wear on their helmets. Stationed here was the Ninth legion under Lentulus Marcellinus, the *quaestor*, with Fulvius Posthumus second in command. Antony had general charge of the left wing. The contravallation works consisted of a rampart ten feet high and ten feet wide covered by a trench fifteen feet wide "fronting the enemy," *i. e.*, towards the north. Some six hundred feet back were similar but less strong defences backing on the others—the usual circumvallation line. Caesar had anticipated an attack from the side of the sea and had recently erected these latter defences. The works which were to connect these two ram-parts and defend the left of the line, *i. e.*, those facing the sea, were not yet finished, and this fact Pompey had ascertained from the Allobrogians.

Pompey's attack was prepared at night and delivered at daybreak on the weakest part of Caesar's lines, was excellently planned, stoutly given, and was a complete surprise. The archers and slingers who attacked from the south were very active, and poured a galling fire upon the unprepared defenders, whom they outnumbered six or eight to one. At the same moment the sixty legionary *cohorts* made a desperate onslaught from the north, using their weapons and engines to great advantage; and began to set up their scaling ladders after filling the ditch with fascines. The danger was imminent enough, owing to the front and rear attack; but to make the situation hopeless, a party of light troops discovered the unfinished defences on Caesar's extreme left, and making a gallant dash in between the two lines, took the legionaries of the Ninth absolutely in flank. The Caesarians appear to have been slenderly supplied with missiles, for their chief defence, thus taken unawares, was stones; and the osier headgear of the Pompeians saved them from the effect of these. There appears clearly, from the *Commentaries*, to have been a lack of readiness, against which, after the desertion of the Allobrogians, one would have supposed that Caesar would have provided. He knew his own weakest spot, he knew that the deserters knew it, and he might have guessed that an attack would

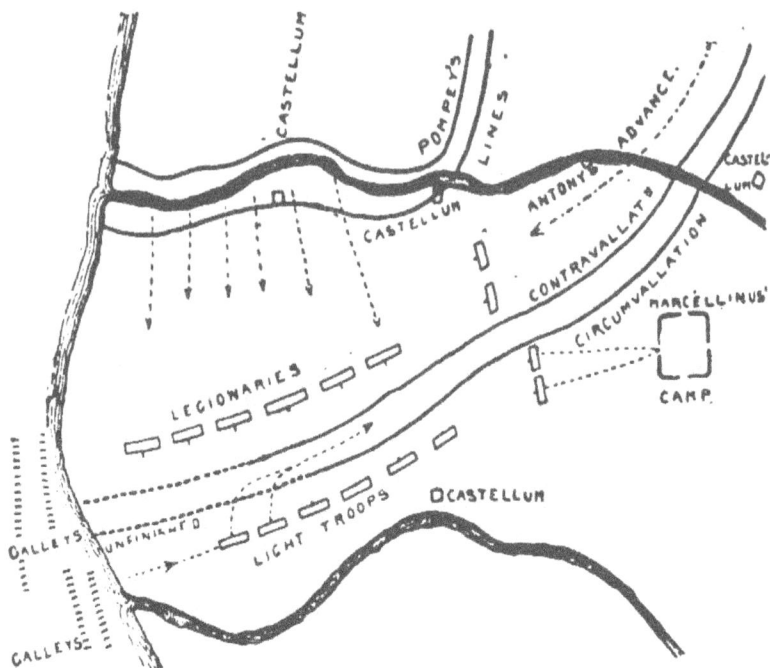

BATTLE OF DYRRACHIUM, POMPEY'S ATTACK

be made here. Caesar had grown to believe that Pompey was loath to fight, and perhaps was careless in consequence. In any event, Pompey's well-conceived attack was fully successful. His men came on with such a determined rush that the Caesarians broke and could not be rallied, and such *cohorts* as were sent to their relief by Marcellinus, whose camp was near the left, also caught the infection and retired in confusion. The Pompeians pressed on; the Caesarians were suffering serious losses, all the centurions but one of the leading *cohort* being killed. He happily was the *primipilus*, and managed to save the legionary eagle. The Pompeians did not stop until they reached the camp of the Ninth legion. There Antony was met debouching from the line of hills where had been erected the circuit of *castella*, with a bold front of twelve *cohorts*, and his brave stand on the enemy's flank checked the latter's onslaught, drove back the enemy, rallied the runaways, and put an end to the present danger.

Caesar, hearing of the disaster by the signals, which were columns of smoke, usual in such emergencies, also came speedily to the ground from the main camp with several *cohorts* collected from the *castella* on the way. But it was too late to save the day or the tactical loss. Pompey had got a foothold from which he could not be ousted and from which he could move in and out at will to forage, or to attack Caesar's rear. The work of months was rendered nugatory. The blockade was practically broken.

At the end of Caesar's late lines, Pompey at once entrenched a new and strong camp, utilizing for the purpose part of the works Caesar had erected. Its location was not far from the seashore and somewhat over a mile south of the river along which lay the right of his line. Opposite this camp, Caesar, nothing daunted and with the hope to neutralize the defeat by a success yet won before the day should close, sat down and entrenched near Pompey. He had with Antony's force and what he could safely and quickly draw from the neighbouring forts some thirty-five *cohorts*. He placed his men between the two lines of circumvallation and contravallation, the former on his right, the latter on his left, and threw up a line between and perpendicular to them within five hundred yards of the enemy.

Pompey's attack had been made at daylight and his initial victory had been quickly won. It was yet early in the day. There were many hours to retrieve the disaster. Pompey had no doubt that the battle was over for that day; not so thought Caesar. Like Sheridan at Winchester, he determined to recover the field. Each of the armies was now divided into two parts. One of each confronted the other at the main camps on the north; one of each lay in fighting contact with the other at the lines on the south plain.

There was nearby this place an old encampment which had an inner work. The latter had been a smaller entrenched camp of Caesar's during the operation of the Ninth legion a week or two back (A), and the outer wall had been added by Pompey when Caesar in changing his lines had been compelled to abandon it and Pompey had occupied it with a larger force. Later again Pompey had himself given up this double camp. "This camp joined a certain wood and was not above four hundred paces distant from the sea." When Pompey occupied the place, he "carried an entrenchment from the left angle of the camp to the river about four hundred paces, that his soldiers might have more liberty and less danger in fetching water," while Caesar's men and his were daily skirmishing over the ground each sought to occupy in constructing their lines. It was now a sort of redoubt, and was half a mile distant from Pompey's camp. This general threw the legion commanded by L. Torquatus into this camp as a convenient link between his north and south camps, to make a wider front and to save his men the labour of constructing a new one. Torquatus marched to the place back of the wood in question.

Caesar, who learned of this movement from his scouts, thought he might attack this post with a good chance of success, and by a brilliant stroke repair the effect of the disaster of the morning. His men had finished their works, but Pompey's had not, and it would take them some time to drop their tools, make ready for battle, and reach the camp. Speed might serve him to crush Torquatus. He headed for this camp with thirty-three *cohorts*, some ten thousand men, among them the Ninth legion, much reduced by the recent fight. He left two *cohorts* in the trenches, which made enough of an appearance of working actively at the rampart to quiet Pompey's apprehensions, and, marching quickly but cautiously, reached the fort before Pompey could have notice of an advance.

Caesar marshalled his men in two wings, each in two lines. The left wing was opposite the camp to be attacked; the right wing opposite the entrenchment which ran to the river. Attacking with the left wing, which he commanded in person, Caesar carried the outer works with a rush, and pushing in, though the entrances were well

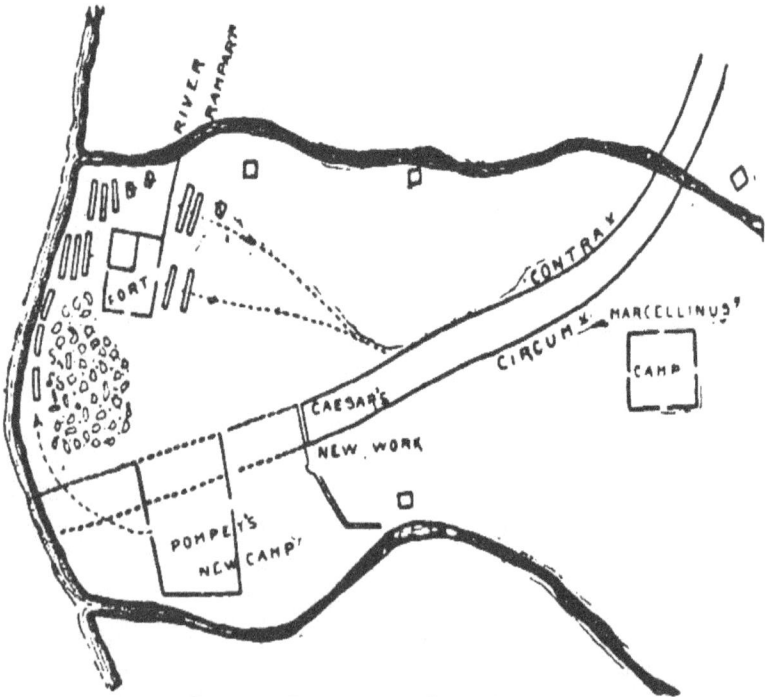

BATTLE OF DYRRACHIUM, CAESAR'S ATTACK

barricaded by an *ericius*, or gate full of sharp spikes, forced the Pompeians from the front rampart of the inner one. So far the attack had succeeded. The right wing, however, in search of a gate by which to enter what they supposed to be part of the wall of the redoubt, and misled by following the new rampart which ran from the fort down to the river and was ten feet high, got separated from the left so far as to produce a serious gap in the line and make mutual support impossible. After following this river rampart a small distance, they climbed or broke through it, followed by the cavalry. This placed them no nearer the redoubt than they had been when in its front, and separated them from the left wing.

Pompey had soon learned of the attack on Torquatus, and recalling his five legions from their work of entrenching he marched to the rescue of his lieutenant. The garrison, now sure of the support of Pompey, made a stout resistance to Caesar's left wing at the *decuman* gate and charged on the Caesarians with a will, while Pompey's cavalry advanced against Caesar's cavalry and his right wing. Caesar's right-wing soldiers by some strange fatality, or else seeing themselves cut off from their leader, were seized with a sudden panic. They had not had time to recover from the morning's disaster and their work was not crisply cut out. The cavalry first caught the infection and fell back through a breach in the river rampart which they had made and entered at. This left the infantry of the right wing unsupported by the horse, and it, too, drifted to the rear even before it had come within sight of the enemy's line, and in retiring over the river rampart in disorder lost a vast number of men by being trodden underfoot in the trenches.

"Most of them, lest they should be engaged in the narrow passes, threw themselves down a rampart ten feet high into the trenches; and the first being trodden to death, the rest procured their safety and escaped over their bodies."

Others, with no better result, tried to get round the north end of the river rampart. It was clearly a stampede. The men of the left wing, made aware that the right wing and the cavalry were melting away, thus leaving their own flank naked while they themselves had the garrison to contend with, perceiving from the wall the advance of Pompey in line of battle with bold and steady front, and fearing to be inclosed between the outer and inner ramparts, were seized with like terror and fell back in like confusion before the enemy had hurled a single spear. Not even when Caesar laid hold of an eagle and personally called upon his men to follow him could the panic-stricken troops be rallied. One man, on whom Caesar laid hands to restore him to a sense of duty, is even said to have lifted his sword against him in the violence of his fright. The men continued to run in the same manner; others, through fear, even threw away their colours, nor did a single man face about. At the *praetorian* gate of the outer redoubt the same scene of confusion and disaster was repeated. But as good luck would have it, Pompey suspected an ambuscade and did not rapidly advance. So sudden a success from so sudden a defeat constrained him to caution. His cavalry, eager to pursue, could not push through the breaches of the river rampart or the camp gates, which were all choked up with dead and wounded men. Caesar was enabled to get the rest of his troops out of action without incurring the penalty of a pursuit, though he saved his *cohorts* from the enemy's cavalry, which finally came up, only just in time behind the contravallation wall.

In the two actions of this day Caesar's losses were nine hundred and sixty men, several Roman knights, thirty-two military *tribunes* and *centurions*, and thirty-two *maniple* ensigns. Most of the men had been crushed to death in the ditch. All the prisoners who fell into Pompey's hands were put to death by Labienus with cruel taunts. Such was the hatred of the man whom Caesar had delighted to honour. This heavy list of casualties, about eight *per cent,* in killed, cannot be counted as a battle loss in comparison with other general engagements. The men had scarcely fought. They had been cut down or perished in their flight.

The description of these two actions is somewhat lacking in clearness in the *Commentaries.* The terrain explains the story, however, and the few items given enable us to sketch out the scene of the combat very distinctly. This much is certain,—Caesar was badly beaten, worse than he had ever been before. He himself came near losing his life. His troops had become utterly demoralized and could not be rallied, and as he is himself reported to have said, had Pompey known how to win a victory, he would have been fatally defeated. There is not even an attempt in the *Commentaries* to gloss over the matter. The two battles of this day had been reverses which had been saved from becoming irretrievable disasters solely by Pompey's lack of enterprise. Excuse enough for the defeat existed in the disparity of forces; there was no excuse for the demoralization of the troops.

All old soldiers know how irrational is the conduct of a mass of fleeing soldiery; how each man seeks his own safety, and all idea of discipline is for the moment lost. Caesar's descriptions give one a picture of an army very badly demoralized. There is a tendency in all old writers to make the light and shade of their sketches very marked. The gallantry displayed in unimportant affairs is brilliant; the fear in slight reverses is excessive. Whether this habit of statement overdraws the matter or not is doubtful. Disciplined and seasoned troops have been much the same in all eras. Caesar's men unquestionably lost heart at times in a discreditable way. But Caesar was always able to hold them in hand and to shame their defeat into an encouragement for the future. What the troops lose in honour, Caesar gains in courage and skill.

By his temerity in attempting a task, the impossibility of which he should earlier have recognized, Caesar had lost three good months and all power of offense at this place. He was back at his starting point, and with his communications with Italy severed. He had failed in every sense, strategically and tactically, and with Pompey's large force of cavalry released he might be logistically compromised. His opponent's all but blameworthy deliberation had proven successful. Time did not work against him as against Caesar. His troops had behaved well; he had every reason to believe they would do so again; and he could now credit Labienus' assertion that Caesar's Gallic veterans had disappeared. If Pompey should rouse himself for once and push home, Caesar might be fatally struck. But Pompey did not do so. Fortune stood by Caesar as she never has by any one; and the character of the two men now plainly appeared.

AQUILIFER

133

CHAPTER 34

Retreat from Dyrrachium
May, 48 B. C.

Caesar retired from Dyrrachium with great skill. He so markedly impressed his own bearing on his soldiers as to shame them into the desire again to meet the enemy and retrieve their unsoldierly conduct. Pompey sought to pursue, but was not rapid enough. Caesar picked up his detachments and headed towards Thessaly to concentrate all his legions and try conclusions afresh. Heretofore-friendly Greece now turned against him; and he was forced to capture Gomphi by assault. Other cities opened their gates. After some manoeuvring between the rival lieutenants of either, Pompey and Caesar both concentrated their forces and reached the neighbourhood of Pharsalus. Caesar had some thirty-five thousand men all told; Pompey, at least twice as many; while his cavalry was seven thousand to Caesar's one thousand. Despite this superiority, Pompey waited for Caesar to move upon him. Some manoeuvring supervened for position near Pharsalus. Caesar endeavoured to bring Pompey to battle, but could not do so on even terms. He was about to shift his ground, when Pompey showed a disposition to fight. Caesar at once accepted the challenge.

This double victory so elated Pompey and his party that he imagined the war already over. He was saluted as *Imperator*. He did not consider the difference in forces or the attendant circumstances. Caesar, on the contrary, with the elasticity of the great soldier, rose to the occasion. By no means disheartened, he determined to change his plan, and at once. He was not slow to recognize that he had failed in his object. He was afraid to risk another battle here, lest from the recollection of the prior defeats his men should again grow demoralized. Even his hardened legionaries had shown that they were not above disgraceful panics. He concluded to give over what, after all, was practically an impossibility,—the task with a much smaller force of shutting Pompey up in his lines; to move away and to lure him out into the plain country where he might outmanoeuvre him as he could not on the entrenched hills. In the open field he felt a superiority he had been unable to show at Dyrrachium, where lines and redoubts of such vast extent limited his movements and his capacity to develop his resources.

Caesar could not overlook all the acts of cowardice which had been at the root of the Dyrrachium defeat. He selected those on whom reliance was wont to be placed, but who in this instance had failed in their duty, and punished several of the standard-bearers by reducing them to the ranks. This sufficed as an example. He then addressed his men in such wise as to rob them of the sting of defeat and inspire them with fresh confidence. Indeed, so soon as Caesar's legionaries had recovered from their first demoralization, they became themselves and eager for a battle. They begged Caesar to lead them against the enemy instead of leaving Dyrrachium, promising to give a good account of them-selves. But Caesar mistrusted not their good will but their steadiness; he deemed his own plan wiser and adhered to it, promising his men a victory the next time they struck the enemy. The question of victualling was, moreover, becoming difficult, and it was time to move away.

After taking only such few hours as were necessary to collect and care for the wounded, Caesar quietly massed on his left all his men and material, and sent forward at nightfall on the day of the battle all his baggage and the wounded and sick, in conduct of one legion, to Apollonia, ordering them to make the distance in one march. Then keeping two legions under his own orders as rearguard in the camp, he started the other seven on several roads, before daylight of the next day, in the same direction, without signals or sound of any kind. When they had got well on the way, he gave the usual signal for decamping, broke up with his two legions and rapidly followed the column. This sensitiveness as to the point of honour involved in giving the signal for the march is interesting. Caesar was unwilling to slink away; but he came very close to doing so. It was the only wise thing to do.

Caesar had a perilous task before him,—to retire from a victorious enemy over two bridgeless rivers, the Genusus and Apsus, both with rapid flow and steep banks. He reached the Genusus after about a five hours' march. Pompey sent his cavalry in pursuit, and followed with the entire army. The horse reached Caesar's rear of column near the Genusus. But it accomplished nothing. Caesar detached his own horse, intermixed with some four hundred legionaries, against Pompey's cavalry and threw it back with loss. He then put his legions across the Genusus, which was done without too much difficulty. This was the day's march he had planned, and he was now safe from Pompey's immediate pursuit, whose cavalry could not readily cross, as Caesar had collected all the boats and the banks were very steep. He took up his post opposite Asparagium, in the old camp, whose wall and ditch still stood, with unusual precautions. He must steal another march on Pompey if he was to elude him. To induce Pompey to believe that he would stay where he was for a day or two, his horse was allowed to go out to forage; but it was soon quietly ordered in again. The infantry had been kept in camp ready to march. Pompey, who had followed Caesar across the river, and had likewise camped in his old defences at Asparagium, was deceived in effect. About midday, when Pompey's men were resting, and many of them had strayed back towards the old camp to collect their hastily left chattels, and were generally dispersed, owing to laxness of discipline, Caesar stole his march on the enemy, and, making some eight miles before dark, got that much start. Then after a brief rest, at the opening of the night Caesar sent forward his baggage, and followed by daylight with his legions. And this he did on the third day also, "by which means he was enabled to effect his march over the deepest rivers and through the most intricate roads without any loss." On the fourth day, Pompey gave over the pursuit, Caesar having steadily out-marched him, and returned to Asparagium.

Immediately after the battle, Pompey had the choice of several plans by which to make use of his victory. He might cross to Italy, where he could count on a better reception now that Caesar was defeated. He might sharply pursue Caesar's army and perhaps destroy it before it could recruit, or, failing to reach it, might follow it inland and bring it to battle before it had recovered its tone. Having begun by pursuing Caesar, though to no good effect, Pompey kept to the plan of a campaign in Greece. But he deemed it wise to reassemble his forces, which the pursuit had much scattered.

Caesar had stopped at Apollonia only to leave his wounded under a suitable garrison and arrange for an indefinite absence. He left there June 1. He had determined to join Domitius, who, with the Eleventh and Twelfth legions, had succeeded in recovering all Macedonia,—a conquest Caesar hoped not to forfeit, as its possession would enable him to concentrate his forces in a friendly country.

Domitius was on the Haliacmon, where he had towards the end of April been anticipating the arrival of Scipio from Syria with two legions and cavalry which the latter was bringing to Pompey. Scipio, about May 1, had reached the vicinity of Domitius, and had then turned south to surprise Longinus, who was in command of only a legion of recruits in Thessaly, He left his baggage under Favonius on the Haliacmon, near Servia. Longinus, catching the alarm, retired across the Pindus Mountains to Ambracia. Scipio, sure of his prey, was about to follow, when Favonius called him back to present resistance to Domitius, who was threatening him. Returning thither, Scipio and Domitius indulged in several slight passages of arms, in which Domitius showed himself the more ready for combat; but nothing came of these exchanges. This was about the time when Caesar had reached Apollonia.

So far as the general strategic scheme went, Caesar's duty was plain. If Pompey pursued him, he would be cut off from his fleet and his *dépôt* at Dyrrachium,—from corn and war material,—and be thereby placed on equal terms with Caesar. If Pompey crossed to Italy, Domitius and Caesar would be forced to follow him through Illyricum to defend Italy, however difficult the task. If Pompey attempted to take Apollonia and Oricum, Caesar would attack Scipio and compel Pompey to come to his relief. No other alternatives were apt to complicate the problem.

Caesar left four *cohorts* at Apollonia, one at Lissus, and three at Oricum, not counting the wounded. This left him seven old legions, one of which had had three *cohorts* taken from it,—say eighteen thousand men. He expected two more legions from Italy; but these were intended to guard Illyricum under Cornuficius.

Pompey, on June 2, ascertained Caesar's movements and elected to join Scipio. He feared that Caesar had designs against his lieutenant and proposed himself to cut off Domitius if he could reach him before Caesar. Many of his lieutenants strongly advised crossing the Adriatic and reconquering Italy, which they said would be the death-blow to Caesar; but Pompey felt that he could not abandon Scipio and the many persons of note adhering to his cause who were still in Thessaly and Macedonia. The majority approved his course.

Accordingly, leaving Cato with fifteen *cohorts* and three hundred vessels to guard the seashore and Dyrrachium, Pompey started from Asparagium June 3, towards Macedonia. Caesar's prompt action had forced Pompey to follow him. It was he still, who, despite defeat, imposed the time and place of future manoeuvres. Pompey's was the weaker will.

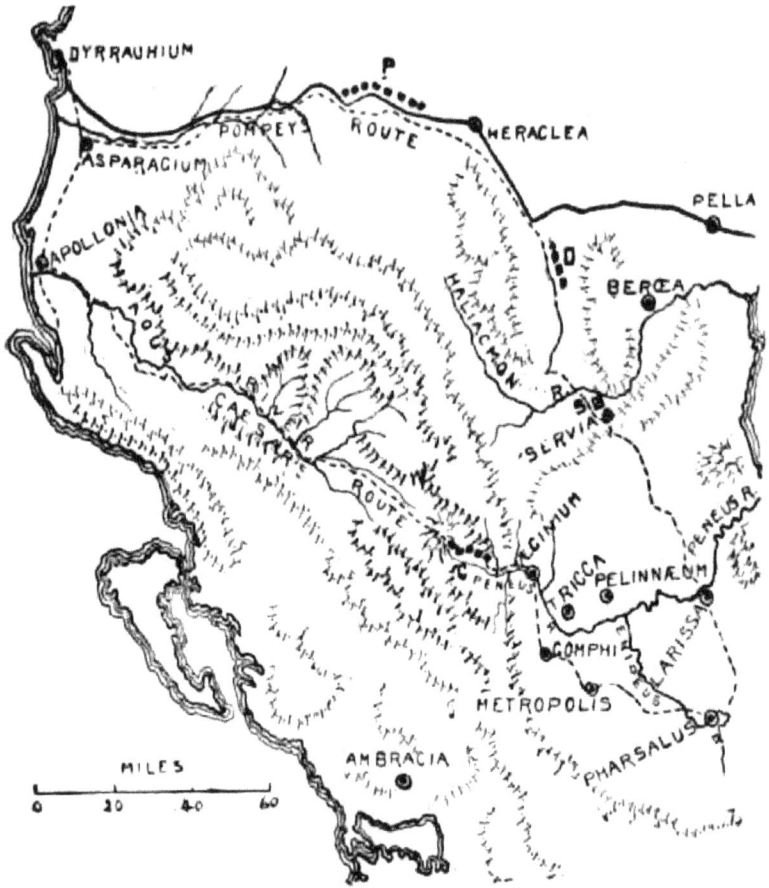

SITUATION JUNE 6

The situation about June 6 was curious. Pompey was marching along the Egnatian highway to join Scipio. Caesar was marching up the River Aous by a difficult road to join Domitius. The latter, in search of victual and ignorant of the recent events at Dyrrachium, was on the point of falling into Pompey's clutches by a march on Heraclea.

The exaggerated rumours of Caesar's defeat had weakened the allegiance of many states in Greece. His messengers had been seized, and it had been impossible for him to communicate with Domitius. Pompey, marching on the direct road, reached Heraclea on June 8. As we have seen, Domitius had been facing Scipio on the Haliac-mon. When the latter declined to come to battle, Domitius, pressed for rations, had headed for Heraclea, where he thought he could revictual. On the 9th of June he was close to the place. But just as he was about to blunder into Pompey's column, some of the Allobroges who had recently deserted to Pompey, and who were with the latter's scouting parties, were captured by Domitius' vanguard and revealed to him all the facts. Domitius quickly changed his course and filed south towards Thessaly.

Caesar had marched with clear purpose and corresponding rapidity. His route was somewhat the same as that pursued by Alexander when marching on Thebes. He reached the watershed of the Aous and Peneus, and descended to Æginium in Thessaly, June 7. Here Domitius joined him June 13. Pompey had followed with for him unusual speed. Fortune was kind to both. The threatened lieutenant of neither was compromised. The situation had cleared itself.

Having joined his lieutenant, Caesar had nine legions, of which one was short three *cohorts*,—in all some twenty-four thousand men. He had a few light troops and one thousand horse. He decided to remain in Thessaly to recruit the physique and *morale* of his army. He was where at need he could rally his legates under Calenus, who had fifteen *cohorts*.

The alluvial plain of Thessaly, was broad and well watered by the Peneus and its affluents, was fertile and well-fitted for the operations of armies. The towns were active in partisan-ship of either Pompey or Caesar, and as Scipio, on learning the movements of the rival generals, had marched to Larissa, Caesar could scarcely count on much support after his late defeat. On debouching from the mountains he was confronted with four strong places lying on the foothills of Thessaly athwart his path,—Pelinaeum, Trieca, Gomphi, Metropolis,—a quadrilateral of importance, but less then than it would assume today.

Caesar left Æginium June 15 and marched to Gomphi, twenty miles distant. Here he found the gates shut on him, the news from Dyrrachium having in fact changed the minds of many of the Thessalians, who previously had been his allies. The inhabitants had sent for help to Scipio and Pompey; but Scipio had marched to Larissa, and Pompey had not yet reached the border of Thessaly.

Caesar camped. His men had made a longer march than usual that day and had entrenched the camp; but he determined to assault Gomphi without delay. The men showed great alacrity. They were anxious to prove that the late defeat came not from lack of stomach. They prepared penthouses, scaling-ladders and hurdles, and were ready by four o'clock. After exhorting his *cohorts* to retrieve themselves, and win reputation and the provisions they needed at the same moment,

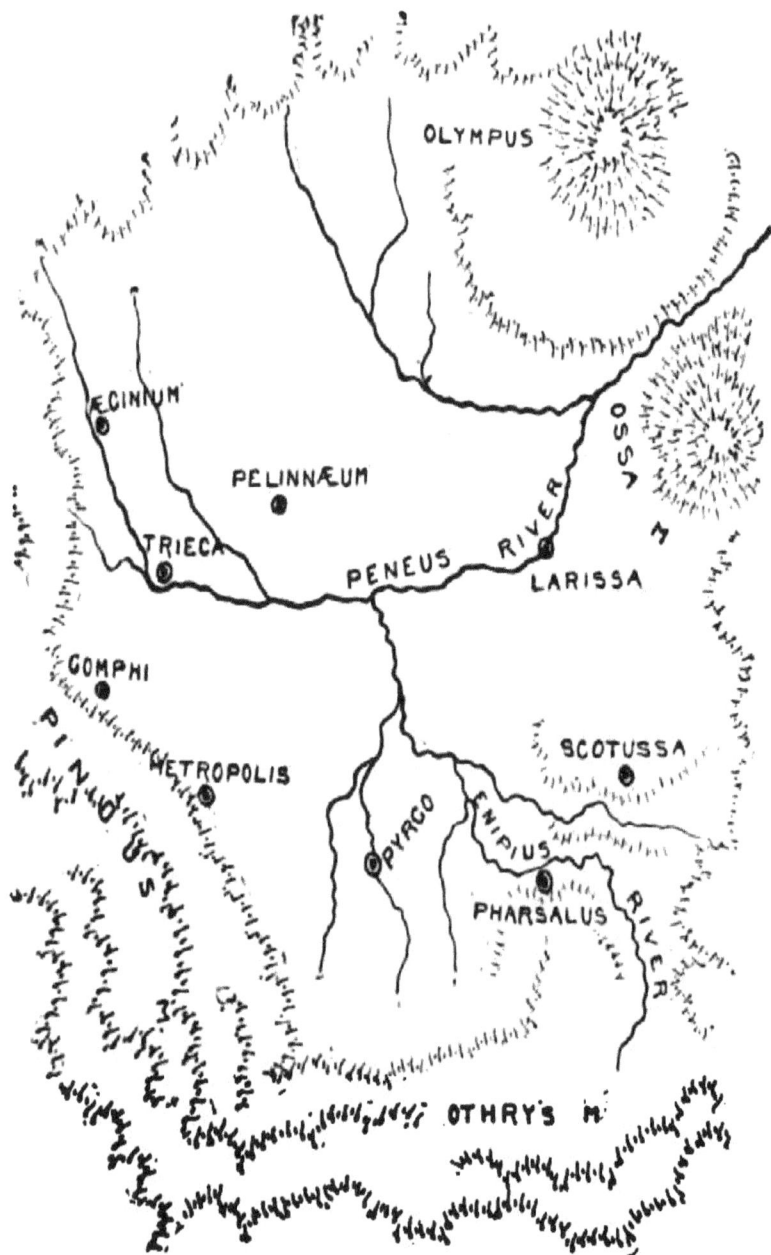

PLAIN OF THESSALY.

Caesar commanded an assault of the town, though it was protected by very high walls; and in the three remaining hours of the afternoon captured it. Then, as an example, and as encouragement to his men, he gave it up to plunder.

Next day he marched to Metropolis. Here, too, the inhabitants at first shut their gates, but on hearing of the fate of Gomphi, were wise. enough to change their minds. Caesar scrupulously spared the place, and thereafter all towns in Thessaly, except those near Larissa, where Scipio was quartered, awed and persuaded by the examples of Gomphi and Metropolis, opened their gates on his approach.

Caesar was cheered by the conduct of his men, and felt that he might again trust to their steady bravery. He made up his mind to await Pompey's arrival, while resting his troops. He headed to the east, crossed the Apidanus at Pyrgo, moved on farther into the level country and camped north of Pharsalus in the plain on the left bank of the Enipeus. The camp appears to us to have been illy chosen, but Caesar's reasons for placing it where he did are not given.

Pompey, when he found that Domitius had escaped him and that Scipio was safe, kept on his course with slow marches, southeast towards Larissa. It is hardly probable that he marched by way of Pella, as has been assumed. He at least knew that Scipio had been on the Haliacmon, and had probably heard that he had marched towards Larissa.

The event proved that Pompey would have been wiser to move into Italy. But he not unnaturally looked upon another victory as the certain consequence of his last, and we can but commend his purpose in following up an enemy whom every indication warranted him in believing he could overwhelm.

Again we see that the plan and sequence of the campaign were dictated by Caesar's movements. Pompey might, by a diversion on Italy, have had things his own way, but he was too lax and indecisive. Even now he was giving his opponent too much time to recruit.

Pompey joined Scipio June 21, at Larissa, and assumed command of both the armies. Why Caesar had not attacked Scipio before Pompey's arrival has been frequently asked. But such an act was not in accordance with ancient practice. Larissa was too strong a town to assault, and a siege was not possible at the moment when speed was of the essence. There may have been political grounds which we do not know. To attack a divided enemy, as we understand the phrase, is rather a device of the modern art of war than a habit of Caesar's days. It had been done by Hannibal and by Alexander, but more often such an opportunity was neglected than improved. Moreover, Caesar was reluctant to assault a well-defended city. Larissa, with Scipio's two legions, was a different task from Gomphi with its native population.

At all events, Caesar remained *in situ* and awaited his enemy. Larissa was but twenty miles distant. The harvest was near at hand. His supplies were now certain and he was in open country where he could manoeuvre at will. On the other hand, Pompey was in command of fifty thousand legionaries, seven thousand horse, and many light troops,—a force large enough to justify his belief that Caesar was at his mercy. So certain was everyone in Pompey's camp of victory, that already they saw their chief at the head of the Roman state, and quarrelled about the disposal of honours, offices and spoils. The estates of the rich men in Caesar's camp were cut up and divided,—on paper. Much wrangling was the result, and the cries to be led against Caesar grew among soldiers, politicians and courtiers alike.

Labienus appears to have been the very worst of counsellors for Pompey. Whatever his motives for his present hatred of Caesar, the feeling was pronounced. He could scarcely himself believe, but he certainly led Pompey to believe, that Caesar's troops were not of the best; that there were few Gallic veterans in the ranks; and that his young soldiers—*teste* Dyrrachium—would not stand fire. He dwelt on the fact that Pompey's cavalry was undoubtedly superior to Caesar's; and alleged that with the preponderance of numbers there could be no doubt whatever of victory so soon as Caesar was attacked. It is certain that Pompey was firmly convinced that he must now win. And there existed abundant reason for his conviction. There was but one weak premise in his argument. He forgot that he had Caesar in his front, and that the personal factor is always the strongest in war. He took no steps to counterbalance the weight Caesar's personality would have in the coming fray. The defect in Pompey's army was the lack of one head, one purpose to control and direct events.

Caesar, on the other hand, *was* his army. The whole body was instinct with his purpose. From low to high all worked on his own method. He controlled its every mood and act. He was the mainspring and balance-wheel alike. And as he now felt that he could again rely upon his legions,—perhaps better than before their late defeat,—he proposed to bring Pompey to battle even though he had but half the force of his opponent.

Both armies had as by mutual consent approached each other and lay in the vicinity of Pharsalus. Caesar, as we have seen, had first moved to this place and been followed at an interval of a few days by Pompey.

The forces of each can be fairly estimated. Some authorities claim that between three and four hundred thousand men faced each other on this field. This is absurd. Nearly all the ancient historians agree that Pompey had one hundred and ten *cohorts*, Caesar, eighty-two *cohorts*, and that each had some auxiliaries. Pompey, whose *cohorts* were nearer the normal strength than Caesar's, had not far from fifty thousand *legionaries* (the *Commentaries* state them at forty-five thousand men), some four thousand bowmen, seven thousand cavalry, and a host of auxiliaries,—a total certainly exceeding sixty thousand men. Caesar's *cohorts* were small, scarcely more than three hundred men each. They had been much depleted and he had not been able to recruit them up to normal strength. He numbered in all not over twenty-five thousand legionaries (the *Commentaries* say twenty-two thousand), had but one thousand mounted men, and fewer auxiliaries than Pompey,—a total of some thirty thousand. All authorities are agreed that Pompey out-numbered Caesar substantially two to one.

There is again, as so frequently occurs in ancient battles, some dispute as to which bank of the river the battle of Pharsalus was fought on. A study of the topography of the country and the field makes the matter perfectly clear. Pompey had come from Larissa, which lay north from Pharsalus; Caesar had come from Metropolis, which lay to the west. These facts must be borne in mind; as also that the Enipeus, according to Strabo, springs from Mount Othrys and flows past Pharsalus; that the battle, according to Appian, was between Pharsalus and the Enipeus; and that according to the *Commentaries* Pompey's right and Caesar's left flanks leaned on the river. We must find a site on which Pompey could suitably camp his large army and build certain *castella* we are told about, and a battle-ground between the rival camps which fits the relations which have come down to us. Unless we satisfy these points, as well as military probabilities, we are all at sea. The following theory of the battle is consistent with all these facts, and no other is. It has been the custom to throw aside one or other of these statements as inconsistent with the rest; but that theory which agrees with all of them is manifestly the best; especially when it accords with the terrain. As in the case of Cannae, there is no need to discard any fact given by any reliable authority.

The Enipeus flows from its source through deep ravines until it emerges into the plain of Pharsalus. Here it turns to the west and incloses heights today known as Karadja Ahmet, some six hundred feet above the river-bed. On all sides, except on the west towards the plain, rises a heavy network of mountains. West of Karadja Ahmet there projects from this network the hill of Krindir, and between the two hills, bounded on the south by the mountains and on the north by the river, is a smaller plain, four miles long by two miles wide.

The Cynocephalae Mountains—a range of gray, serrated peaks— lie to the north. On his way from Larissa Pompey had come across the plateau, leaving the Cynocephalae hills on his left. He could not have camped here, with a view to battle, as alleged by Mommsen; it was far too rugged for operations. Pompey needed a battle-ground on which he could use his large body of cavalry. He sought a place whose slope was such that he could induce Caesar to attack him, which on the rough and cut-up heights of Cynocephalae Caesar would certainly not have done. His enemy was already encamped in the narrows between the Enipeus and Krindir, with the citadel of Pharsalus—perhaps Homer's Phthia, dwelling of Achilles—frowning, with heroic memories, from its two-peaked hill five hundred feet above his camp. Pompey did what it was natural to do; he moved down and across the Enipeus, and pitched his camp on Karadja Ahmet, where he had in his front a suitable slope, with his flanks protected by the river on one side and the hills on the other, and with a good ford across the Enipeus at his back. On the flanking hills to the left of his camp he threw up a number of redoubts.

Caesar faced east, Pompey west. The camps were five miles apart. Caesar was intent on bringing Pompey to battle. He had kept his touch on the pulse of his army, and found that its beat was again strong and regular. This capacity to test the tone of an army's system is distinctly a proof of the great captain. Despite his late defeat, Caesar was not misled in his estimate of his soldiers; despite his victory, Pompey's confidence in his *cohorts* was misplaced.

To bring Pompey to an issue, Caesar each day led out his men and set them in array, at first on their own ground not far distant from Pompey's camp, but on succeeding days advancing up to the foot of the slope on which lay his powerful antagonist. His horse, of which he had but a handful compared to Pompey, he mixed with the most active of the light troops, and habituated them to this species of combat by daily skirmishes. The cavalry, thus sustained, though numerically weaker, felt confidence in its conduct, and in one of its outpost com-

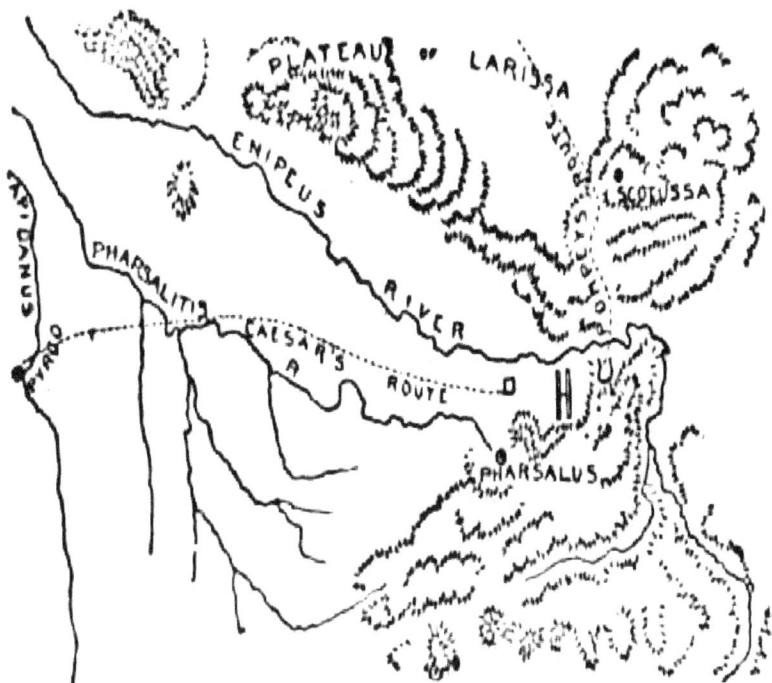

PHARSALUS PLAIN

bats defeated the enemy, killing one of the Allobrogian deserter-chiefs.
Caesar's men thus gained in self-poise from day to day.

Pompey did not leave the hill his camp lay on, but uniformly drew
up on the lower slope, hoping that Caesar would attack him at this
disadvantage; but from his much greater strength, Caesar was far too
wary to do so. Nothing better shows Pompey's weaker *morale* than
his indecision here though every element was in his favour. Nor can
it be said that Pompey was still acting on his old theory of tiring out
Caesar by non-action. For, whether of his own free will or yielding to
the importunities of his friends, he had come hither especially to give
Caesar, sore hit in the late disaster, the *coup de grâce*.

Unsuccessful in his attempt to bring Pompey to battle on equal
terms, Caesar was about to change his tactics. He determined to shift
his ground from day to day, and thus endeavour to catch Pompey
under adverse conditions on the march. For Pompey's men were not
used to hard marching, as were Caesar's, and would be harassed by a
series of forced manoeuvres. And moreover, Caesar, by keeping in motion, could more readily supply himself with corn without detailing a
heavy force from camp each day. On the very morning when Caesar

145

proposed to put his new plan into execution he noticed that Pompey had advanced farther than usual from his camp and down the slope, as if willing finally to test the issue. This was actually the case, for Pompey's friends had unanimously demanded battle.

Pompey, though giving way to pressure, in his inner consciousness still clung to the value of his defensive views. This came partly from lack of initiative, partly from the fact that he was a good enough soldier to see that the victory at Dyrrachium had not been wholly without accident, that Caesar's troops were really better than his own, and that to keep up a Fabian policy was safe, and more apt to win in the end, even if less commendable on the score of enterprise. This was a healthy view; but his lieutenants combated it, and Pompey's vanity yielded to their insistence.

Seeing Pompey's advance, Caesar deferred his march to test the intention of the enemy and drew up over against them. It was the 29th of June, 48 B. C.

COIN WITH CIVIC CROWN

CHAPTER 35

Pharsalus

June 29, 48 B. C.

The Pompeians felt confident of victory. They were two to one, and had won the last fight. Pompey believed that by throwing his cavalry upon Caesar's flank, he could rout his legions before they were able to close for battle. Pompey's right rested on the Enipeus, Caesar's left; the cavalry was on the outer flanks. Each army had three lines, but Caesar made a fourth line, perhaps a sort of a column of chosen troops, and posted it back of his right to hold head against Pompey's cavalry. Pompey allowed Caesar to attack. The legions soon closed in fierce struggle. Meanwhile Pompey's cavalry rode round Caesar's right, defeated his small body of horse, and, confident of victory, pushed in on the flank of the legions. But they were unexpectedly met by Caesar's fourth line and checked; and, lacking cohesion, dispersed. The legions were alone left. Caesar ordered in his third line. Its charge was stout, and the Pompeians gave way. Pompey fled. Following up his victory, Caesar captured or dispersed the entire force. Pompey made his way first to Asia Minor, thence to Egypt, where he was assassinated. Caesar followed him.

Pompey had vauntingly declared to his men that he would make Caesar's legions fly before their infantry came to action, and was unwise enough to explain to them how he proposed to do it. His plan was to place his heavy body of cavalry in one column on his own left wing and have it sally out and envelop Caesar's right and rear, and charge in on the uncovered side,—of which all Romans had a dread,—before Caesar's legions could reach his line of foot. It was his cavalry in which he particularly gloried. Nor did this seem an idle boast, for his horse was seven to one of Caesar's and much of it was supposed to be and was indeed of high quality. Had he been an Alexander, and had he handled the cavalry himself as the Macedonian did at the Hydaspes, his theory would have been carried out in practice. Labienus, too, addressed the soldiers and told them that not only had the fight at Dyrrachium robbed Caesar of all his best men, but that none of his old *legionaries* had come back with him from Gaul. Pompey and he and all the officers took an oath to return from the battle victorious or to perish. The Pompeians were in the highest elation and confidence.

Caesar carefully reconnoitred Pompey's position. Pompey, instead of remaining on his inexpugnable heights, had descended to the plain and left his camp over a mile in his rear. Caesar saw that Pompey's right wing leaned on the river where were steep banks which, with a force of six hundred cavalry from Pontus, abundantly, protected it. This wing under Lentulus was composed of the Cilician and Spanish *cohorts*; these latter Afranius had brought from those discharged at the River Varus. Pompey considered these his steadiest troops. His left wing, under Domitius Ahenobarbus, contained the two legions sent him in the previous year by Caesar, numbered the First and Third, and was accompanied by Pompey in person. The left flank was near the rising ground. Scipio held the centre with the two Syrian legions. Seven *cohorts* guarded the camp, which, as stated, was flanked by some redoubts. Many auxiliary and volunteer *cohorts*, including two thousand *veterani*, were interspersed in the line. Pompey's cavalry, under Labienus, and his archers and slingers, were on the left wing, which was in the air, for the hills were too easy to be any particular protection. The entire force comprised one hundred and ten complete *cohorts* of heavy troops numbering, according to Caesar, forty-five thousand men in line, and stood in the usual three lines and ten-deep formation. The cavalry, light troops and auxiliaries swelled this number by one half. "*Hercules Invictus*" was the password.

Caesar, as was his wont, drew up his legions in three lines of *cohorts*, four in the first line, three in the second and third lines. The men may have stood eight deep. At all events, Caesar must have deployed his *cohorts* so as to extend his front to equal that of Pompey. Had he not done so, the *Commentaries* would have stated the fact, as it would have had a marked effect on the tactics of the battle. It is to be regretted that we do not know how Caesar covered so much front, Pompey so little, for the force each had in line. Caesar placed the Tenth legion, despite its heavy losses, on the right, and the Ninth legion on the left. The depletion of the latter had been so severe that he placed the Eighth close by to support it and make up, as it

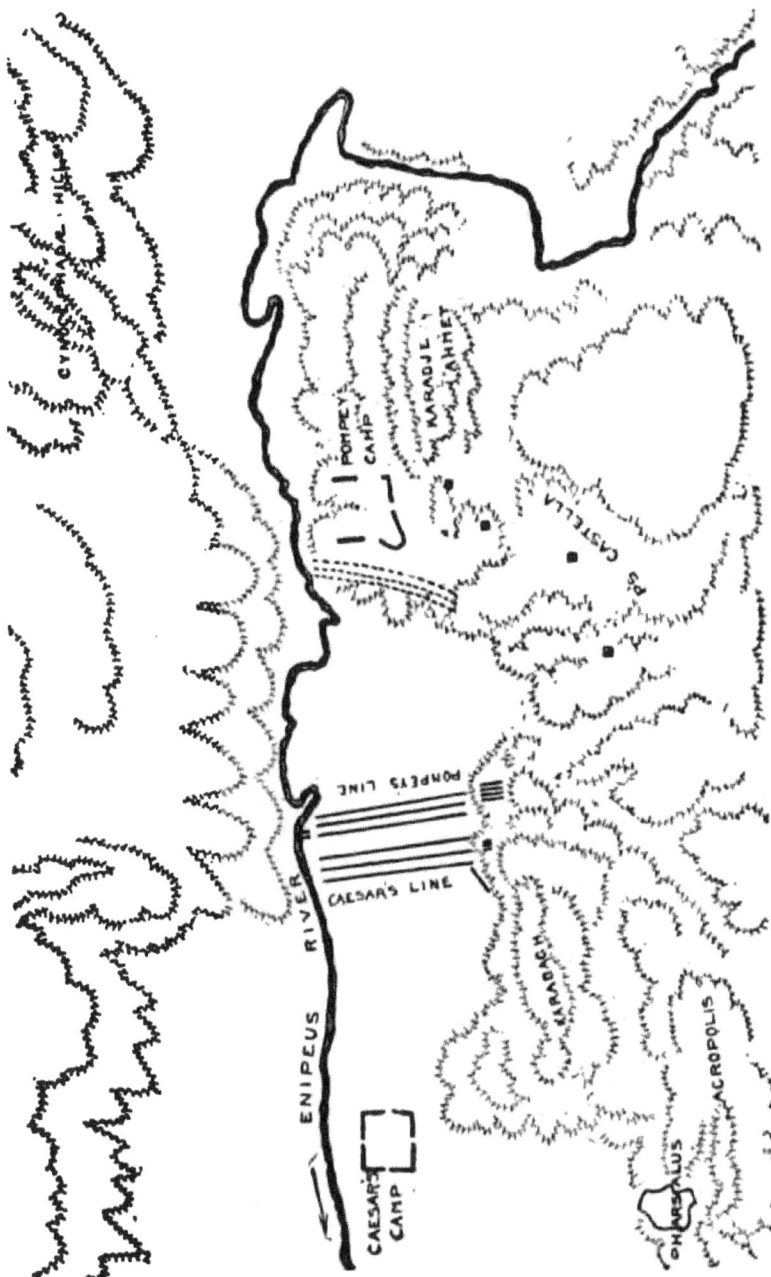

BATTLE OF PHARSALUS

were, one legion. Two *cohorts*—or as some think two thousand men, say six or seven *cohorts*—guarded the camp. Antony commanded the left; Sylla the right; Domitius the centre. Caesar himself took post opposite Pompey, with the Tenth. He had eighty-two *cohorts*, including those in camp. Those in line numbered twenty-two thousand men, as he states in the *Commentaries*. With his cavalry, light troops and a few auxiliaries, he may have had thirty thousand men facing the enemy. The two lines stood within some three hundred paces of each other. Caesar was outnumbered two to one. His situation and purpose recalls vividly to mind the iron will of Frederick who so constantly faced these and yet greater odds, and by unmatched determination wrested victory from the very jaws of disaster.

Caesar foresaw that the main danger would come to his right flank from Pompey's cavalry force, for his left leaned on the steep river banks and was safe from such attack. Pompey at all events should not take him unawares. Recognizing the danger, he quickly made up a fourth line by drawing a choice *cohort* from the third line of each legion except the Eighth and Ninth, and placed this fourth line of six *cohorts* in support of his small body of horse on his right,—"opposed them to Pompey's cavalry, and acquainted them with his wishes." He gave this *corps d'élite* to understand that on their steadiness, courage and rapid action would depend the result of the day. He also distinctly required of his main lines that they should not charge until ordered; and especially so the third line, which he proposed to hold strictly in reserve, lest he should have need of it to repair an unexpected disaster. He then, as was usual, addressed his army, exhorting them to display their ancient courage; which had won on so many hotly contested fields, and called on them to witness that it was not he who spilled Roman blood, but Pompey, who persistently refused his overtures of peace. We have no record of his words, but the enthusiasm of the legionaries was marked. It was well typified by one Crastinus, a volunteer who had been *primipilus* of the Tenth, who, stepping from the ranks, voiced the ardent spirit of the rest: "I will so act, Caesar, that thou shalt be grateful to me, living or dead,"—which promise he redeemed with his life. The trumpet signal for battle was then sounded. The battle-cry was "*Venus Victrix*."

There was space enough between the armies for each to advance part way upon the other, as was the usual manner in ancient battles. But Pompey had ordered his legions to await Caesar's onset and to strike when the enemy should reach them tired with the rapid charge

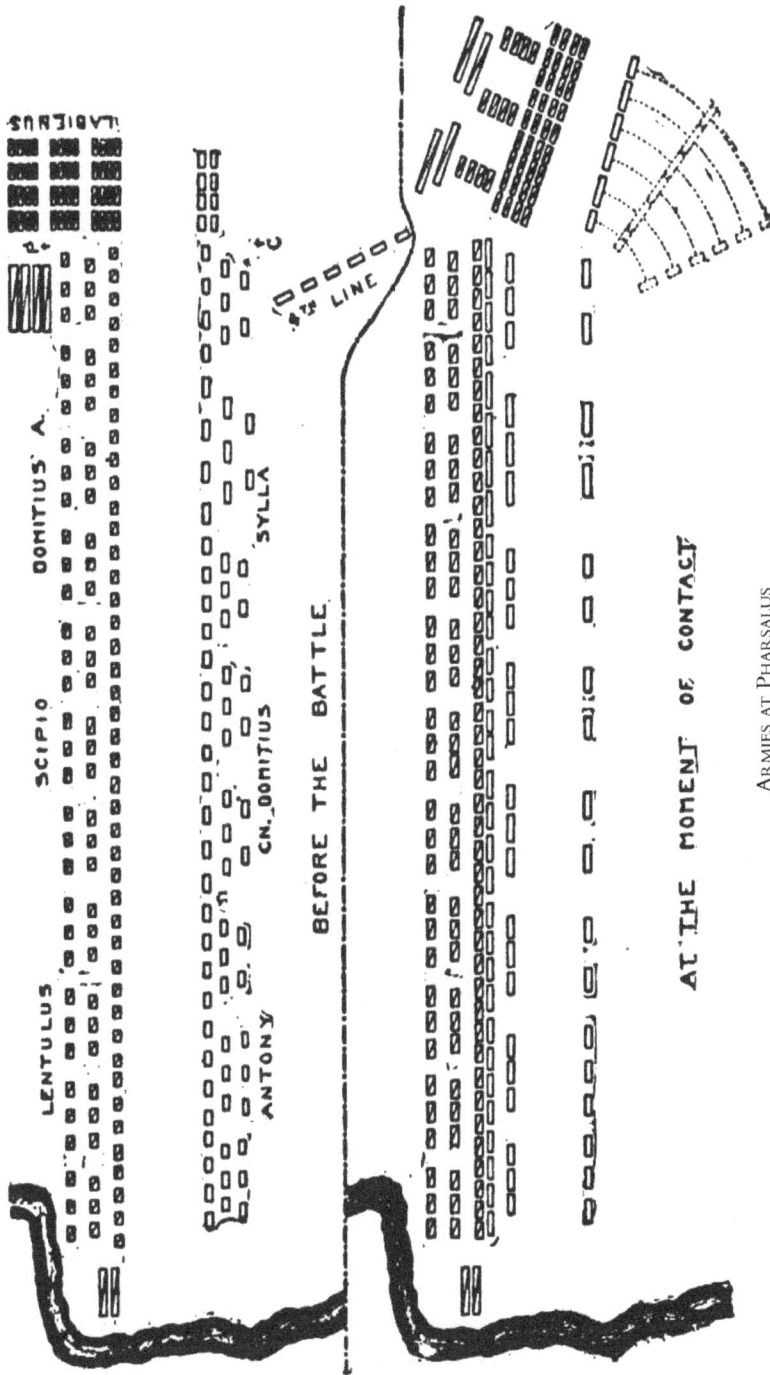

LABIENUS

DOMITIUS A.

SCIPIO

LENTULUS

4th LINE

SYLLA

CN. DOMITIUS

ANTONY

BEFORE THE BATTLE

AT THE MOMENT OF CONTACT

ARMIES AT PHARSALUS

and with ranks presumably disordered. Pompey thought "that the jave-lins would fall with less force if the soldiers were kept on their ground, than if they met them in their course; at the same time he trusted that Caesar's soldiers, after running over double the usual ground, would become weary and exhausted by the fatigue." But Caesar knew well the value, moral and physical, of impetus.

"There is a certain impetuosity of spirit and an alacrity implanted by nature in the hearts of all men, which is inflamed by a desire to meet the foe. This a general should endeavour not to repress, but to increase; nor was it a vain institution of our ancestors, that the trum-pets should sound on all sides, and a general shout be raised, by which they imagined that the enemy were struck with terror, and their own army inspired with courage."

Every great general has understood this. Caesar knew that his men could endure the fatigue and that they would be the more inspired by Pompey's line awaiting their attack, as if from fear.

The Caesarians rushed forth with great bravery. It was Crastinus, with one hundred and twenty chosen volunteers on the right, who charged first. This was the place of honour, given to such men as, hav-ing discharged to the state all their military obligations, still preferred the career of arms. The Caesarians, perceiving that Pompey's men did not advance of their own accord, and with the experience bred of many battles, paused as with one consent midway, lest they should reach the enemy out of breath. "After a short respite" they again ad-vanced. When within distance they paused to let the front rank men cast their javelins, "instantly drew their swords, as Caesar had ordered them," again sent their battle-cry resounding to the clouds and rushed upon their foemen with the cold steel. Pompey's legions received them manfully and with unbroken ranks, hurling their *pila* and quick-ly drawing swords. The battle was engaged with stanchness on either side. The two lines mixed in one, each intent on breaking down the other's guard, and swayed to and fro in the deadly struggle, neither able to wrest from the other an advantage which foretold success.

At the instant of the crash of meeting legions, the cavalry-was launched from Pompey's left upon Caesar's small body of horse, fol-lowed by his whole host of archers and slingers. The effect of the impact was never doubtful. Weight was superior to courage. Caesar's cavalry was borne back, slowly but surely. It fought well, remembering the many fields on which it had held its own; but it soon began to lose formation, to melt into a disorganized mass, and finally broke up. The enemy, believing success within their grasp, commenced to file off in small troops to get into the rear of the army. The moment was critical. Was it a battle lost or won?

The foresight of Caesar now proved his salvation. His fourth line of six *cohorts*, hitherto held behind the other three, came into play. We must presume them to have been either deployed, or so disposed that they could readily deploy, to face the probable direction of the charge of Pompey's horse. And *cohorts* such as they were had no dread of mounted men, in whatever number. Rushing forward at Caesar's command when the Pompeian cavalry approached, this splendid body of men, who knew not fear nor ever doubted victory, charged with desperate purpose upon the front of the Pompeian cavalry, which, unsuspecting and in loose order, were wheeling in on the flank of the Tenth as if they believed the battle won. The Pompeian horse, startled at the unexpected sight of this firm array, at once drew rein. They were made up of many bodies from countries scarce knowing each other's names; and however effective as separate columns, they were bound together by no common purpose. Their speed once checked, their momentum was gone. There was no one again to launch them on the foe. Each squadron looked at the bold front of Caesar's advancing men, paused, balanced. Who hesitates is lost. Caesar's bold *cohorts* kept on until they reached the line of horse, and then, instead of hurling their *pila*, they closed with the enemy and, using them as spears, struck at the horses' breasts and the men's legs and faces. Not a man of all the seven thousand stood. Discountenanced, the squadrons, losing their heads, turned and fled towards the hills. Pompey's right arm was para-lyzed. What a contrast to the cavalry at the Hydaspes, which, under Alexander's tremendous impulse, charged, and charged, and charged, and yet again charged home, until they pounded the flank of Porus' huge army to a jelly!

The cavalry disposed of, the six *cohorts* immediately advanced upon the slingers and archers, who, deprived of their mainstay, could offer no resistance, fell savagely on them and cut them to pieces where they stood. Then once more wheeling about upon the Pompeians' left wing, while the main lines were still locked in their bloody struggle, this gallant body furiously attacked the enemy's foot on the left and rear. The tables were turned.

Caesar's plans had been welcomed by the smile of Fortune. The Pompeians, astonished beyond measure at the defeat of the horse, were visibly wavering under the blows of the flank attack. The second lines had already advanced into the fighting front. The moment had arrived for the home-thrust. Caesar, who had until this moment directed his *corps d'élite*, now galloped over to his reserve third line and ordered it into action. Advancing with steady stride and perfect front upon the enemy, while the first and second lines fell back through the intervals and sustained them from the rear, these fresh and undaunted veterans deployed into battle order, and with one charge, delivered only as veterans can do it, broke through the Pompeian line as if it were but lacework, and tore it into shreds. It has been said that Caesar's orders to his third line were to cut at the faces of the Pompeians, many of whom were young Roman fashionables, who dreaded a visible scar worse than a deadly wound. This lacks the semblance of truth; but true or false, no further resistance was attempted. Every man fled towards the camp. Nor was this all. When Pompey "saw his cavalry routed and that part of the army on which he reposed his greatest hopes thrown into confusion, despairing of the rest, he quitted the field and retreated straightway on horse-back to his camp," ordered the gates closed and retired to his tent in apathy and despair.

The battle was won. Pompey was not only beaten but incapable of further action. But the camp must still be taken. Exhorting his men not to pause midway, Caesar led them to attack its entrenchments. Though wearied by the heat, for they had fought from morn to mid-day, the *legionaries* obeyed with their wonted cheerfulness. The *cohorts* left in Pompey's camp fought well, but the best defence was made by the Thracians and auxiliaries, for the Pompeians who had taken refuge in it had mostly thrown away their weapons and standards, intent on further flight. The camp was captured, the foe fleeing to the hills beyond Karadja Ahmet.

The camp was full of the evidences of security and luxury. Tables loaded with plate and viands, tents covered with ivy and floored with fresh sods, testified to their false estimate of Caesar's men, "distressed and suffering troops, who had always been in want of common necessaries." Pompey, so soon as the Caesarians had forced the trenches, throwing aside his dress of general, mounted and fled to Larissa and thence to the coast, which he reached with but thirty horse, and embarked. He felt that his men had betrayed him.

Caesar once again urged his legions not to pause for plunder, but to make an end of the whole war by capturing those who had fled to the mountain. In the persistency of his pursuit upon this field he resembles Alexander. Pursuit was not as a rule his strong point. The

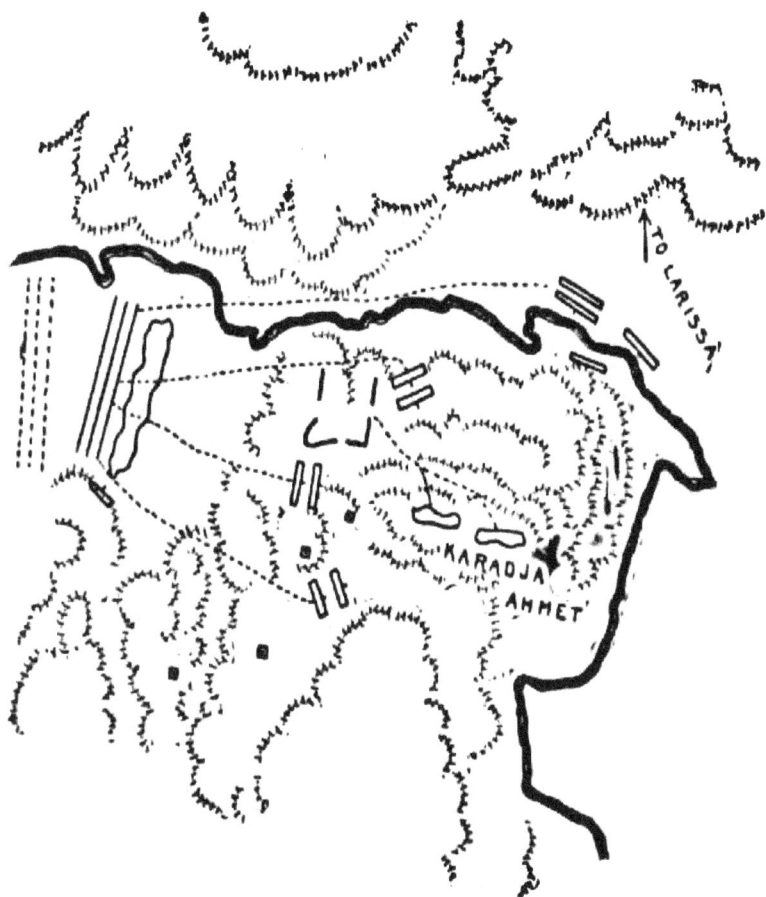

AFTER THE BATTLE OF PHARSALUS

men were most amenable to discipline. They left Pompey's camp un-
plundered and followed Caesar, who set about drawing a line of works
at the foot of the hill where the runaways had taken refuge. Foreseeing their danger, as Caesar's men threatened to surround them and
were advancing on three sides, there being no water on the hills, the
Pompeians sought to retreat by a circuit to the river where it makes a
bend. Here they hoped to cross and get on the road to Larissa, in which
place they might undertake renewed defence under another leader, or
failing this, might better plead for terms. But Caesar, leaving a force
in Pompey's camp and another in his own, took four legions, made a
smart march up the river along the plain, and at a distance of six miles
from his camp cut the fugitives off also from this retreat. The mass took
refuge on still another part of the same hill. Though Caesar's men were

greatly exhausted, having fought and marched all day, he encouraged them to draw a work between the river and hill at the only available approach, to prevent the enemy from getting water during the night. This brought the Pompeians to immediate terms. They sent to treat for surrender. A few leading men of senatorial rank escaped.

Next morning all were ordered down from the hill and bid to pile their arms. Expecting retribution, they found clemency. Caesar pardoned all, and forbade the soldiers to harm a man or take from them anything they had. Then, sending his weary troops to camp, and taking fresher ones, he pushed forward to Larissa.

In this noted battle Caesar lost but thirty centurions and two hundred men killed,—a noteworthy proportion of officers,—while of Pompey's army there fell fifteen thousand men; twenty-four thousand prisoners were made; one hundred and eighty standards and nine eagles were taken. Domitius Ahenobarbus was killed while fleeing. The prisoners were sent to Asia and organized into new legions by Domitius Calvinus.

This splendid victory was won by Caesar's admirable dispositions, the lack of vigour of Pompey's soldiers, and the want of steadfastness of Pompey's cavalry. Had this body done its duty the victory would have been more dearly purchased. Caesar's quick detection of the weak point of his line; his disposal of the six chosen *cohorts* to resist the cavalry; and upon their overthrowing this body, his hurling them on Pompey's left flank, was a superb exhibition of grand tactics. It was entirely unexpected by Pompey, who believed his left flank to be his winning one, and upset all his calculations. It shows how a small body of determined men, well handled and thrown upon the foe at the critical instant, can change the tide of battle.

During this time at sea, Brundisium had been blockaded by Decimus Laelius, one of Pompey's admirals; and another of them, Cassius, had captured the harbour of Messana in Sicily, had destroyed by fire Pomponius' fleet and had later captured Vibo in Italy and in like manner damaged the fleet of Sulpicius. All these places would have fallen to the Pompeians but for the news of the victory of Caesar at Pharsalus, upon receiving which Laelius and Cassius speedily decamped with their respective fleets.

Calenus, meanwhile, reduced much of Phocis and Boeotia; and after Pharsalus, Calenus and Cornuficius remained to complete the conquest of Greece and Illyria.

From Larissa Caesar pursued Pompey with his cavalry to Amphip-

olis. Here he saw that Pompey had escaped him. The Sixth legion
having come up, he kept on along the shore of Thrace; reached the
Hellespont July 24; stopped to collect means of crossing; and finally
put over in frail *barks*,—a most foolhardy operation. On the passage
hazard threw in his way one of Pompey's minor fleets of ten galleys
under L. Cassius. By good rights Caesar should have succumbed; but
the news of Pharsalus so utterly stupefied the Pompeian that Caesar,
with his matchless audacity, took the whole squadron prisoners. This
windfall facilitated his progress to a degree.

Pompey had fled to points in the Ægean and Asia Minor, hoping in
each place to rim across friends and help. He dreaded to encounter Cato
and his other lieutenants, after his disgraceful flight from Pharsalus. Caesar felt that he must pursue him whithersoever he might fly, and finish
the war without allowing him the opportunity to collect a fresh army.
He marched on his track as fast as he was able, but was hampered by
being tied down to an infantry column. He left Mark Antony behind to
command the army, with orders to cross to Italy so soon as the enemy's
fleet would permit it, and hold the peninsula. Caesar took with him
only the Sixth legion, and ordered Calenus to send him while *en route*
another legion of young troops. He had a few hundred horse.

In his flight Pompey stayed one day, July 2, at Amphipolis, where he
issued a proclamation calling all men to arms; and collecting moneys
from the tax-farmers there, set sail for Mitylene, and thence to Pam-
phylia, Cilicia and Cyprus. Antioch having refused to receive him, he
gave up a half-conceived design of going to Syria and thence to the
Parthians; but collecting in Cyprus more money, and brass for military
use, and raising two thousand troops, he sailed to Pelusium in Egypt,
which he reached toward the end of September. Here he found the
ten-year old Ptolemy, son of Ptolemy Auletes, engaged in war with his
sister Cleopatra, who was seventeen, for the sole possession of the Egyptian throne. Cleopatra had taken refuge in Syria, and Ptolemy was at
Pelusium holding the approaches to Egypt against her. Their respective
armies now lay near the desert. To Ptolemy, Pompey applied for a refuge
in Alexandria. Ptolemy received his application with openly expressed
kindness, but fearing to associate with misfortune, he, or rather his tutor,
the eunuch Photinus, caused Pompey to be put to death by Achillas,
captain of the king's guard. L. Lentulus was likewise assassinated.

Thus miserably died in his fifty-ninth year, Pompey, surnamed
the Great when but twenty-six years old. He had been the popular
hero of the Romans. He had conducted seventeen successful cam-

paigns. He had thrice entered Rome in triumph. He had thrice been consul. With Caesar he could have divided the world. To what a pass had he come, indeed! Mommsen says:

"A good officer, but otherwise of mediocre gifts of intellect and heart, fate had with super-human constancy for thirty years allowed him to solve all brilliant and toilless tasks; had permitted him to pluck all laurels planted and fostered by others; had presented to him all the conditions requisite for obtaining the supreme power,—only in order to exhibit in his person an example of spurious greatness to which history knows no parallel."

This contest for sovereignty between Caesar and Pompey shows marked characteristics of the men themselves. Whether right or wrong, Caesar made great efforts to keep the appearance of right on his side, and succeeded in so doing. In this sense were made his reiterated appeals to Pompey for a personal interview. He may, soon after the refusal of the first one, have seen that his appeals would be fruitless, but he nevertheless persevered, and no doubt his persistency, coupled to success, gave him the shadow of right in the eyes of many who had previously opposed him. For the same purpose of persuading people to his cause Caesar was generous towards all Roman citizens who came under his control, as prisoners or otherwise, even when they had been active foes. Caesar was not less inhuman than other Romans, but he was wont to be politic in his actions, and he knew when and how to be generous.

In warlike qualities the two generals are distinctly contrasted. Caesar's broad and solid views, foresight and power of reasoning out his course of action, were as marked as his persistency, his wisdom and his strength. During much of his Gallic campaign he had foreseen and been preparing for this final struggle between Pompey and himself. And he had not reckoned in vain on the splendid legions he had created, nor on Gaul, which had afforded him his base for operations in Italy. Even Caesar's foolhardy exploits never carried him out of the generally wise scope of his original plan. Pompey, on the contrary, while anticipating the coming struggle with equal certainty, had done absolutely nothing to enable him to cope with Caesar. He had apparently not comprehended that he must undertake to hold Italy or forfeit the first and most important innings of the game. He had made preparations elsewhere for resistance, while he had failed to do so at the centre of the empire. He did not make use of his resources when collected. Instead of facing Caesar and forcing him to pay dearly for success, he allowed him to snatch Spain from his lieutenants with apparently no effort to check him. One can scarcely imagine conduct more impotent than this. One can scarcely recognize the Pompey who conducted the war against the pirates.

Caesar's directness of purpose in contrast to this is wonderful. In sixty days from crossing the Rubicon, he had conquered Italy. Then, shielding himself by a curtain of forces on the Adriatic, he turned to Spain in order to protect his rear and base from Pompey's legions in the peninsula. In six weeks more after reaching Iberia, this gigantic labour was also accomplished, and his course against Pompey was made clear. Then followed a period during which his hands were tied by Pompey's control of the sea. It was many months before he could cross both his detachments to Epirus, join them and stand face to face with his foe in command of such a force as would warrant him in fighting.

Caesar knew his enemy. Though he was justified in relying on his inertia, he was unquestionably rash in moving with half his force, as he did, across the sea and running the chance of being beaten in detail. For if Pompey had but put forth his strength in a creditable manner, he could have crushed Caesar and all his hopes. The position of Caesar at Dyrrachium was a false one, brought on by conduct rash rather than judicious; and though its outcome was the victory of Pharsalus, it must be distinctly condemned as unsound military policy. This can scarcely be called the art of a great general, whose province is to play a bold but not rash part. Nor did Caesar accomplish any substantial good by his haste in seeking Pompey in Epirus. The same time spent in Italy would have enabled him to prepare means of shipping his entire force at once to Greece, and thus have saved the grave risk he ran. Or better still, in much less time, he could have marched through Illyricum. The legions he needed all came from Spain and Gaul; they concentrated in the Padane country; it was not much farther from there to Epirus than to Brundisium. He would, indeed, have saved time if from this latter place he had made the overland march through Illyricum. This was his true road, for Illyricum was committed to his interests while Pompey held the Adriatic. There was no real danger of Pompey's crossing to Italy when he knew Caesar was advancing to meet him in Greece. It was not his way. Good fortune alone saved Caesar from the disaster which all but followed on his rashness in crossing to Greece by sea.

Caesar's boldness in endeavouring, with his small force, to blockade Pompey near Dyrrachium, while it compels our admiration for its unwonted audacity, was none the less a reckless undertaking which of necessity sooner or later must and actually did come to grief. It entailed the loss of a large part of the flower of his army, not to mention the demoralization which it took no less than Caesar's fluent tongue and able discipline to overcome. To undertake such an operation shows rather an excess of animal than a well-balanced moral courage,—or else an inexpertness in gauging his task which we know Caesar was not subject to. In this operation, Caesar was conducting war more on the physical than on the intellectual plan. It was not a case of necessity, which always excuses a desperate act, for he afterwards successfully tried another and better scheme, that of luring Pompey into the open country. His allowing his valour to override his discretion met with its proper check. Nothing but his luck saved him from fatal disaster. It was well that he was released from his false situation by a defeat which was not a final one.

An interesting circumstance in the campaigns of Caesar, which cannot but impress itself on every American soldier, is the handiness exhibited by Caesar's *legionaries* in the use of pick and shovel. Every Roman soldier knew how to use a spade. But Caesar's men were even more expert. These entrenching tools, quite apart from the daily camping-work, seemed to be as important to the legions as their weapons or their shields. They dug their way to victory on more than one occasion.

The best illustration of Caesar's character in the campaign against Pompey is his determination to fight at Pharsalus. Not every general is called upon or is ready to fight a decisive battle, which must make or mar his cause, against an army of twice his strength. In this determination one must recognize character sustained by intelligence of the first order. Caesar had taken post at Metropolis, expecting to manoeuvre with Pompey until he could place him at a disadvantage. Pompey, however, moved on him, and Caesar without hesitation determined to take the initiative. This he boldly did; his men backed his courage by their gallantry, and leader and legions won. Pompey, on the contrary, while his plan of battle was good, showed in its execution that there was no stamina in his men, no such *esprit de corps* as emanates from contact with the great commander. His cavalry lacked the first elements of stanchness or discipline. It had no unity of action in the absence of a proper commander; and this was Pompey's fault. Orientals could not have behaved worse. And there appears to have been no mutual confidence which might be called on to resist disaster on the field. So soon as the first contrary incident occurred, there was neither head nor heart to stem the tide of defeat. Pompey beaten showed himself incapable of further exertion, mental or moral; his adherents decamped like a terror-stricken herd. Caesar's loss in killed measures the fighting of the Pompeian army, and this measures the loss of *morale* of the great general.

In eighteen months from taking up arms Caesar had made himself master of the world by defeating the only man who claimed to dispute this title with him. The Battle of Pharsalus was fought just seven months from the landing in Epirus.

It must be said in Caesar's honour that few conquerors of the ancient world made use of clemency after victory as did he. He knew its value, no doubt, but we must believe that with victory disappeared all feelings of animosity. This side of his character stands in curious contrast to that which urged him unnecessarily and by treachery to slay four hundred and thirty thousand defenceless Germans in one day.

The most marked result of the victory of Pharsalus was the transfer of allegiance by the provinces from the vanquished to the victor. These all recalled their military and naval contingents and refused to receive the refugees. Juba was the only man of consequence who stood to his guns. Most of the leading men escaped from Pharsalus and made their way to Cato at Corcyra,—part of them by sea, part over the mountains. Here was held a conference at which Scipio, Labienus, Afranius, Cnaeus Pompey and others were present. Greece manifestly was lost. Pompey's whereabouts were unknown; large parts of the fleet had been recalled by their respective provinces. On the other hand, Spain was largely favourable to Pompey. In Africa Juba was a strong centre-point; the Pompeian fleet was still larger than Caesar's. There was no chance in surrender,—there was one chance left in a partisan war. But the Pompeians no longer existed. It was the aristocrats who continued the war.

ANCIENT HELMET

161

CHAPTER 36

Alexandria

August, 48, to March, 47 B. C.

Caesar now committed another of those foolhardy acts of which his career is full. He followed Pompey to Alexandria with but four thousand men, and attempted to dictate the succession to the throne of Ptolemy, about which Cleopatra and her brother were disputing. He was resisted by an Egyptian army of five times his force, and found himself beleaguered in Alexandria. He had great difficulty in holding himself. He sent for reinforcements, and managed to keep the eastern harbour and the Pharos tower. He burned the Egyptian fleet, and utilized his own fleet to great advantage. In a naval battle he defeated the Egyptians. These then essayed to cut off his water supply by pumping sea-water into the canals which supplied him; but Caesar saved himself by digging wells. One legion soon reached him, and some vessels from Rhodes. In a second naval battle he was again successful; and he then captured the entire island of Pharos. But in a fight on the mole between the island and city Caesar was defeated, as also in a third naval battle. Finally, Mithridates of Pergamos, with an army of relief, came to the Nile; Caesar marched up the Delta, joined him, and, in a battle of considerable difficulty, decisively defeated the Egyptians, and recovered all the ground he had so nearly lost. But he had wasted the better part of a year by his carelessness in moving to Alexandria with so insufficient a force.

Caesar, in pursuit of Pompey, whom he thought to find in Ephesus, had crossed to Asia Minor. Here he heard that Pompey had been in Cyprus, and divined that he had gone to Egypt. He had with him the Sixth legion, and the one Calenus had been ordered to send him joined him August 8, at Rhodes. With these and eight hundred horse, he set out for Alexandria. He had ten ships of war from

Rhodes and a few from Asia. The foot amounted to about thirty-two hundred men; the rest of the *legionaries*, "disabled by wounds received in various battles, by fatigue and the length of their march, could not follow him." With the eight hundred horse he boasted a bare four thousand men.

"Relying on the fame of his exploits, he did not hesitate to set out with a feeble force, and thought he would be secure in any place."

Reaching Alexandria about August 20, he was informed of the death of Pompey. This was less than two months after the battle of Pharsalus. He anchored in the great or eastern harbour, and took possession of the royal palace, which was half a fortress, situated near Cape Lochias, to the east of the artificial mole which divided the old and new harbours, and likewise of the arsenal, which was close by. Caesar had supposed that to the conqueror of Pompey many troops would be unnecessary, but he was speedily and rudely undeceived. The *tumult* of the populace caused by the troubles raging in the land made even Caesar unsafe. His entry into the place, preceded by the consular fasces, had in fact almost bred a riot, as the populace deemed such a display an infraction of their king's prerogative. Caesar was called on to send immediately to Asia Minor for more legions, which he ordered collected by Domitius from some of the disbanded levies of Pompey.

Meanwhile Caesar found himself in a most embarrassing situation. The troops he had sent for might be a long time reaching him. He himself had been detained by the periodical winds. But he was not the man to look back when his hand had been put to the plough. With the scanty means at his disposal, he determined to hold his ground. He could have at once retired before allowing a quarrel to breed. But Caesar always settled all civil questions which came under his hand, *pari passu* with the military. He had undertaken to dictate a settlement of the troubles between young Ptolemy and Cleopatra. The late king had left his kingdom jointly to Ptolemy and Cleopatra, as king and queen, and had made the Roman people executors of his will. On this ground Caesar, as consul representing the Roman people, deemed that he had the right to order these princely claimants to plead their cause before him and to disband their armies until he decided between them. Alexandria was a large, independent, turbulent city, full of able men. The population at once took alarm. It is possible that Caesar might not have been able to get away had he been so inclined; he had run some personal danger

ALEXANDRIA

from the populace in landing; and the Alexandrians had a large fleet, while he had next to none. Other motives than the Ptolemy-Cleopatra quarrel, or than the desire to gain his point, may have been the prevailing ones.

Cleopatra shortly arrived from Syria, and Caesar's mandate was at first accepted; but Ptolemy and the eunuch Pothinus, his tutor and regent during his minority, soon adopted a less peaceful policy, secretly appointed Achillas, the captain of the guards and intimate friend of the king, commander of the army at Pelusium, and ordered it to advance on Alexandria. While the succession was being pleaded before Caesar, news came that the king's army and all the cavalry were marching on the city.

Achillas had a motley force of eighteen to twenty thousand foot and two thousand horse, largely made up of freebooters, slaves and runaways, but among these were many of Pompey's disbanded legionaries. The Roman army of occupation had been largely Pompeian, and easily sided against Caesar.

"Caesar's forces were by no means so strong that he could trust to them if he had occasion to hazard a battle outside the city. His only resource was to keep within the town in the most convenient places."

So soon as Caesar learned of the approach of Achillas he caused the king to send envoys to him. On these being assassinated by Achillas without even a hearing, Caesar saw through the plot and seized on the persons of both Ptolemy and Pothinus, who had not left Alexandria, and held them as hostages, "both supposing that the king's name would have great influence with his subjects and to give the war the appearance of a scheme of a few desperate men, rather than of having been begun by the king's command." Pothinus was later executed by Caesar.

Achillas had five times Caesar's force, but the material of his army was poor. The old legionaries even, by long residence in Egypt, and many intermarriages with the native women, had lost all ideas of Roman discipline. Still Achillas was able to take possession of the larger part of the city of Alexandria, all except that small section which Caesar had occupied on his arrival, and which was as much as his handful of men could defend. The part he occupied Caesar at once put in a state of defence. He saw that his situation was questionable. However illy disciplined the Egyptian army, it was formidable in more than one way, and it was backed up by public sentiment.

Achillas' first effort was to force the palace, but he was unable to do so. Caesar had occupied and barricaded all the streets leading to it.

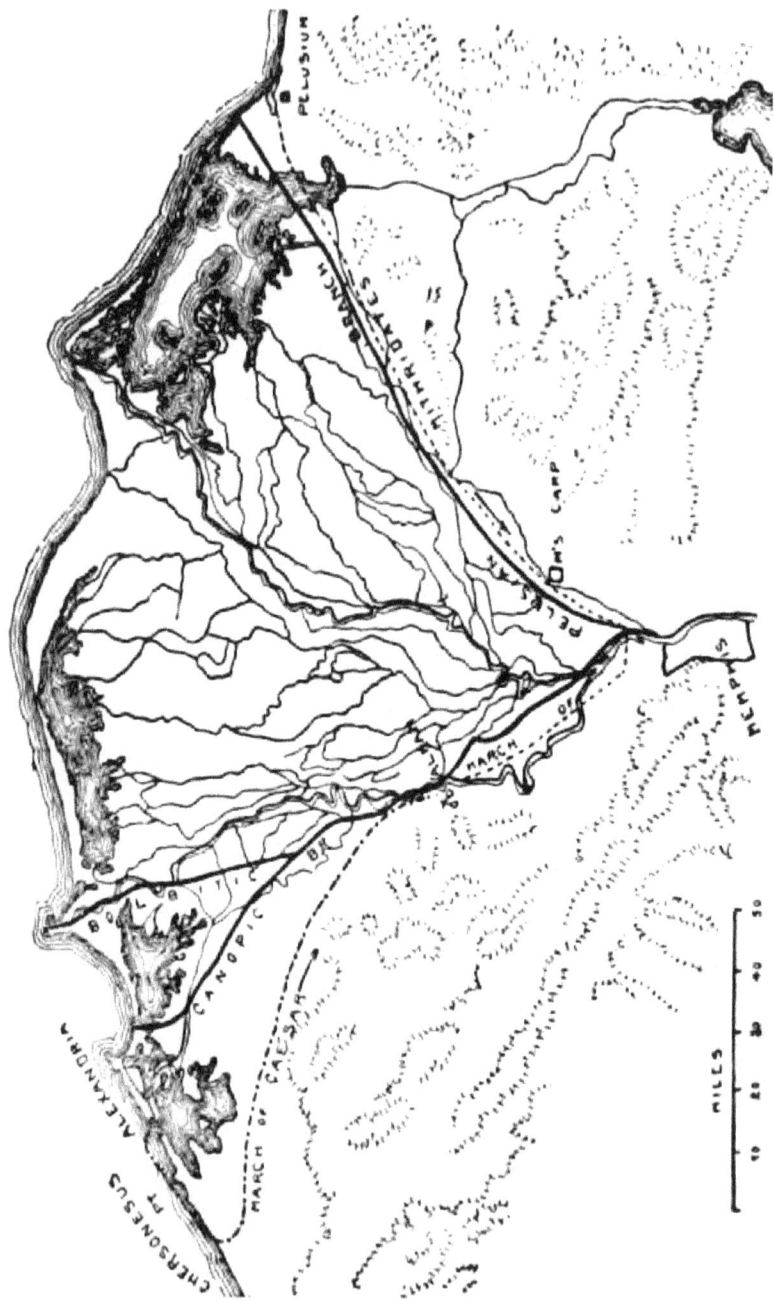

EGYPT

ALEXANDRIA

CHERSONESUS PT

MARCH OF CAESAR

BOLBITIC BR.

CANOPIC BR.

MARCH OF

PELUSIAC BRANCH

SEBENNYTIC BRANCH

PELUSIUM

B

IS

OM's CAMP

MEMPHIS

MILES
10   20   30   40   50

At the same time there was a desultory and obstinate combat at the port side of the town, fought in many streets at once and along the wharves, and difficult to manage. Achillas attempted to get possession of the Alexandrian war-galleys in the harbour, of which there were seventy-two, including many *triremes* and *quinquiremes*, but was foiled in his efforts. For fear they should fall into the enemy's hands, as he could not well guard the vessels, Caesar put the torch to the entire fleet. It was in the conflagration thus begun that the Alexandrian library perished, together with many other public buildings and treasures. Had Achillas succeeded in getting hold of the ships, he could have closed the harbour and cut Caesar off from receiving reinforcements or victualling the palace. Caesar's act, however disastrous in its results, was a necessary method of protecting his position.

The action at this point was fraught with grave danger.

"Accordingly that spirit was displayed which ought to be shown when the one party saw that a speedy victory depended on the issue, and the other their safety."

Caesar held his own, and took early occasion to occupy the Pharos tower. At that time, the Pharos was "a tower on an island, of prodigious height," claimed by a later historian to have been four hundred ells, or nearly six hundred feet,

"Built with amazing works and taking its name from the island. This island, lying over against Alexandria, forms a harbour; but on the upper side it is connected with the town by a narrow way eight hundred paces in length, made by piles sunk in the sea, and by a bridge. In this island some of the Egyptians have houses and a village as large as a town; and whatever ships from any quarter, either through mistaking the channel or by the storm, have been driven from their course upon the coast, they constantly plunder like pirates. And without the consent of those who are masters of the Pharos, no vessels can enter the harbour, on account of its narrowness. Caesar being greatly alarmed on this account, whilst the enemy were engaged in battle, landed his soldiers, seized the Pharos, and placed a garrison in it. By this means he gained this point, that he could be supplied without danger with corn and auxiliaries; for he sent to all the neighbouring countries to demand supplies."

By holding the Pharos tower Caesar commanded the entrance to the harbour, which secured his rear.

But though Caesar had gained a footing in the harbour, he could gain nothing in the town. Here Achillas had a more than equal holding,

Caesar merely keeping what he had got, and fortifying the most neces-sary posts. Achillas, who, through the inhabitants, held all the Pharos is-land except the tower, as well as the Heptastadium, or mole, continued to push the attack on Caesar by whatever means he could devise. Cae-sar strongly fortified the theatre as a citadel, and the adjoining wing of the royal palace, so as to command the avenues to the port and docks.

Meanwhile Ptolemy's youngest daughter, Arsinoë, fled to Achillas in the camp, hoping herself to control the succession. But Achillas and she soon quarrelled, which bred dissension in the native army, much to Caesar's advantage.

Caesar saw that lie was in a perilous case, and that he must speed-ily gather more troops, or he could not rescue himself. By his utter lack of caution he had again blundered into a dilemma similar to the one he had barely escaped from at Dyrrachium. But Caesar had one singular quality,—a certain test of the great captain. He was capable of the most reprehensible recklessness. But when, from the results of such conduct, he had forfeited almost every chance of success, he always rose to the occasion with a force, an intelligence which commanded the situation. When we have all but lost patience with his heedlessness, Caesar compels our admiration by his energy, his courage, his resourc-es. He was indomitable. When another man would have considered the question of surrender, Caesar began to exert his splendid force, his absolute reliance on himself. Doubt as to eventual success never found rest in his unflinching soul.

So now. At the head of the Roman state, he had at his disposal the forces of the world; yet he was cooped up with four thousand men in one of the client-cities of Rome. But Caesar was not for a mo-ment doubtful of his ability to cope with the Egyptians. In how great soever danger he actually was, he gave no sign of it to his troops. His demeanour was at all times calm and self-poised, and no one could have read in his countenance or actions the least doubt as to the issue of the matter. He sent to Rhodes, Syria and Cilicia for all his fleet; to Crete for archers, and into Arabia Petraea, to Malchus, king of the Nabatheans for cavalry. Domitius, from whom he expected two le-gions from Asia Minor, was to send at the same time victual, material of war and military engines. Caesar called on Mithridates, king of Pergamos, to march an army by way of Syria to his aid. He himself set to work to make ballistic machines and to collect from every source corn and soldiers. In Alexandria he took means to hold himself until relief should come. He razed many houses to the ground in order to gain elbow-room, and fortified the streets leading to the arsenal and palace, or wherever his line seemed weak, with sheds and mantelets, thus inclosing the entire smaller part of the town he had occupied. The walls were perforated for rams and missiles. The town, being built of houses whose floors were all vaulted, without wood of any kind, was peculiarly adapted to creating a good scheme of defence.

The smaller part occupied by Caesar was "separated from the rest by a morass towards the south." This was a low and narrow piece of meadow land running north and south from the sea to Lake Mareotis, between the low hills on which the city is mainly situated. This lowland could be made to furnish the army both water and forage if it could be controlled. By dint of pushing forward works on either side of it from his own position southerly, Caesar gradually gained a hold on a part of this lowland. Its possession in entirety would result in his being in a central position between the two wings of the enemy.

The Alexandrians, thoroughly roused by the seizure of their young prince, were equally active in collecting troops and material of war. From every part of Egypt which they could control, they levied troops. They accumulated and manufactured vast quantities of darts and engines in their part of the town, and increased their forces by a great multitude, including peasants and slaves. The raw levies they stationed in the least dangerous parts of the inclosing line; the veteran *cohorts* in the open squares. They shut up all the avenues and passes by a triple wall of hewn stones forty feet high, and built a number of ten-storey towers in the lower part of the town. Some equally tall ones were made to move on wheels along the flat Alexandrian streets by horse-power. The people were very ingenious, and not only imitated the Romans in all they did, but devised many new things themselves. The old art of the days when Archimedes studied here was far from having died out. They had resolved to be rid, for once and all, of the Romans, who they felt were trying to reduce Egypt to a mere province, as they had so many other lands. And their chiefs led them to believe that Caesar would soon be starved into surrender, because the stormy season prevented him from getting supplies by sea. Caesar made an attempt to conciliate the Alexandrians through the mediation of the young king; but the Alexandrians believed that what Ptolemy said was at Caesar's dictation, arid would not listen to him.

Achillas was now murdered by the machinations of Arsinoë, assisted by the eunuch Ganymed, her governor, whom she raised to the command of the army. Ganymed was a man of fertile invention.

169

He determined to cut off Caesar's water-supply. A good-sized canal or branch from the Nile Delta ran into the quarter of the city held by the Alexandrians, and yielded them abundance of water, though rather thick and muddy. The supply of Caesar's part of the town was stored up in cisterns which were filled through aqueducts, likewise leading from the Nile. The water was allowed to settle and clarify in the cisterns. Caesar's narrow system of defence had cut him off from the canal and reduced him to use the cisterns alone. Ganymed went to work on a large scale. He diverted the river water from these aqueducts and reservoirs, by which he also cut off his own cistern supply, and was forced to rely on the canal water. But this was not a grievous hardship. Then, by water-wheels and other engines, he raised sea water in large quantities and poured it in a steady stream into the aqueducts leading to Caesar's cisterns. By this clever means all the cisterns in the upper town became gradually tainted and unfit for use. The water in that part of the lower town which was occupied by Caesar was not reached by the salt water, but became brackish and unhealthful.

The impending danger of a water famine came close to occasioning a panic among the troops, which Caesar had some difficulty in allaying. He could not safely retreat, for his small force, so soon as he left his defences to embark, would be at the mercy of the Alexandrians, whose multitude could easily crush the retiring Caesarians.

"Caesar laboured to remove his soldiers' fears by encouraging and reasoning with them. For, he affirmed, 'that they might easily find fresh water by digging wells, as all sea-coasts naturally abounded with fresh springs; that if Egypt was singular in this respect and differed from every other soil, yet still, as the sea was open and the enemy without a fleet, there was nothing to hinder their fetching it at pleasure in their ships, either from Paraetonium on the left, or the island, Pharos, on the right, and as their two voyages were in different directions, they could not be prevented by adverse winds at the same time; that a retreat was on no account to be thought of, not only by those who had a concern for their honour, but even by such as regarded nothing but life; that it was with the utmost difficulty they could defend themselves behind, their works; but if they once quitted that advantage, neither in number or situation would they be a match for the enemy; that to embark would require much time, and be attended with great danger, especially where it must be managed by little boats; that the Alexandrians, on the contrary, were nimble and active, and thoroughly acquainted with the streets and buildings; that, moreover, when flushed with victory, they would not fail to run before, seize all the advantageous posts, possess themselves of the tops of the houses, and, by annoying them in their retreat, effectually prevent their getting on board; that they must, therefore, think no more of retreating, but place all their hopes of safety in victory."'

The wonderful confidence of the troops in their leader put an end to fear. Caesar's promise was redeemed by setting all hands which could be spared to digging wells. These he knew would be an effective means, and in fact, during the very first night, the wells yielded plenty of fresh, good water. "The mighty projects and painful attempts of the Alexandrians were, with no great labour, entirely frustrated."

The Thirty-seventh legion, part of Pompey's forces which had surrendered to Caesar, and were sent by Domitius Calvinus with full equipment of victuals, arms and enginery, now arrived off the coast from Rhodes; but adverse east winds kept it from making the harbour. It got blown westerly from the mouth. The ships could, however, safely ride at anchor, and the commander sent a rowing galley to notify Caesar that they had arrived, but were in want of water. The winds made no great odds to the rowing galleys. The transports, which relied upon sails, were at their mercy. Caesar determined to go to the fleet to take proper measures to bring it into port. He left all the land forces at their posts, unwilling to deplete the garrison. He embarked, and set out with such galleys as he had ready, in search of his transports.

Sending some men on shore for water, as he was cruising along the coast near Point Chersonesus, some seven leagues west of Alexandria, these were captured, and the Alexandrians learned that Caesar was on board the squadron, and without legionaries. Here was too good a chance to miss. Ganymed collected all the available ships and sallied out from the Eunostos or western harbour, which the Alexandrians had always held, to attack and haply capture him. Caesar would much have preferred not to fight, as he was intent on other things. When, on his return towards Alexandria with his fleet, he encountered the enemy, he at first declined the combat, as it was towards nightfall, and the enemy knew the coast better than he did. He, moreover, felt that he could get better work out of his men by daylight, and he had no soldiers on his war-galleys. The Thirty-seventh legion was in the transports. He drew in towards the shore.

But circumstances forced him to do battle. One Rhodian galley rashly separated from the fleet, and was attacked by several of the enemy's ships. Caesar was forced to go to her relief, "that he might not suffer the disgrace of seeing one of his galleys sunk before his eyes." The Rhodians, always noted for naval pluck, here outvied each other in their gallantry. The Alexandrians could hold no head against them. The victory, largely by the good conduct of Euphranor, the Rhodian admiral, was complete. The enemy suffered grievous loss. Caesar would have destroyed the enemy's entire fleet but for the approach of night. The adverse winds having happily abated, the transports, under convoy of Caesar's galleys, reached their moorings in the Great harbour of Alexandria without mishap. Caesar had now nearly doubled his force both on land and at sea.

At first this disaster to the Alexandrians appeared irremediable. They had lost one hundred and ten vessels since Caesar came to Alexandria. They were peculiarly disheartened, because their defeat was not by soldiers but by seamen, and they prided themselves on their skill at sea. They "retired to the tops of their houses, and blocked up the entrances of their streets as if they feared the Caesarian fleet might attack them on land." But this people was naturally a maritime race, and with great zeal, under the cheering words of Ganymed, they set to creating a new navy. They saw that to blockade Caesar by sea was their only sure means of reducing him. They brought together all the old vessels which could be refitted and made seaworthy, all those used as custom-house ships in the mouths of the Nile, and from whatever source they could gather craft, and equipped them as best they might, putting into use everything which could float in the harbour. To find material for oars they unroofed the porticoes, academies and public buildings, and made use of the plank thus obtained. They expected to fight in the port, where craft useless at sea would do well enough. In a few days they had fitted out twenty-two *quadriremes*, five *quinquiremes* and a vast number of small craft. These were manned by excellent seamen and the proper complement of soldiers. Caesar had but ten *quadriremes*, five *quinquiremes* and, counting smaller ones without decks, thirty-four sail in all. Of these, nine were the Rhodian (one had been wrecked), eight from Pontus, five from Lycia, twelve from Asia.

Caesar carefully made ready for a fresh naval engagement; for he saw that the Alexandrians, unless their fleet was dispersed, might succeed in blockading him in the harbour. He represented to all his troops the necessity of conquering. In case of defeat he showed them that each and every man was unquestionably lost. After due preparation, he sailed round Pharos and drew up in line facing the enemy opposite the Eunostos harbour. The Rhodians had the right, the Pontus galleys the left. Between these wings he left a distance of about four hundred paces for manoeuvring, and marshalled the rest of his vessels in reserve, appointing to each ship in the fighting line another in the reserve for succour. The Alexandrians brought up their fleet, greatly more numerous, with abundant confidence. The twenty-two *quadriremes* were in front; the rest were in a second line. A vast number of small craft accompanied the fleet. They had prepared a supply of flaming darts and combustibles on board the small craft to set Caesar's vessels on fire.

Between the fleets lay certain shallows through which were crooked channels. They are the same today. Each side waited for the other to pass these shallows, as each deemed it to be dangerous to fight with them in their rear. The fleet of Caesar was commanded by Euphranor the Rhodian, who had been so useful in the late naval contest, and who was a man of no little ability and courage. After some hesitation, Caesar, at Euphranor's suggestion, resolved to attack, and allowed the Rhodian galleys to lead the way through the shallows. The rest of the fleet followed hard upon. When the lines came into action, there was so little space to manoeuvre that it became a question of bravery alone. This was an advantage for the Romans. The fight was witnessed

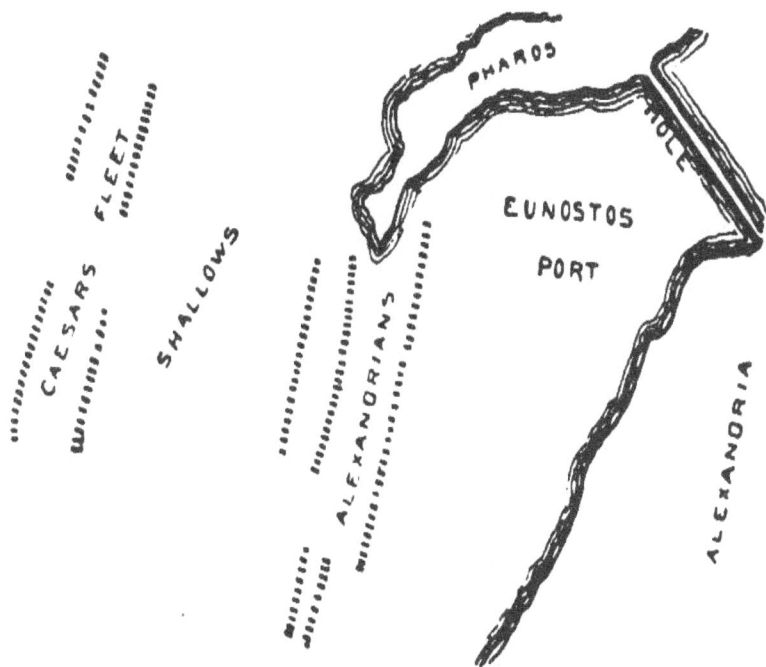

SECOND NAVAL BATTLE

from the housetops of Alexandria by Romans and Egyptians, people and soldiers alike. The Romans were really fighting for existence. If they lost this battle they would surely be shut off from the sea. This knowledge spurred them on to exceed even their accustomed valour. After a long and rather irregular battle, the Egyptians, despite their well-earned reputation for gallantry at sea, and their far greater number of ships, were signally defeated. A *quinquireme* and a *bireme* were taken with all on board, and three were sunk, without loss of a ship to the Romans. Measured by the loss, the battle does not appear to have been as severe as one is apt to infer from the wording of the *Commentaries*. The rest of the Egyptian craft were driven into their port, where they took shelter under the protection of the bowmen on the mole and ramparts.

To deprive the enemy of this resource in the future, Caesar determined to make himself master of the entire island of Pharos, and of the Heptastadium, which connected it with the mainland. He already had the Pharos tower. He had so far finished his works in the town as to think himself able to hold his position there, and the mole and island as well. He embarked in small vessels ten *cohorts*, a chosen body of light troops, and some Gallic horse especially fit for the work, and sent them against the south side of the island, while with a few of the vessels of his fleet he attacked the north side, promising rich rewards to those who should first make themselves masters of it. The bulk of the ships had to watch the Alexandrian fleet and keep it in the western harbour. The defence at the Pharos village was stout, slingers and bowmen being stationed on the tops of the houses along the shore, and it was difficult for the *cohorts* to land. The coast was rocky, and every crag and inlet was defended by boats and men, while five galleys patrolled the shore. But at last a footing was secured, and the Pharians driven to the town. On the harbour side of the island they had also resisted the landing parties with some success; but Caesar's men pushed on vigorously, and though the town walls were fairly strong and flanked by many towers, and the *legionaries* had no ladders or fascines, a panic ensued among the inhabitants and they yielded up the town, with considerable loss in killed and six hundred taken. Caesar gave over the town to plunder, and ordered it to be razed.

There was a fort on the island next the mole. This Caesar took and garrisoned. But the fort on the mainland at the south end of the mole was held by the Alexandrians. It was stronger than the other and situated in a large open place outside the city proper. This he felt that

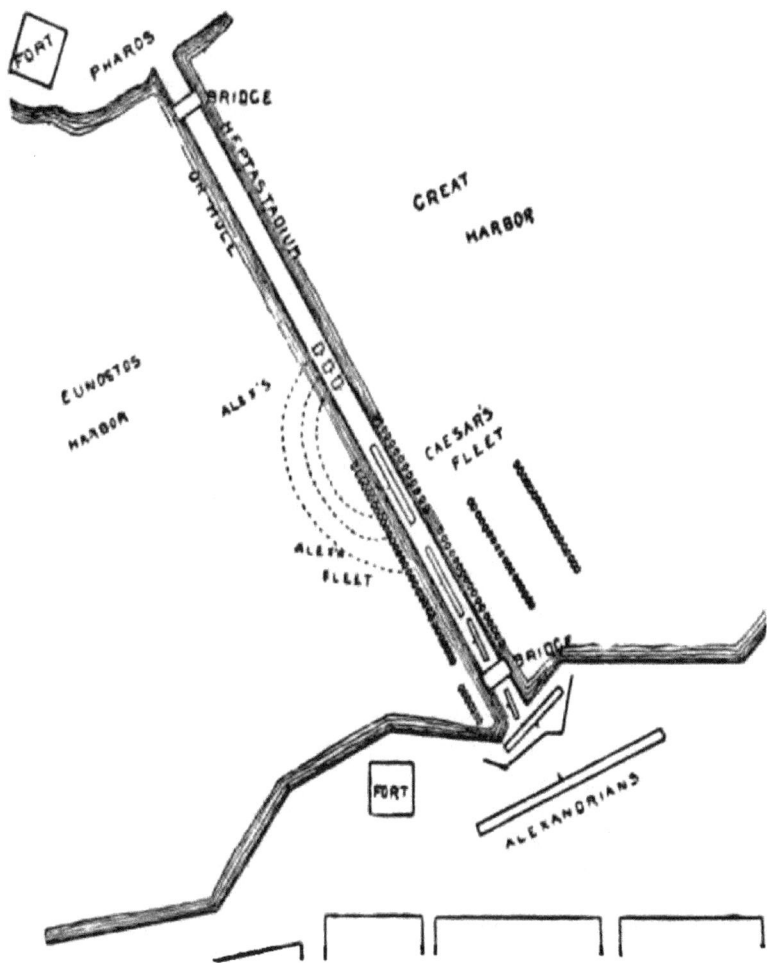

BATTLE AT THE MOLE

he must have, for by holding both ends of the mole he would substantially control both the harbours. Next day he attacked it. At first by a heavy fire of missiles he drove the garrison out of the fort and towards the town and landed three *cohorts* to occupy the mole and entrench, leaving the rest of his force in the boats. There was not room on the mole for a larger force to operate to advantage. The mole had near each end a bridge built over an arch, through which the vessels could pass to and from one harbour to the other, by which means the Alexandrians could keep the Great port in a constant state of uneasiness. Caesar threw up a work below the south bridge and set the men at filling up the arch, so as to cut off this communication.

175

While this was being done, the Alexandrians sallied out, deployed in an open space opposite the end of the bridge, and attacked the working party and force protecting it at the bridgehead they had made. At the same time they sent the ships which they had in the west harbour alongside the mole to attack the Romans on it, and seek to set fire to the fleet on the other side. The Caesarians held the mole and bridge; the Alexandrians attacked from the open space facing the bridgehead and the ships.

While Caesar's affairs were thus working to his advantage, some additional men—rowers and mariners—landed from the Roman galleys on the mole, unordered. This diversion at first materially aided the enterprise, for the men drove off the enemy's ships, but being after a while taken in flank by some enterprising Alexandrians who seized a footing on the mole from small boats, this party, not under control, made a hurried escape to their ships. Seeing the success of this flank attack, more Alexandrians landed on the mole and took Caesar's three *cohorts* at the bridge in the rear. The soldiers in the galleys, seeing the Alexandrians in force on the mole, and fearful that they might board the galleys, withdrew the ladders and put off from shore. The unusual commotion in their rear of necessity produced among the three *cohorts* at the bridge a flurry of which the Alexandrians were not slow to take advantage; and pushing in heartily they forced Caesar's men back in marked disorder.

They now had Caesar and his small force between two fires, and though Caesar himself was with them, the old spirit of panic came up. Perceiving that the ships were shoving off from the mole, and fearing that they would be left to their fate, the *cohorts* began to fall back. Retreat soon became flight, each man endeavouring to reach a vessel. Some made for such galleys as were still alongside the mole and crowded into them in such numbers as to sink them. Some swam out to the galleys at anchor, buoying themselves upon their shields. Some cast away their arms and swam out to the fleet. Caesar did his best to hold them in hand, but their demoralization was as complete as at Dyrrachium. He could not arrest the panic. It was another *sauve qui peut*. Reaching his own galley, he found that so many had crowded aboard her that she could not be got off the shore, and afterwards in effect she went down with all on board. Caesar was himself obliged to dive from the mole and swim for his life out into the harbour to another ship. It was this occasion on which he is said to have swum with one hand, holding aloft a manuscript in the other lest he should lose it. Reaching a galley, he sent small boats to the rescue of those who were floating in the water. Many were cut to pieces on the mole; more were drowned. In all the loss was four hundred legionaries, twice as many as had bit the dust at the great victory of Pharsalus. More than that number of sailors perished. This was the usual fate of the defeated in ancient times, whether in a combat or a pitched battle. This victory enabled the Alexandrians to retake and thenceforth to hold the fort at the south end of the mole, the defences of which they made too strong with enginery and works to again assault. They then reopened the bridge so as to have access through it to the east harbour.

The Roman soldiers appear to have been more ashamed than disheartened by this untoward defeat and anxious to wipe out their disgrace. They became so bent on fighting the Alexandrians, whom they assaulted on every possible occasion by sallies and cut off whenever they ventured beyond their works, that Caesar was compelled to restrain rather than encourage them. For this quality of quick recovery from the demoralization of a defeat, Caesar's legionaries were always distinguished. They had shown it markedly before Dyrrachium. They had caught the recuperative spirit of Caesar.

In the peculiar elasticity which enables troops to recover their equipoise after a repulse, no soldier has ever equalled the American volunteer. All veterans of our civil war will remember occasions where, after being driven back from a position or an assault, in a disorder apparently fatal, the line, having reached shelter, would of its own accord recover, and in a few minutes be ready to renew the charge or retake the position, in better spirits than before the repulse. Nor was this so much due to the efforts of the officers as to the natural character of the men. So, in a lesser degree, with Caesar's *legionaries*. They did get demoralized; but they speedily recovered their tone.

Seeing, then, that defeat neither weakened the enemy nor success threw him off his guard, some of the Alexandrians sent a secret deputation to Caesar to ask that their young king be restored to them, for they were weary at the government of a woman and the tyrant Ganymed, promising that if they could have Ptolemy back they would shortly place themselves in a position to make terms with Caesar. To this they solemnly bound themselves.

Caesar had little faith in these promises, but thought that if the king were returned to the Alexandrians these would probably be less well led than they now were by Ganymed, in case they continued the war. He could not see in what manner he profited by Ptolemy's retention. Moreover, he had fully espoused the cause of Cleopatra, and with the young king well off his hands, he could the better place her in authority when he should have reduced the Egyptians to reason,—as he never for a moment doubted that he could do. Many thought that Caesar had been overreached in these negotiations, but he probably saw through the matter with clean-cut purpose. He gave Ptolemy his freedom, and the young king left him with tears and vows to be grateful and friendly. But no sooner had he returned to his people than he in reality became more bitter than any one of the Alexandrian chiefs. As the courage of the Alexandrians was by no means raised by the recovery of their king, nor that of the Romans lowered, the surrender bore no part in the events which ensued.

The Alexandrians heard about this time a true rumour of an army marching overland to Caesar's assistance, and a false rumour that a convoy of troops and victuals was on its way to him by sea. They took steps to intercept the latter. They ordered their fleet to cruise before the Canopic branch of the Nile, where they thought it could best watch its movements. Hearing of their expedition, Caesar sent out his fleet to fall upon the Egyptian squadron, placing Tiberius Nero in command. Aboard the Rhodian galleys, which were with the fleet, was also Euphranor, who had rendered such exceptional services in the last naval battles. But fortune was unkind. In an action ensuing upon the fleets coming into each other's vicinity, Euphranor behaved with conspicuous gallantry and handled his own vessel to advantage; but for some reason not clearly set forth, he was not efficiently aided by the rest of the fleet. He was surrounded by the Alexandrian vessels and went down with his galley. The action had no particular result in affecting the war.

In January, 47, after Caesar had for four months been carrying on this luckless war, which had been thrust upon him against his will, but as a result of his carelessness, Mithridates of Pergamos arrived across the desert from Syria with reinforcements for the Romans. This man, who had taken his name from Mithridates, king of Pontus, whose son he claimed to be, had warmly embraced Caesar's cause in the Civil War, and enjoyed the consul's confidence. He had raised his army in Syria and Cilicia. Among the soldiers was a large body of Jews under Antipater. Mithridates began his campaign by assaulting and capturing Pelusium, where the Alexandrians had a small force, and leaving a garrison there, marched up the right bank of the Pelusian Branch towards Memphis, which was the nearest point where he could to advantage cross the Nile on his way to Alexandria, conciliating the regions he traversed, and gaining their allegiance to Caesar "by that authority which always accompanies a conqueror." He soon approached the head of the Delta. King Ptolemy, on learning of his coming, dispatched a force from Alexandria, partly by boats up the Nile, partly up the left bank, to check Mithridates, whose advent threatened to transfer the balance of power into Caesar's hands. This force crossed to the right bank, fell upon Mithridates in his camp, which he had fortified according to the Roman method, some thirty miles below Memphis. After repulsing them, Mithridates sallied out and inflicted on them a crushing defeat. But for their knowledge of the country and their vessels, none would have escaped. Mithridates was then enabled to get word to Caesar of what had happened. This was near the end of January.

Caesar and Ptolemy, on receipt of this news, both set out, Caesar to aid, Ptolemy to destroy, the new arrival. Mithridates, meanwhile, marched to the head of the Delta and crossed the Nile. The king had sent his fleet up the Nile with the bulk of his army. Caesar could not well march that way. Leaving a suitable garrison in his works at Alexandria, his fleet conveyed him along the shore to the west, where, disembarking at a convenient place on the coast, he marched around the south of Lake Mareotis, across the desert, and joined Mithridates. on the fourth day, before the king could attack him, or was, indeed, aware of Caesar's whereabouts. How considerable an army he now commanded we cannot tell.

Ptolemy had encamped on a hill protected by the Nile on one side, by a morass on the other, and steep access on a third. Such a place is found near modern Alcam. Between this camp and the road upon which Caesar was marching was "a narrow river with very steep banks," probably one of the numerous canals into which the Nile channel is constantly overflowing. To this river, seven miles from his camp, Ptolemy sent his cavalry and some choice light infantry to oppose Caesar's crossing and annoy him from the opposite bank. This force "maintained an unequal fight from the banks, where courage had no chance to exert itself and cowardice ran no risk." Caesar found it an annoying undertaking to cross in the face of these troops, but he speedily sent some German cavalry upstream to make their way by swimming to the other shore and to take the enemy in reverse, and the legionaries, at the same time, felled some trees across the stream and forced the passage. The enemy's cavalry fled in confusion, but were overtaken and mostly killed. The light troops were cut to pieces.

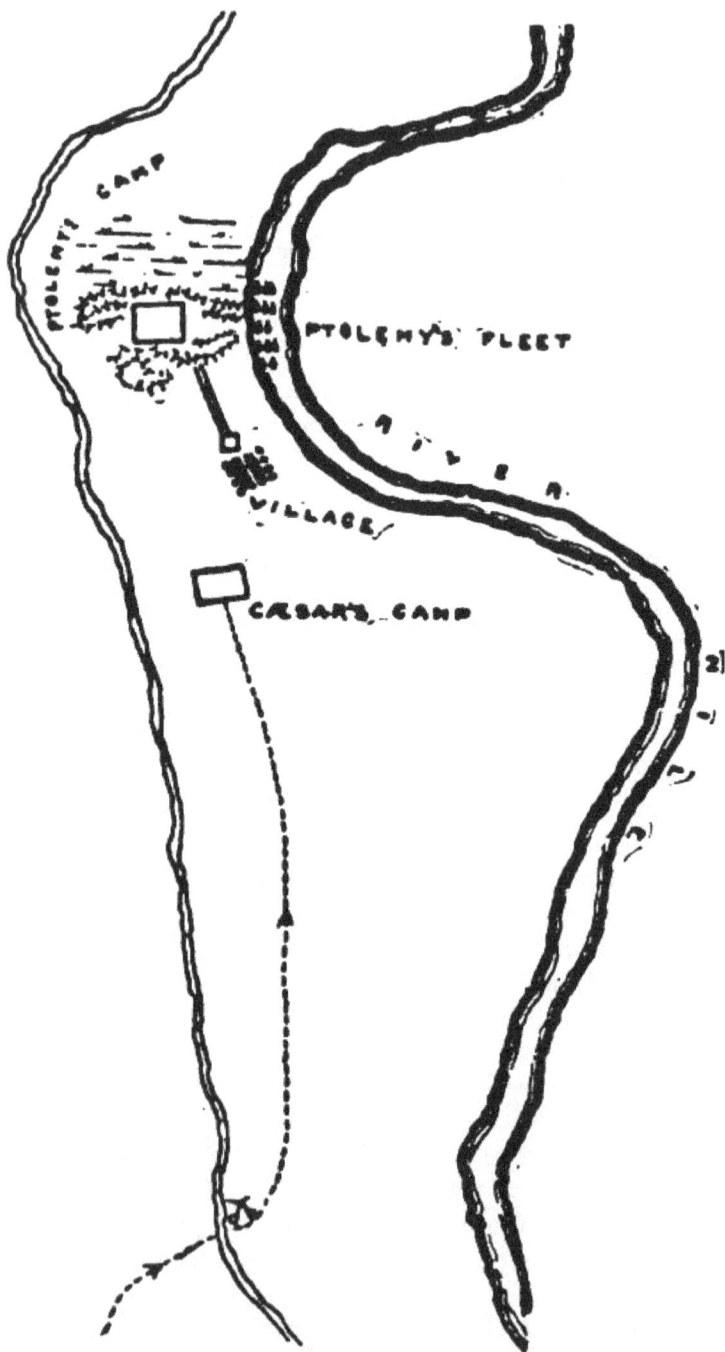

BATTLE OF THE NILE (TERRAIN)

Caesar followed them up and at first blush thought he might assault their camp, as they seemed too much demoralized to defend it stanchly; but on arrival he found it so strongly entrenched, and the troops so alert, that he declined to risk the operation for the moment. He camped. There was a village and fort nearby communicating with Ptolemy's camp by a line of works. Caesar next day made a demonstration here and forced an entrance to the village. In the confusion resulting in the Alexandrian camp from this unexpected manoeuvre, he ordered a general assault upon the latter. The camp had but two approaches, one in front from the plain and a narrower one facing the Nile. The former approach was held in great force, as it was here the attack was anticipated; the latter was exposed to darts from the hill and from the ships in the river, on which the Alexandrians had stationed a large number of bowmen and slingers. When the troops made no headway, despite their utmost ardour, Caesar, noticing that that side of the camp which had rugged sides—the southerly one—was illy protected, "for the enemy had all crowded to the other attacks, partly to have a share in the action, partly to be spectators of the issue," ordered a select force under Carfulenus, a soldier of ability and experience, to scale the rocks in that place, where an attack would be apt to fall on the defenders quite unprepared. With the greatest effort the men were able to make the ascent at all, but they succeeded in doing it in secrecy. Taking the Alexandrian camp in reverse, they produced a panic that enabled the *legionaries* who were delivering the front attack to succeed beyond expectation. The enemy fled in marked disorder, and in rushing over the ramparts towards the river, where they hoped to escape to their fleet, the trench was filled by men who fell and were trampled to death. There was fearful slaughter of the fugitives before they reached the river, and in the attempted escape to their ships a yet greater number perished by drowning. Among these was the king, whose ship was loaded down by terror-stricken men and sunk.

No sooner, was the battle over than Caesar advanced straight overland with his cavalry to Alexandria. Here the garrison and inhabitants, on hearing of the king's defeat, opened the gates of that part of the city which they had held and humbly sued for pardon. Caesar placed the younger son and Cleopatra on the throne, as Ptolemy the late king had by will requested should be done, banishing Arsinoë. After remaining two months longer than necessary,—held, according to many ancient authors, by the blandishments of Cleopatra,—Caesar departed by sea for Syria with the Sixth legion. He left the two legions which

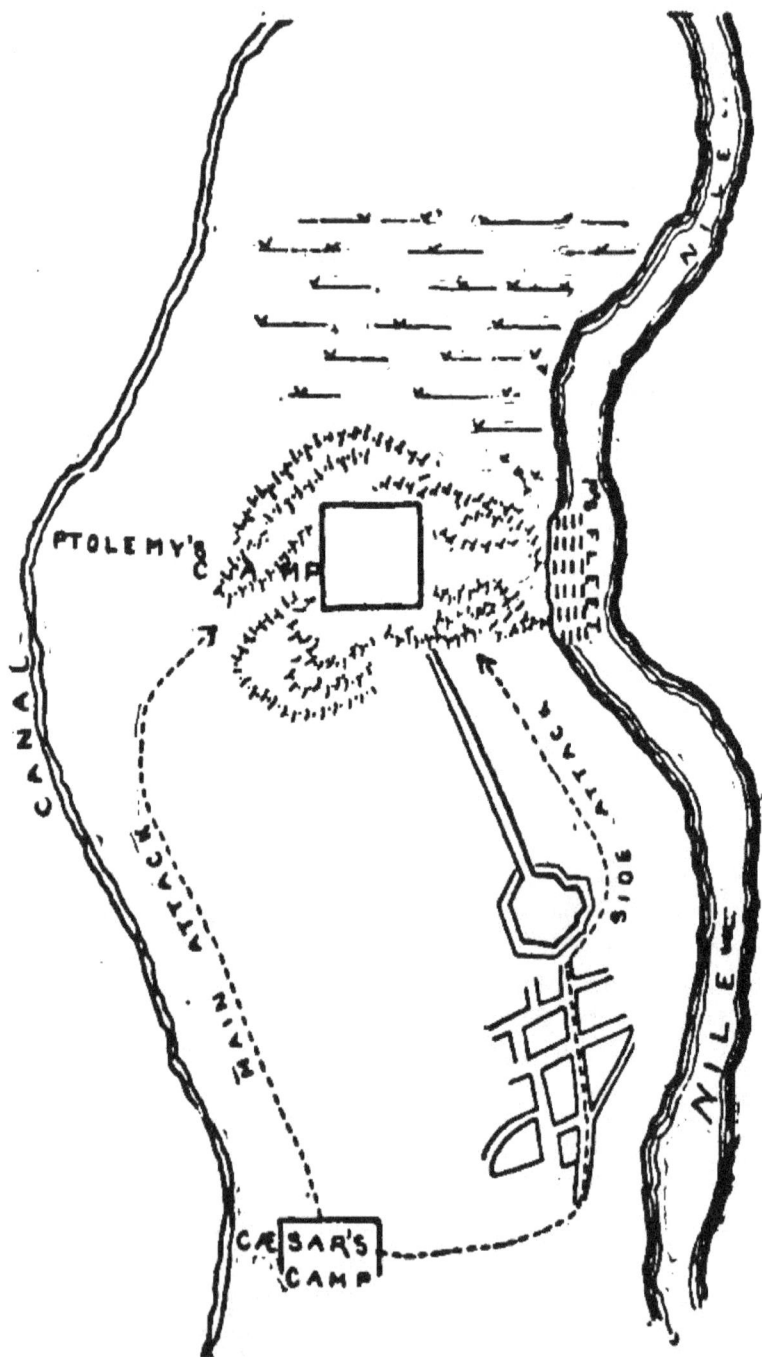

BATTLE OF THE NILE

had been with him, and a third one from Syria, under Rufio, to sustain the new government of Egypt, for the young monarchs were unfavourably regarded by the people.

The Alexandrian war lasted six months. During the first five months Caesar had been forced to hold himself on the defensive. This method he had largely transformed into offensive-defensive by his activity at sea. In the sixth month, on the arrival of reinforcements, he had assumed the offensive and ended the war by the battle of the Nile. He had not, on leaving for Egypt, anticipated being caught in the toils of a war; but from its inception he had foreseen that, with his mere handful of men, he would be cooped up until he could receive reinforcements. He made his plans accordingly, first to defend himself and then to carry on such an offensive as would forestall the offensive of the Alexandrians. As usual, he himself was the moving spring of action of both parties.

The six months thus spent, owing to Caesar's lack of caution, and the two additional months given perhaps to Cleopatra, perhaps to political demands we do not know, afforded the Pompeian party a breathing spell, and the opportunity of taking firm root in Africa. This necessitated two additional campaigns, one in Africa and one in Spain. Had Caesar, immediately after Pharsalus, turned sharply upon Pompey's adherents; or had he taken four or five legions with him—as he should have done in any event—to Alexandria; or had he for the moment put aside the question of the rule of Egypt by a temporizing policy and turned to the more important questions pressing upon him, he would have saved himself much future trouble.

The force he carried with him was so inadequate as to savour of foolhardiness. By crass good fortune alone was he able to seize the citadel and arsenal, and the tower on the Pharos, and save himself from utter ruin. It was a month after he arrived before the Egyptian army came from Pelusium and sat down before Alexandria. His own first reinforcements reached him shortly after. There seems to be nothing marvellous about the campaign, says Napoleon. And in view of the two months of unworthy dalliance, after the long and uncalled-for campaign had been ended, and other campaigns had become imperatively necessary, Egypt might well have become, but for Caesar's wonderful good fortune, the very grave of his reputation.

CHAPTER 37

Veni, Vidi, Vici

May And June, 47 B. C.

Pharnaces, king of Bosphorus, taking advantage of the civil broils of Rome, had seized territory not his own. Caesar's lieutenant had advanced against him and been defeated. Caesar sailed from Egypt with a mere handful of men along the coast of Syria and through Cilicia to Pontus. With such troops as he collected on the way, he had but a few *cohorts*, of which all but one thousand men were raw levies. With this corporal's guard he set out to subdue the rebel,—another of his foolhardy operations, doubly so, because unnecessary. But Caesar's luck did not desert him. In the Battle of Zela, at great risk and with splendid courage, he snatched a victory and settled the Pontus question. Once on the ground, it had taken but four days. When he reached Rome, he found matters in Italy in much confusion. He suppressed a mutiny of the legions, who, deeming themselves the masters, had become unreasonable in their demands. He was then called to Africa, where the Pompeian chiefs had rendezvoused, and, owing to the defeat of Curio, had full sway. There was here a gigantic problem to solve.

Pharnaces, son of the great Mithridates, king of Pontus, had some years before risen against and made war upon his father, and on surrendering himself to Pompey had been made king of Bosphorus. On the outbreak of the Civil War, Pharnaces deemed the occasion suitable for acquiring further dominion, and had taken to threatening Armenia and Cappadocia. He had already made considerable headway with his conquests, when Pompey was defeated at Pharsalus, on which he became still more hardy, and laid his hands on everything within his reach. Deiotarus, king of Armenia and *tetrarch* of Galatia, and Ariobarzanes, king of Cappadocia, appealed for help to Domitius Calvinus, whom, from Epirus, Caesar had sent to Asia, after the great vic-

184

ASIA MINOR

tory. Domitius, who had detached two of his three legions to Caesar and was correspondingly weakened, sent a deputation to Pharnaces, commanding him to withdraw from Armenia and Cappadocia; and, knowing full well that the command alone would be ineffectual, he at once backed up the embassy by arms.

He rendezvoused, the end of October, 48 B. C, at Comana in Pontus, with the Thirty-sixth legion and two others which Deiotarus had drilled in the Roman fashion; he sent P. Sextus to C. Plaetorius, the *quaestor*, for a legion which had been raised in Pontus, and Quinctius Particius in quest of auxiliaries in Cilicia. He had but two hundred horse. To Domitius' message Pharnaces returned answer that he had quitted Cappadocia, but that he claimed Armenia as his inheritance; and that he would submit to Caesar's decision when he should personally arrive. Domitius gave no credit to these protestations. He saw that Pharnaces had merely vacated Cappadocia the better to concentrate his forces on ground in Armenia, which was more easily defended. He sent the monarch word that he would wait only when matters were put on their old status, and at once marched on Armenia. This was in the winter of B. C. 48-47.

The route lay along the very rugged mountain chain which from Comana runs east and west, parallel to and south of the River Lycus, and is a spur of Anti-Taurus. Domitius chose this route because he would be less apt to be surprised on the road and could the more readily victual from Cappadocia. Pharnaces sought to conciliate him by various flattering and costly presents, but Domitius kept on his way and in due time reached a point west of Nicopolis, in Lesser Armenia, and camped seven miles from the town. Nicopolis lay in a plain flanked by mountains.

Between the Roman camp and Nicopolis lay a dangerous defile. Here Pharnaces placed his cavalry and best foot in ambush, but kept the flocks and herds in sight, so that if Domitius "entered the defile as a friend, he might have no suspicion of an ambuscade," "or if he should come as an enemy, that the soldiers, quitting their ranks to pillage, might be cut to pieces when dispersed"—a neat ruse quite in the style of Hannibal. Meanwhile he sent repeated messengers to Domitius to allay his suspicions. Domitius kept to his camp, fancying that negotiations might avail, and Pharnaces' clever design to entrap him failed. In a few days Domitius advanced on Nicopolis and entrenched a camp nearby. Pharnaces drew up his army in line in front of the camp, "forming his front into one line, according to the custom of the country, and securing his wings with a triple body of reserves," rather a curious order of battle for that day. No action supervened.

Rumours now arrived from Alexandria that Caesar was in a strait and had recalled Domitius to his aid, ordering him to move via Syria to Egypt. Pharnaces, who had learned the news from captured couriers, thought to embarrass Domitius by deferring battle, for delay would compromise him as well as Caesar. He entrenched his position near the town with two ditches four feet deep, and between them daily drew up his foot in one long phalanx sustained by three bodies of reserves, with his cavalry on his flanks beyond the ditches, where they could charge to advantage. This was a clever defensive scheme and lacked not originality.

Domitius, more concerned for Caesar than for himself, felt that he could not retreat without forcing and winning a battle against Pharnaces, equally as a measure of reputation and security. He accordingly drew up in front of his camp. The Thirty-sixth legion was posted on the right, that of Pontus on the left and Deiotarus in deep order in the centre. His front was narrow and his wings were protected with the cavalry and the *cohorts* not belonging to the legions named. Battle engaged. The Thirty-sixth seems to have been a fine body of men. Rushing upon the enemy, they entirely demolished Pharnaces' cavalry,—as Caesar's fourth line had done Pompey's at Pharsalus,—and drove it back to the very walls of the town; then, turning, struck the foot in the rear. The Pontus legion, on the left, was of no such stuff. Its first line quickly gave way, and the second line, advancing to its support and making a circuit around the enemy's flank, was, though at first successful, finally overwhelmed by the multitude of darts. Deiotarus' legions offered scarcely a respectable resistance. Pharnaces' victorious right wing then swung round on the flank of the Thirty-sixth. Thus abandoned, this gallant body,

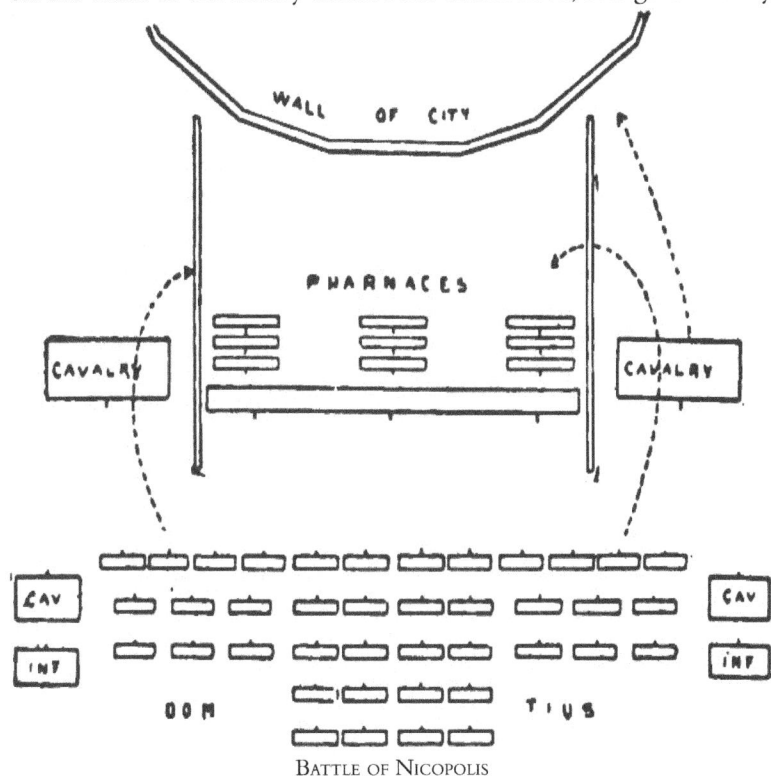

BATTLE OF NICOPOLIS

187

undismayed, drew up in a circle, and, though with great loss, successfully retired from the field and retreated to the slope of a neighbouring mountain, where Pharnaces, abashed by its firm aspect, did not see fit to pursue. It had lost two hundred and fifty killed and many Roman knights. The legion of Pontus was cut off and for the most part destroyed, as well as the bulk of the men of Deiotarus. Amid great hardships, Domitius retreated to Roman Asia.

In this battle, the difference between stanch and poor troops was made apparent. Pharnaces, expecting that Caesar would be destroyed in Egypt, now marched into Pontus, inflicted cruelties and mutilations of the most galling atrocity on the Romans and leading Pontic citizens, and re-established in his own name the ancient limits of his father's kingdom.

The defeat of Pompey at Pharsalus by no means broke up the combinations of the Pompeian party,—or rather of the aristocrats. While Caesar was still working out the Egyptian problem in Alexandria, the Roman arms all but received a fatal check in Illyricum. Q. Cornuficius, with two legions, had established himself strongly and prudently in that region, where hordes of runaways from the beaten army at Pharsalus threatened trouble. Gabinius was sent from Italy by Caesar to join him with two additional legions, newly raised. But Gabinius, undertaking an ill-advised winter campaign, was so harassed by the small-war of the Illyrian men and many officers, and was happy to make good his retreat to Salona with the relics of an army. Here he was shut in while Octavius, Pompey's lieutenant, overran half Illyricum. The situation was, however, retrieved by the vigour of Vatinius, then at Brundisium. This officer collected boats, made his way, despite the fleet of Octavius, to Illyricum with a small force of convalescent veterans from the hospitals, and obliged Octavius to raise the siege of Epidaurus. Then, near the Isle of Tauris, though much weaker in numbers and vessels, he inflicted on his opponent a stinging naval defeat,—a very noteworthy act, as he had only a few hastily fitted merchantmen to oppose to Octavius' war-vessels. Thus having cleared the coast, Octavius retiring with a few vessels to Greece and thence to Africa, Vatinius turned over the province to Cornuficius and returned to Brundisium. Illyricum was saved to Caesar.

From Alexandria, as already stated, Caesar had taken ship to Syria. He arrived at Antioch May 23. Here was not much to do except to settle sundry political disputes and encourage the states in their

ILLYRICUM

dependence on the democratic party,—*i. e.*, on himself. He paused only when he must, for his presence was not only urgently needed in Pontus, but the affairs in Rome demanded his coming; and he must dispose of the Pontus question before he could return to the capital. Leaving Sextus Caesar in command of the legions in Syria, he sailed to Cilicia on the fleet he had brought from Egypt. Summoning the states to meet him at Tarsus, he transacted the necessary business of the province and started at once for Pontus, *via* Mazaca in Cappadocia. Turning aside to Cappadocian Comana, he appointed a new priest for the temple of Bellona, pardoned and received again into favour Deiotarus, who had been seduced to join the cause of Pompey. Caesar required him to join the army with all his cavalry and the two legions he had drilled in the Roman manner, but which had behaved with so

189

little courage at Nicopolis. The relics of these had been collected and again recruited up to standard. With the Sixth and Thirty-sixth, this made a force of four legions,—two thirds of question-able stuff.

Of Caesar's few men only the Sixth legion, which had been reduced to one thousand men by the drain of its campaigns, were veterans. Pharnaces, nevertheless, fearing a terrible retribution, at once sent in his submission and begged hard for forgiveness. This Caesar granted upon certain promises of good behaviour and restitution. But Pharnaces, foreseeing that Caesar must soon leave for Rome, felt that he could afford to be slack in his performance, for he intended to keep none of his promises. Caesar, well understanding his treachery, determined summarily to punish him, despite the fact that he had only the one thousand reliable men of the Sixth legion as a leaven to a small force of other troops to oppose to Pharnaces' considerable numbers. This was quite in Caesar's style; it accords well with his bold disposition. When he had anything to do he felt that he could do it with the means at hand,—a marked characteristic of the great captain. When the able leader can readily concentrate larger numbers, he prudently does so. When he has but a limited force and work which must be done, he supplements his numerical weakness by his moral intelligence and strength instead of waiting for impossible reinforcements. But Caesar was much at fault in entering into this campaign so illy equipped. It was not necessary, and to this extent he is blameable. No feature in his life is more peculiar than this habit of insufficient preparation.

Pharnaces lay encamped in a strong position, some miles north of the town of Zela. Here was the field on which his father, Mithridates, had vanquished Triarius, the lieutenant of Lucullus. Zela, fifty miles westerly of Comana, was a town of great natural and artificial strength, in a plain among the mountains, but with walls built upon a natural eminence. Caesar approached, and camping, June 11, five miles from Pharnaces, and south of Zela, reconnoitred the ground. He ascertained that near the height fortified by Pharnaces was a hill separated from it by a steep ravine, and very suitable for defence. He was impressed by its natural tactical advantages, as well as felt that its possession would yield him a certain moral advantage over Pharnaces; for the latter's father, Mithridates, in his victorious battle against Triarius, had held this latter hill; but Pharnaces had neglected to occupy it.

Caesar quietly caused everything to be prepared for quickly entrenching a camp, and then by a night march passed over the Zela plain and,

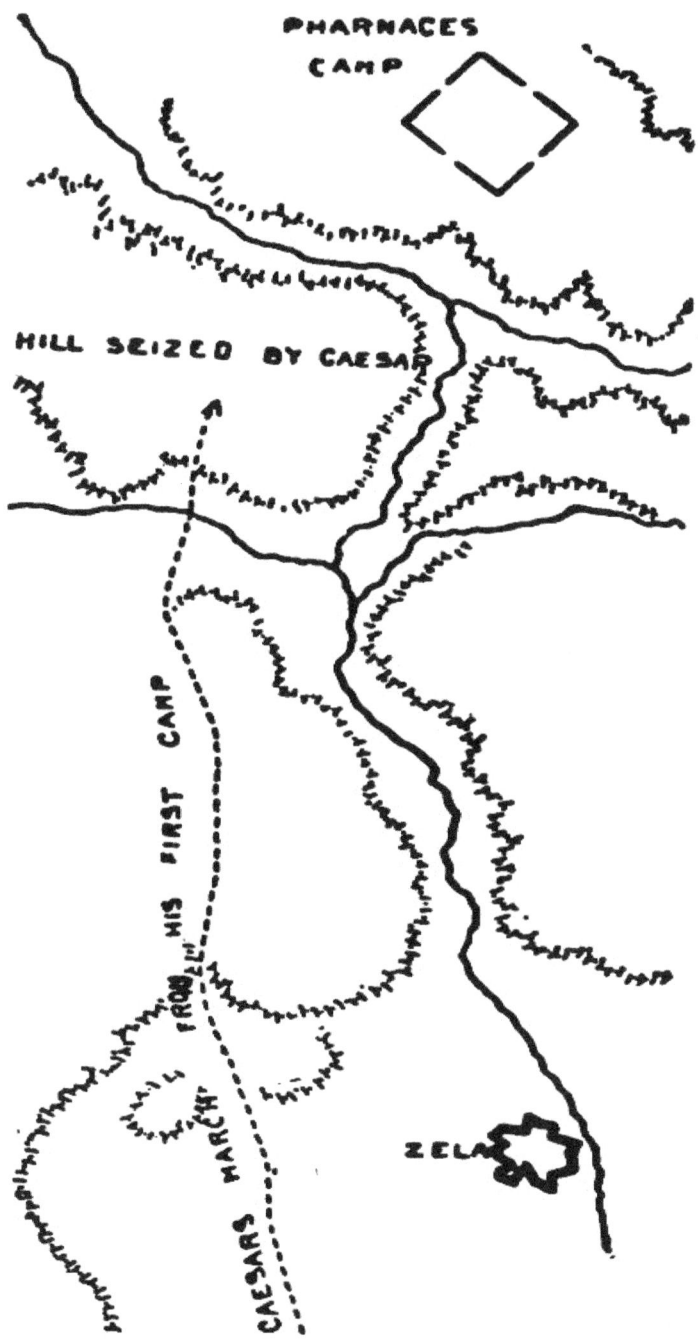

PHARNACES CAMP

HILL SEIZED BY CAESAR

FROM HIS FIRST CAMP

CAESARS MARCH

ZELA

THEATRE OF ZELA

approaching the debouches on the other side, seized the height in question, unknown to Pharnaces. The material was speedily carried over to the new location by the camp-followers, while the *legionaries* to a man worked on the fortifications. Caesar's idea was probably to prepare a thoroughly strong camp, from which as usual he could develop his plans and seek to wrest an advantage from the enemy. Pharnaces, seeing the non-combatants carrying material, thought it was the *legionaries* who were thus engaged, and deemed the occasion good to surprise the enemy.

Secure in his preponderating strength, and anxious to attack before Caesar could complete his entrenchments, he drew up in four lines and advanced down his own slope and up the one on which Caesar was at work, expecting to overwhelm him, though the position was strong (June 12). He felt that the fortune of his father would run in his favour; he remembered his own late victory, and he had had good omens in his sacrifices. Still the act was a foolhardy one.

At first Caesar declined to believe that the attack was intended. He considered it a mere threat to interrupt his entrenching, and made the very natural mistake of only ordering out his first line. The Romans were almost unprepared when the shock came. They had really allowed themselves to be surprised.

The enemy's scythed chariots opened the action, but their advance was partially arrested by a heavy fire of darts. Caesar's new troops were much alarmed at the suddenness of the attack, and threatened to become unmanageable. Pharnaces' infantry line soon closed in. The men came on with the utmost impetuosity, shouting their war-cry, as if victory was already secure. The impact was severe. The Sixth legion, on the right, stood like a stone wall, and the enemy recoiled from it; but in the centre the shock of the chariots had immediately broken through Caesar's first line and, followed up by the infantry, the rush placed the Romans in the gravest danger; it required all Caesar's presence of mind and skill to keep the troops on the left flank at work, and to fill the gap thus made in the centre. After a long and obstinate contest, the discipline of the Sixth legion—though but one thousand strong—prevailed over all odds; these brave men clung to their ground with a tenacity beyond words to praise, and by their example held the rest of the line to its work. Pharnaces, despite the splendid energy of his *cohorts*, could no longer maintain his ground, and was driven down the hill with great slaughter. The steadiness of this mere apology for a legion shows what a handful of good men may accomplish in the face of almost certain disaster. The Roman troops pursued the enemy to the camp, which, despite its strong location, they captured out of hand. Pharnaces escaped with a small troop of horse. His army was annihilated. Caesar gave the enemy's camp up to plunder and the men found considerable spoil in it. The defeat was complete. The king's army was quite broken up. Some months later, Pharnaces lost his life in battle against his brother-in-law, Asander, who had risen in opposition to his rule.

Having thus by the intervention of rare good fortune put an end to what promised to breed serious complications, Caesar left two legions under Caelius to guard Pontus; sent the Sixth legion to Rome as a reward for its distinguished services; disbanded the *cohorts* of Deiotarus, and started the day after the battle with a cavalry escort for Rome. He paused only so long on the way as was essential to leave matters well settled in the several states through which he passed. Among other executive acts, he appointed Mithridates, who had served him so well in Egypt, king of Bosphorus and *tetrarch* of Gallograecia, practically investing him with the dignities of Pharnaces.

It was with reference to the Pontus campaign that Caesar, in a letter to his friend Amantius in Rome, made use of the words, "*Veni, vidi, vici!*" "Happy Pompey!" exclaimed he, "these are the enemies, for overcoming whom thou wast surnamed The Great!"

Caesar always made great speed in his journeys. In going from Italy to Gaul and back, when in haste, he had the habit of travelling in a chariot or litter, and, alternating with riding or walking, moved day and night at the average speed of four miles an hour, or one hundred miles a day. Probably he did the same thing elsewhere. In the East he could get over still more ground. No doubt litter-bearers were then, as now, good travellers. His route was *via* Nicea (June 30), Athens (July 18), Tarentum (July 30), and Brundisium (August 2). He arrived in Rome August 11, much sooner than he was expected.

It was nearly two years since Caesar had been in Rome when he again trod the sacred soil. It was time he should return. The Senate was his tool. He had been made dictator, and Antony was his *magister equitum*, so that the latter during his absence had exercised full sway. But Antony, though officially a good servant, had subjected himself to grave reproach for many breaches of decorum, legal, social and political, and there was widespread discontent. The legions which had fought in Gaul and Greece had not been paid. To be sure they had all agreed to trust Caesar for their largesses until the end of the war, but there was no doubt cause for complaint. The Second legion refused

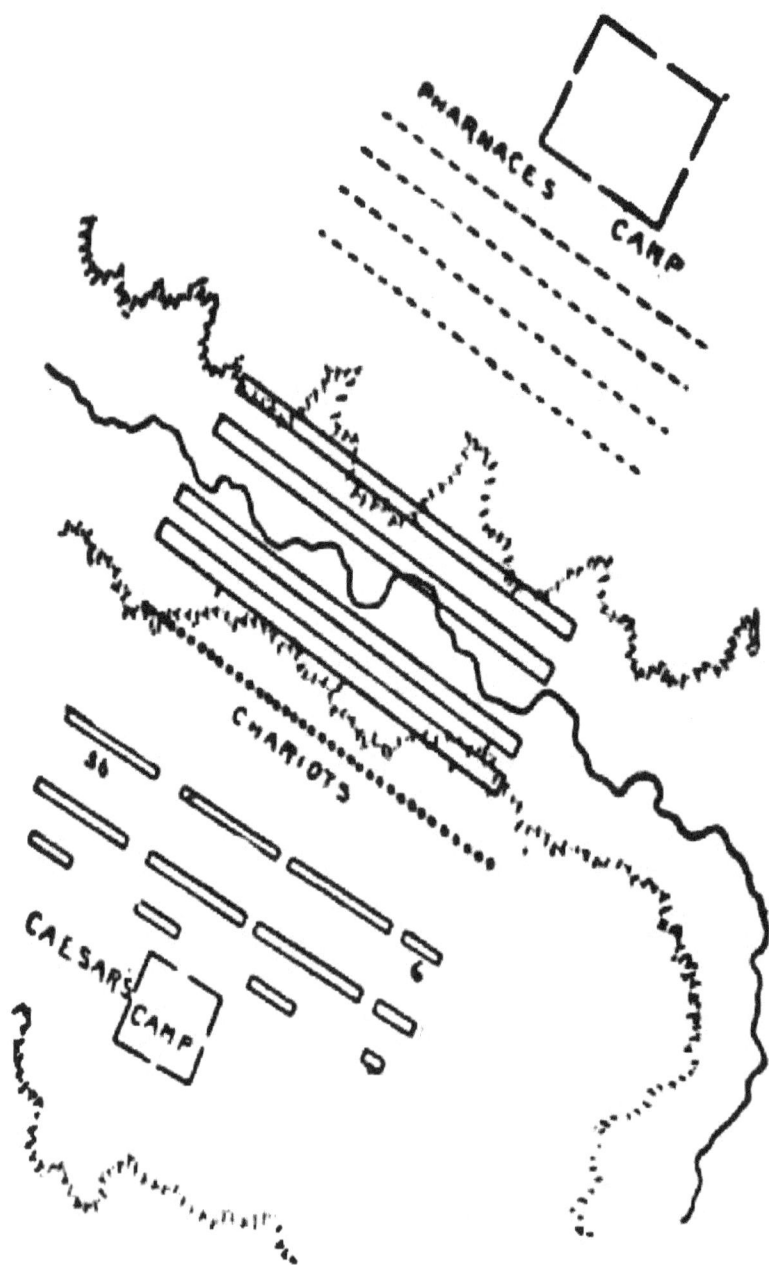

BATTLE OF ZELA

to march to Sicily; others followed its example. Caesar arrived in the midst of all this tumult. He at once took measures to settle the difficulties. For a time his presence sufficed to restore quiet, but shortly a still graver trouble broke forth. The legions which were stationed near Rome mutinied, murdered a number of their officers, who had tried to appease them, seized their eagles and marched on Rome. They had conceived the notion that Caesar could not continue in power without them; that they really were the fountain of authority; perhaps they flattered themselves that they could gain greater rewards and more speedy payment by their threats. The old legions which had placed Caesar on the pinnacle of fame and power felt that they were, in a fashion, masters of the earth. Under Caesar's sole charge they were tractable and ready; under his lieutenants they had grown self-opinionated and overbearing. Their officers grew to fear them, and acts of violence even against these had become common. The luxury of Campania had done them more injury than all their campaigns, more than Livy alleges that sensuous Capua did to Hannibal's veterans. Grave danger was imminent. A spark might light the fire in this body of combustible soldiers and inaugurate a reign of terror.

Caesar, on learning of their approach, caused the gates of the city to be shut upon them and guarded by some *cohorts* Antony had at hand; but when the legionaries asked leave to assemble on Mars' field they were allowed to enter without helmets, breastplates or shields, but wearing each his sword. Disregarding the advice of his friends and scorning personal danger, Caesar at once went out to them, and, facing the turbulent, seething mass, asked their leaders sternly what it was they desired.

"We are covered with wounds," cried they, "we have been long enough dragged about the world, and have spilt sufficient of our blood. We ask our discharge."

"I give it you," replied Caesar, with chilly deliberateness. He then added that in a few weeks he was going on a new campaign, that he would defeat the enemy with new legions, and that when he returned and triumphed with a new army, they, the old ones, should have the presents which had been promised them "on his triumph," and unpromised land beside. Expecting nothing less than that they would actually be discharged, and thus forfeit participation in the glories of Caesar's triumph,—the one thing to which every Roman soldier looked cravingly forward,—and awed by the cold demeanour of their great commander, the legionaries at once showed signs of weakening. As Caesar was about to go, the legates begged him to say a few kind words to his veterans, who had shared so many dangers with him. Caesar turned to them again, and quietly addressed them as "Citizens!" (*quirites*) instead, as usual, as "Comrades!" (*commilitones*). "We are not citizens," they exclaimed, interrupting Caesar, "we are soldiers! Their ancient devotion to the splendid chieftain who had so often led them to victory came welling up; the cutting word of *quirites*, to them who were soldiers first of all, and who had lost all pride in being burgesses of the Roman republic, in an instant changed the current of their purpose. A single word had conquered them whom arms could not; Caesar's indifference was their punishment. They could not bear that he should go forth to war with other troops. They crowded round him, and begged forgiveness and permission to continue in service and to accompany him whithersoever he might go. Caesar, it is said, forgave all but the Tenth legion, his old favourite, whose mutiny he could not condone. All the ringleaders had a third docked from their largesses, and he threatened to muster out the Tenth. But later the Tenth followed him to Africa, and there did its service as of yore. Still one sees in after days that it was no more the Old Tenth of the times of the Gallic War.

The accounts of the suppression of this mutiny do not strike one as being so dramatic as Arrian's story of Alexander's suppression of the mutiny of his Macedonians, which threatened to be of even graver danger. But as both are but embellished statements of an actual fact, they can scarcely be compared as a measure of the men themselves. And each case was characteristic. It was certainly a great role for one man to appear before and control scores of thousands by the mere force of his disdain and his iron will.

TRIUMPHAL CAR.

CHAPTER 38

Ruspina

October and November, 47 B. C.

Caesar commanded the resources of the world; yet he entered on the African campaign with his usual reckless disregard of suitable means. The Pompeians had assembled their forces in Africa, had accumulated a huge army and had been joined by King Juba as ally. Caesar got together his legions in Sicily and set sail for Africa without giving his fleet any place as rendezvous. A storm dispersed his vessels, and he landed on the coast at Ruspina with but three thousand men, the rest having been blown he knew not whither. For weeks he lay on the seashore awaiting the rest of his forces, and, but for the hebetude of his enemies, in a state of greatest peril. Despite this blameworthy negligence, we are forced to admire the remarkable manner in which he imposed on his enemies and saved himself harmless from attack. From his camp near Ruspina he sent in all directions for victual and troops, and by and by—with Caesar's own luck—the scattered fleet turned up, and ended the suspense. A battle shortly supervened, in which Caesar ably rescued himself from a grave peril coming from too distant an advance inconsiderately undertaken. Scipio soon after came up with the bulk of the Pompeian forces. More serious work then supervened.

At this time the northern part of the African continent, which alone was known to the Romans, was divided into Mauretania (Morocco), Numidia (Algiers), Gaetulia (the Great Desert) and so-called "Africa" (Tunis). Libya was sometimes used as a name for all Africa, Egypt and Ethiopia. "Africa" was now a Roman province, ruled by a praetor in Utica. The country was in the hands of Pompey's adherents. The sovereign of Numidia, King Juba, was committed to the interests of the Pompeian party and held a large place in its councils.

Because Pompey was dead there was no reason why his followers should not assert the rights which he had represented. Whatever their dissensions among themselves, they were a unit in opposing Caesar. The chiefs of the party, now a coalition of aristocrats rather than Pompeians, had severally fled to Africa. What they had lost in strength they gained in fanaticism. They could expect to make no terms with Caesar. After Pharsalus, Metellus Scipio had collected the relics of the Pompeian Army and shipped them to Africa; and Cato, Labienus, Cnaeus and Sextus Pompey, Afranius, Petreius, Octavius and others had joined him there. In Leptis, which they reached after great privations, these Pompeians spent the winter. Cato became praetor and took up his quarters in Utica. He unwisely declined the command in chief, luckily for Caesar; for though Cato was not a soldier, he was a man of exceptional strength. Scipio was made commander of the armies. A new senate of "three hundred" was elected and convened. Juba was independent, but lent friendly assistance. This coalition of the aristocrats summarily called for Caesar's presence in Africa.

The Pompeian army, as Caesar was informed, consisted of a vast cavalry force; four legions, armed and drilled Roman fashion, under Juba, and a great number of light-armed troops; ten legions under Scipio, eight of which were from refugees and conscripts;

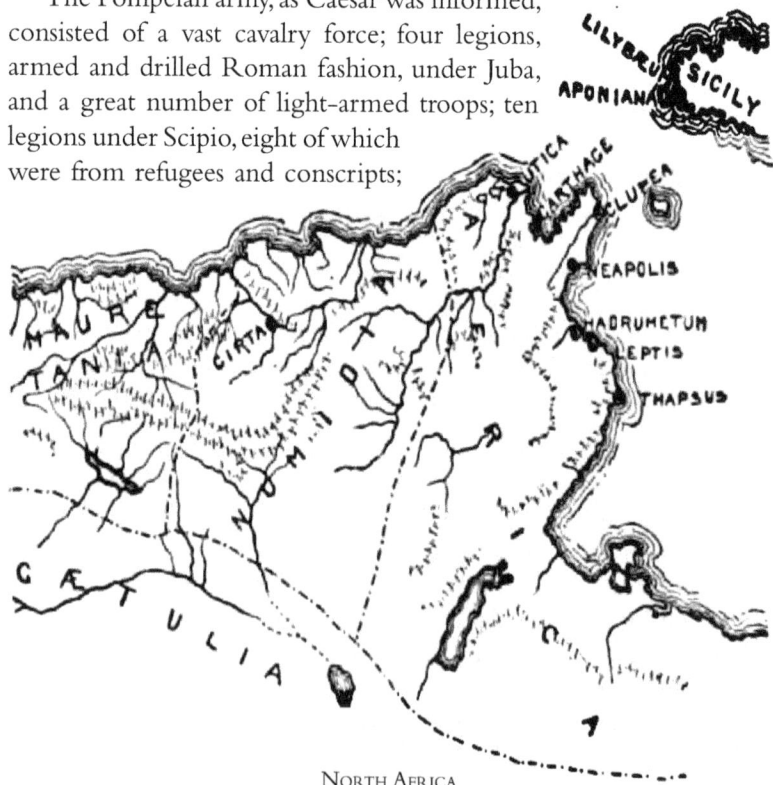

NORTH AFRICA

198

one hundred and twenty elephants; and a numerous fleet, which under Octavius, Varus and Nasidius controlled the African and Sicilian shores and contained fifty-five war-galleys. This force, both on land and sea, was capable of immense mischief. Caesar had thus far paid so little heed to the gathering danger that his enemies in Rome had feared that Scipio would invade Italy. This would have been practicable had Scipio worthily borne his name,—if his opponent had not been Caesar. While Caesar was in Alexandria and Asia Minor, what might not these legions, well led, have accomplished in Sicily and Italy? By a descent on Sicily and the occupation of its waters, Scipio could have practically nullified Caesar's attempt to cross to Africa.

But boldness was no part of Scipio's programme. He contented himself with a mere holding of the African province. For this purpose his plan was to gather all obtainable victual in his cities, so as to rob Caesar of the power to feed his troops, and to fortify all the coast towns. He was, however, unable to carry through his plan. Many of the towns were distinctly in Caesar's favour, and Scipio's measures lacked both decision and efficacy.

With his main army, Scipio lay near Utica, protecting his magazines. Afranius, Petreius and other old Pompeian generals were stationed on the coast within concentrating distance. The cavalry scouted the seashore for many scores of miles. The fleet was cruising partly on the African and partly on the Sicilian coast. Apparently these precautions were well taken. But neither the fleet nor the cavalry were sufficiently alert to fend off Caesar's attack. It was not numbers they lacked; it was discipline and proper command. There was not that push from headquarters which alone keeps subordinates to their work.

Before leaving Rome, Caesar divided up the provinces. Allienus received charge of Sicily, Sulpicius of Achaia, Sextus Caesar and Dec. Brutus of Syria and Transalpine Gaul, and M. Brutus of Cisalpine. After collecting all the transports he could lay his hands on, towards the end of October, B. C. 47, Caesar gave a rendezvous to them and to his army at Lilybaeum. He had at the time but one legion of raw levies and six hundred horse at this port. He expected four legions to come to Africa from Spain, to work in connection with Bogud, king of west Mauretania. The wind was contrary, but such was his anxiety to reach Africa that he kept his men in the ships ready to sail, and himself watched them from his tent pitched on the seashore. After some days of impatient waiting, his levies and ships gradually began to come in. He soon had assembled six legions and two thousand horse, among the legions the Fifth, a veteran body. Leaving Allienus, the praetor, strict orders to forward more troops without delay, and having rendezvoused his vessels at Aponiana, he set sail, October 30, for the promontory of Mercury (Cape Bon), hoping to land well south of Scipio, whom he knew to be at Utica. The troops were embarked in light order, without servants or camp-kits, the foot in galleys, the horse in transports.

The irregular winds of the season—they blow today as they did then—separated his fleet. He had failed to give orders to his captains where to assemble in such a case,—a very reprehensible oversight. He was, says the author of *The African War*, in the *Commentaries*, unaware of the location of the enemy's forces, and could not give a rendezvous.

"Some blamed his conduct on this occasion, and charged him with a considerable oversight, in not appointing a place of meeting to the pilots and captains of the fleet, or delivering them sealed instructions, according to his usual custom; which being opened at a certain time, might have directed them to assemble at a specified place. But in this Caesar acted not without design; for as he knew of no port in Africa that was clear of the enemy's forces, and where the fleet might rendezvous in security, he chose to rely entirely upon fortune, and land where occasion offered."

This is a lame excuse, which Caesar himself would never have made. While he could not perhaps have assigned a very definite rallying point, he knew where lay the bulk of the enemy's forces, and, therefore, what ports to avoid; and in any case he might have given better instructions than none at all. He himself, after four days of tossing on the treacherous waters of the Mediterranean, came in sight of land, attended by a few galleys, sailed south along the coast past Clupea,—where he saw the cavalry of the Pompeians and about three thousand Moors scouting the shore,—past Neapolis, and anchored near Hadrumetum (modern Sousa), November 3. Here was a Pompeian garrison of two legions and seven hundred horse, under C. Considius. Having reconnoitred the coast and seen no enemy, though he had in his company but three thousand men and one hundred and fifty horse, the rest having been blown he knew not whither, he concluded to land.

It was here that, in leaping on shore, Caesar accidentally fell, and lest the omen should dispirit the legions, he arose with the cry, "Africa, I have embraced thee!" He encamped where he had landed (a). He then made a reconnoissance, in person, of Hadrumetum, whose inhabitants

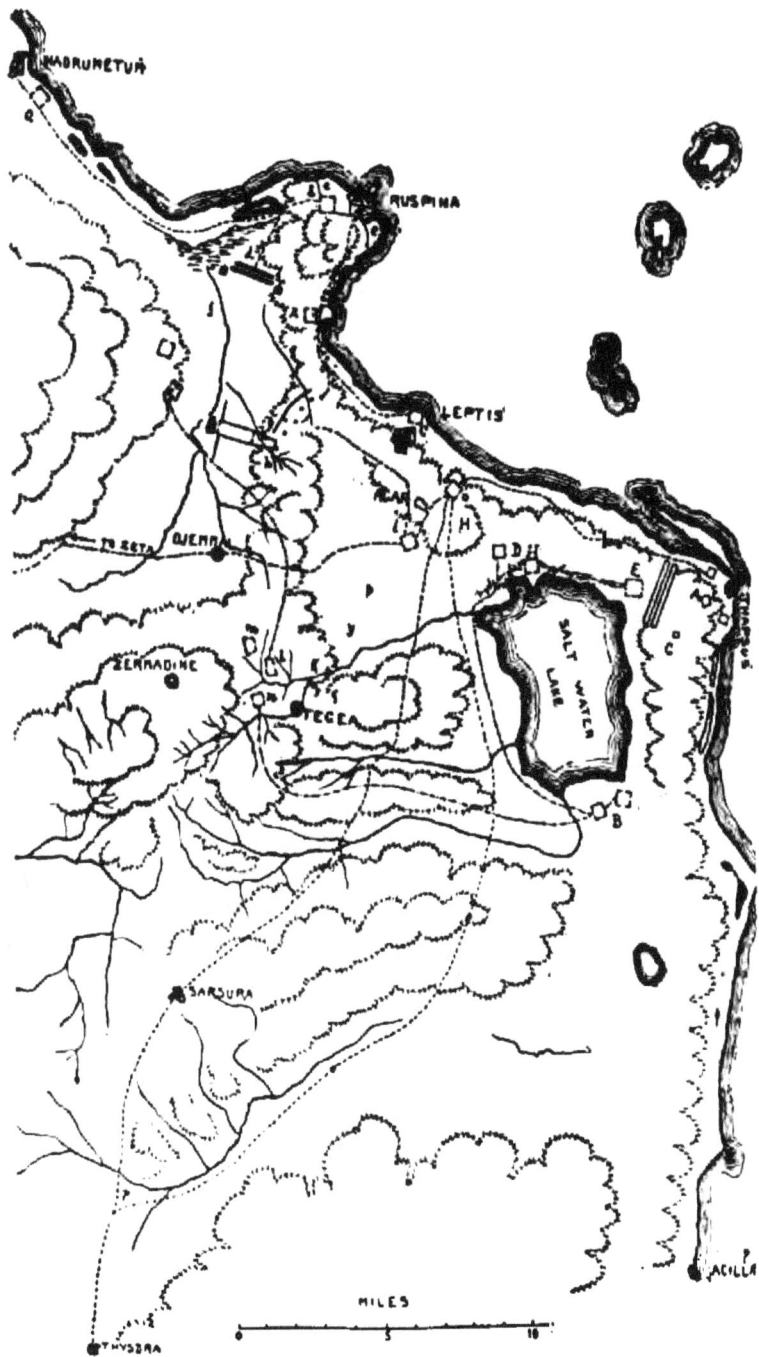

THEATRE OF AFRICAN CAMPAIGN

at once manned the walls and prepared for defence. Desirous not to offend the population, he forbade any plunder to be taken by the men. L. Plancus, one of the legates, attempted to treat with Considius, by letter, but the advances were rejected by the sturdy Pompeian.

"The rest of the forces had not yet arrived; his cavalry was not considerable; he had not sufficient troops with him to invest the place, and these were new levies; neither did he think it advisable, upon his first landing, to expose the army to wounds and fatigue; more especially as the town was strongly fortified, and extremely difficult of access; and a great body of horse was said to be upon the point of arrival to succour the inhabitants; he therefore thought it advisable not to remain and besiege the town, lest, while he pursued that design, the enemy's cavalry should come behind and surround him."

After remaining a day and night before the town, Caesar retired down the coast to a more suitable place to collect his scattered fleet, perhaps thinking that he might find some city already committed to his interests, or which might be persuaded to join his cause.

He was in fact in a graver danger than at Alexandria. Considius' legions were ten thousand strong, and this force was soon increased by the arrival of Cnaeus Piso with three thousand horse. The enemy had happily not attacked Caesar, but had adopted means of defence themselves. It was part of his good fortune—even Alexander never boasted such—that he met so lax opponents on his first landing.

On Caesar's retiring, Considius made a sally from the town, seized on the camp he had left and followed him up, sustained by Juba's cavalry, which had just come in to draw their pay; but Caesar halted, and throwing his small body of horse sharply upon the Moors he drove them back to the town. "An incredible event occurred, that less than thirty Gallic horse repulsed two thousand Moors." Incredible indeed! Mixing some *cohorts* of infantry with his horse as a rearguard, Caesar retired to Ruspina (modern Monastir), a well-located and prosperous town on a headland, and camped (b). It was the 5th of November. Thence Caesar, invited by its inhabitants, next day removed to Leptis, "a free city governed by its own laws," but far from a good place for defence, being situated on a flat part of the sea-shore. Leptis opened its gates to him. Caesar posted guards to protect the town from the soldiery, and camped between it and the seashore (c). He kept his cavalry on board the transports, to prevent their roaming about and plundering the inhabitants, whom he wished to conciliate,—a matter which speaks poorly for the discipline under which he held them.

Many towns came forward, furnished him victual, and assured him of their fidelity. Caesar had by crass luck escaped the most serious danger. Shortly, a part of the fleet came up by the merest accident and reported the rest to be probably on the way to Utica, supposing Caesar to be in that vicinity. Utica, since the destruction of Carthage, was the principal city on the coast, and, it will be remembered, was a usual place for a Roman army to disembark, when invading Africa from Sicily. Caesar's failure to give a rendezvous to his ships was sending them into the very clutches of the enemy.

The Moorish horse appeared to keep afoot, and on one occasion fell from ambush upon a watering party from Caesar's ships. Otherwise there were no armed exchanges.

Caesar was compelled to remain near the coast to collect his scattered vessels, a fact which prevented his foraging largely in the interior, and threatened to cut his victual short. But he kept actively at work. He dispatched ten vessels in search of the missing fleet. He sent into Sardinia and elsewhere for men, corn and stores, with stringent orders to comply with his requisition. The vessels in which he had come he emptied and sent back to Sicily for a new load of troops. He gave strict orders to his men by no means to leave camp. He sent out a naval force to take possession of the well-filled magazines on the island of Cercina. He reconnoitred and informed himself from natives and deserters of the status of Scipio's army.

On the 7th of November, finding Leptis less available than he had thought it, Caesar left six *cohorts* there under command of Saserna, and with some nine thousand men returned to Ruspina, "whence he had come the day before." He took steps to make this a *dépôt* for corn, of which he collected a large supply by using his soldiers and the inhabitants with all their wagons and sumpter-animals to forage. He was anxious to have an ample supply ready against his fleet should be collected. Ruspina was much more suitable for his purposes. It was nearer Sicily. It stood well out to sea so as to give a free view to a considerable distance. The anchorage, then as now, was on the south, and protected vessels from the north and west winds, which are those to be most dreaded.

Caesar began to foresee trouble from the non-arrival of his vessels. He made up his mind to leave the bulk of his men in garrison in Ruspina and Leptis and to go himself in search of the missing fleet; failing to find which he would sail for Sicily to bring more legions. On the same day, therefore (November 7), the ten galleys sent after his fleet not having returned, Caesar took seven of his choice *cohorts*, some of those which had behaved so well in the naval actions under Sulpicius and Vatinius, and embarked. He fully understood the danger in which he had placed himself. He said nothing of his destination to his army, which consequently felt much troubled at this proposed absence.

For "they saw themselves exposed upon a foreign coast to the mighty forces of a crafty nation, supported by an innumerable cavalry. Nor had they any resource in their present circumstances, or expectation of safety in their own conduct; but derived all their hope from the alacrity, vigour and wonderful cheerfulness that appeared in their general's countenance; for he was of an intrepid spirit, and behaved with undaunted resolution and confidence. On his conduct, therefore, they entirely relied, and hoped, to a man, that by his skill and talents all difficulties would vanish before them."

Just as Caesar was on the point of sailing next morning, the fleet appeared unexpectedly in view. This event was a fair sample of Caesar's luck, to which he owed so much throughout his life. To whom else did such things ever happen? The troops were disembarked and encamped west of but close to Ruspina, and near the coast. His situation was now improved, having twenty thousand foot and two thousand horse; but it was still far from satisfactory. He was no longer in grave peril, but it seems inexcusable that he, practically the ruler of the world, should, by his own default, be so far beneath his opponents in strength. Scipio, Caesar knew, was in Utica, nearly one hundred miles distant.

The whole coast here is flat. From the beach back there runs, as a rule, a line of slight hills, fifty or sixty feet high, and back of these, a flat country very slightly accentuated. The roll of the plain is no greater than the average of prairie land. Ruspina stands higher than most places on the coast.

So soon as the camp had been entrenched, on November 8, Caesar, with thirty *cohorts*, one hundred and fifty archers, and four hundred horse in light marching order, set out at nine a. m. on another foraging expedition, and "advanced into the country." He could not send small parties, lest they should be cut off. Due south from Ruspina runs a line of coast hills. West of these hills is a flat plain, once the bed of an inlet of the sea. It is today just what Caesar described it. Easy to march along and leading to a fertile section, he chose this plain for his advance. Some three miles out from camp a great dust announced the approach of an army. The Pompeians had moved up to his vicinity, camped, and were now coming out to meet him under command of Labienus, Petreius and other lieutenants of Scipio.

Caesar's scouts and an advanced party of cavalry had but just discovered and reported this fact. The scouting service was apparently far from being good. It was well for Caesar that Scipio had not been able to collect his force and reach the field a day or two before, when he was disembarking his troops. Scipio's legions had been occupying an extensive territory and had needed time to concentrate. He had heard of Caesar's arrival from Considius, and of his lack of troops. He fancied he had an easy prey. He had probably expected Caesar to land near Utica, and had only watched the gulf of Carthage.

It was too late to retire. Nor was it Caesar's way. Ordering the horse forward, supported by archers, of whom but a few had accompanied the column, Caesar himself rode out to reconnoitre, and ordered the legions to follow in line of battle (d). He soon saw that he had to do with a very large part of the enemy's force, and instructed the men to prepare for battle. His total number present was perhaps twelve thousand men. The Pompeians had marched with such precaution as not to be discovered, and had surprised Caesar with an overwhelming body of men, stated in the *Commentaries* at ten thousand five hundred horse, forty-four thousand foot and a large array of light troops which were mixed in the line of battle with horse. Labienus was in command. He had conducted his march with ability. Despite the defeat at Pharsalus, Labienus was full of courage and believed that he could crush Caesar by numbers. He proposed to use his Numidian cavalry in their own hereditary fashion, by skirmishing round Caesar's foot and tiring it out without even coming to combat; and fight was the very thing the legionary must do, if he would succeed. Labienus had trapped Caesar on the level, where his work was clear and easy.

Caesar sent back for the rest of his horse,—sixteen hundred in number. The terrain was a perfectly flat, open plain somewhat over one and a half miles wide, and growing wider in Caesar's front. On Caesar's left were the slight hills of Ruspina; on his right was marshy ground, the relics of the old inlet. The enemy was drawn up in deep order, with heavy bodies of cavalry on the wings and Numidian horse interspersed with the light-armed Numidians and bowmen in the centre. Labienus intended to put horse rather than foot into action. His line was much longer than Caesar's and overshot his flanks. Caesar imagined that he would have only infantry to fight in the enemy's, main line, but the latter had mixed horse with the foot so cleverly that at a distance it looked like an infantry line. To gain space, his numbers being small, Caesar was obliged to draw up his army in one line. This he did by moving the fifteen *cohorts* of the second line up into the intervals of the first, or else by opening intervals between the *cohorts*, or by ordering the men to take open order. His line was covered by archers, out as skirmishers, and flanked by Caesar's few horsemen on the wings. These were ordered to be particularly careful not to charge to a distance or to allow themselves to be surrounded. His line was probably about a mile long. His left wing and Labienus' right leaned on the Ruspina hills, but these were so very slight in elevation that they afforded scant protection. Why Caesar did not send back to camp for the balance of his force is not explained. It may be of a part with his usual over self-reliance. Or he may have thought that in case of disaster he would be better off to have in camp a strong force of fresh and undemoralized men on which to retire. At all events, he concluded to fight it out against the odds before him.

CAESARS 30 COHORTS

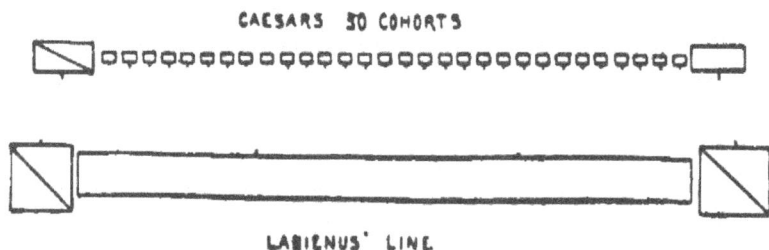

LABIENUS' LINE

BATTLE OF RUSPINA (FIRST PHASE)

Caesar, owing to his limited numbers, was unable to take the offensive, but waited for the enemy to advance. He saw that he must depend more on tactics or stratagem than on strength. Presently the Pompeians began to extend their line to the right and left to lap Caesar's flanks and surround his horse, which soon had difficulty in holding its ground. At the same time the centre of horse, interspersed with foot, adopted a new tactics, the horsemen rushing forward and casting their darts and, so soon as opposed, retiring under cover of the infantry through their intervals. When the *legionaries* would advance beyond their line to drive off the horse, they would be taken in flank by the Numidian infantry and many wounded, while the horsemen easily escaped their darts by flight. And when the Caesarians retired, the horse again advanced to the attack. This is similar to the tactics by which Hannibal's Numidians so frequently puzzled and defeated the *legionaries* of the Second Punic War. Labienus had boasted of this tactical attack by the novelty of which he believed he would certainly overwhelm Caesar's *legionaries*. Caesar was obliged to forbid the men to advance more than four feet beyond the line of ensigns,—which from this we should imagine to be in the first rank.

Soon Labienus' force swept so far beyond Caesar's flanks that the cavalry was crowded back upon the foot, many of the horses being wounded. The movement continued until the entire army of Caesar was surrounded by the Pompeian hybrid squadrons. The *cohorts* "were obliged to form into a circle, as if inclosed by barriers." This they did rapidly and in good order. Despite all which, the battle had not yet advanced to hand-to-hand fighting; for these operations had been accompanied by only a skirmishing contact, and what Caesar's men desired was to get at the enemy with the sword. They were placed at a grave disadvantage by this method of attack.

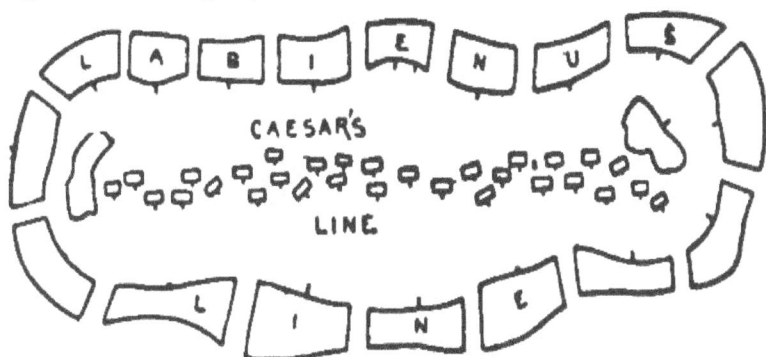

BATTLE OF RUSPINA (SECOND PHASE)

Caesar's position was difficult and dangerous in the highest degree. The young soldiers appeared to be much demoralized, and looked only to him for countenance. Many, no doubt, thought of the massacre of Curio's army. But they found that in Caesar's bearing which gave them confidence in him and in themselves. He was omnipresent, cheerful, active, full of encouragement. From him and the few old soldiers interspersed in the ranks the new levies took heart, and bore themselves like men.

Labienus made himself conspicuous by advancing beyond the line and taunting Caesar's men, over whom he imagined he was surely to obtain a complete and telling victory. In this vainglorious boasting he all but received a fatal check from a soldier of the old Tenth legion, who advanced, hurled a javelin at him, and wounded his horse. But Labienus was slow in attacking his old chief. He probably waited for a break in the lines so as to turn defeat into massacre. Caesar saw that he must undertake some manoeuvre to extricate his *cohorts* from their dilemma, or that he would soon succumb from some unexpected accident. As it was, it was becoming a question how long he could hold his new men in hand.

Caesar's brain was fertile in expedients. What he did is explained at length in the *Commentaries*, but in such a manner as to be susceptible of several readings. In fact, many tactical manoeuvres have been constructed to explain Caesar's movement. Rüstow and Göler have each made an elaborate evolution, savouring, perhaps, a little too much of the drill-ground, of what was done. One thing may be assumed as certain. With new troops, Caesar would be apt to undertake no very difficult tactical manoeuvre; but to do that which was the simplest, and therefore most likely to work under the rather demoralizing circumstances.

The *cohorts* were huddled together so much that the men could not use their weapons to advantage. Caesar saw that he must break the circle of the enemy, and was well aware that his interior position, so long as the *cohorts* kept their head, was much the stronger. He ordered alternate *cohorts* to face to the rear, and back up each against its neighbour, so as to form two fronts. The flank *cohorts*, presumably, as usual, of old troops, pushed their way to right and left, so as to give greater intervals to the centre *cohorts*; and by vigorous charges by horse and foot together, the circle of the enemy was ruptured at its two extremes. There were now two bodies of the enemy, which could not act together, and Caesar could see that they, in their turn, were growing uneasy, while his own men, cheered by success, began to recover their elasticity. Seizing the proper moment, Caesar ordered both fronts to charge the enemy with a will. The result justified the order. The Pompeians turned and fled in all directions. Caesar then faced the *cohorts* of the original front, which he had personally commanded, to the rear, and retired towards camp.

This manoeuvre produced a temporary lull in the battle. It looked as if Caesar could extricate himself. Just at this juncture a considerable body of foot and a select and fresh column of eleven hundred Numidian horse under M. Petreius and Cnaeus Piso came up and rehabilitated matters for the enemy. Caesar, during the lull, had begun to retire upon his camp in order of battle, and with unbroken ranks. The enemy's newly arrived cavalry endeavoured to harass his retreat and disorganize his line; but Caesar's men had gained confidence in their chief, and in their own fighting capacity. Far from being nervous un-

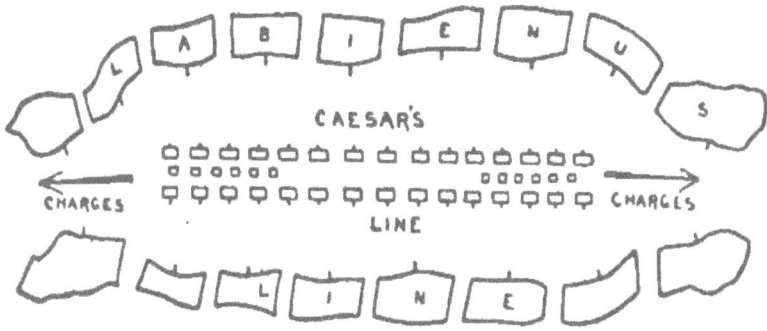

BATTLE OF RUSPINA (THIRD PHASE)

der the stress of their difficult situation, they promptly and cheerfully obeyed every order. There was no sign left of giving way. At command they sharply faced about and made bold to renew the battle in the middle of the plain. Labienus pursued the same policy of not coming to close quarters, but kept up a sharp skirmishing attack. Despite his boast, he seemed careful not to get within the reach of his old chief's arm. His presence was, however, harassing to a degree.

Caesar saw that a supreme effort was essential if he would keep his forces so well in hand as to permit a retreat to camp. His cavalry was all tired out. On a given signal, and with a vim which only the true commander could impart, the whole force made about face, paused, and moved as one man forward at charging pace upon Labienus' line, which was now somewhat carelessly dispersed. Taken by surprise at this bold front by an enemy they supposed beaten and were waiting to see dissolve its ranks, the Pompeians were completely broken, and retired with loss beyond the hills on the west of the plain. The Caesarians followed, and, taking possession of an eminence, held it until they could retire in order of battle. They then returned to camp in good condition. "The enemy, who in this last attack had been very roughly handled, then at length retreated to their fortifications," *i. e.*, their camp. The battle had lasted from eleven o'clock till sunset.

Caesar's tactical manoeuvre has been worked out by Rüstow to be something like this. From his one line of thirty-*cohorts* he withdrew the even-numbered ones into a temporary second line, thus affording him a more open order which could better manoeuvre. These latter *cohorts* then wheeled into two columns, those of the right wing to the right, those of the left wing to the left; and so soon as they were ready to charge, the horse retired around their flanks to the rear. The odd-numbered *cohorts*, now alone in the first line, also wheeled into column right and left, thus making two heavy columns facing outwardly to each flank. At the word of command these columns charged home right and left upon the wings of Labienus which had outflanked Caesar's line, driving them well back but not advancing too far. Meanwhile, Caesar collected the cavalry, which had retired behind the columns, into two bodies in the centre, and charged Labienus' centre to create a diversion there. The surprise of the whole manoeuvre, particularly by troops which Labienus thought were all but defeated, was what gave it its success. So soon as the enemy had been thrown back, the *cohorts* again returned to their places in double line, and Caesar began to withdraw. It cannot be said that this is accurate. It is one plausible explanation of the tactical manoeuvre, and fits the description of the *Commentaries*,—as indeed more than one will do. But the manoeuvre first given is more probable, as being simpler.

Many deserters came to Caesar's camp. These reported that Labienus had expected to surprise and demoralize Caesar's new troops by his unusual tactics, and then cut them to pieces as Curio had been. He had relied on his numbers rather than on discipline and his own ability, and had miscalculated Caesar's resources of intelligence and courage when pressed. And yet he knew his old chief full well.

Caesar had not won a victory, but he had, after being surprised, saved his army from possible annihilation by a very superior force. "Had Ruspina not been near, the Moorish javelin would perhaps have accomplished the same result here as the Parthian bow at Carrhae," says Mommsen. But Caesar was not a Crassus.

Caesar now fortified his camp with great care, inclosing it with entrenchments flanked by towers which ran from the outer flank of Ruspina and that of the camp down to the sea, beside joining the town and camp (e). He could thus safely receive victuals and enginery of war and have safe access to his fleet. However strong Caesar might make his works, the strength of his position lay in the man himself. His own legions recognized his confidence and partook it; and in the enemy's camp, it may be presumed, the aristocrats equally felt the presence over against them of a great captain.

Caesar did not deem it expedient just now to risk an attack on the enemy in the open field. Needing light troops, he armed many of the Gauls, Rhodians and other mariners in the fleet as slingers and archers, and drew from the fleet many Syrian and Iturean bowmen, who were serving as mariners. Though not very effective, they added a certain value to the army. He put up workshops to make engines, darts and leaden bullets, and sent to Sicily for corn, hurdles, wood for rams and other material of war. He insisted strictly on the performance of guard duty, saw to every detail himself, constantly visited the outposts, encouraged his men, and looked out for their wants with the utmost energy.

But Caesar was unfortunate about his victual. Corn in Africa was scarce, for all the labouring population was under arms. He could not forage in the neighbourhood; no corn had been left by the enemy. Many of his transports were taken by Scipio's fleet, for, not knowing where Caesar was, the transports were uncertain where to land. Caesar had to keep part of his fleet hovering along the coast to guide his incoming vessels. The question of subsistence taxed him to the utmost. The motif of the entire African campaign may be said to be the lack of victual in Caesar's camp.

Scipio was heard to be on his way to reinforce Labienus with eight legions and three thousand horse. Caesar, with his late arrivals, had less than thirty thousand men. Scipio and Labienus together had thrice the number. After the late battle, Labienus had sent his sick and wounded, many in number, to Hadrumetum, and made ready

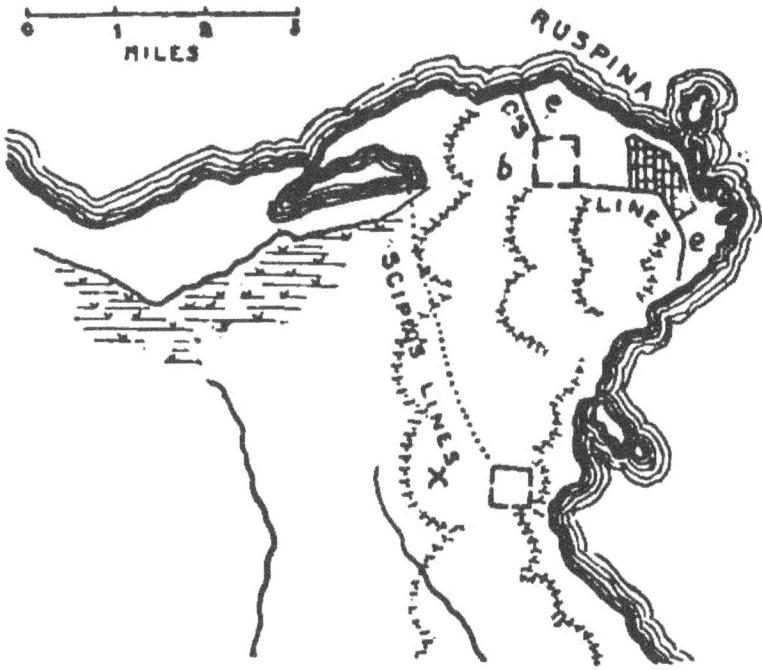

RUSPINA CAMP

211

for a junction with Scipio. He posted cavalry outposts on all the hills around Ruspina to prevent victual from reaching Caesar. Scipio's intention had been to attack Caesar before he got entrenched at Ruspina, but he was tardy. Caesar's expedition was too great to allow of much delay by Scipio upon the march. Scipio had left Utica with a strong garrison and marched to Hadrumetum, where he arrived November 13. Thence, after a few days, he joined the forces under Labienus and Petreius, and all three fortified a camp about three miles south of Caesar's works (x) before Ruspina. Scipio, no doubt, reconnoitred, but apparently did not care to attack Caesar's entrenchments. They were too formidable. He thought he would try on Caesar the same proceeding Caesar had tried on Pompey at Dyrrachium,—blockade. In this he had a fair chance of success with his overwhelming odds. But he did not carry out his purpose with acumen nor with sufficient force. His guard-duties were laxly performed, and he had not the eye to seize on the salient topographical advantages of his position, though he established, apparently, a cordon about Caesar's lines. Still, what he did soon began to interfere with Caesar's foraging,—a serious matter, as no provisions had yet arrived from Sicily or Sardinia, and Caesar "did not possess above six miles in each direction" from which to get corn. That he kept so much reflects small credit on Scipio's activity. Just what "six miles" may mean is subject to question. The circuit of Caesar's inclosure was about six miles, but that he could forage much beyond is improbable in view of Scipio's great force of cavalry. The horses and cattle were largely fed on seaweed washed in fresh water, a fact which proves the considerable difficulties he was under. Caesar was blockaded in earnest.

Young Pompey, meanwhile, in Utica, urged by Cato to do something worthy of his name, got together thirty sail, and, embarking two thousand men, invaded the land of King Bogud in Mauretania. Landing near Ascurum, the garrison allowed him to approach; then, sallying out, drove him back with confusion. Disheartened, he sailed to the Balearic Isles. Bogud was merely irritated into giving more earnest support to Caesar, who made use of every means to which he could put his hand. P. Sitius, a soldier of fortune expatriated by the Catalinian *fiasco*, had collected a force of motley legionaries and served various African potentates for pay. Him Caesar set to influence King Bogud to invade Numidia, whose king, Juba, was on the march to join Scipio. In this he succeeded. Sitius and Bogud advanced into Numidia, took Cirta (Constantine), put the citizens to the sword, and captured Juba's stronghold of provisions and war material. Juba was summarily called to defend his own territory. This defection was a serious blow to Scipio. Juba left but thirty elephants with the Pompeian army, out of the large number he had brought. Juba's approach had threatened to add the last straw to the load Caesar had to bear; his change of mind distinctly modified the danger.

CHAPTER 39

Entrenched Advance
December, 47 B. C.

Caesar strongly entrenched himself in Ruspina to await the arrival of the rest of his legions. The country towns and people were mostly favourable to him, but under the control of the Pompeians. Scipio lay in a large camp three miles down the coast, with an outpost in Ucita, a small town in the middle of a plain surrounded by rolling hills. Caesar was anxious to bring Scipio to battle, but on his own terms. All through this campaign he appeared to avoid a general engagement. He moved the bulk of his forces out to the heights east of Ucita, and entrenched. Between him and Ucita, in the plain and on the hills on its west, a number of skirmishes ensued, but no approach to a battle, though Caesar frequently offered it. Caesar determined to capture Ucita, which had been made the centre of Scipio's defensive line. He advanced a series of fieldworks from his entrenchments on the hills across the plain towards the town, so that he might not be attacked in flank. With a force all but equal, if not quite, to Scipio's, Caesar, for some reason, did not force the fighting, though he restlessly manoeuvred against the enemy.

So soon as the province of Africa was convinced of Caesar's arrival in person,—this had not been believed, owing to the allegations of the enemy that only a legate was in command, until Caesar communicated with the important towns himself,—many persons of rank sent in their offers of allegiance and complained bitterly of the cruelty of the Pompeian coalition, which had sucked the life-blood out of the land by their rapacity. Caesar determined to undertake active operations as soon as the season would admit, and sent word to Alienus, the praetor in Sicily, that the troops must be forwarded, whatever the weather, if he was to preserve Africa from utter ruin. "And he himself was so anxious and impatient, that from the day the letters were sent he complained without ceasing of the delay of the fleet, and had his eyes night and day turned towards the sea." Meanwhile, the enemy continued to ravage the country, which Caesar was forced to watch, and could not prevent owing to his small force. But he increased his works, and made his camp almost impregnable with redoubts and defences, and carried the lines quite to the sea.

Caesar's constrained position was due to his own overeager act in attacking the African problem with insufficient means. However justly we may admire Caesar as perhaps the greatest man of ancient days, as indisputably one of the world's great captains, we cannot justly overlook his errors. Caesar must be tried by his peers. His habit of undertaking operations with inadequate forces was a distinct failing from which only "Caesar's fortune" on many occasions saved him. This characteristic of his military life cannot but be condemned. It is beyond question that all the danger and delay to which he had been subjected since sailing from Lilybaeum were attributable to a carelessness which militates as much against his character as a captain as his subsequent splendid efforts to save himself from ruin and to defeat his enemies redound to his credit. His energy and skill in saving himself from self-imposed dangers are thoroughly admirable.

A great captain must face any odds of numbers or conditions when it is essential. But sound preparation is one of the corner-stones of his reputation. Foolhardiness may show courage; but it shows equal lack of discretion. Overhastiness is still worse. In the mixed caution and boldness of the captain, Hannibal far outranks Caesar. But Hannibal had not the help of Fortune as Alexander and Caesar always had.

It would seem clear that Scipio's best policy was the one which Cato urged upon him,—to move into the interior and, if possible, lure Caesar away from the coast to a point where he would find it not only harder to victual, but to keep his array up to fighting level. But Scipio was not gifted with military sense. Instead of this course, he garrisoned Hadrumetum and Thapsus, and sought to shut Caesar in. He spent much time in drilling his elephants in mock battles so as to train them to face the enemy. He knew that, as a rule, elephants in battle had proved as dangerous to one army as to another,—but Scipio could not give up his desire to put these beasts to use in his line.

As usual, the cavalry outposts of the two parties continually skirmished, and the German and Gallic cavalry occasionally exchanged greetings on a prearranged truce. Labienus tried on several occasions to surprise Leptis, but was beaten off by the three *cohorts* then in garrison under Saserna. The town was strongly fortified and well supplied with catapults and *ballistas*, which made up for its situation on the flat seashore where it had no natural defences.

On one of these occasions when a strong squadron was before the gates, their chief was slain by a shaft from an engine which pinned him to his own shield. The whole body, terrified, took to flight, "by which means the town was delivered from any further attempts,"—a fact which argues illy for the cool-headedness of Labienus' squadrons, and is a curious commentary on the value of the nomad cavalry of antiquity. When such a man as Hannibal headed it, it was alone effective; and then it was an arm of exceptional power.

When Scipio had finished his preparations and felt strong enough to fight Caesar, he began about the 20th of November to draw up on successive days some three hundred paces from his own camp and to offer battle. This was invariably declined. Caesar was awaiting his veterans and supplies, and could not be provoked into paying any attention to Scipio's taunts; and his works were impregnable. This "forbearance and tranquillity gave him (Scipio) such a contempt of Caesar and his army" that on one occasion in a boastful spirit Scipio advanced with his whole army and towered elephants up to Caesar's very ramparts. But Caesar merely ordered in his outposts of horse when the enemy advanced to dart-throwing distance, called in his fatigue parties, posted his men, ordered his reserve cavalry under arms, and awaited the assault if they were foolish enough to make it.

"These orders were not given by himself in person, or after viewing the disposition of the enemy from the rampart; but such was his consummate knowledge of the art of war, that he gave all the necessary directions by his officers, he himself sitting in his tent and informing himself of the motives of the enemy by his scouts."

This is the first instance in ancient military books where a commanding general is described as managing a battle just as he would do today. The Roman general was always at the front in person. Caesar knew that the enemy would not dare to assault his works, for he had cross-bows, engines and other missile-throwing devices, besides abatis and *trous de loup* in plenty; but he was ready to receive them should they really attempt the storm. He did not desire a battle until he could make it a crushing defeat, and to insure this he waited for the veterans who were to arrive on the next embarkation. Scipio, out of this caution, made loud a claim of cowardice against Caesar, exhorted his troops and promised them speedy victory. Caesar resumed his work on the fortifications, and "under pretence of fortifying his camp, inured the levies to labour and fatigue."

But meanwhile many deserters, Numidians and Gaetulians, came to Caesar "because they understood he was related to C. Marius, from whom their ancestors had received considerable favours" during the Jugurthan wars. Many of these returned home and wrought up their friends to favour Caesar's cause. Caesar had spies in Scipio's camp in plenty and kept abreast with his purposes. Many tribes sent in offers of allegiance. Deputies came from Acilla, which perhaps has been identified with El Alia, some twenty miles south of Thapsus, and from other towns, requesting garrisons and promising supplies. Caesar sent a small force to Acilla under C. Messius, who had been *aedile*. On the way, this body was all but intercepted by Considius, who was apparently on a general reconnoissance from his headquarters at Hadrumetum, with eight *cohorts*; but the garrison reached the town before him. Considius returned to Hadrumetum, whence, securing some horse, he again made his way to Acilla and laid siege to it.

About November 26 there arrived a large supply of corn from Cercina on board the fleet of transports which Caesar had sent thither; and equally to be desired, the Thirteenth and Fourteenth legions, eight hundred Gallic horse, one thousand archers and slingers, and a great deal of war material from Alienus, the praetor at Lilybaeum. The fleet laden with these troops had had a favourable wind and had made the passage in four days,—a distance of somewhat less than two hundred miles. This double arrival "animated the soldiers and delivered them from apprehensions of want." The *cohorts*, after a proper rest, Caesar distributed on his works. He also ascertained that those of his ships which had not yet arrived were only detained by adverse winds, and that none had been taken by the enemy.

This failure to move greatly puzzled Scipio, all the more from Caesar's usually all but abnormal activity. He sent two Gaetulians as spies in the guise of deserters, and with promises of great rewards, into Caesar's camp to discover what they could about the pitfalls and entanglements Caesar had made; In what manner he proposed to meet the elephants, and what his dispositions were for battle. This only resulted in the men remaining in Caesar's service and in increasing the number of real deserters. Of these there was daily a large number. But Cato at Utica supplied these gaps by the recruits he sent from there. These were mostly freedmen, Africans or slaves. The neighbouring towns aided Caesar as much as possible. Tysdra (modern El Djem), a town thirty miles to the south, pointed out to him a store of three hundred thousand bushels of corn belonging to Italian merchants, which he was, however, unable to seize. P. Sitius, still active, made an incursion into Numidia and captured an important castle of King Juba's, holding much victual and war material.

Caesar now dispatched six of his transports to Sicily for the remainder of the troops. Though still far weaker in numbers he had enough men to face the enemy, and determined to manoeuvre for a good chance to bring him to battle.

South of Caesar's works at Ruspina lay "a fine plain, extending fifteen miles and bordering upon a chain of mountains of moderate height, that formed a kind of theatre." It is the same today as Caesar describes it (f). The width of the valley is from two to five miles. The hills surrounding it vary from three hundred to six hundred feet. The northern outlet leads to a marsh near the sea. Six miles from the coast, in the centre of the plain, lay Ucita, a town held by a strong garrison of Scipio's. On the highest of the hills were watch-towers, and at various points of the valley Scipio had infantry guards and cavalry outposts. Caesar did not propose to allow Scipio to inclose him in siege lines; he must break the growing circle, and this was a good place to do it. If Caesar could gain possession of this plain it would also go far towards cutting Scipio off from Leptis, which he could then reach only by a long circuit and make it easier to hold this place. This would secure him two good harbours, Ruspina and Leptis.

As Caesar's good fortune would have it, Scipio was hard up for water in his camp south of Ruspina, and determined to move to a point where there was a better supply. He gave up his camp November 27, and made for the hills on the west of the Ucita plain (s s). This afforded Caesar his opportunity, and he followed.

Caesar's main purpose was probably to feel the enemy and by a series of movements seek to put him at a disadvantage so as to draw him into battle on terms helpful to himself. Accordingly, on the last day of November, leaving a suitable force in the Ruspina lines, he broke camp at midnight with the rest of the infantry and all the cavalry and marched (t t) away from Ruspina along the seashore, left in front, and, striking the hills on the eastern side of the plain, he filed to the south along them until his head of column neared Scipio's cavalry outposts (g). He was careful to avoid the plain, for fear of the Numidian cavalry, of which he had had so serious a taste in the last encounter.

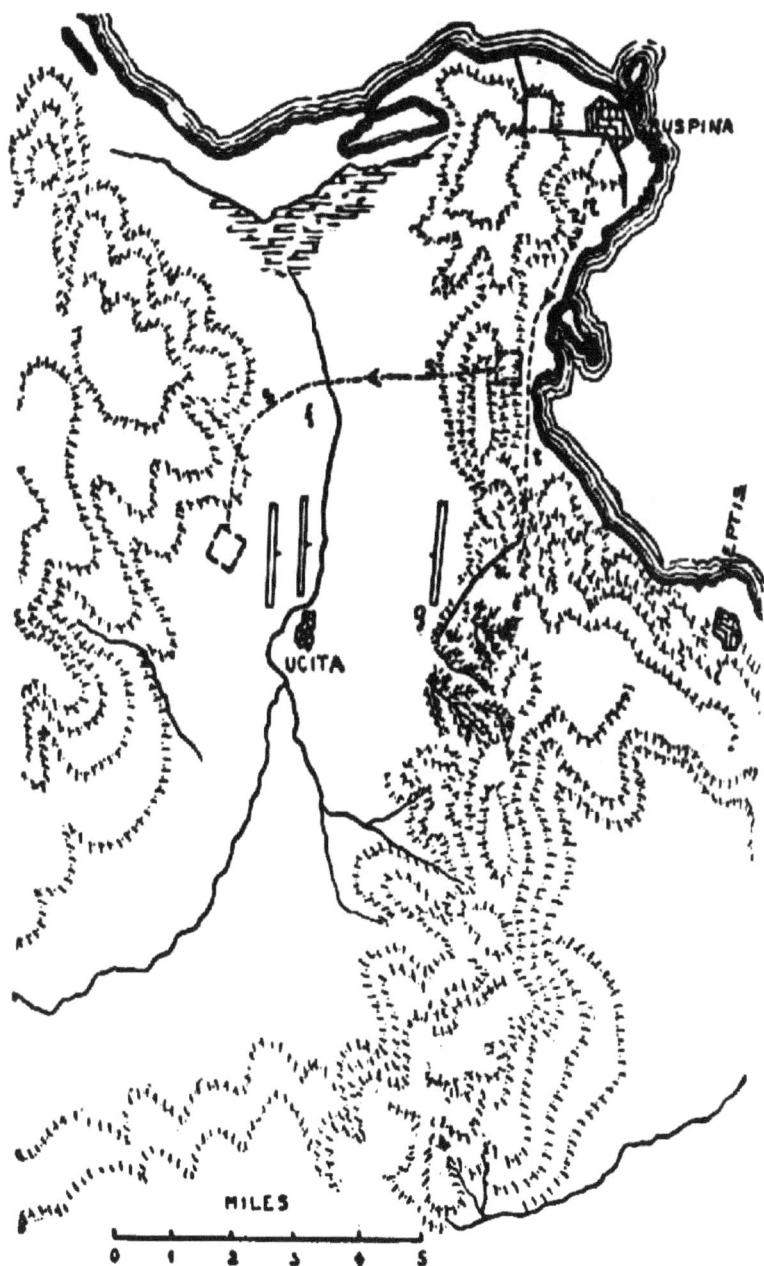

UCITA PLAIN

Here Caesar began to fortify the most available line "along the middle of the ridge, from the place at which he was arrived to that whence he set out;" that is, he threw up works (u) crowning the slope of the hills and facing substantially west. He was so placed as to prevent the enemy from cutting him off from Ruspina.

The "mountains" Caesar refers to in all these operations in the triangular theatre of Hadrumetum, Thysdra, Thapsus, do not exist today, and from very evident geological conditions never did exist. There has been no change of topography since Caesar's day. The highest point in this theatre is six hundred feet; the highest point on which operations were conducted is half that height. The ridge Caesar occupied is less than one hundred and fifty feet above the Ucita valley. Where Caesar drew his lines is half way down the ridge, which here is cut up by ravines and is very stony. To read the *Commentaries* without knowledge of the topography is very misleading.

When dawn came on, Scipio and Labienus became aware of Caesar's operations. Scipio's new camp was to the west of the valley, and Labienus appears to have had a supplementary camp near Ucita, between that town and the hills. The Pompeians at once determined to intercept the work. They advanced their troops in two lines, the cavalry in front about a mile from their camp opposite Ruspina, the infantry one half mile in its rear. Scipio imagined that Caesar's men would be exhausted by the night's work, and would fall an easy prey to an attack. When Caesar saw that they had come within fifteen hundred paces,—a mile and a half,—a distance too small for him safely to continue his work on the entrenchments, he ordered some of his Spanish cavalry and archers to attack the party of Numidian cavalry which held a post on a hill near his own left, but on the enemy's right. This was done in good form and the Numidians were quickly driven off. Seeing this, Labienus led all his horse from the right wing of his advance line to the assistance of this retiring force. So soon as this last detachment was separated from the main army of Scipio, Caesar threw forward his own left wing to intercept them, and advanced a body of cavalry to the right.

In the plain east of Ucita was a large villa and grounds (v) which lay west of the hills where the cavalry skirmish had just taken place. These grounds happened to hide from Labienus the view of the movement of Caesar's cavalry. Under cover of this obstacle Caesar's horse advanced, and when Labienus had passed beyond the villa, presenting to it his naked left, it wheeled round upon his flank and rear, and charged

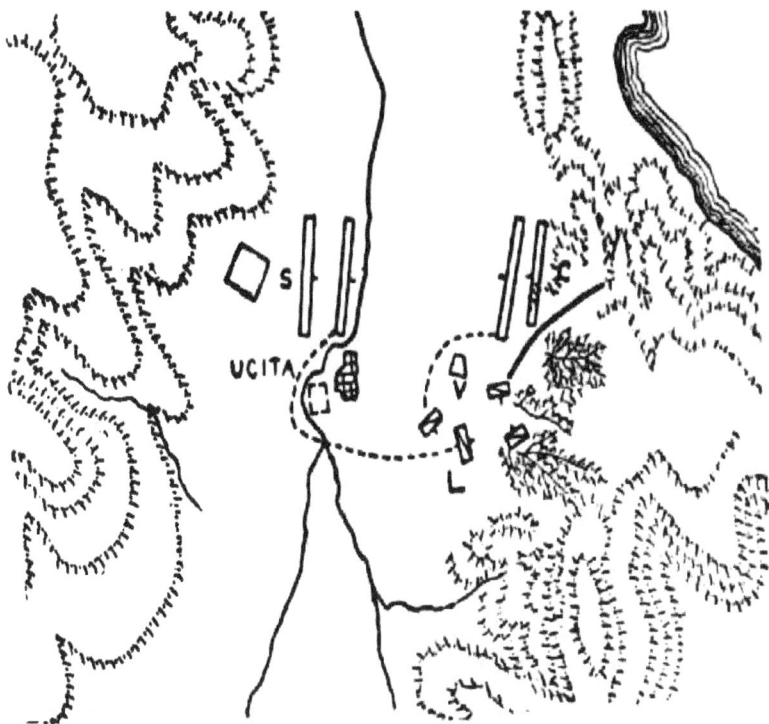

home with a will. The astonished Numidians at once broke and fled; but a body of Gallic and German cavalry which Labienus had induced to accompany him from Gaul, having stood their ground, Caesar's men fell upon this detachment, surrounded and cut it up. The sight of this defeat so demoralized Scipio's legions that they could not be held in hand, but retired in disorder from the plain and even the hills. His loss had been very large. 'Caesar did not pursue, but retired to his lines and again set to work to complete his entrenchments.

This was an auspicious beginning. Caesar had gained possession of a foothold in the plain and a marked moral advantage over Scipio. About December 4 he moved his entire army, except the Ruspina garrison, into the new entrenchments, which completely covered Ruspina and practically Leptis.

Next day Caesar marched out from the new lines, drew up and of-fered battle. He was anxious to see what Scipio would do. He had gained a strong point the day before and wanted to assert it for the influence on his young troops. But the Pompeian, discouraged by his defeat, declined the offer. Caesar marched along the foot of the hills to within a mile of

Ucita, hoping he might take it by a *coup de main*; for not only had Scipio accumulated great stores in the town, but here, too, were the wells from which he drew the bulk of his supply; and good water was so scarce along the coast that it was for this he had left his old camp.

Perceiving Caesar's movement, Scipio, fearing to lose the place, at once marched out with his entire army to its defence, and drew up in four deep lines, "the first of cavalry, supported by elephants with castles on their backs." His depth made it impossible for him to outflank Caesar. Caesar stopped and waited for Scipio's advance. The latter, however, keeping Ucita as if it were a fieldwork in his centre, merely advanced his two wings on either side of the town, and remained in line. He had none too great confidence in his troops. Caesar did not see a good chance of attacking both the town and the army on either side of it at the same time, and as it was now sunset and his men had fasted since morning, he withdrew to the entrenchments. But one good result of the last few days' manoeuvring by Caesar was to

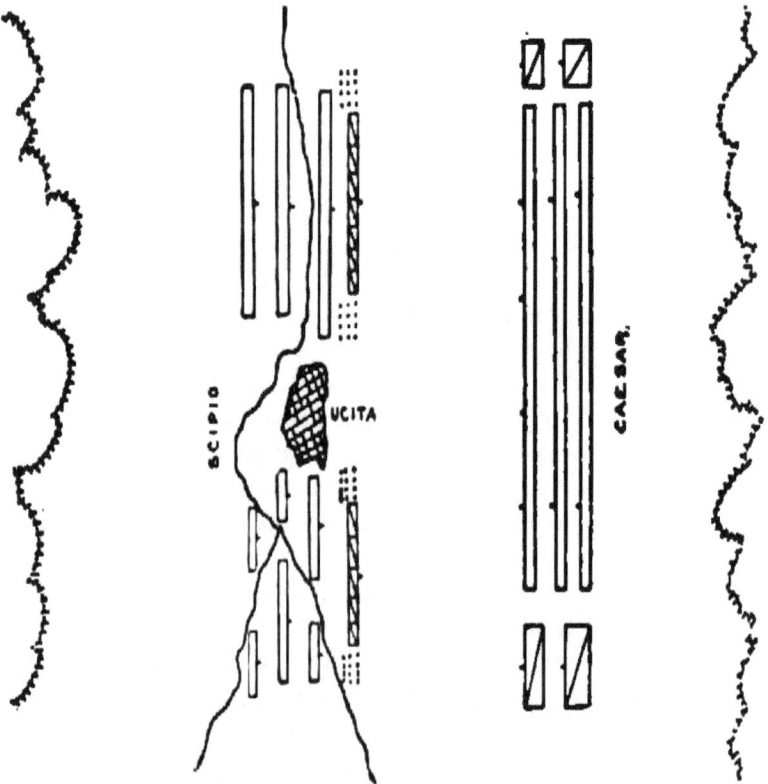

LINES OF BATTLE AT UCITA

222

constrain Considius to abandon the siege of Acilla, ably defended by Messius, from which he retired with some loss to Hadrumetum by a long circuit "through the kingdom of Juba."

Nothing exhibits the fidelity of Caesar's soldiers better than the capture about this time of one of his transports and a galley with some legionaries on board. These men were sent to Scipio, who offered them freedom and rewards if they would join his banner. Among them was a centurion of the Fourteenth legion. He answered Scipio's promises by a firm refusal to serve against Caesar. He told the Pompeian that he quite underrated Caesar's soldiers, and in proof challenged him to pick out the best *cohort* in his army and give him but ten of his comrades, and he would agree to destroy the *cohort* in open fight. The penalty of this faithful boldness was the death of all these veterans. Incensed at the capture of this transport, Caesar broke the officers whose duty it was to patrol the coast to protect the landing of his vessels.

Caesar's forces on this campaign, as already stated, were unprovided with baggage. So strict had he been in prescribing light order that even officers had been forbidden to take slaves or camp-kit. Moreover, he shifted his ground every few days, and thus prevented the men from thoroughly housing themselves from the weather, as they would have done if put into winter-quarters. They were reduced to making huts of brush, and to employing clothing or mats or rushes as tent covering. One severe hailstorm is mentioned in the *Commentaries*, as occurring early in December, which destroyed all the huts, put out the fires, soaked the rations, laid the whole camp under water, and obliged the soldiers to wander about with their bucklers over their heads to protect themselves from the hailstones. It reminds one of the great storm which came so near demoralizing the *phalanx* of Alexander in the Hindoo Koosh.

Despite his numbers, Scipio felt that he was weak, and he earnestly urged King Juba to join him. The latter, well aware that he ran greater danger from Caesar's winning in Africa than from any efforts of Sitius, left Sabura with part of the army to protect his territory against this partisan chief and King Bogud, and started with three legions, eight hundred regular and much Numidian horse, thirty elephants and a vast number of light troops towards the Pompeian camp. His arrival had been heralded with loud boasts which produced a certain uneasiness in Caesar's camp, where daily deserters spread all the rumours of Scipio's. But when, about December 20, Juba actually arrived, the legionaries, after a glimpse at his undisciplined rabble, saw that they

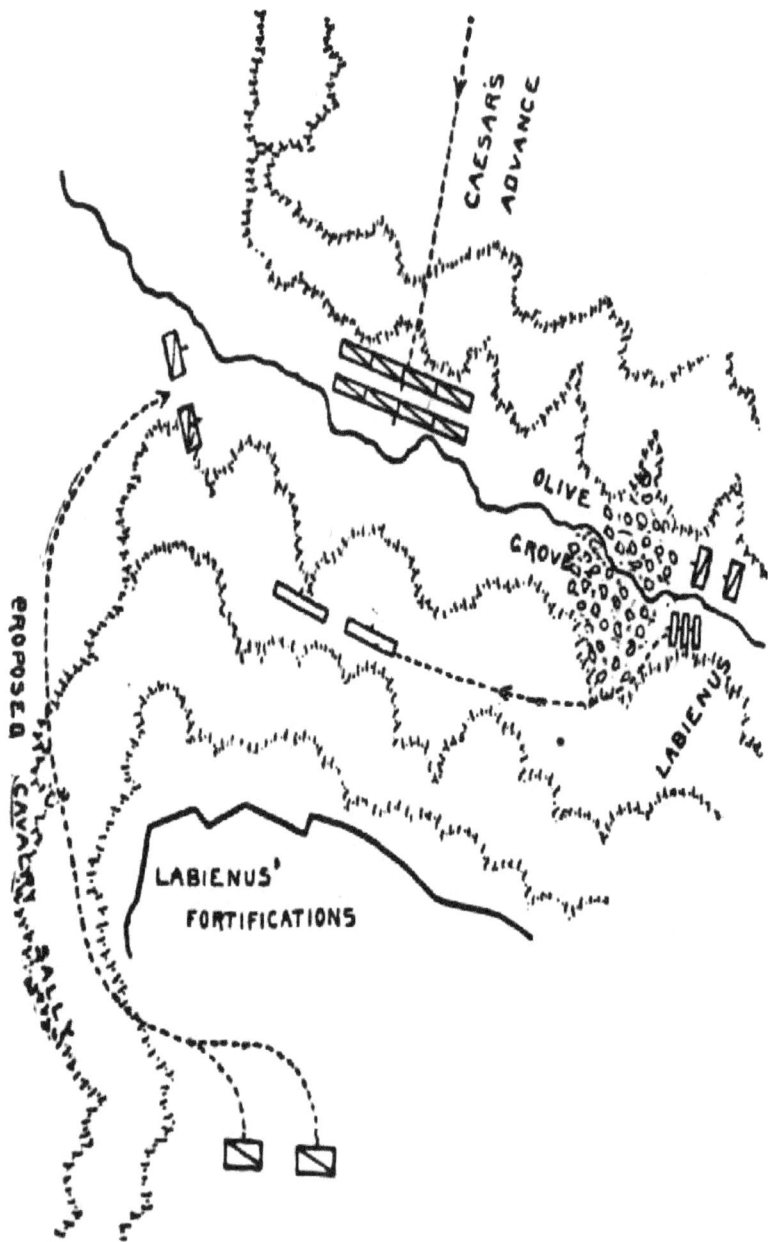

CAESAR'S ADVANCE

OLIVE

GROVE

LABIENUS

PROPOSED CAVALRY SALLY

LABIENUS' FORTIFICATIONS

Ravine fight

might despise his numbers. Scipio, however, celebrated this reinforcement by drawing up in line with the entire joint forces and ostentatiously offering battle to Caesar. The only response of the latter was a quiet advancement of his lines along the ridge towards the south. Juba camped north of Scipio (j).

Scipio had now received all the reinforcements he could expect and Caesar believed that he could be brought to battle. He had camped opposite Ucita, between two ravines, each of which protected a flank. He "began to advance along the ridge with his forces, secure them with redoubts, and possess himself of the hills between him and Scipio," who still had outposts on the east slope of the valley, south of Caesar. The latter could gain marked advantages by obtaining possession of this entire range of hills. He would be rid of the cavalry outposts of the enemy which interfered with his watering parties. He would secure his left flank in case he desired to advance against the enemy. He could seriously impede the enemy's offensive movements, and perhaps, out of some of the minor encounters, develop a general engagement under favourable conditions. This advance of Caesar's lines Labienus sought to arrest by fortifying one of the hills beyond Caesar's left (h). To reach this hill Caesar had a rugged, rocky valley to pass, at the bottom of which was a thick grove of old olives. Here Labienus, anticipating Caesar's manoeuvre, about December 24 placed himself, with some horse and foot, in an ambuscade under cover of the grove, which lay well to the rear of the valley, and sent a body of cavalry to lie in hiding south of the fortified hill so as to be able to debouch on Caesar's rear if he advanced so far as to attack it. Unaware of either ambush, Caesar sent forward his cavalry, but Labienus' foot soldiers, fearing to encounter Caesar's horsemen in the plain, began too soon to break out of cover in the olive wood in order to oppose them on the south bank of the ravine, where they had the advantage of height. This utterly upset Labienus' stratagem. Caesar's horse easily dispersed this body of infantry in its scattered formation; the cavalry ambuscade also went wrong, and Labienus barely made good his own escape. This retreat having drawn from hiding the whole of Labienus' party, the Caesarians captured the hill beyond as they had set out to do, and there Caesar at once threw up a work and garrisoned it strongly. His camp was now inexpugnable.

Caesar made up his mind to capture Ucita, a town which "stood between him and the enemy, and was garrisoned by a detachment of Scipio's army." But Scipio, with his numbers, was able to protect the town by such a long line of battle, that Caesar's flanks would be exposed in advancing on Ucita across the plain. This led him to undertake another of those remarkable feats of field fortification for which the time was noted, and in which he especially excelled and carried out in all his campaigns. It is curious to see how Caesar, who was capable of doing such hazardous things as to come to Africa with a mere handful of men, would resort to such hypercautious means of accomplishing an object, when his strength was greater, if properly gauged by quality, than the enemy's. We are not able to weigh all the existing conditions; we do not know them. But taking the *Commentaries* as the basis of our information, we are as much surprised at Caesar's caution here as we were at his boldness in the operations at Dyrrachium. Still, we understand the situation fairly well; the topography and facts are before us, and we can only ascribe Caesar's caution either to mood or to distrust of his newly raised legions. To give orders for a battle is as often a matter of inspiration as of calculation and preparation. Here Caesar had an easier task than at Pharsalus, in luring Scipio into battle on the Ucita plain; and Scipio's troops were no better than his own. In Alexander there was but one mood: "*de l'audace, encore de l'audace, toujours de l'audace!*" In Hannibal's caution, when we know the facts, there is always a consistent reason and one which appeals to us. Caesar's caution we are often put to it to explain. It was not perhaps so much the capture of Ucita at which Caesar was aiming, as the chance in some manner of placing Scipio at a disadvantage so as to lead up to his defeat in a decisive engagement,—without too much risk.

To carry out his plan, about December 26 Caesar began to throw out westward two parallel lines of works, facing north and south, from his camp at the foot of the slope across the plain in such a direction as to strike the outer corners of the town of Ucita. This, say the *Commentaries*, he did so that he might have his flanks amply protected from the enemy's vast force of cavalry in case he should besiege or assault the town; or, indeed, from any attempt by Labienus to outflank him. The proximity of these works facilitated desertion from the enemy to Caesar. Within these lines he could sink wells, the plain being low, and he was in want of water at his camp upon the hills, and had to send to a distance for it.

The prosecution of the work was protected by a body of horse backed by some *cohorts*, which fended off the Numidian cavalry and archers. The entrenchment was begun after dark, and was so far completed on two successive nights as to be occupied by the troops before

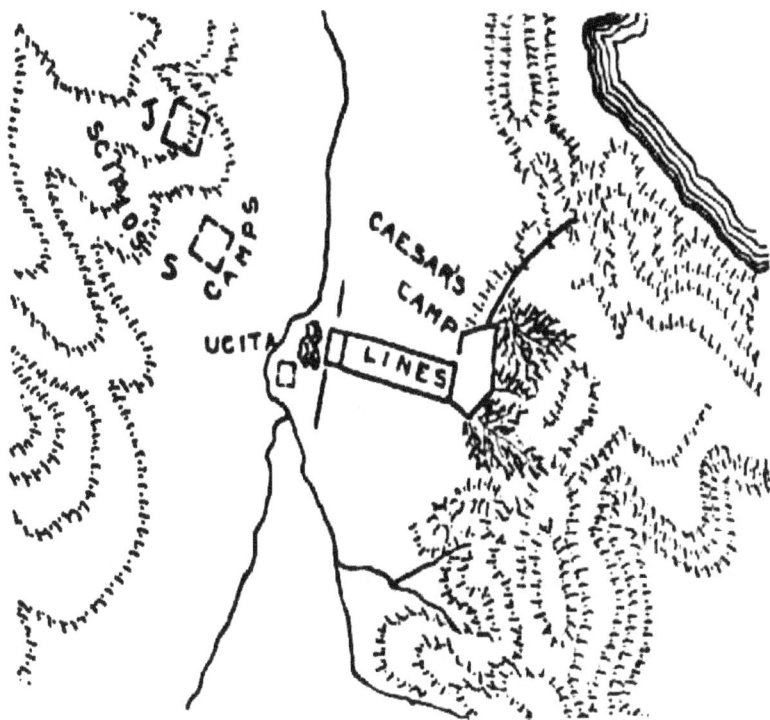

UCITA LINES

the succeeding morning. During this work his men held frequent
intercourse with the enemy's soldiers,—as, indeed, at all times when
they could safely approach each other,—the result of which was almost invariably desertion to Caesar. But of desertions from Caesar
there may be said to have been none. The *Commentaries* at least acknowledge, no desertions, and their number was in any event small. A
number of cavalry exchanges took place, in the majority of which the
troops of Caesar had the upper hand. Scipio's horse was much more
numerous, but far from being as well drilled or steady. Nor had it that
instinct which enables cavalry under a born leader to accomplish the
wonders it sometimes does.

One day towards evening,—it may have been December 29,—as
Caesar was drawing off the fatigue parties, Juba, Labienus and Scipio,
at the head of all their horse and light troops, fell upon the cavalry
outposts and drove them in. But Caesar quickly collected a few *cohorts*
of legionaries, who always had their arms at hand, and leading them
up to the assistance of the horse, re-established the combat. Seeing
themselves well supported, the cavalry turned with a brilliant charge

upon the Numidians, who were scattered over the plain by the pursuit they had just undertaken, slew a large number, and hustled the rest into rapid flight. Juba and Labienus barely escaped capture under cover of the dust. The result of this handsome interchange was that still more numerous deserters from the Fourth and Sixth legions came over to Caesar, as well as a large number of Curio's horse.

Gaetulia, roused by the leading citizens whom Caesar had sent back to their homes for this purpose, now revolted from King Juba. This monarch, with three wars at once on his hands, was constrained to detach a considerable part of his force to protect his own borders. But he himself remained in the Pompeian camp with the remainder and made himself obnoxious by his insolence, meddling and vanity.

The Ninth and Tenth legions, on the last day of the year, arrived from Sicily, after a narrow escape from capture as the result of their own imprudence. The relics of their old spirit of mutiny were still evident in their undisciplined conduct. One of the military tribunes, C. Avienus, had gone so far as to fill one transport exclusively with his own slaves and camp-equipage. The legions had too long been on easy duty near Rome. In order to bring these men under curb, Caesar resorted to sharp and decisive measures, and took the case of Avienus as a pretext. He broke this and one other tribune and several centurions, and sent them out of Africa under guard. Among the Romans, to be cashiered was all but the heaviest penalty which could be inflicted. It was a deprivation of all the culprit's civil rights, honour and character. The *cohorts* of the Ninth and Tenth were put into the trenches, with no more equipage or rations than the other men.

Counting in the new arrivals, Caesar's heavy infantry force of five veteran and five new legions was nearly if not quite equal to Scipio's. The latter had more light troops, but these were practically worthless in battle. Caesar still looked for two more legions from Sicily, and Juba, having been obliged to send away part of his army, depleted Scipio's numbers. The new year opened with Caesar's chances fully equal to those of the enemy.

CHAPTER 40

Ucita

January, 46 B. C.

Though Caesar's lines had reached Ucita, he still waited for more of his troops. These shortly arrived, though barely escaping capture. Each of the commanders daily drew up for battle, but neither attacked; and meanwhile further fortifying was their only activity. It had become difficult for Caesar to victual his army. In foraging he was often reduced to fighting his way to and fro. Finally, between lack of corn and lack of a chance of battle on favourable terms, Caesar gave up his designs on Ucita, and moved down the coast to near Leptis. His entrenchments had been made for naught. To all appearances Scipio had won the game. In a bold raid on Zeta, in which he ran an exceptional risk to procure victual, Caesar had a brisk combat with the enemy; but nothing decisive came of it. He was still aiming to get a certain chance to thrust home. Scipio neither gave him an opening nor improved his advantages. Finally Caesar determined upon a siege of Thapsus as a means of compelling Scipio to battle, and marched thither, reducing several towns on his way.

In the early days of January, 46 B. C, having finished his works up to a point just beyond dart-throwing distance from Ucita, Caesar built a line across the head of the works, mounted on the parapet and towers a number of military engines, and constantly plied these against the town. He brought five legions to the west end of the lines from the large camp at the east. The lines were almost two miles long. It speaks well for Caesar's activity, skill and care that he was able to build and man such extensive works without affording an opportunity to Scipio to break through at any one point while incomplete. But Caesar was the ablest engineer of his age, almost of any age.

When the lines were finished he was secure. It was generally deemed impossible to capture well-manned entrenchments, and Scipio was not the man to try. We have seen how reluctant Caesar was to attempt such an assault, even when the defenders were savages. The successful completion of the lines produced other desertions of men of decided consequence to Caesar's camp, and at the same time furnished him with one thousand more horse. Scipio, meanwhile, was not idle. He also undertook to fortify all available and useful points on his own front, and prepared for a vigorous and stout defence when Caesar should attack Ucita.

The Seventh and Eighth legions now sailed from Sicily, and Varus at Utica thought there was a promising opportunity to intercept them. He weighed anchor with fifty-five vessels for this purpose and sailed to Hadrumetum. Caesar had sent twenty-seven sail, under L. Cispius, to Thapsus, and thirteen sail under Q. Aquila to Hadrumetum with orders to anchor, watch for, and protect the convoys. Aquila's part of the fleet being unable to double the cape, they took shelter in an inlet nearby. The mistral, or west wind on the Mediterranean, has always been a fruitful source of annoyance. Today, large steamers often cannot land passengers at either Sousa (Hadrumetum) or Monastir (Thapsus). The balance of the fleet at Leptis was left riding at anchor; but the mariners were mostly ashore, some buying provisions, some wandering about,—a matter indicating poor discipline. A deserter notified Varus of these facts. He left Hadrumetum at night,—the mistral blew in his favour,—and next morning, January 9, reaching Leptis, came suddenly upon Caesar's fleet in the same unprotected condition, burned all the transports, and carried off two five-benched galleys, "in which were none to defend them."

Caesar heard of this misfortune while engaged inspecting his works at Ucita. Roused at the prospect of losing his men and victuals, he summarily took horse and rode to Leptis, happily only six miles distant, went aboard the most available galley, ordered his fleet to follow, joined Aquila, whom he found much demoralized in his retreat, pursued Varus, who, astonished, tacked about and made for Hadrumetum, recovered one of his galleys with one hundred and thirty of the enemy aboard, took one of the enemy's *triremes*, which had fallen astern, and drove Varus into Hadrumetum. Caesar could not double the cape with the same wind, which suddenly shifted; but, riding at anchor during the night, on the next day, when the east wind sprang up, he sailed near the harbour of Hadrumetum and burned a number of the enemy's transports lying outside. Aboard the captured galley was P. Vestrius, a

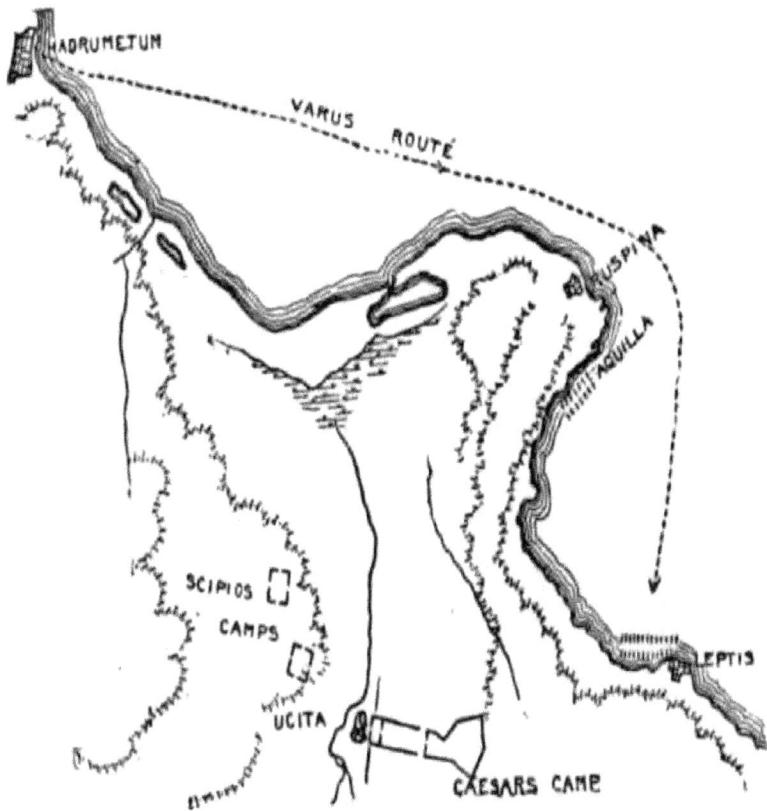

CAESAR AND VARUS

Roman knight, who had been in Spain under Afranius, and after being paroled, had again joined Pompey in Greece, and later Varus, without exchange or ransom. Him Caesar ordered to be executed for breach of his oath. This fact shows that the paroling of prisoners was well understood, with at least some of its rights and liabilities.

This short expedition of Caesar's exhibits the marvellous audacity, decision and skill of the man. Everything he undertook in person was carried through with an active intelligence which insured success. Whomever he attacked he was sure to defeat. Had he not done just this and done it in person, probably his transports, his fleets, his corn, his enginery, his legions would all have been liable to be cut off. Some of these minor expeditions of Caesar show that if he had not been a great general, he would have made the very pattern of a partisan officer. All the more wonder that occasionally, as now before Ucita, Caesar was almost a McClellan for his want of incisiveness.

231

Each commander now essayed to bring the other to battle on advantageous terms. Scipio, on a day shortly after the completion of Caesar's lines,—January 7,—marshalled his army on a slight elevation running along the west bank of the brook which bisected the plain. Caesar did the like on a parallel rise in the ground, but awaited the attack. On the floor of this valley can now be seen but slight indications of these eminences. It is nearly level. But a very little slope in the ground was of marked advantage to the Roman soldier, and the *Commentaries* often speak of hills which we should scarcely notice.

The enemy exceeded Caesar in numbers; they had a strong garrison in Ucita opposite his right wing, so that if he defeated them and pursued beyond Ucita he might be compromised by a sally from the town; the ground in front of Scipio was rough and thoroughly bad for

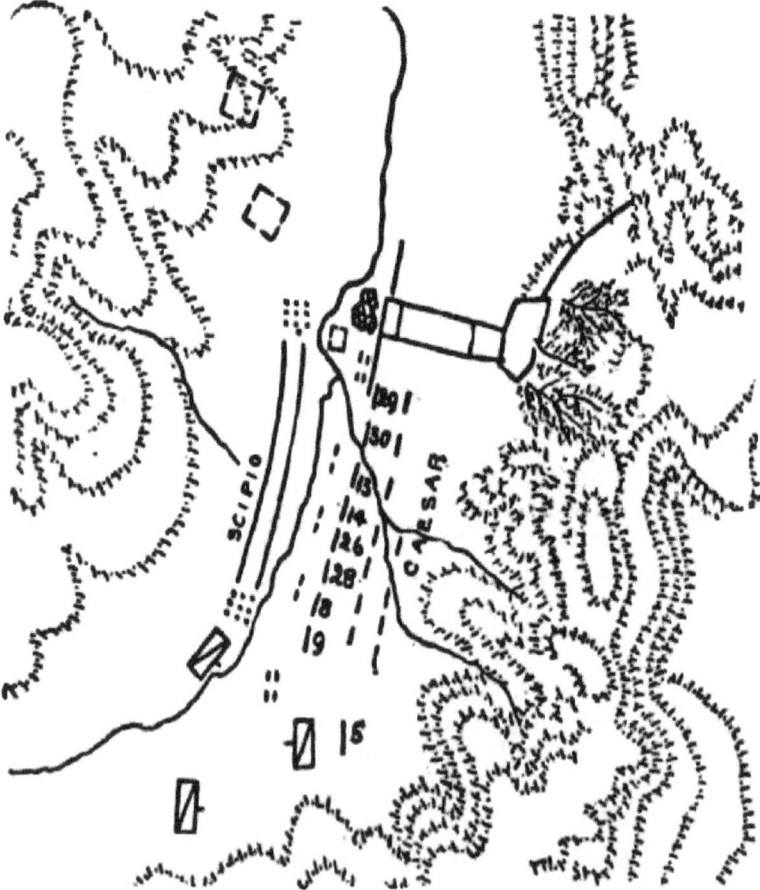

IN LINE OF BATTLE

a charge. The valley in places is very stony. Where the brook had worn its way it was more so; and to attack required Caesar to cross the brook. The two armies were marshalled within three hundred paces of each other. Nothing divided them but this slight depression in the ground. Scipio's left leaned on the town, which was an advanced redoubt, as it were, affording it ample protection. His own and Juba's legions were in the front, the Numidians in a second line in reserve, but in an extended thin formation. "At a distance you would have taken the main body for a simple line of *legionaries* doubled only on the wings." On the right and left at equal distances Scipio placed elephants supported by light troops and auxiliary Numidians. The regular cavalry was on the right in one body, not being needed or available near Ucita. The Numidian and Gaetulian horse,—irregulars, "without bridles,"—sustained by a great body of light troops, formed a flying right wing one thousand paces from his right extending out towards the hills. Scipio's intention was to envelop Caesar's left with all his cavalry and "throw it into confusion by their darts," when the action should begin.

In Caesar's front line the Eighth and Ninth veteran legions were on the left, today the post of danger; the Thirteenth and Fourteenth, Twenty-sixth and Twenty-eighth, in the centre; the Twenty-ninth and Thirtieth on the right, leaning on the Ucita works. His second line was composed of the new levies, mixed with *cohorts* from the legions above named. His third line, composed of the third-line *cohorts* of the right legions, withdrawn for the purpose and replaced by some new *cohorts*, extended only from the centre of the line to the left, as the right was so strongly posted at the entrenchments opposite Ucita as to need no reserve. His right wing was thus in two, his left in three lines. All his cavalry stood on his left, opposite the enemy's, mixed with light foot; and because he put no great reliance on these, the Fifth legion was placed in reserve in their rear. The archers were principally on the wings, but bodies of them stood in the front.

The two armies thus drawn up remained in line all day, but three hundred paces apart, neither party willing to advance across the low ground,—a most unusual spectacle. It strikes one as curious, indeed, that Caesar, who was so prompt in his attack at Pharsalus, where he had but half Pompey's force, and where excellent Roman legions under an able leader confronted him, should have been so slow at opening the battle here, when he was about on a par with his antagonists, a large part of whose troops were far from good either in quality or discipline. This is especially so as Pompey had recently beaten him at

Dyrrachium, and in any event was far superior to Scipio in ability. Fighting a battle is, with any commanding general, often a matter of temporary vigour or lack of it, and Caesar's indecision on this occasion may have depended on his state of health. An inspection of the terrain shows that there was nothing in any respect as disadvantageous to Caesar as the hill at Pharsalus. And we seem to have all the details.

The simple fact is that Caesar, in tactical attack, had far inferior initiative than Alexander, or than Hannibal, so long as the latter's conditions gave him anything approaching an equality to the Romans. In almost all Caesar's battles, unless forced on him, he was slow in attack. In strategic initiative, on the contrary, Caesar was admirable. It was one constant, never-ceasing push.

At night, when Caesar was retiring to camp, the flying cavalry wing of the enemy moved out towards the works upon the hill. The heavy horse under Labienus remained opposite the legions. Seeing this, part of Caesar's horse and light foot sallied out without orders to attack the Gaetulians, and advancing through a morass, probably made by the brook, but which does not today exist, were driven in with a loss of a number of men and many horses wounded. Scipio, rejoiced at this success, retired to camp. This check was compensated for next day, when a party of Caesar's horse, on their way to Leptis for corn, killed or captured an hundred of the enemy's troops who were straggling from camp.

Both armies now busied themselves with advancing their lines and entrenching new positions opposite each other. Scipio sought to strengthen his holding on the hills back of Ucita. Caesar's especial endeavour was to cut Scipio's right off from the hills on his own left. He therefore "carried a ditch and rampart along the middle of the plain to prevent the incursions of the enemy." This phrase has been translated "*quite across the plain*," but that cannot be explained by anything which the probabilities or later events show us to have been done. There is no evidence that a ditch and rampart were carried across the Ucita plain from east to west; nor was there reason for it. The passage probably means that opposite Ucita Caesar extended the head of his works in a long line north and south,—"along the middle of the plain." Scipio sought to anticipate any attack by Caesar. The cavalry skirmished every day between the two parties.

The inhabitants of Africa, then as now, were wont to keep their corn in little *caches* or underground vaults for safety in time of war. Caesar, who was in constant want of victual, sent out a party of two

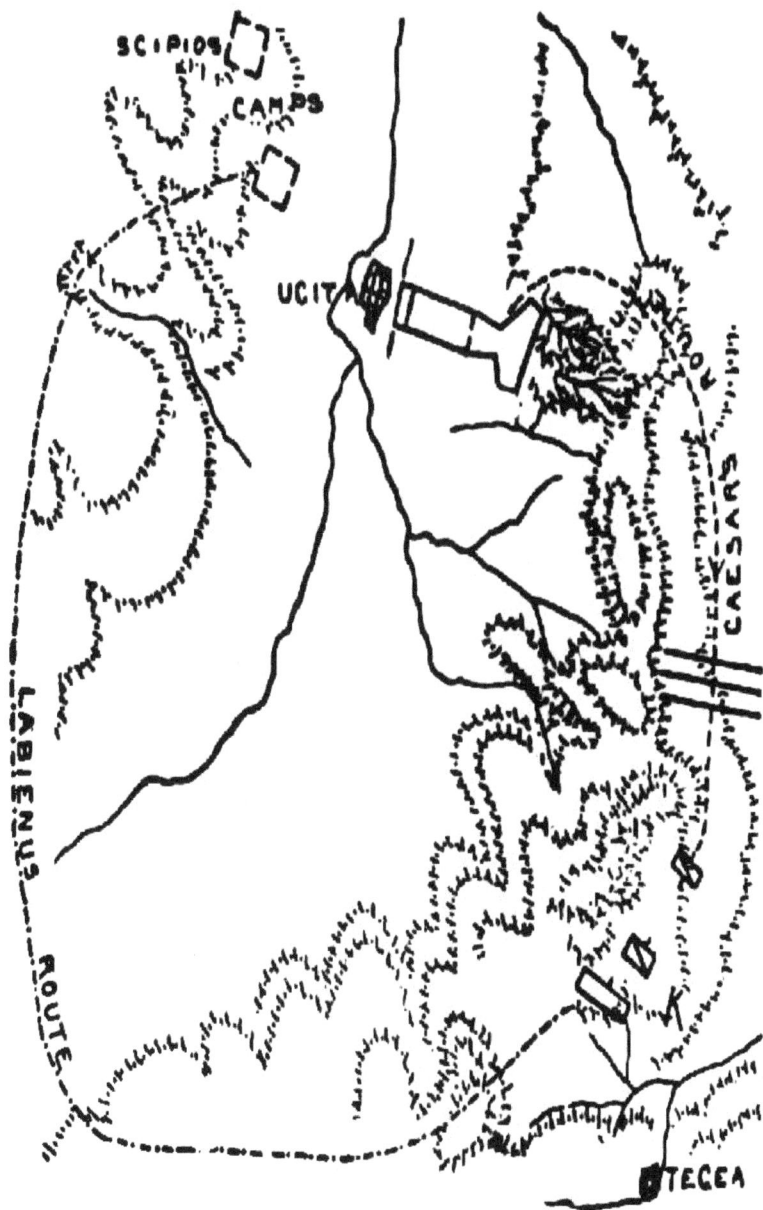

LABIENUS' STRATAGEM

legions and some cavalry one night, which within a radius of ten miles in the fruitful region south of Agar collected a large supply of corn from these hiding-places and returned to camp. Labienus, expecting that Caesar would again pursue the same road for the same purpose, laid an ambuscade for him on January 12 about seven miles from the plain where operations were being conducted. This was presumably in the vicinity of Tegea, where the plain narrows between two lines of hills (k).

Caesar became aware of this stratagem through the medium of deserters. He waited a few days until Labienus' men should become a trifle careless. Sending forward part of his cavalry, he followed with eight legions and the rest of the squadrons. The cavalry came unexpectedly upon Labienus' outposts of light troops, which were taking their ease in their cover and paying small heed to the duty they were sent on, fell on them and broke them up with a loss of five hundred men. Labienus, nearby, hurried up to their assistance with his own horse, and, by weight of numbers, had routed Caesar's cavalry, when he suddenly ran against Caesar's line of legions, which compelled him to beat a summary retreat to the west. His ambuscade had been a failure. Juba crucified all the Numidian runaways as an example.

Caesar, despite all his efforts, was unable to collect the corn he needed to feed his men. He was reduced either to shift his ground or else to make an attack on Scipio in his defences. On estimating the chances, Caesar deemed the risk of the assault greater than the possible loss of morale incident to a change of base and the abandonment of the position gained by so much exertion and sacrifice. Besides, he knew how easy it was to him to persuade his army that they retired with honour, and the labour had really been useful in hardening the legions.

The whole matter is somewhat puzzling. Caesar must have long ago foreseen that his supplies would be precarious. He had gone to incredible exertions to create works from which he could fight a battle with Scipio to advantage. The army opposing him was by no means as good and scarcely larger than his own. He had pushed his manoeuvring at Ilerda; he had boldly attacked Pompey at Pharsalus, who had a superiority much more marked; here he declined the combat. It is unlike the Caesar we are apt to believe in; and yet not unlike the real Caesar. The best explanation lies in the probability that his entrenchments had been made in the hope that he could lure Scipio out into the open and there defeat him; that Scipio had erected excellent works and that Caesar did not

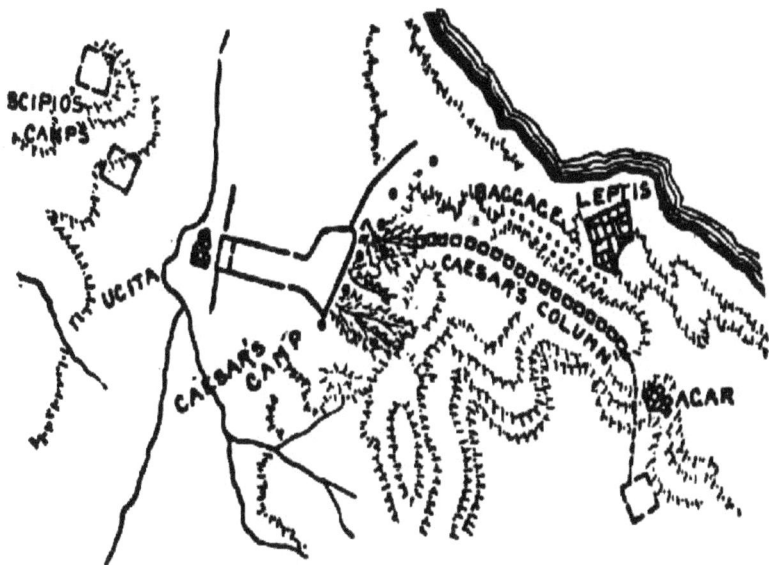

MARCH TO AGAR

care for an assault. We must remember, too, that Caesar did not
have the same splendid body of men he had trained in the wars in
Gaul and which he still commanded at Pharsalus, though relatively
he was now better placed than then. The lack of initiative looks
much like that of Napoleon in his later years. Was Caesar tiring of
war? Or was war sapping Caesar's energies?

Leaving the garrisons at Leptis, Ruspina and Acilla, which were
all strongly fortified, Caesar ordered his fleet under Cispius and Aquila to blockade Hadrumetum and Thapsus and narrowly watch the
coast to forestall attack on coming transports during his movements,
set fire to his camp at Ucita, and started, January 14, before daylight,
in column left in front and with baggage-train between his column
and the sea, and marched easterly along the coast between the hills
and the shore to Agar, a town near Leptis, on the southerly slope
of the first line of small coast-hills. He was thus basing on Leptis
rather than on Ruspina. He camped in the plain before Agar (i). In
the neighbourhood he found a large supply of barley, oil, wine and
figs, with some wheat. Scipio did not attempt to disturb the retreat,
or even send his horse in pursuit; but soon followed along the hills,
and, reaching the vicinity, camped a few miles away and farther from
the sea (1). His evident purpose was to shut Caesar out from getting
corn in the interior. His force lay in three camps about six miles
from Caesar's on the heights which stood back of the town of Te-

237

gea (l m n). The Numidian cavalry was posted on all advantageous heights, to head off foragers from Caesar's camp. But, for all their care, Caesar was able to collect a fair supply of victual, by sending out large bodies on this duty.

It is evident, not only from the *Commentaries*, but from the circumstances narrated, that Caesar was very close-pressed for rations; for, in order to fill his depleted magazines, he now undertook one of the most hazardous operations of all his campaigns. The town of Zeta (modern Bourdjine) in rear of the enemy was ten miles from Scipio's camp, some seventeen from Caesar's. Deeming it secure beyond a peradventure, Scipio had made it a great magazine of corn and had sent two legions to those parts to forage and protect the corn collected. Of this fact Caesar had notice by a deserter. He made up his mind to try a raid on Zeta. To accomplish his purpose he was forced to make a flank march past Scipio's camps and to return by the same or an equally perilous road. Only famine staring him in the face, and the fact that supplies could not be got in sufficient quantity in the region to the south of Thapsus, explain the risk he took. He established his men in a new camp on a hill east of Agar (o) for greater security to the comparatively small number he was to leave

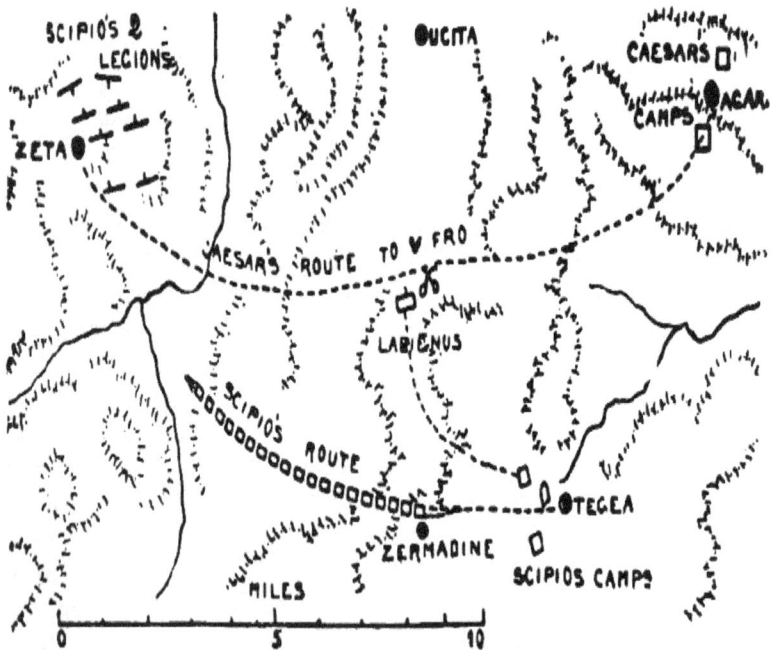

ZETA RAID

behind in it, broke up January 17 at three o'clock a. m., with his entire cavalry force and a large body of foot, passed around Scipio's camp unobserved, reached and took the town of Zeta out of hand, with a number of prominent Pompeians, loaded an enormous train, including twenty-two camels, with breadstuffs, and put a garrison under Oppius in the place, with instructions to shift for itself as best it might. Not content with this success, he moved on to attack the two foraging legions; but, on reaching their vicinity, Caesar found that Scipio had learned of his diversion, and had marched to their support with his whole army. He wisely desisted from attack and began to retire with his booty.

Caesar was obliged to pass nearby Scipio's camp on the way back to his own. Here a heavy force of Numidian horse and light troops under Labienus and Afranius had been placed by Scipio in ambush for him among the neighbouring hills about modern Djemmal. Just after he had got beyond them they sallied out and attacked his rear. So far, Caesar had had extraordinarily good luck, but this diversion threatened trouble. He at once faced his *cohorts* towards the enemy, and, moving the baggage to their rear, he threw his cavalry out in their front, and prepared to defend his rear-ward march. No sooner did Caesar's cavalry, sustained by the legions, fall boldly upon the enemy than the troops of Labienus and Afranius turned and fled; but when Caesar resumed his march they renewed the attack. These Numidians were wonderfully active and expert at their own method of fighting. They so effectually harassed Caesar in his effort to retire that he "found he had not gained a hundred paces in four hours." Moreover, he lost many horses, which he could ill afford to spare. The enemy's purpose was to force him to camp in that place, where there was no water; and Caesar's men had had nothing to eat from their start at three a. m. till now, about three of the afternoon. Finally his cavalry grew so exhausted with its efforts that he was compelled to send it on ahead and make his rearguard of infantry, which could better impose upon the Numidians. The legionaries, though the ground was not much cut up, were really more fitted for rearguard than the tired horsemen. The baggage was hurried on ahead. Caesar was thus able to advance, though with extreme slowness. For, if only a handful of the *legionaries* faced about and flung their darts, thousands of the Numidian light troops or cavalry would fly; but so soon as the march was resumed, these warriors again approached and showered darts, stones and arrows upon the rear of column.

Some of these worked their way around to the flanks and van of Caesar's column, and gave him the greatest trouble. Labienus and Afranius made an effort to inclose Caesar's army by marching round his wings and through the hills to head him off, but unsuccessfully. Caesar preserved his formation, which may have been the square usual in such cases, in unbroken order. "Thus Caesar, at one time moving forward, at another halting, going on but slowly, reached the camp safe," about seven in the evening, a total march of over thirty-six miles, with a loss of only ten men wounded.

To judge from the description in the *Commentaries* one would have gauged the loss an hundred-fold this sum. It is not improbable that the number is erroneously given by the historian. Labienus, he says, had thoroughly tired out his troops and lost three hundred men, beside the wounded. The disparity in numbers is incompatible with the description of the raid. Caesar was in a position to lose the larger number.

The distance marched in sixteen hours seems incredible. Assuming that the capture of Zeta, the loading of the train and the diversion against Scipio's two legions consumed but two hours, we have a large army, harassed by the enemy part of the way back, and delayed four hours by fighting, making a march of thirty-six miles in the remaining ten hours. There is probably exaggeration somewhere. Few bodies of foot can cover three and one half miles an hour except for a short stretch. Still, that the march was made from shortly before day to some evening hour is scarcely to be denied.

This raid exhibits in marked contrast the character and ability of Scipio and Caesar. It is probable that Caesar would not have dared undertake such a movement against an opponent more his equal. Scipio distinctly showed want of power to seize an advantage. Caesar had passed over a range of hills to the plain of Zeta, and must return through the same path to regain camp. What more natural than for Scipio to draw up his forces on suitable slopes and, by disputing his passage, bring him to battle on disadvantageous terms? And during such an engagement, which Caesar would be forced to accept, Scipio had two legions at Zeta which could fall upon his rear. But instead of this simple plan, Scipio, apparently losing his head, marched off to the assistance of the two legions on such an eccentric line that he opened to Caesar the very road of retreat which he should have closed. Nor was Labienus any more skilful. He should have disputed Caesar's passage of the hills by attacking his head of column and not his rear. Instead of so doing he allowed Caesar's column to regain the road to camp, and contented himself with simply attacking his rearguard. It looks a trifle as if Caesar had really sustained something more of a defeat than the Commentaries are willing to acknowledge. But the defeat was not a fatal one. Caesar had a way of extricating himself from desperate straits.

In justification of Caesar's movement on Zeta it may be said that the character of the country is such as to afford more than one route for retreat. The whole surface of the land is covered with carriage and mule roads now, and presumably was so then, when the population was larger and even more intelligent. He could have returned by way of modern Zermadina, Scipio being left at Zeta. He could have moved north along the Ucita plain to his old camp and thence to Agar, for on his left he would have Ruspina, strongly garrisoned by his own troops, as a refuge in case of danger.

Caesar's own luck and the paltry conduct of his foes had again saved him harmless. It is all the more strange that, with such contemptible opponents, this great captain, who was daring enough to undertake expeditions which might compel him to do battle with all the chances against him, should have so long delayed forcing on his enemy a decisive engagement which might terminate the war. For he now had twelve legions, and the difficulties of subsisting them were enough to make him above all desire a definite outlet to the matter. He indeed shortly undertook it in a way he had not before attempted.

While Labienus was fighting Caesar on his retreat, Scipio, after returning from Zeta, had apparently drawn up before his camps, while Caesar was filing by the flank in his front laden with baggage. But on Caesar's approach he withdrew. This lack of force is of a part with Scipio's entire conduct. Caesar had run a grave danger, but at all events his legions had refilled their corn-bags.

Caesar was obliged to instruct his men in new tactics to meet the new conditions thrust upon him. The enemy's light troops were so nimble as seriously to annoy the heavy-armed legionaries in a mere skirmish; and he deemed it wise to bring some elephants from Italy to accustom the troops and horses to their sight, and drilled the men in the best method of attacking them. In Gaul, Caesar's troops had met a frank, courageous enemy who came out and fought hand to hand on the field; here they had to resist the devices of a crafty foe who relied upon artifice, not courage. The *Commentaries* acknowledge that Caesar's horse was no match for the enemy's when sustained by light foot, and frankly confess that Caesar was not certain that his *legionaries* were equal to the enemy's in the open. This again seems inexplicable. We are wont to think that Caesar's raw levies soon became seasoned; Hannibal's did; and we have proof that Scipio's troops were none of them well disciplined.

Caesar constantly marched his troops about the country, not only to drill and harden them, but in hope of compromising Scipio by some manoeuvre and of bringing him to battle against his will. He drew up, three days after the Zeta raid, near Scipio's camp in the open plain south of Agar (p), but this general declined to come out and Caesar did not care to assault his works. As a rule Caesar was fortunate in securing the towns in the vicinity of which he was campaigning. Vacca sent to him for a garrison; but in this case Juba anticipated him, captured and razed the town. Too great fault should not be found with Scipio's apparently inactive method. It was Fabian. Famine was doing the work of many a victory. But it was half indecision, half method, which governed Scipio's movements.

On the 22nd day of January Caesar held a grand review of his army, which now numbered some forty thousand *legionaries*, three thousand horse and some auxiliaries, and on the succeeding day, well satisfied with his legions, marched out to a distance of five miles from his camp and to within two miles of Scipio's camp north of Tegea (q) and offered battle. But again Scipio declined it. Caesar saw that he was wasting his time in trying to lure Scipio into the open by merely offering battle, and as a last resort he planned a series of attacks on Scipio's strong places and *dépôts*, such as Sarsura, Tysdra and Thapsus, to provoke him to activity.

Thapsus was on the coast southeast of Leptis, a large magazine of military stores and a highly important point for Scipio, which he had strongly garrisoned and in whose harbour was a large number of vessels, at present blockaded by Caesar's fleet. But to attack Thapsus was to play the great game for which Caesar was apparently not yet ready. He preferred to raid the smaller towns, not only as being an easier prey, but above all because he needed the corn with which they were well supplied. It is altogether probable that at this moment Caesar's legions were all but starving. He was on a tramp for victual. The strategy of the situation must yield to the logistics.

Caesar broke up from Agar January 23 and marched on Sarsura over the eastern slope of the hill below Tegea. To Sarsura he was followed by Labienus who harassed his rear. Caesar had on this occasion detailed three hundred men from each legion as rearguard. These do not, however, appear to have been able to hold Labienus in check, for this officer was able to cut out some of the train from the rear of column—probably animals which were ready to load in case Caesar could capture Sarsura. In a rearguard engagement which ensued, the Numidians proved overanxious to secure booty and were severely punished by Caesar's troops. They lost a number of men, and thereafter Labienus kept his distance, following along on Caesar's right upon the hills. Arrived at Sarsura, Caesar stormed and took it under the very eyes of Scipio and Labienus, put the garrison to the sword, and found a goodly supply of corn, which he distributed to the soldiers or loaded. Scipio observed him from above, not offering to interfere. Thence Caesar marched next day to Tysdra, which he did not attempt to assault, the place having been very strongly fortified by Considius, a brave and stubborn officer who held it with his *cohort* of gladiators. There was no time, nor even engines, for a siege; and Caesar had already got a fairly good supply of victual.

Caesar started back and camped overnight at the stream which ran midway between Tysdra and Sarsura (r). Thence he made his way to his camp at Agar, January 26, probably by a circuit round the foot of the hills he had marched across. Scipio did the like.

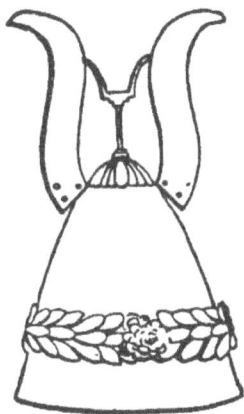

ANCIENT HELMET

CHAPTER 41

Thapsus

February, 47 B. C.

The rest of Caesar's reinforcements having arrived, he was ready, if ever, to try conclusions with Scipio. After some strategic manoeu- vring, Caesar marched on Thapsus, and sat down before it. Scipio and Juba followed, lest they should lose this valuable city. Caesar complet- ed his lines. Scipio essayed to break through these on Caesar's right, failing which, he tried the left, near the sea, and began to entrench a camp near his lines. Caesar drew up for attack, while Scipio was at work, and compelled the latter to do the like. The Caesarians were in high spirits; not so the Pompeians. The former were eager to attack, seeing the indecision of the enemy. Caesar delayed. But the restless Tenth legion, on the right, gave a trumpet blast without orders, and this being repeated down the line, the whole army advanced on the Pompeians. These troops held their own some hours; but victory was finally won, and the ensuing slaughter was terrible. The entire army of Scipio was destroyed; the leaders fled. Caesar had no difficulty in reducing Africa to his sway. The African campaign had been the direct result of Caesar's going to Alexandria with an insufficient force and of the loss of time there encountered; and it was often characterized by a lack of decisiveness unlike Caesar. The victory of Thapsus, "which Caesar prepared, but his men won," rectified all his errors.

About these days Thabena, a town on the seacoast at the confines of King Juba's dominion, rose against its garrison, murdered it, and sent a deputation to Caesar asking for protection, "as they had revolted from Juba's rule and therefore deserved well of the Roman people." Caesar detailed thither the *tribune* M. Crispus with a *cohort*, some arch- ers, and a number of engines of war.

The balance of the legionary soldiers who, by sickness, leaves of absence, or other causes had been detained in Sicily, arrived towards the end of January in one embarkation to the number of four thousand men, and with them four hundred horse and one thousand bowmen and slingers. Having all his forces in hand, Caesar had no further excuse for not forcing Scipio to a decisive battle. Before resorting to the siege of Thapsus, which he had long contemplated, but had been prevented from undertaking on account of the necessity of procuring corn in towns more easily taken, he made one more effort to bring Scipio out on the open, and on the last day of January moved from his camp to a plain—which the *Commentaries* say was eight miles from his own and four from Scipio's, but the distances are actually less than six and two—not far from Tegea (y) and awaited the enemy.

Scipio was not willing to take any chances. The town of Tegea lay below his camp. Its garrison of four hundred horse he drew up

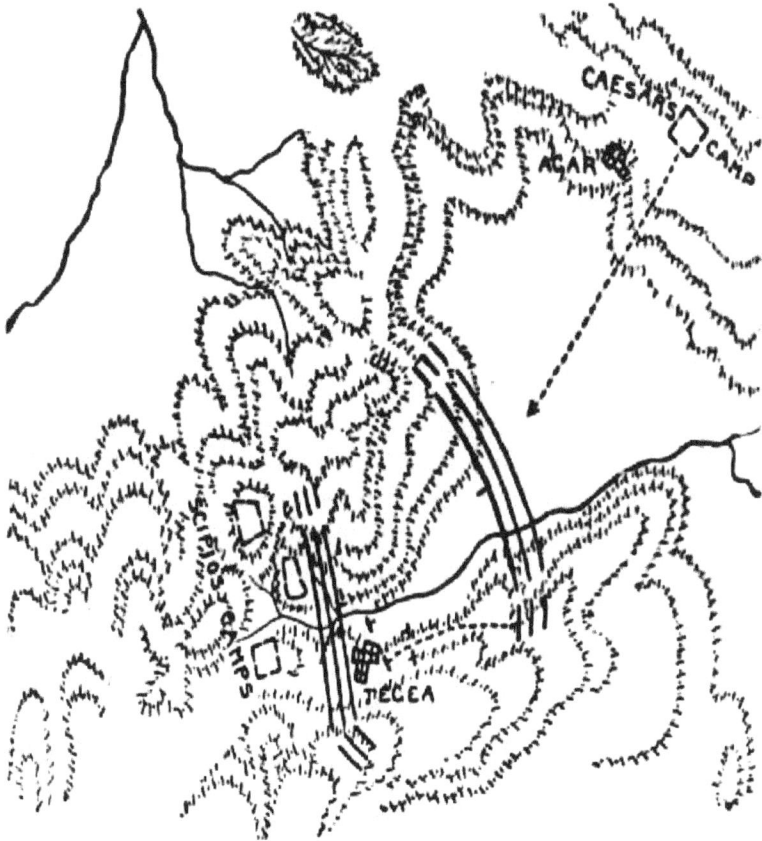

TEGEA

on the right and left of the town, and formed his legions on a hill somewhat lower than his camp and about one thousand paces from it, as a reserve, the cavalry on both flanks, but so placed as to be able to sustain the Tegean horse in their front. From this place Scipio would not budge, nor Caesar attack him in it. Finally, to tempt him out Caesar sent some squadrons, about four hundred men, supported as usual by light troops, to charge the cavalry at Tegea. To meet this partial attack, Labienus sent some of the cavalry of his second line around the right and left of this body to take it in reverse. Caesar ordered forward three hundred of the *legionaries* habituated to sustain the horse. Caesar's men, not only greatly outnumbered but threatened in flank, began to give ground. Each side undertook to throw forward supports, and it looked for a short period as if the battle might become general. When Caesar's line appeared to be all but overwhelmed, a further opportune reinforcement of foot carried the day. After a stout struggle Scipio's horse was broken and pursued, with loss of many officers, three miles to the mountains.

Caesar kept his *legionaries* in line all day; but the enemy's foot, though the occasion appeared to be favourable to Scipio, he being on higher ground, could not be induced to come down to the plain to accept a general battle. Caesar's efforts were all directed to trying to lure Scipio from his position. This, however, he could not accomplish, and as usual he was unwilling to attack equal numbers on ground above him. Though Fortune was wont to be on his side, he was manifestly disinclined to tempt her too far.

Caesar finally withdrew his men to camp, "without the loss of a man," while "the enemy had many of his best officers either killed or wounded." A corresponding loss in men is to be presumed. This statement shows that the historian of the *African War* was subject to the weakness, observable in most chroniclers of modern contemporary military events, of understating the losses of his own side and overestimating those of the enemy. When a combat is presented in considerable detail and severe fighting is reported, we must assume some loss in killed. In most cases the wounded are not taken into consideration. Except in the case of a massacre, there are rarely large losses on one side without some equivalent on the other. It must, however, be remembered that with his good defensive armour and his skill in the use of his shield, the Roman *legionary* could fight, sometimes for many hours, without a wound. So long as ranks were kept unbroken, he was comparatively safe.

THAPSUS AND VICINITY

The siege of Thapsus now appeared to be the only means left of forcing Scipio into such activity as to give Caesar a chance of fighting on at least even terms. If anything would bring Scipio to battle, the danger of losing this town and port would do so. And, water being scarce near Scipio's Tegean location, so that he could not sit down before him there, Caesar broke camp in the night of February 3-4, "marched sixteen miles beyond Agar to Thapsus,"—the distance is really ten,—and seizing the elevations back of it, immediately began to draw lines of contravallation about the city to invest it, as well as lines of circumvallation with redoubts in proper places to prevent succour from reaching it (A).

Thapsus is situated at that point in the coast where, after having run to the southeast from Hadrumetum, it turns suddenly south. It was an old Carthaginian city and very strong. The ruins found today on the site of the city proper cover nearly one hundred and fifty acres.

It had triple walls, and its harbour, natural and artificial, was excellent. The town lay on low land, but hills up to one hundred feet in height ran to the west and to the south along the coast. Thapsus could be approached only from the south or west, on account of a large salt lake three miles inland and seven miles long.

Caesar's movement on Thapsus drove Scipio into action, "to avoid the disgrace of abandoning Virgilius and the Thapsitani who had all along remained firm to his party." After several councils of war in the Pompeian camp, it was determined to follow Caesar along the line of the hills, and to avoid an attack unless on ground favourable to them. This was done, and the enemy entrenched eight miles south of Thapsus in two camps, one for Scipio and one for Juba (B).

There was, as stated, west of the town of Thapsus a salt-water lake,—the modern Sebka di Moknine,—separated from the sea by a strip of dry land from one to two miles wide. Caesar had camped and thrown up his line around the entire town, but along this strip of land between the lake and the sea Scipio imagined that there was still access from his camps and that he could carry succour to the inhabitants. After renewed councils, it was determined to make a move in force up that way,—Juba remaining in his own camp to protect both. But Caesar with his usual foresight had anticipated this very manoeuvre, and had forestalled Scipio by the erection of a fort (C) in the centre of the strip of land and had placed a triple garrison in it which was ample to check the approach of an enemy as cautious as Scipio.

Scipio broke camp, and marching right in front up the narrow strip in question with his back to the sea, instead of being able to penetrate to Thapsus was astonished to run against Caesar's redoubt. It is altogether probable that vigorous measures might have captured or masked the fort, but its presence so entirely brought Scipio out of countenance that he scarcely knew what course to adopt. He remained *in situ*, taking no action of importance during the entire day and night, but probably returned to his camp south of the lake. He now resolved to try the approach from the north, and early next morning he advanced round the lake to near Caesar's camps. Here, had he acted with vigour, he might have cut Caesar off from Leptis and Ruspina, or by an attack on his works have added immensely to his task. But Scipio dallied, gave Caesar time to finish his entrenchments, and undertook no diversion whatever.

Caesar, in a day or two, got his army well entrenched and extended in a semicircle around the whole town from shore to shore.

The enemy was definitely excluded from Thapsus. Scipio set about constructing two camps north of the lake (D), one for Juba and one for himself, having done which, he marched his troops to a point about fifteen hundred paces from the sea and an equal distance from Caesar's lines, and there, on the 6th of February, he began to entrench still another camp (E). Just what his object may have been does not appear from the relation in the *Commentaries*, or from the topography. Scipio's manoeuvres were apt to be indefinite. There were plenty of things to do, but Scipio was not given to vigour, and he was loath to approach Caesar except under cover of heavy works.

Caesar could not permit an entrenched camp to be placed m such dangerous proximity to his own lines, and determined to attack Scipio at once, though he would have preferred to defer a battle till he had taken Thapsus. The time for attack was manifestly before Scipio had completed his new works. Leaving Asprenas, the proconsul, with two legions, to look after the trenches of Thapsus, Caesar drew out and marched upon Scipio with the rest of his forces. One half of the fleet he left before Thapsus, but ordered the other half to sail out beyond Scipio's camp, make in near the shore, and, upon a proper signal, to begin a noisy demonstration in Scipio's rear by shouting and getting ready to land men.

Scipio was drawn up before the half-made entrenchments in three lines, the third of which only was at work; the elephants, sustained by light troops, were displayed before his right and left wings. The Numidian cavalry was on the left, the rest of the cavalry and light troops on the right. His left all but reached the coast. Caesar advanced likewise in three lines, with the Second and Tenth legions on the right, the Eighth and Ninth on the left, and five legions in the centre. His flanks opposite the elephants he covered each by five chosen *cohorts* of the Fifth legion aided by archers and slingers. His cavalry was mixed with light foot. He himself went on foot from legion to legion to encourage the veterans by reminding them of their past victories, and to stimulate the new levies by urging them to win equal glory. All perceived with glowing ardour that finally the battle was to come for which they had striven for so many weeks.

Not so the enemy. Scipio's men were seized with the trepidation of a surprise; they saw Caesar about to attack when their camp was but half finished. They had been weakened by being kept behind entrenchments. There seemed to be no head or order. Caesar's men could see the lines moving in and out of place as if entirely unpre-

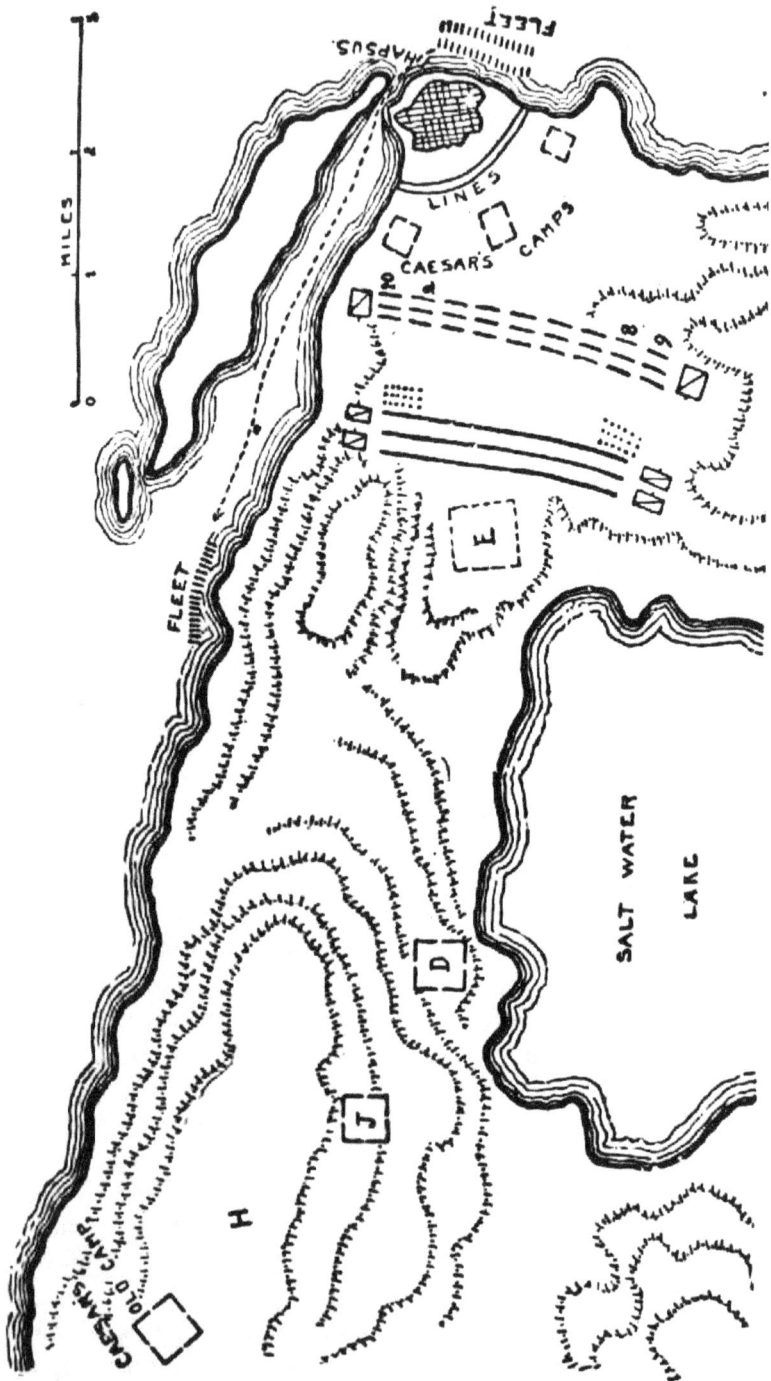

BATTLE OF THAPSUS

pared for the deadly work at hand. His *legionaries* and officers begged for an instant order to advance, for they saw in this uncertainty a sure sign of victory. Caesar was anxious to be deliberate, for the elephants were strange and awful to the young troops, the Numidian cavalry was vast in number, and had bred all but disaster at Ruspina, and the light troops of the army were brave and nimble. While the captain was thus hesitating, the men acted; the attack was actually precipitated by a trumpeter of the right wing, whom the soldiers of the Tenth legion compelled to give the signal before Caesar commanded it. This is one of the most extraordinary instances of slack discipline in all history. It reminds one of the charge on Mission Ridge,—though, indeed, at the latter place there was no actual breach of orders, but only an excess of spirit in carrying them out.

The signal being repeated in the usual manner down the line, the *cohorts* rushed forward, and could not be restrained. Seeing this and taking advantage of his troops' enthusiasm, Caesar gave "Good fortune" (*Felicitas*) as the battle-cry, "spurred on his horse" and joined the fray. The archers and slingers and the *cohorts* on the right flank, set for this particular duty and now well-trained to encounter elephants, speedily overwhelmed these brutes with a shower of darts and stones, and drove them trumpeting back upon their own lines, where they trampled numberless men under foot, made their way to camp, closed up the entrances, and utterly demoralized the Mauretanian horse in the left wing, which fled incontinent. The lines of foot now clashed. That the Pompeian legions despite their surprise fought well is demonstrated by the fact that they held their own some hours. It was sunset before Caesar's legions could call the day their own. But after a gallant struggle, Scipio's right wing partook the growing demoralization; then followed the centre. In a short time thereafter the entire line was melting away towards the half-completed camp (E). The *legionaries* of Caesar's right and left wings soon wheeled around the enemy's flank and captured the entrenchments which there was scarcely an attempt to defend. The principal officers, fearful of their own fate if captured by Caesar, and appalled at this sign of disaster, without an effort to rally their men, themselves fled from the field. Perceiving this desertion by their chiefs, the whole army, seized with utmost panic, dissolved into formless squads and made its way from the field as best it might. The struggle at the new camp was a short one. The soldiers of Scipio were cut down *en masse*; all who could still flee started towards the old camp north of the lake (D).

The garrison of Thapsus had, meanwhile, made a sally along the shore, wading through the surf to aid their friends; but were beaten back by the camp-followers and non-combatants in the siege lines, which Caesar had left to attack Scipio.

Caesar's *legionaries* followed hard in pursuit. Scipio, Labienus, Afranius, and other generals had already got away; no sign of defence was made; their army was a mass of fugitives. The men endeavoured to rally at the old camp, where they could still have shown a stout resistance, but there was no one to head them. Seeing none of their officers at this spot, they imagined that they had gone to Juba's camp nearby (J), and made their way thither to seek them. Finding this camp already in the hands of Caesar's men, who had flanked them on their left, they at once fled to an adjoining hill (H), intending to defend themselves. On the approach of their pursuers they became panic-stricken, "cast down their arms, and saluted them in a military manner," *i. e.,* made the usual signal of surrender.

But surrender availed naught. Caesar's soldiers were too much wrought up to heed the signal. The Roman people were by nature cruel; in common with all men of their trade in ancient days, Caesar's *legionaries* partook the national spirit and had long reproached him for clemency; they had been at war three long years; they now proposed to put an end to the matter, and broke quite beyond control. Caesar, though anxious to spare Roman blood, was unable to stem the tide. The *legionaries*, glutted with passion and blood, not only slaughtered the armed men, pursuing them in every direction and cutting them down wholesale, but in their frenzy they killed a number of Roman citizens in their own camp, against whom the cry was raised that they were the authors of the war, or secret adherents of Pompey's cause.

"This made several Roman knights and senators retire from the battle, lest the soldiers, who after so signal a victory assumed an unbounded license, should be induced by the hopes of impunity to wreak their fury on them likewise. In short, all Scipio's soldiers, though they implored the protection of Caesar, were, in the very sight of that general, and in spite of his entreaties to his men to spare them, without exception put to the sword."

This escape from control by his legionaries is the most serious criticism on their discipline which can exist. One can scarcely associate such laxity with *cohorts* which had been even weeks under Caesar. Plutarch says that several authors have claimed that Caesar was not in this battle at all, but was down with an attack of epilepsy. This scarcely accords with the facts elsewhere set down, or with the probabilities; but if anything lends countenance to it, it is the remarkable lack of hold upon his men shown by Caesar on this field, both at the inception and close of the engagement. Their conduct at Pharsalus stands out in marked contrast to it.

At least ten thousand men were slain and sixty-four elephants were taken. Scipio's whole force was annihilated. Caesar's army, it is claimed in the *Commentaries*, lost not over fifty killed and some wounded. Fancy a decisive battle in the nineteenth century won by an army of forty odd thousand men at such a paltry cost!

The flight of the leaders, Scipio, Juba, Labienus, Afranius, Petreius and the others, availed them little. Most of them were unable to escape pursuing fate, whether by land or sea, and either fell that day or within a few weeks. Labienus made his way to Spain. Scipio reached his shipping, but was overtaken by bad weather, driven into Hippo, attacked by Sitius, and fell in the ensuing action. Some lesser chiefs reached Utica.

As Thapsus did not surrender after this signal victory, though formally summoned to do so, with a display of the captured elephants, Caesar left the proconsul C. Rebellius with three legions to continue the siege, sent Cnaeus Domitius to invest Considius in Tysdra with two, and having been lavish in praises and rewards to his troops,—the Fifth legion was allowed to adopt an elephant as ensign,—he set out for Ucita and Hadrumetum, which he took February 10 and 11, and where he found Scipio's stores and much military treasure. Thence he marched on Utica, with Messala commanding the cavalry in the van. He was anxious to capture Cato and a number of Scipio's lieutenants who had fled for refuge to its walls.

Scipio's cavalry escaped in a body from the battle as the foot could not, and started for Utica. On the way they were refused entrance to the town of Parada, but forced the place. In revenge for the refusal, they built a huge fire in the forum and into it cast the whole population bound hand and foot, with everything which they could not carry away as plunder. After this signal act of barbarity they marched to Utica, where they in like manner began to plunder and slaughter, and were only stopped by being bought off with money by Cato and Sylla Faustus. Cato endeavoured to arouse the inhabitants to resist Caesar, but, unable to accomplish more than to gain permission from the city for all adherents of Pompey to leave for Spain, on February 12 he committed suicide.

Cato was Caesar's most able opponent. Had he not yielded the military command to Scipio, Caesar might not have put so easy an end to the campaign. After his death, L. Caesar, his *quaestor*, determined to throw himself and the town on Caesar's clemency. Sylla collected a body of men and retired into Juba's territory.

Messala, with Caesar's cavalry-van, soon reached the city, and placed guards at the gates. Caesar followed close upon his heels. Reaching Utica February 16, he was easily prevailed on to pardon the rebels their lives, but he amerced them in a heavy money-penalty of two hundred thousand *sestertia* to be paid the republic for having, while Roman citizens, furnished Varus and Scipio with funds.

King Juba and Petreius made their escape together, and hiding by day and travelling by night reached Zama, where were all Juba's treasures and his family. His subjects refused him admittance and appealed against him to Caesar,—for Juba had threatened to consume himself, all his goods, and all the Zamians in one great conflagration should he return from this war other than victorious. On receiving this message Caesar himself set out towards Zama. On the way many of Juba's officers and nearly all his cavalry came in and surrendered. Caesar's pardon of all made them his firm adherents. Juba and Petreius killed each other. Reaching Zama March 6, Caesar confiscated all the king's goods and those of Roman citizens who had borne arms against him and turned the kingdom into a province, leaving Crispus Sallustius as proconsul in command.

Considius, meanwhile, had abandoned Tysdra. On the retreat his forces assassinated him, seized his treasure and dispersed. Virgilius at Thapsus surrendered to Caninius. Sitius defeated Sabura, and on his return to Caesar ran across Faustus and Afranius, who had escaped from Utica with the body of troops which tried to plunder the place, some fifteen hundred strong, surrounded and captured the entire force. The two chiefs were slain in a mutiny which occurred a day or two after. The services of Sitius were recognized by the gift of Cirta (Constantine) in which to settle his irregular *cohorts*.

Caesar confiscated and sold the estates of the rebels in all the towns which had opposed him; and fined Thapsus and Hadrumetum and their merchants fifty thousand and eighty thousand *sestertia* respectively. Other towns were fined in proportion. He then embarked, April 14, for Sardinia, where he went through the same form of amercement of his enemies, and thence sailed for Rome, which city he reached on May 25. He had been absent six months, of which four and a half in Africa. ,

In Rome from June to November, Caesar celebrated four triumphs, for his victories over the Gauls, Pharnaces, Egypt and King Juba. No triumph, under the Roman constitution, could be had for victories in civil wars. During the days of the triumphs Caesar gave to the Roman people the most magnificent spectacles that had as yet been seen. Over four hundred lions and fifty elephants fought in the arena. The promised largesses were distributed to the soldiers, some nine hundred dollars to each old *legionary*, the *centurions* double, the *tribunes* and the chief of cavalry quadruple. Besides this, lands were distributed, though they had not been promised. For the next year, B. C. 45, Caesar was elected consul and was made dictator for ten years. But his stay in Rome was short. Seven months after his return from Africa—November, 46 B. C.—he was called to Spain to suppress the relics of the Pompeian insurrection in that peninsula.

The African war is perplexing to gauge. From one point of view it seems to have been a most difficult undertaking and to have taxed Caesar's ability to the utmost. From another, when we note the low quality of the generals and the legions opposed to him and the unusually cautious manner in which he handled his problem, it does not appear to be a campaign as marked in excellence as others. That the African war was ever waged was due to Caesar's being caught in unnecessary political and discreditable personal toils in Alexandria. This delay gave the Pompeian conspirators the better part of a year to hatch out their means of resistance, and enabled them to organize and carry through a campaign in Africa and still another in Spain. Both these campaigns could have been avoided if at once on Pompey's death Caesar had turned against Cato and Scipio, his stoutest opponents; or if he had at the outset gone to Alexandria with a number of legions instead of less than one. We are not estimating an ordinary man. We are gauging the work of perhaps the greatest man the world has ever seen, of a soldier who has few peers. What would escape notice in the average general, forces itself on our attention in the case of Caesar.

At the root of all this lies Caesar's reprehensible habit of undertaking work with insufficient means. He moved to Greece with half his force, and was compelled to wage a defensive war for months. He sailed for Alexandria with but four thousand men, a reckless act which gave rise to a long and arduous struggle there. He moved into Pontus with a ridiculously insufficient force and was saved from disaster as by a miracle. He came to Africa under circumstances which, without Caesar's own luck, must have resulted in his defeat. This more than foolhardy conduct brought in its train vastly greater complications than could have resulted from a careful opening of each campaign. If the months be counted, it will be seen that more than half of all Caesar's campaigns were consumed in extricating himself from the results of his own mistakes.

It was either unnecessary delay or uncalculating haste which made most of Caesar's campaigns essential. At the same time we cannot forget that it was these campaigns which brought out his great qualities as a soldier, which have taught us so many lessons in the art of war.

When Caesar woke up to the danger of the African *imbroglio*, his impatience to seize upon and carry through the matter led him to neglect the commonest precautions. He must have known, or at all events he could have ascertained, the numbers opposed to him in Africa. But apparently without consideration, just as he had before started from Brundisium against Pompey with half his force, he now set sail from Lilybaeum with but six legions and two thousand horse, on a weaker fleet than Scipio's, at a season of the year when storms were common, and, most extraordinary of all, without a rendezvous if the transports should be separated, as was not only probable but actually occurred. It needed all Caesar's luck to overcome such carelessness. It would have been a much more expeditious plan to wait till he got his forces together, till a season of better winds prevailed; he could then have crushed out the opposition with a blow. Most of the African campaign was taken up with manoeuvring to avoid the natural results of Caesar's numerical weakness,—Caesar's, who controlled the vast resources of Rome,—or else in search of corn which he should have collected for shipment before he himself set sail. In this particular characteristic—lack of preparation—Caesar stands on a lower plane than any of his compeers. None of the other great captains was so unnecessarily reckless, ever tempted fortune so far; none ever had the fortune to be extricated from such dilemmas.

There is so curious a mixture of daring and caution in Caesar that we are often tempted to believe that we do not understand the conditions under which he worked. The historian of the African War has an indefinite way of stating things which obliges us to complement much of his meaning by a study of the terrain. That the man who was bold enough to blockade Pompey at Dyrrachium with half his force, to attack Pompey uphill at Pharsalus with like odds against him, should be unwilling to attack Scipio under conditions far more favourable, is hard to explain. That the man who undertook and carried through the Zeta raid—the operation of a partisan corps by an entire army like that of Alexander at the Persian Gates—should have been unwilling to cross the valley at Ucita, or at least to attack Scipio when he had dug his way across, we can scarcely understand. Still the historian and the topography agree. We understand the conditions better than those under which Hannibal and Alexander worked. We are forced to ascribe Caesar's hesitancy to mere mood.

Caesar's manoeuvring was always good. His reason for entrenching, instead of fighting, is harder to comprehend. Caesar was a fighter, in his way; not like Alexander, not like Frederick, but still an able and antagonistic tactician. But often, without reason, he appeared to be disinclined to fight, even when his men were in the very tone to command success. He was so clever at manoeuvring that he apparently desired for the mere art of the thing to manoeuvre his enemy into a bad position before he attacked him. His pausing at Thapsus has led to the remark that, while he prepared for the battle, it was his men who won it. When Caesar was weak in numbers, his caution was justifiable; but his caution was often less great with a handful than when his force was respectable. His opponent in Africa was far from being an able man; Scipio's legions were less stanch than Caesar's, yet hypercaution gives Caesar distinctly the appearance of having had more difficulty in mastering Scipio than in overcoming Pompey the Great. What difficulties he had were largely of his own creation. It is because he was Caesar that we wonder at his hesitation.

This is one aspect of the case. On the other hand, Caesar's activity, his intelligence, his skill and brilliant dash in the minor operations, his broad conceptions of the strategic necessities of the case, as well as the execution of all his plans, stamp him with the seal of genius. And if we consider the element of time, Caesar is unapproachable. In the Civil War, from his arrival on the field, the Italian campaign lasted but sixty days; the Ilerda campaign six weeks; the Epirotic seven months; the Alexandrian six; the Pontus campaign a bare week; the African a little over three months; the Spanish an equal time. When we note that in the Epirotic and Alexandrian wars it was Caesar's over-hastiness which consumed the bulk of each period, this record, added to the splendid work in Gaul, in this sense stands unequalled in the history of great captains.

CHAPTER 42

Spain

December, 46, to August, 45 B. C.

The Pompeians had taken root in Spain, in doing which Caesar's lieutenants had aided them by mismanaging his affairs. Pompey's sons,
Cnaeus and Sextus, were in command of large forces there. Caesar,
after triumphing in Rome, proceeded to Spain. The first manoeuvring
was near Corduba, with no marked advantage on either side, though
Caesar suffered a defeat in a combat near the bridge over the Baetis.
Caesar then moved away and attacked Attegua, and around this town
there was a long interchange of hostilities, with frequent conflicts. Attegua finally surrendered. Ucubis was the next point of contest. Caesar,
as usual, skirmished for an opening, which Pompey was clever enough
not to give. But unsuccessful at all points, and having been worsted in a
battle of no great importance at Soricaria, Pompey finally determined
to leave this part of Spain and retire to Carteia in the south.

Spain was divided by the Romans into Tarraconensis, or Hispania
Citerior and Ulterior, in the north, Baetica in the south, Lusitania
in the west. In this peninsula, while Caesar had been preparing the
defeat of Pompey in Greece, Q. Cassius Longinus, who, as tribune
of the people, had so ably served him in the early months of the
Civil War, and whom Caesar had left in command, with the legions
of Varro, after its conquest, had been acting with grave indiscretion.
He had fallen into serious disfavour with the population, though he
had kept the affections of the veterans in the army by exceptional
largesses,—a course tending to the destruction of discipline. He had,
for some time, by cruel extortions from the people, been raising
moneys, which he squandered in needless equipments for his troops,
and in supplying them with absurd extravagances. He had raised a
fifth legion and three thousand horse, which he sumptuously paid

and clad. Some time before the Battle of Pharsalus, Cassius received orders from Caesar to march through Mauretania on Numidia, where Juba was still in Pompey's favour, and was raising fresh troops to aid the cause. He was getting ready-to march, for he lacked not vigour if there was work to do, when he was all but assassinated by some of the men he had injured. He was, however, rescued, and caused all the conspirators to be tortured and put to death, except some few whom he allowed to purchase their lives for sums varying from ten thousand to fifty thousand *sestertii* each. After this experience he became more tyrannical than ever. A mutiny and revolt ensued, which threatened to place Spain in the hands of the Pompeian faction; for these atrocities by one of Caesar's lieutenants had brought the adherents of Pompey again to the front. At the request of his Spanish friends, Caesar sent Trebonius, the conqueror of Massilia, to displace Cassius. The latter, in sailing away from the province where he had earned so much hatred, was drowned in the Ebro.

Young Cnaeus Pompey, after his *fiasco* in Mauretania, had sailed for the Balearic Isles, and finally reached and taken possession of Baetica in southern Spain, where he had been well received by the larger part of the people whom Caesar's lieutenants had alienated, and had been saluted *imperator*. He had driven Trebonius out of that part of the country. By seizing the wealth of many private citizens and by general rapacity and high-handed measures, he managed to collect a large army. After the defeat at Thapsus, many of the fugitives—his brother Sextus, Labienus and Varus among them managed to make their way to young Pompey, with such small relics of the army as they had saved. By all these means a nucleus of parts of thirteen legions was collected and put under supreme command of Cnaeus, then a young man of twenty-four, by no means lacking in boldness or ability.

In Baetica, which is a territory much cut up by hills and rivers, with excellent resources, and strong towns and positions, there was a promising chance for Pompey to drag out a war of defence for an almost indefinite time. This necessitated Caesar's at once leaving Rome. He had imagined the Civil War to be at an end, but he was rudely undeceived by the news from Spain, received during October and November, 46 B. C. He first dispatched Q. Fabius and Q. Pedius to Spain with troops, and Didius with a fleet. Didius beat Varus at sea and drove him into Carteia. Caesar left Rome early in December, 46. By what route he went is not known. Appian, Strabo and Eutropius assert that he reached his camp in Obulco (Porcuna) in twenty-seven days from the city. It is thought that the trip was by sea to Saguntum, which he reached in somewhat less than three weeks, and thence to Obulco in a week more. One thing alone seems clear, that he reached Spain in less than a month after starting from Rome, certainly before he was expected, and in advance of his troops. He was on the ground prior to the rumour of his approach.

On arrival, Caesar learned by ambassadors from Corduba (Cordova) that the town was weakly defended by Sextus Pompey and might be captured out of hand. Pompey had sent out scouts to ascertain Caesar's coming, but these had all been captured. Cnaeus Pompey was besieging Ulia (Montemayor, twenty miles south of Corduba), the last town which had held out against him in Baetica. To the relief of Ulia Caesar sent a force of eleven *cohorts* and a good body of horse under L. J. Paciecus, a man well known and acquainted with the province. Paciecus managed to enter the place during a storm which was accompanied by such darkness that the enemy was careless and readily deceived as to his presence and purpose. With this additional garrison, Ulia could

THEATRE OF SPANISH CAMPAIGN

probably have held out in any event; and moreover, to draw Pompey from the siege, Caesar, about January 8, marched on Corduba, which he had some hope of capturing out of hand. He sent his cavalry on ahead, accompanied by a body of chosen heavy-armed foot, and adopted the stratagem of mounting a number of these behind the cavalrymen when they approached the city, so that their presence was not perceived by the enemy. The Cordubans thereupon sallied forth to attack what they supposed to be only horse intent on ravaging the country. The infantry, dismounting and forming, fell on the enemy with such effect that few returned to the town. But the victory obtained no result.

The presence of Caesar near Corduba and the relief of Ulia, obliged Cnaeus to raise the siege when Ulia was on the point of surrender and to march to Corduba, which was important as being the capital of the province, and which his brother Sextus had sent him word he feared he could not hold against Caesar. It is very apparent that Cnaeus had illy prepared for opposing, as well as little anticipated, Caesar's arrival.

The description of the events which now took place is given in the *Commentaries* in a manner very difficult to understand. These *Commentaries*, like the African War, were formerly ascribed to Hirtius Pansa, but it is certain that he did not write either; their author is unknown. One must decipher the matter as best one can. The bulk of the text is devoted to utterly trivial details, and the important movements are passed over with a word or altogether omitted. The topography is the only reliable guide so far as one can guess the localities or as they have been established by careful research and comparison of data. Few excavations have been made. It is necessary, sometimes, to do slight violence to the text in some one place in order to make the statements coincide with others equally positive. On the whole, however, we may feel reasonably sure of our general ground; but the details are wanting and any narrative of the campaign somewhat lacks sequence.

When, about January 10, Caesar reached the Baetis (Guadalquiver), he found that the Pompeians held the only bridge (A), and that the river was too deep to be forded. He accordingly built a number of piers for a bridge below the town (B) by sinking for foundations baskets of stones; and laying his roadway on these, crossed to the right bank in three successive divisions (C, D, E) and camped each in a suitable location strongly fortified. He then built a good bridgehead on the left bank (F). When Cnaeus arrived from Ulia, he camped over against Caesar's bridgehead, on the heights south of the town (G), hoping to get access to Corduba by the old bridge.

CORDUBA

Caesar began operations by an effort to cut Cnaeus off from the town and prevent his entering it. "He ran a line from the camp to the bridge " (H) in such a manner as firmly to hold his bridgehead while threatening to cut Pompey off from easy access to the city and thus from his provisions. He might, perhaps, have thrown a force, by a night surprise, on the south end of the bridge and have quickly fortified it; but Caesar was always fond of the security of earthworks. He ran his lines along the river towards the bridge at the foot of the hills on which sat Pompey.

Pompey's plan was of course to obtain control of his end of the bridge, whose farther end was near a tower of the town, a fact which would make his access all the safer. It would have been a simple matter for his brother Sextus to fortify the bridge at its southern extremity, but he kept comfortably within the town walls. Perceiving Caesar's works, Pompey began a line of his own from his camp to the bridge (I). So long as neither cared to fight for the bridge, it became a question of speed in building works.

CORDUBA TO MUNDA

As a result of this entrenched race, a series of serious struggles occurred for the possession of the bridge. Skirmishes nearby were of daily occurrence, in which neither side could boast the upper hand. But it is evident that finally, about January 20, Cnaeus broke down Caesar's defences by an attack in force and fought his way to the bridge. The battle here was desperate. The legionaries fought hand to hand. Hundreds perished not only by the sword but by falling from the bridge into the river. "On either side were heaps of slain." Despite stout fighting, it seems clear that Caesar was defeated. Cnaeus gained the bridge, and his entrance to Corduba. Caesar stayed on awhile, hoping to force Pompey to an open-field engagement, which might terminate the war; but finding that he could not bring him to battle on advantageous terms, he gave up the hope of capturing Corduba, and, as a long siege was not advisable, he drew off his forces. When Caesar left, Pompey strengthened Corduba by many engines.

Caesar rightly believed that he could make better headway by attacking Pompey's minor strongholds to the south, and perhaps seize an opportunity for battle during the operations. Moreover, to get hold of some of these *dépôts* of provisions was the easiest way to ration his army. Southeast of Corduba lay Attegua (modern Teba), a town well fortified in a naturally strong and high position. This place he selected for a first attempt. On the 20th of January he quietly drew in his forces, after lighting the usual evening fires in the camp to deceive the enemy, crossed the river by night and marched on Attegua. There were plenty of provisions in the place, and as usual Caesar lacked rations. The country was hilly and the town lay on a height a mile or so back from the River Salsum (modern Guadajoz), a narrow and not deep stream. Caesar reached the place next morning and at once laid siege to it; he camped on the hills to its west (A), constructed strong lines about it with many redoubts to afford a shelter to the cavalry and infantry outposts, cast up a mound (B), brought up his *vineae* and engines and made ready to storm. The watch-towers built on nearly every height by the old inhabitants as a means of security against the barbarians came readily into play in Caesar's work.

Pompey, on ascertaining next morning that Caesar had decamped, at first entered Corduba amid much rejoicing. He felt that he had scored a point against the great soldier. Moreover, having possession of most of the towns, the winter season would work in his favour and not Caesar's. Attegua, against which he guessed Caesar had marched, was strong and could hold out. But when he heard that the place was

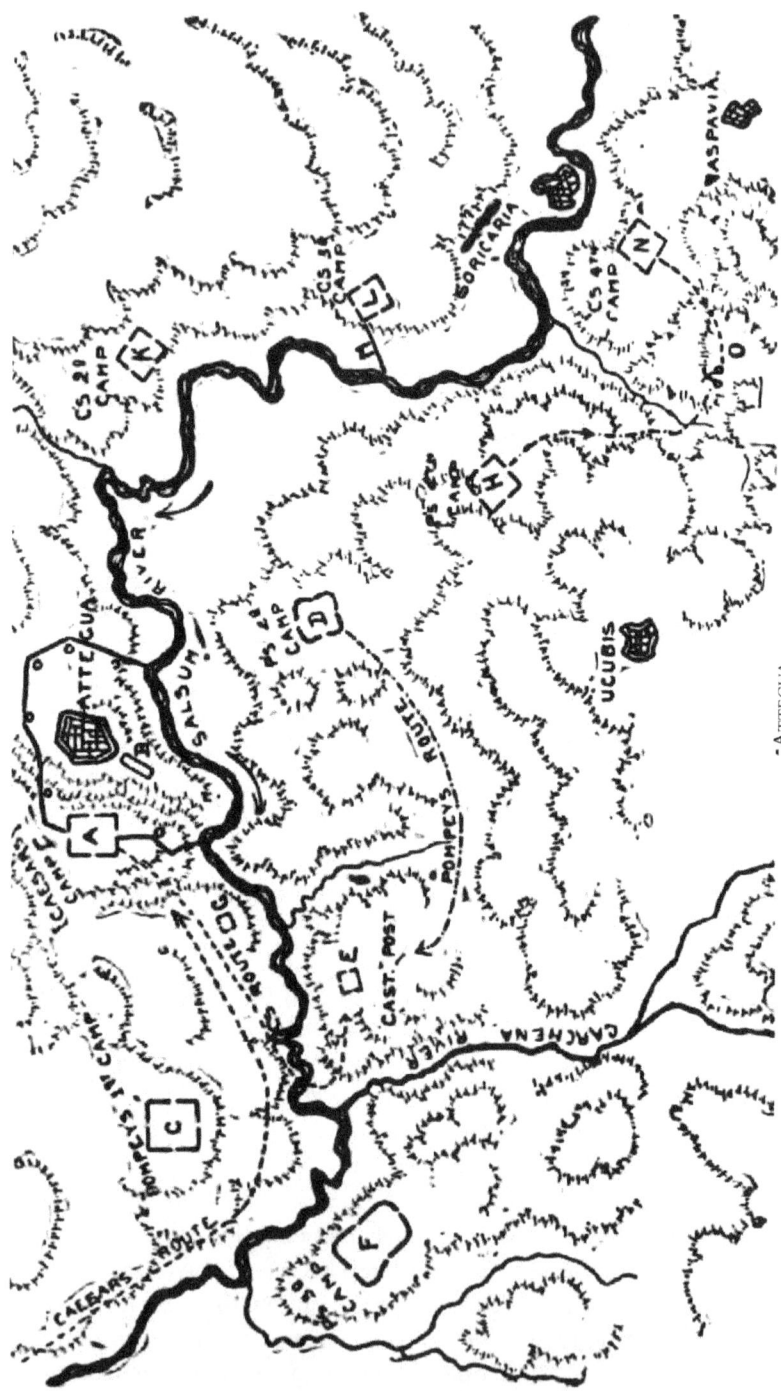

- ATTEGUA

actually invested he followed Caesar up and reached Attegua a week later, before the siege operations had advanced too far. By his sudden arrival on a foggy day he caught some stray parties of Caesar's outpost horse and cut them to pieces. Not wishing to lose his communications with Corduba, he pitched his first camp on the hills to the west of Caesar (C), but still north of the river Salsum. Changing his mind next day, perhaps January 28, he set fire to this camp, crossed the Salsum, and took up a new camp (D) south of Attegua, and in view both of it and of Ucubis (modern Espejo), another of his strong places to the south. But though his presence near Attegua with thirteen legions gave Caesar and his troops much work, if not anxiety, Pompey could bring no assistance to the town, and in the outpost conflicts the Caesarians generally had the best of it.

Pompey, to be sure, "had the emblems and standards of thirteen legions," but none of these were full, nor were they of good material. Two were native, had been under Varro, had deserted to Caesar, had been given by him to Longinus and Trebonius, from whom they had revolted in favour of Cnaeus Pompey; one was recruited among the Roman colonists in Spain; one had been in Africa with Afranius; the rest were mostly made up of fugitives from Pompey's old army, deserters and Spaniards. Thus four of his legions may be said to have been veteran, the rest raw. He had some thousands of horse, and about twelve thousand auxiliaries. Caesar had eight legions, and with later reinforcements eight thousand cavalry. His light troops were probably of better quality and quite as many as those of Pompey. Each general had some fifty thousand men, not counting auxiliaries. The feelings of the old and weary legionaries were very bitter. The war promised not to lack atrocity.

The nature of the country, which is mountainous, with the towns built on easily defended heights, was such that Pompey was able to camp in positions to make an easy and protracted defence. Spain has always been noted for its defensive wars. The sharply accentuated country lends itself peculiarly to defence. Every small place remote from cities was built on an eminence, was fortified, and sentinels were kept constantly on the lookout. Whomever the native population befriended had strong and able allies.

Standing on any one of the numerous watch-towers of the country, one sees on every hand numberless round, woodless eminences, "like an immense city whose roofs are all cupolas." Nearly all these hills are fit for camping, and at every turn is a position easy to hold, difficult to capture.

In order to strengthen his own position, keep a good outlook, and hold more territory, Caesar had taken possession of a suitable eminence—Castra Postumiana—some four miles from his main camp and fortified it (E). It was separated from his own camp by the River Salsum and was so placed as to be a threat to Pompey's camp. This general harboured the idea that Caesar could not readily come to its relief in case he attacked it. It could be approached from his camp through the valleys without the troops being seen. He planned to fall upon this fort by night, as a means of creating a diversion in favour of Attegua, and, moving at midnight of February 4, reached the place without the *cohorts* being discovered. But before it was too late the garrison took alarm, flew to arms, and rained such numberless missiles on the Pompeians from the walls that Pompey was much delayed in his operations. Caesar learned quickly of the attack, and with three legions hurried to the fort, already manfully defended by the garrison, where he inflicted a heavy loss on Pompey's troops and drove them off.

Caesar at this time received reinforcements, especially of cavalry. Pompey, who again appears to have feared that Caesar's position might enable him to move on Corduba and seize it out of hand, once more—on February 6—set fire to his camp and made signs of retiring in the direction of that place, crossing the Carchena and actually camping south of his first location (F). He had been much harassed by Caesar's cavalry in bringing victual from Corduba, and he appears to have retired the more readily to ration his men, for all his provisions were sent to him from the capital. Most of these convoys reached him, but Caesar's cavalry on one occasion intercepted a train and pursued the guard back to the very walls of the city.

Caesar pushed his works against Attegua. He daily added *castella* to his lines, and his terrace, surmounted by a tower, would shortly be able to fire upon the defenders of the city walls. To destroy these works the besieged made almost nightly sallies from Attegua, but these always resulted in their being driven back with loss. They employed every device to set fire to Caesar's towers and engines. Pompey, who had not really left the vicinity, made sundry efforts to interfere with the siege, but to no serious effect. The besiegers proceeded with their operations, undermined and threw down a good part of the wall.

Pompey continued his activity. He seized a height on Caesar's side of the river and erected a fort (G), hoping to place Caesar at a disadvantage, and in many skirmishes near the town showed himself to be an efficient and capable soldier. A select body of his infantry one day lay in ambush for some of Caesar's horse and suddenly attacked them. These troopers dismounted to fight on foot, and, not being as good infantry as cavalry, were as a consequence driven in nearly to Caesar's lines; but being here reinforced they rallied and pushed back the enemy with a loss of some hundred men.

The garrison in the town was not only active but very obstinate and cruel. Caesar's men were none the less so. The garrison consisted of Roman soldiers, and, mindful of the massacre of Thapsus, they dreaded any terms with Caesar lest he should not be able to control his men. The soldiers murdered a great number of the citizens who were favourable to Caesar, throwing some headlong from the walls. Flaccus, the commander of the garrison, organized the defence with skill, and a vast number of darts and missiles and much inflammable stuff was thrown at all times from the ramparts upon Caesar's works.

One sally on February 15, at a time agreed upon with Pompey,— he being able occasionally by shooting darts or slinging bullets into the town to communicate with the garrison,—was made with particular vigour. The garrison had for object to cut its way out to join the main force. After having thrown a large number of fire-pots and flaming arrows upon the besiegers' lines at various places to create a diversion and uncertainty, they issued at midnight by the gate nearest Pompey's camp, carrying fascines to fill up the ditch, and mural hooks and fire to destroy Caesar's works and the barracks of the men, which latter were mostly built of reeds. They were sly enough to carry with them a large supply of silver and fine apparel with the intention of scattering these valuables in places where they would divert Caesar's men from their work of resistance by thoughts of plunder. Pompey was in the fort he had erected on the Attegua side of the River Salsum, and bore his part in the fray. He remained all night in line to protect the retreat of the Atteguans, should they cut their way out. The military enginery of the town proved very efficient. One of Caesar's wooden towers was battered so severely as to give way above the third story, and in fact the besiegers fired that and an adjoining tower. But the gallantry of the besieged was of no avail. The courage of the men and Caesar's good leadership sufficed to drive them back into their lines and to hold Pompey in check at the same time.

The inhabitants now sent ambassadors to ascertain if Caesar's clemency could be procured, and at the same time Pompey determined that he could do no more to afford the garrison relief. As a result, on February 19, the gates of the town were opened to his army. Caesar behaved with conspicuous generosity.

When Cnaeus learned of the surrender of Attegua, he felt convinced that Caesar would advance on Ucubis. He moved his camp again up the river to a point northeast of the place, where he threw up works on all the hills around it which appeared to lend it strength. His weak conduct in not relieving Attegua had bred lack of confidence in him, and induced numberless desertions. These Pompey determined to punish. He selected a number of citizens of Ucubis supposed to be favourable to Caesar's cause and put them to death. In all the towns and territories controlled by him similar cruelties were practiced. This was a shortsighted policy on his part, and materially helped Caesar's cause.

After the capture of Attegua Caesar moved his camp up the river nearer to and opposite Pompey's (K). He was puzzled how to proceed to draw Pompey into battle, which he sought as keenly as Pompey avoided it. Pompey, under the guidance of Labienus, was wisely avoiding open-field work and seeking to reduce Caesar by famine. The experience of Africa and Greece was telling.

Caesar within a few days (March 4) moved his camp somewhat nearer Pompey's, but still on the other bank (L), and his men drew an entrenched line to the river (M). This work, the object of which is not apparent, gave rise, after a while, to some heavy outpost combats.

On Caesar's line was the town of Soricaria. Pompey had entrenched a *dépôt* at Aspavia, south of this place. The stores therein Caesar wished to divert to his own uses. He moved to Soricaria, crossed the Salsum, and established a camp (N) whose position resulted in cutting Pompey off from his communications with Aspavia. Pompey broke camp and endeavoured to reach the place, but found Caesar athwart his path and entrenching his camp. Cnaeus, thereupon, determined to offer battle, though on unequal terms to Caesar's troops, as he sought the protection of the higher ground, in Caesar's front (O). But Caesar was on the alert. He sharply advanced on Pompey's *cohorts*, which were climbing the hill from the west, attacked them smartly, drove them from the heights and downward to the plain, occupied the upper ground himself, and, following down the slope, fell upon them as they were crossing the valley back to camp and defeated them with a loss of five hundred killed.

On the next day, March 6, Pompey, intending to retrieve himself, advanced on the same hill, anticipated Caesar in its possession, and sent his cavalry to attack Caesar's men, still working at their camp. Caesar marched out and, drawing up on lower ground, invited Pompey to battle. This Pompey declined. After thus remaining some time, Caesar retired to camp. Pompey attacked his rear with his cavalry, which bred a very severe combat, in which Caesar's light troops had to mix to extricate the squadrons. The battle went no farther.

Soon after this action, Pompey retired to and held himself in Ucubis, and daily skirmishing was kept up between the armies, chiefly by the cavalry.

Desertions from Pompey grew in number alarmingly. To arrest these Pompey resorted to perversion of facts by writing to the towns which still held to him that Caesar would not come down to the plain and fight, but stayed on the hills where he could not be attacked on anything like equal terms. Pompey was in his way energetic, and would have liked battle; but he was afraid of Caesar. He determined to move from town to town, encourage some and punish others, hoping to gain some advantage by drawing out the war.

Roman cuirass

271

CHAPTER 43

Munda

March, 45 B. C.

The *Commentaries* are very inexplicit on many of the facts of this campaign; they are made up of shreds and patches, which can be put together into one whole only by a knowledge of the topography. Caesar followed up Pompey, and heading him off from crossing the Singulis, forced him to retrace his steps. Following him to Munda,—which place cannot well be at modern Monda, as it is usually assumed,— Caesar attacked Pompey, and in a battle which came very close to being lost, by a happy accident cleverly utilized he eventually won a decisive victory. The entire Pompeian army was destroyed. It still took some five months for Caesar to finish the settlement of Spain. He then returned to Rome.

About the 10th of March, Pompey, according to the *Commentaries*, which here become exceedingly sparse of details and unsatisfactory, broke camp and marched toward Hispalis, a place which, despite the name, cannot be modern Seville. Caesar destroyed the camp at Ucubis, took Ventisponte, and following Pompey, marched to Carruca, still seeking opportunity to bring him to battle. Pompey moved to Munda. Caesar followed and camped over against him. It is greatly to be regretted that the historian gives us no details of these manoeuvres. Caesar was evidently trying his best to drive Pompey into some position where he could have him at a disadvantage. And that he finally succeeded in so doing is evident from Pompey's concluding to fight at Munda. But the reasons for the marches and counter-marches, as even these themselves, we have no means of positively knowing. All that we are sure of is that Caesar finally succeeded in forcing Pompey into a position where the latter saw that subterfuge and retreat would no longer avail him; but that, in order to hold his allies to his cause, he must do battle for it. We are put to our inquiry from the topography and the probabilities.

Let us see whether we can supply the gap left by the historian of the Spanish War and reconstruct these manoeuvres. The interest of the campaign justifies a digression from our narrative. First we must disprove some of the theories already advanced as to the location of Munda.

The entire Spanish campaign is involved in difficulties. As soon as we approach the battle of Munda, these difficulties multiply indefinitely. The question where Hannibal crossed the Alps is sufficiently puzzling, though it seems that the route of the Little St. Bernard may be considered as fairly established. In any event, there are but a few passes over which he could possibly have frayed a path. But within a radius of one hundred miles from Attegua and Ucubis there is scarcely a ruin-surmounted hill with a brook at its foot which has not laid claim to being the scene of Caesar's great Spanish victory. And there are all but as many heights crowned by Roman ruins in Spain as in Italy.

The location of the Battle of Munda has been the source of hundreds of essays and books, some indeed crowned by the Spanish Academy; it has been the subject of many topographical surveys and researches by the engineers of the Spanish army; it has been the cause of endless controversy. There is good reason to believe that the locality was not so far from that of the operations around Attegua and Ucubis as it is wont to be placed; certainly not so far as modern Monda, Osuna, or Ronda. There are dominant reasons for the belief that the battle was fought north of the Singulis (Xenil), rather than south of it. Let us glance at these.

Caesar was constantly on the offensive, Pompey on the defensive. This was Caesar's strategic habit, or, at least, it was his habit to actively push his enemy by operations of some nature until he could force him to battle under suitable conditions. With none of his enemies did he long dally on the side of defence. We may fairly presume that this rule of conduct obtained in the present case. As we learn from the *Commentaries*, after the battle of Soricaria, "since which the enemy had been under continual alarms," and the succeeding operations, Pompey decamped. Caesar followed, and "afterwards laid siege to Ventisponte, which surrendered; and, marching thence to Carruca, encamped over against Pompey, who had burned the city because the garrison refused to open the gates to him." Thence "Caesar, still pursuing his march, arrived in the plains of Munda, and pitched his camp opposite to that of Pompey."

Now, none of these places have been identified by excavations or otherwise, and it is well not to give much heed to a similarity of names. It is safer to rely on military probabilities and to weigh each little item and word in the very short and unsatisfactory accounts which have been preserved to us.

There is an infinite number of arguments of more or less value, which can be framed to explain or sustain any given theory of the movements of the rival armies at this time. Let us keep in mind the leading statements concerning and characteristics of the campaign lest we go astray. These all point to the battlefield of Munda being not far from Corduba.

After his lack of success in the late operations, Pompey would not unnaturally determine to retire towards the sea, so as to have the proximity of his fleet to lean upon. Caesar had a keen eye for the intentions of the enemy, and to have Pompey thus escape him would be the last thing he desired. It is altogether probable that he narrowly watched his adversary and sought so to manoeuvre as to head him off before he could cross the Singulis, which was a marked barrier between Pompey and the sea. Caesar based on Obulco, and could hope to succeed better if he penned Pompey in the triangle made by it with the Rivers Singulis and Baetis.

It is, therefore, a fair assumption that, so soon as Pompey showed the intention of definitively retiring from the theatre so marked out, Caesar marched towards the River Singulis to head him off at the fords and compel him to do battle before he got away.

Had the rival armies passed the Singulis, the historian would have been likely to mention the fact as he does the passage of the Baetis. He does not mention the passage of the Salsum, because the latter is easily forded in many places. The Singulis has few fords, and at that time had doubtless few bridges, and is more or less difficult to cross.

Again: after the Battle of Munda, the beaten Pompeians, we are told, took refuge in the cities of Munda *and Corduba*. Naturally enough in Munda, which they had at their back during the battle; but if we allow that Munda was far beyond the Singulis, and that Pompey was retiring from Corduba, while Caesar followed him, how could large numbers of the Pompeians reach Corduba, through a country cut up by mountains and rivers and in possession of Caesar's forces? Would they not rather have taken refuge in the towns nearer the battlefield, many, most of which, in fact, still held to Pompey's cause? That a very considerable number did reach Corduba appears plainly from what is told us about the siege of the town following the battle. A few stray fugitives from battle have often been known to reach very out-of-the-way places even through the enemy's lines, but not large bodies of men.

The text of the Spanish War is susceptible of meaning that some of these fugitives—among them Valerius—reached Corduba the night of the battle. This alone would prove Munda to be near Corduba. The text might also be held to imply that part of Caesar's army marched from the battlefield to Corduba between the evening of the morrow of the battle and the next following noon, showing that but a short distance intervened. The text may be read to mean that Valerius escaped to Corduba, and that Cnaeus took the road in the other direction, to Carteia (near modern Gibraltar), one hundred and seventy miles from Corduba,—as if Munda was near Corduba and Carteia very far away. But the text should not be forced. Let us consider some other items.

Cnaeus Pompey, after the battle was lost, "attended by a few horse and foot, took the road to Carteia, where his fleet lay, and which was about one hundred and seventy miles distant from Corduba." He arrived there exhausted, showing that he had made a long journey, as his taking but a small party implied that he had a difficult march to make,— one much more tedious than the road from modern Monda to Carteia would be. Now, if the battlefield was not near Corduba, at least in the province of which Corduba was the capital, but far south of the Singulis, why should the historian give the distance of Carteia *from Corduba*, and not from some other well-known city nearer the battlefield?

Again: as Pompey's intention, unquestionably understood in the ranks of his army, was to make his way to Carteia, if he had passed the Singulis on his way thither, it seems certain that the fugitives would have sought to reach Carteia rather than distant Corduba. But except Cnaeus, the historian speaks of no soldiers reaching any places other than Munda and Corduba.

The historian gives no details whatsoever of the march from Ucubis to Munda, except to say that Caesar went to Ventisponte and Carruca. Had the distance been great, would not he have said something about it, especially as to pass the Singulis with an army is quite an operation, and the country beyond is very mountainous? He does describe the country near Attegua, and when he comes to speak of Munda he says: "*as we have observed before*, this country is full of hills which run in a continued chain without any plains intervening," as if Munda were still in the same section.

Again: Corduba surrendered easily after the news of the battle had reached it, as if from panic arising upon the presence of Caesar's army nearby. Orsao (Osuna), on the contrary, near which town many place Munda, stood a siege. May it not be assumed that it was too far off to be subject to immediate panic?

As to modern Monda, neither the topography of the section, nor the narration of the Spanish War, can be held to justify making it the locality of the battle. Mommsen is clearly wrong in this.

Ronda or Ronda la Vieja are still less available for both reasons. A few only have advocated these places.

The vicinity of the Rosa Alta mountains has been suggested. This will not do, because had this been the theatre of the battle, the town of Orsao would certainly have been a refuge for the beaten army. Nor does the topography of any particular place there correspond to what we are told of the battlefield.

Again: Many have claimed that Munda must be near Orsao, because the military engines used at Munda were brought to Orsao:

"Fabius Maximus, whom he had left to continue the siege of Munda, conducted it with great zeal; so that the enemy, seeing themselves shut up on all sides, sallied out, but were repulsed with great loss. Our men seized this opportunity to get possession of the town, and took the rest prisoners, in number about fourteen thousand. Thence they retreated towards Orsao, a town exceedingly strong both by nature and art, and capable of resisting an enemy. Besides, there is not, within eight miles of the place, any spring but that which supplies the town, which was a decided advantage to the besieged. In addition to all this, the wood necessary for building towers and other machines had to be fetched from a distance of six miles. And Pompey, to render the siege more difficult, had cut down all the timber round the place, and collected it within the walls, which obliged our men to bring all the materials for carrying on the siege from Munda, the nearest town which they had subdued."

But the Roman military engines were not difficult to transport. Alexander always carried his engines with him, like our field artillery. The legionary *onagra* were carried. Within six miles of Orsao there was wood left for the large framework, so that to carry all the parts of the big engines from Munda to Orsao was optional, and the operative parts could be carried almost any distance with ease. Orsao is, moreover, not on the road from Corduba to Carteia, the line of Pompey's retreat, but on that from Seville to Malaga, so that Munda can scarcely be assumed to have been near it. The *Commentaries* refer to Orsao as "the nearest town which they (*i. e.*, the besiegers of Munda) had subdued." But this does not necessarily imply that Munda was in the vicinity of Orsao. These two towns appear to have been the stoutest in their resistance to Caesar. Had they been close to each other, it is probable that Caesar would have done more than leave the sieges of Munda and Orsao to the management of Fabius, lest the one town should interfere with the siege of the other.

So much for the most important of the various places which lay claim to be the scene of this great battle. We can adduce only negative evidence at best to disprove their claims. The military probabilities furnish a stronger argument.

There is noticeable a certain similarity in some of Caesar's campaigns, showing a method of work,—a type,—which it may be allowable to appeal to as a guide when we can find no certainty in the narration left to us. For instance, in the Ilerda campaign, Caesar constantly kept Afranius and Petreius within certain bounds by manoeuvring. He did not permit them to get beyond his easy reach. In Africa, too, all his manoeuvres were within a comparatively small area. Without proof positive that the Battle of Munda was fought south of the Singulis, may we not by analogy claim that it is more like Caesar to have kept his opponent within the boundary prescribed by the Baetis and the Singulis?

If Pompey crossed the Singulis and made for Carteia, and Caesar followed him and forced battle on him, how had he time to besiege Ventisponte on the way? For while he was doing so, Pompey would have certainly escaped him. Does it not seem more probable that Caesar had headed Pompey off from crossing the Singulis on the way to Carteia, and had thus gained time for the siege? Is it not much more according to a Caesarian model to imagine the great captain manoeuvring Pompey into a place where he must fight, than to consider him as conducting a stern chase?

Such considerations as these make it altogether probable that the battle of Munda was fought north of the Singulis. The town of Montilla has been pointed out as a probable location. The topography is as satisfactory as we can ask, in view of the fact that the historian's description is not very close; and the strategic features tally well with what we may imagine Caesar to have done. In order to construct a homogeneous whole out of the shreds of historical statement, we are compelled to assume something.

For the purpose, then, of planning a campaign which shall tally both with probability and with what we are told, let us assume that the three unidentified locations are: Ventisponte, modern Puente Vieja; Carruca, modern Puente Xenil; Munda, modern Montilla. The two former places are the only fords over the Xenil in this section, and have ruins of Roman bridges; the latter has a battlefield which chimes well with the narrative of the Spanish War. On his way towards Carteia after the battle of Soricaria, Pompey was heading for the bridges or fords of the Singulis. He chose Carruca for a crossing, but was stopped there by the garrison. Caesar, meanwhile, moved on Ventisponte, took it, and moved against Pompey to Carruca. Thus cut off from his retreat towards Carteia, Pompey chose the only other alternative, turned in his tracks and headed by his left towards his old capital, Corduba. Caesar met this manoeuvre by moving by his right to cut him off from that city. Around modern Ecija are plains to which Caesar may have been hoping to drive him. Pompey had told his allied cities so frequently that Caesar would not fight when he offered him battle on equal terms, that he now felt compelled to make good his word. It is not impossible, too, that he saw no means of longer avoiding Caesar's pursuit. In this way both armies reached Munda.

Caesar had no special hope that Pompey would stand, but was surprised to see that his enemy had determined on battle. This was the thing he welcomed of all others.

The assumption thus made bears the stamp of accuracy, for it accords closely with the historian's relation, and still more closely with the military probabilities. No other does.

It was on the 15th of March that Pompey camped under the walls of Munda. Caesar arrived next day and camped to the eastward, on a brook, today the Carchena. Back of Pompey lay his own entrenched camp and the town of Munda as a retreat in case of disaster. He did not feel that his position was disadvantageous.

The next day after Caesar's arrival, March 17, as he was preparing for the route,—for he did not believe Pompey would fight,—he learned from spies that Pompey had been standing in battle array ever since midnight waiting for his approach. Caesar "at once ordered the standard to be raised" for battle. Pompey had so long alleged that Caesar preferred not to come to battle because his troops were raw levies that he had ended by half believing it; which idea, coupled to his present excellent tactical position, made him the more ready to chance matters on the result of a general engagement.

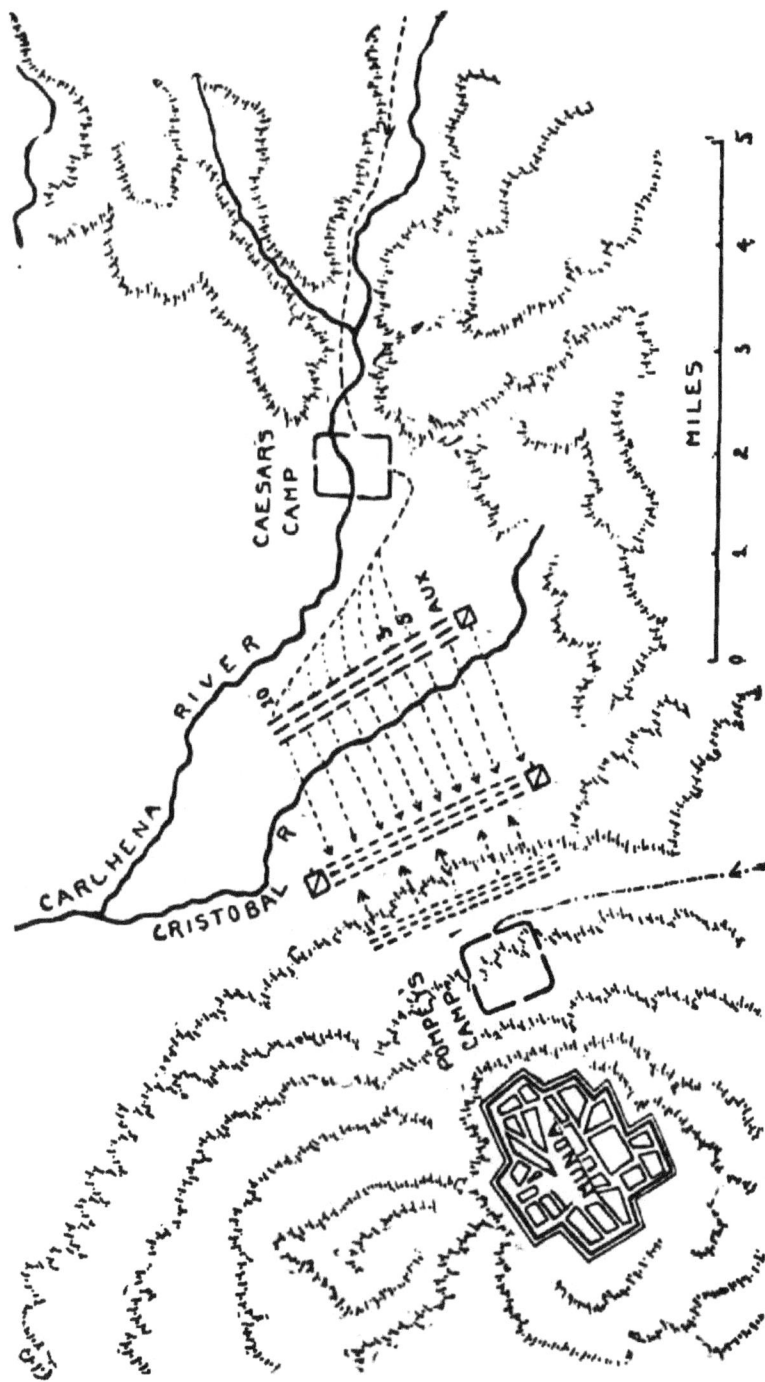

BATTLE OF MUNDA

The town of Munda lay on a hill sloping towards the east. Between the two camps lay an undulating plain about five miles in width, through which ran a small rivulet, the modern Cristobal. Caesar had had in mind some other plans for outmanoeuvring his opponent, but on hearing that Pompey had prepared for battle, he himself drew up in line and waited for the enemy to descend to the plain, as he believed he would do; for Pompey had some cavalry which on the plain could act to better advantage than on the slope. But Pompey kept close to the hill and near the town on which his legions backed. His position was exceptionally strong, and he did not propose to forfeit it. He had all his thirteen legions in line. The cavalry was on his wings with six thousand light infantry and six thousand auxiliaries. He had probably been able to make good his losses, and may have still numbered fifty thousand men. The slope on which the Pompeians lay was rugged, excellent to defend, bad to attack. At its foot, on Caesar's right, was low and marshy ground, fed by the brook. Caesar had eighty heavy armed *cohorts* and eight thousand horse,—in any event under forty thousand effective. His light troops may have been eight thousand more.

As Pompey did not show any sign of advancing, Caesar, on his part, marched across the plain to a point opposite Pompey, as a means of luring him forward. When the legions had reached the low ground and the brook, beyond which the hill where Pompey was posted began to ascend, and before crossing the brook, Caesar halted the line and, calling together his officers, pointed out to them and to his troops the disadvantage under which they would attack if they did so now. As we have seen, Caesar never favoured attacking positions, and was reluctant to undertake an assault here. He had caution in certain contingencies equal to Hannibal's; but, unlike Hannibal, he alternated hypercaution with the extremity of recklessness.

"The army murmured greatly as if they had been kept back from a certain victory, when this was told them." The men were in excellent spirits and demanded but a chance to fight. The order to advance was accordingly issued, and the line promptly moved forward as with the will of one man, and crossed the brook. The pause which had thus occurred in the advance of the Caesarians encouraged the enemy to believe that Caesar's legions were hesitating from fear, and induced Pompey to order his line to move a short distance down the hill; but though they thereby yielded part of the strength of their position, the advantage still remained indisputably with them. Nor did they advance far from the protection of the walls of Munda, which was not exceeding a mile in their rear. Pompey proposed in any event to have this city as a harbour of refuge.

Caesar's Tenth legion was on the right; the Third and Fifth legions were on the left with the cavalry and the auxiliaries drawn up beyond them. The other legions held the centre. The battle was engaged with extraordinary enthusiasm. The shout on each side came from men determined and expecting to conquer,—men who proposed to give no quarter. Caesar's legions charged up the hill with consummate gallantry. Pompey's line met them at javelin-throwing distance by a storm of *pila* and a counter-charge. Caesar's men were superior in discipline and went at their work with cheerful courage; Pompey's troops fought with clenched teeth, in the belief that their only salvation depended on winning this battle. They remembered Thapsus.

At the instant before the impact the shower of darts was so heavy from above that the young troops wavered, and there was serious danger of Caesar's line being broken before it had fairly engaged the enemy. Then came the charge down from the higher ground which struck like the blow of a ram. Its momentum fairly staggered Caesar's line; the onset was checked. The two lines, like wrestlers, with a firm hold, swayed to and fro in fierce opposition. This lasted while the successive ranks and lines relieved each other and fought with lance and sword. But the position of Pompey's men was much in their favour. They pressed Caesar's *cohorts* hard. After many hours, of this close-locked fighting, Caesar's line began to show serious signs of weariness; there were hints of that disintegration which appals the stoutest-hearted leader. Caesar was taken aback. So grave, indeed, was the danger at this instant, that Caesar afterwards stated that while he had often before fought for victory, this, his last battle, was the first occasion on which he ever fought for his life. He had forgotten the Sabis. But that wonderful magnetic energy of his was roused to its highest pitch by the imminence of disaster. Never, since the day when the Nervii all but annihilated his legions,—save perhaps at Alesia,—had he been called upon to put out his every power, physical and moral, as now. He rushed through the ranks, shaming some, stimulating others, reproaching the backward, praising the brave, and rousing the courage of his men by every appeal. He fought, as at the river Sabis, like a common soldier, with sword and shield in the front rank before the ensigns. By his personal endeavours the men were kept at their work.

There is no question that victory or defeat, for hours perhaps, hung by a hair. It was Caesar, and Caesar alone, who kept the *cohorts* from stampede. It has been alleged by some historians that at the most dangerous period of the battle Caesar, in despair, was about to take his own life. But this is so thoroughly unlike the man that we cannot accept it as true. Caesar was capable of falling at the head of his legions, but not by his own hand in battle, unless he was taken prisoner.

Evening was approaching. The last man on both sides had been put in. Not a *cohort* of reserves was left. The battle was anybody's. No one could predict the result. Caesar's men had rallied, but they were fighting uphill, and Pompey's men had been encouraged by holding their own so long. The auxiliaries on both sides had fled. There was no chance for manoeuvring. It was a mere question of discipline and valour. An accident might break either line, and such a breach would be surely fatal. Caesar was still omnipresent. His efforts had never slackened. He clung to his ground like one possessed. He would not face defeat. He made a last appeal to his old favourite, the Tenth legion. "Are you not ashamed to deliver your general into the hands of boys?" he cried to his veterans. Stung to the quick by the taunts of their general, for whom they had wrested victory from desperate straits so many times before, these battle-scarred men now rose to their old standard of enthusiasm, and pressed the enemy hard. The rest of the line gained courage for redoubled effort. Pompey was compelled to draw a legion from his right to help sustain his left, which was battered by the heavy blows of the Tenth. Caesar's cavalry of its own motion fell upon this depleted wing and created a distinct impression. The fighting "was hand to hand, foot to foot and shield to shield." On whose banners was victory to perch?

Finally chance decided the day. King Bogud with his Numidians, after the charge of the cavalry, made a circuit of the Pompeian right and marched upon their camp. Perceiving this, Labienus, who commanded on this wing, detailed five *cohorts* to head him off. Catching sight of these troops moving to the rear, Caesar, who was in the thickest of the fray, though he comprehended the manoeuvre, seized on it as an omen and shouted to his men: "Look you, comrades, the enemy flees!" The Pompeians at the same moment saw this rearward movement, and conceiving the idea that their line was somewhere broken, began to waver. This bred confusion in their ranks and enthusiasm in Caesar's,—as small things will often do upon the battlefield. Here was Caesar's opportunity. Under his powerful influence, the line was roused to one more almost superhuman effort. It was all that was required; the effort prevailed; the Caesarians broke the Pompeian line and drove the enemy towards the town.

The victory was won, but the battle was not yet ended. Caesar's eight thousand cavalry, which had so far done small work, now put in its heartiest blows, and soon broke up the *cohorts* of the aristocrats. Great slaughter ensued; thirty thousand Pompeians were cut down, among them Labienus and Varus, and three thousand Roman knights. Caesar lost, according to the *Commentaries*, but one thousand killed, and five hundred wounded. This last item is another of those curious discrepancies between killed and wounded which make it so difficult to gauge the Roman losses in comparison to those of modern times. In some battles it can, from their peculiar tactics, be understood how there might be less wounded than killed; but at Munda the reason does not so plainly appear. It may have been due to the hand-to-hand fighting, which gave a wounded man small chance of getting to the rear.

Caesar took the eagles of the thirteen Pompeian legions, an immense number of standards, and seventeen higher officers. The victory was overwhelming; the massacre decided the war. Most fugitives from Pompey's army made for Munda, which it became necessary to besiege. So heated were the passions of the Caesarians, that the dead bodies of the slain were used as ramparts, and their javelins as palisades, and on these their bucklers were hung as breastworks. The heads of many were stuck on pikes and placed along the investment lines to strike terror into the besieged.

At Pharsalus Caesar lost, according to the *Commentaries*, two hundred killed; at Thapsus, fifty; at Munda one thousand. The enemy, on the contrary, practically lost their entire army in each of these engagements. While these figures may not be accurate, it remains true that in ancient battles the vanquished lost to an extent impossible today. Defeat always meant massacre,—except to a Caesar. There was no attempt to restrain the troops. To kill was one of the main purposes of an ancient battle; today, killing is an unfortunate incident of war, which is ended as soon as the army of the enemy is put as far as may be beyond usefulness for the campaign. Despite such fearful slaughter, the total losses of a campaign in ancient times were apt to be much less than they are today, when constant deadly fighting, with daily loss on both sides, is going on.

Cnaeus Pompey fled from the field towards his fleet at Carteia, "which was about one hundred and seventy miles distant from Corduba," one hundred and forty-five from Munda; but, after some time, was overtaken and killed. Caesar left Munda invested by Fabius Maximus, and marched to Corduba. Sextus Pompey had decamped. Here Caesar was arrested some time by the gallant defence offered by the Thirteenth legion. We have no details whatever of the operations. But the adherents of Caesar within the walls set fire to the place. Caesar made his way in, and slew twenty-two thousand men, many of them runaways from the battlefield of Munda. This slaughter was uncalled for. It adds to the list of holocausts for which Caesar was responsible.

The battle of Munda had by no means crushed out opposition. Pompey's adherents defended themselves to the last. Hispalis was the next city to be reduced. This occupied some time. Asta and Munda followed. Each was a task of some difficulty. Carteia had seized Cnaeus Pompey. One party in the town wanted to give him up; one to assist him. His adherents got the upper hand, and, laying hands on all his adversaries, remorselessly slaughtered them. Cnaeus escaped by sea, but Didius followed him up with Caesar's fleet, and, after a series of romantic adventures and a brave fight for life, he was captured and killed. Didius' success was, however, short-lived; he was shortly after caught in an ambuscade and his fleet destroyed by the Lusitanians.

Fabius, after a long siege, took Munda, and later the city of Ursao fell to the Caesarian arms. But the stanch defence of the towns adhering to Pompey is best shown by the fact that it took Caesar or his lieutenants many months to accomplish their reduction.

The Spanish war was the last in which Caesar was engaged. Having reduced the whole of Spain, there was now no organized opposition to his rule in any quarter of the world. He started for Rome the end of July. But his glory was short-lived. He was assassinated next Ides of March.

The sons of Pompey had many conditions in their favour at the beginning of the Spanish campaign, but they did not use them to advantage. One of their chief errors was of a kind not unusual at that day; they devastated the land and robbed the population of a country already half Caesar's. This conduct incensed both their friends and foes, and enabled Caesar to tamper with Pompey's adherents, who listened the more readily to him for having suffered at the hands of Pompey. Cnaeus, who was the ruling spirit, conceived his military projects in a manner far from perfect and carried them out in still worse form. When the execution of a plan of campaign brought either Cnaeus or Sextus into the presence of Caesar, he seemed to be still less capable of intelligent action. Few generals shine when they are opposed to men like Alexander, Hannibal or Caesar. Except Vercingetorix, scarcely one of Caesar's opponents came out of the struggle with military reputation unscathed. Pompey had been a great man; but he was no longer such in Caesar's front.

Caesar never had to face such men as Marcellus, Nero and Scipio. Even in contrast with the greatest captain of antiquity, perhaps of all time, these Romans earned an abiding fame. Caesar was never called on to oppose such generals; nor, indeed, such legions as were made up of the burgesses of the Second Punic War.

Caesar encountered semi-barbaric tribes much as did Alexander, but not in as overwhelming numbers; he never encountered civilized armies under conditions by any means as unequal as Hannibal.

A marked distinction in ancient times between the great and the mediocre captain lay in the ability of the former to rescue himself from disaster if he happened to suffer defeat; to keep his men within the bounds of demoralization; to save them from a massacre. Alexander scarcely knew failure. Hannibal often looked defeat in the face, but never disaster, until Zama. Caesar always rescued himself from defeat. Disaster never overtook him.

If, after the Battle of Munda, Cnaeus had not lost his head, he might have saved a portion of his army; have retired to one of half a dozen provinces or cities, and have raised troops to continue the struggle. He might not have been able to alter the outcome of the war, but he could have protracted it indefinitely, at this time a highly undesirable thing for Caesar, who was needed at Rome to allay serious political troubles, and could not well afford military difficulties. Neither Cnaeus nor Sextus were in any sense worthy antagonists of Caesar. The former must not be underrated. He had some good points, and, under better conditions, might have shown for more. Sextus must be gauged lower. They could not expect to equal Caesar; but they might have made his task a harder one.

The fact that Caesar took from March to August after Munda to reduce Spain to complete subjection shows how strong a grasp the Pompeian element had got upon the peninsula, and proves that a good soldier, despite defeat, might well have held out an indefinite time. While it is true that Caesar's luck generally pitted mediocre men against him during the Civil War, his genius was demonstrated as much in taking advantage of their shortcomings as it was in his so cutting out and doing his work as to reduce the length of his campaigns to such exceptionally short limits.

CHAPTER 44

The Man and Soldier

Caesar was tall and slight, but strong and uniformly well. He was a good fencer and rider, and well up in athletic sports. His features were large but refined. In his last years he showed his age and grew bald. His dress was always elegant. Cicero was his only superior as an orator; in ordinary converse he was unequalled. His power of work and endurance were wonderful. He is charged with many *liaisons*, but they were the custom of the day. His domestic habits were simple, but he was extravagant in art. Some ancient authors charge him with many vices; he was, indeed, not perfect; but the sum of all is a well-balanced character. He was a good friend and bore no malice to enemies. He had no bigotry; his intellectual equipment was splendid. He did more cruel things than Alexander, but he was personally kind and generous. He had projected many great works in addition to those he had already performed when the end came. As a soldier, Caesar's art was inborn. The ancients knew nothing beyond tactics and logistics. Strategy was not a recognized science. Caesar was his own pedagogue; he learned from his own errors. The conception of the plan of the Civil War was on as high a plane as its execution; the rapidity of its campaigns has no equal; but it was marred by repeated instances of overhasty action barely pardonable in a tribune, inexcusable in a great captain. A large part of the time consumed by his work was due to these mistakes. Caesar's objectives were always well chosen; he invariably struck at the key-point. His manoeuvres and blockades were on a big scale. In adversity he was elastic; he never lost *morale*. His tactics was simple; such battle-tactics as that of Epaminondas, Alexander, Hannibal, we never see. His strategy was broad. Caesar's opponents were not as a rule strong; but he made good use of their mistakes. Pompey was able; he was never great, and Caesar's *morale* overrode him. Caesar's influence over his men was marked. In peace he allowed laxity; in war he demanded strict discipline. With few exceptions his legions reflected his own splendid qualities.

"Caesar was born to do great things," says Plutarch. First of all a statesman, arms were to Caesar a means of carrying out his political scheme, rather than statecraft an aid to his military policy. The portrait of this great man has been painted by able hands and in many colours. It is only sought to add to this portrait some touches which pertain to his military career.

Caesar was tall and of slight but well-knit frame. Constant exercise and exposure had made him hardy; and his constitutional and nervous strength could not be overtaxed. Except that he had at times attacks of "the falling sickness," no illness save *quartan* ague is recorded of him during a life of infinite toil. He was skilful as a fencer, and in many of his battles exhibited an ability to wield arms, coupled to a personal gallantry and magnetic power rarely shown by the captain. To his boldness in swimming he owed his life in Egypt. He was a fine horseman. As Alexander had his Bucephalus, so Caesar owned and rode in the Gallic War a much prized horse of his own raising who allowed no other man to mount him, and whose "divided hoof," which, it is said, resembled a human foot, made him singular, if adding no value to his other qualities. That Caesar had great physical endurance is shown by the exceptional speed of his journeys. He often travelled day and night and worked on the road as if he had quietly sat in his tent.

Refinement and strength rather than beauty of feature characterized Caesar's face. His portrait busts show a strong intellectual development with an abundance of will-power; and in some of them there is a singularly sweet expression of the mouth; but this detracts naught from its force. In the last few years he showed in the deep-cut lines of his face the severe strain to which he had so long been subjected; and his carriage was not as erect nor his gait as elastic as that of many men of his age. In middle life, much to his regret, his hair grew thin; and as he never quite lost the instincts of the dandy, he combed his locks forward with noticeable care, and to conceal his baldness was glad to wear upon his head the golden wreath of laurel voted him by the Senate. His eyes are variously spoken of as dark gray, or black and piercing. His face was pale when not bronzed by exposure; his dress had a touch of elegance all through life. He was a constant bather and never lost his liking for the niceties of the toilet.

Caesar may not have possessed the grace of demeanour of Alexander; but he had the force of Hannibal, and a power of impressing himself on all who approached him in which neither the Macedonian nor the Carthaginian was his superior. His simple directness, his aptness at saying the right word in season, his persuasiveness, his broad culture and immense resources of thought and language charmed everyone who was cast with him, whether the barbaric king of Gaul or the queen of Roman society. As an orator he was confessedly second to no one but Cicero; his voice was high-pitched and his manner animated. In personal converse he was, perhaps, the first man of his day. His high-bred courtesy and an easy manner never forsook him. He was gifted with a remarkable memory and power of concentration; he often dictated to two or more secretaries at the same time; and we can conceive how such a memory, stored with all that Greek culture and extensive travel could bestow, and drawn on by eloquent lips, must have lent an attractiveness none could approach. He was versatile; without an effort he attained the highest excellence in all he undertook.

Caesar has been blamed for his relations to women. His habits were those of the day. Hannibal may be praised for his fidelity to Imilcea; Alexander for his scrupulous respect of Statira, the consort of fugitive Darius; but Caesar is scarcely blameworthy for being a man of the world when what we call morality was not considered a virtue, and to be continent or scrupulous was to be out of fashion. It is no doubt true that Caesar's *liaisons* extended far and wide. He is charged with intrigues with the wives of many of his friends; but, whatever the truth, it seems clear that his friends and he did not quarrel. He was assuredly not gross in his amours; and his bravery in refusing to divorce his wife at Sulla's nod, when other and then greater men did so, and in taking the consequences, scores a high mark in his favour. It is impossible to say how much of what has been charged against Caesar is due to the idle gossip of the Roman *salons*.

Caesar's domestic habits were not pretentious. When he was virtually king of Rome, when he had been called "the Divine" by an obsequious Senate, he is said to have lived simply, though Plutarch speaks of the general splendour of his manner of life, and he was extravagant in the purchase of statues, pictures, gems, and other objects of art. He kept a generous table, of the best to be had, but without ostentation. As *custos morum* he enforced the sumptuary laws with some severity. One of his tables was laid for his political friends, one for his military.

He himself was moderate in food and drink, but enjoyed the mental friction of enlivening table-talk. That he had indulged in a youth of pleasure cannot be gainsaid; but that it left no trace on his body or mind is equally true. No vices had sapped his powers; his physical and mental structure rendered him proof against their effects.

Caesar owed much to his mother, Aurelia; and he repaid her by the same devotion which Frederick showed to "the queen mother." Aurelia lived under her son's roof until her death. Caesar exhibited equal affection for his sister.

The ancient authorities vary greatly in their estimates of this man. He is charged by some with all the vices; he is credited by others with all the virtues; still others ascribe all vices and virtues to him. It has been the habit until of late years to look upon Caesar as "the monster," which the many-headed in Rome once dubbed him. The pendulum has now swung back, and we are threatened with forgetfulness of what many Roman authors tell us. Among others, Suetonius informs us that Caesar exhibited great animosity as a judge; that he resorted to bribery; that he was hasty and violent; that he was suspected of ridding himself of an enemy by poison; that he lent money without interest in order to cater friendship; that he plundered Lusitania at the point of the sword and robbed temples in Gaul; that he was rapacious in character and extravagant in language; and that he incurred the suspicion of heading a conspiracy to murder his opponents in the Senate and resort to a *coup d'état*. Other authors give us many similar items. There is no certain means of weighing these allegations. We must note them all and give them a proper place in our estimate of what Caesar was. But after so doing, the sum of all that is told us makes up a well-poised character, quite apart from Caesar's gigantic intellect or moral force.

From youth up Caesar avoided quarrels; he had other means of settling disputes, and could either assert his view with reasonable insistence or persuade his opponent by his superior skill. When angry he was easily appeased. When worsted he bore no malice.

Caesar's friendships were sincere and durable, honest and above board. He was generous and kind. To sick Oppius he gave up his couch and slept on the ground. With few exceptions his friends remained his friends. He had no room for suspicion in his broad affection. He would not believe that Labienus meant to desert him. When he did so, Caesar offered any friends of Pompey who might be in his service free conduct to join his opponent if they so chose.

He clung to his friends, not from calculation but affection; though he made use of them as he himself was useful to them. When he had pardoned an enemy, there was no further relic of ill-will. He took as much pride in restoring the statues of Sulla and Pompey as he had exhibited courage in replacing on the capitol-hill the trophies of Marius.

Had he been nothing but a soldier, Caesar would still be the equal of the other great captains. Taking him as the statesman who built on the ruins of the republic the foundations of the empire, as the patron of learning who founded libraries in all the great towns, and filled Rome with men of science, culture and letters, as the legislator who drafted laws which still control the jurisprudence of the world, as the pro-found scholar who dictated the correction of the calendar, as the thinker, for the grasp of whose mind nothing was too intricate, nothing too broad, Caesar was, indeed, "the foremost man in all this world."

Of the men of that generation, no one clung to fact as did Caesar. As Carlyle says of Napoleon, "the man had a certain instinctive, ineradicable feeling for reality." He was no idealist, yet he had an abundant fund of imagination, as every creative mind must have. He coolly dissected things, and could look at them as they actually were. From a given array of facts Caesar rarely failed to draw the correct conclusion. Traditions were of value to him for their influence on weaker minds. As *pontifex maximus*, he was neither bigoted nor over-liberal. The cult of the Roman gods had on his mind the proper influence, no more. It was of distinct value to the state; of no particular value to the individual.

In gifts of intellect and character Caesar was exceptional; his judgment was rarely at fault. He was of a reasonable turn of mind, and the harmony and consistency of his life were marked. In politics he was persuasive rather than dogmatic, but he had a way of carrying his point. His intuitions as well as his power of gauging men and of guessing their actions were keen.

While allowing all this, it must not be assumed that Caesar was perfect in character. It is possible to make a glaring array of faults with which he may be charged. He was utterly unscrupulous as to the means he employed when he made up his mind to do a given thing,—a fact not palliated because it may be said to have been the fault of his age. He would allow nothing to stand in the way of the accomplishment of his purpose. When he deemed the thing he aimed at worthy to be done, every means was proper. He borrowed immense sums of money without other means of payment than what he anticipated might be ground out of the government of a province. Personally of a generous, kindly habit, he is chargeable with holocausts before which the devastations of Alexander shrink to naught. It is said of him that he never murdered a Clitus or savagely mutilated a Batis, or burned a Persepolis; but he executed Acco with extreme if legal cruelty; he put to death the whole Venetan Senate for their patriotic resistance; he again and again visited awful vengeance on the Eburones for the sins of Ambiorix; he cut the hands off all the prisoners taken at Uxellodunum, and in treacherous cold blood he massacred four hundred and thirty thousand defenceless men, women and children in the course of a short afternoon. The sum of his massacres in Gaul overruns a million souls, paying no heed to those who perished by a worse fate than the edge of the sword. Yet, though we view all these things in their proper light, we cannot withhold from Caesar's personal character the meed of our respect and admiration.

Up to middle life, Caesar was purely a statesman. He then had the fact brought home to him that he could no longer win the success he sought unless he had at his command the military resources which his enemies boasted. Those who place Caesar on the plane of pure patriotism, who claim that the regeneration of Rome and Greece was his leading object, must still allow that he sought it mainly by his own elevation. What he sought he won. He was a born ruler, and he became a republican king. The honours and titles which were heaped upon him were lavish to absurdity. The heretofore military title of Imperator became a prefix to his name and was made hereditary in his family. He was styled *Pater Patriae*. He was saluted as *Divus Julius*. He was made consul for ten years. His statue was erected in every town and medals were struck in his honour. Chairs of gold and gilded chariots were presented to him. Triumphal arches arose in his honour, and a temple of Concord or Clemency. He was invested with *tribunician* honours which made it sacrilege to injure his sacred person or character.

It is hard to say what part of all this proceeded from the gratitude of the Senate, what part was fulsome and empty adulation, what part the work of enemies who sought to sap the autocrat's popularity with the people. It is hard to say how much Caesar enjoyed this worship, and how much he despised it. He declined some of the honours; he accepted others. He added his own to the seven statues of the kings of Rome; he appeared in public in the garb of the old kings of Alba. About all he did there was a certain ceremonial, despite his natural personal simplicity. Caesar was sole ruler and the Senate became a mere council. He assumed their political functions. A new patrician nobility was created. Augustus was no more emperor than Caesar.

It is probable that Caesar at heart cared little for much of all this tinsel; it is certain that he felt out of place and far from secure in the city. And yet he was covetous of honour; he enjoyed the applause of the multitude. That he had a certain habit of simplicity is undeniable. He went about alone and unarmed, though well aware how numerous were his enemies. He refused the crown which was offered him,— perchance because he saw therein a snare. Had he lived he would no doubt have openly become what Augustus was, but he bided his time and the time never came.

He had good cause to be satisfied with what he had accomplished. Vast as his work had been, it had borne good fruit. Despite its fearful depopulation, Gaul was again flourishing and commerce and agriculture were on the increase. His changes in the laws were solid,—"the political life of nations has during two thousand years again and again reverted to the lines which Caesar drew." As *custos morum* and in his other judicial characters, he punished severely but judiciously, and despite Suetonius we must believe impartially. It is certain that Rome was the better for his administration, at least for the foundations which he laid.

On Caesar's final return to Rome, his physical strength, which had been upheld by nervous tension, sensibly declined; but his energy remained intact. He made vast projects for the future. He purposed to drain the Pontine marshes, to make a new channel for the Tiber, to improve the roads, to cut through the Isthmus of Corinth. He projected a campaign against the Parthians and was intending soon to start in order to secure this frontier of the state, as he had all the others—when the end came.

At the risk of repeating what has already been said in running comment, it is well to sum up the soldier. Caesar had the inborn qualities of the great captain. When he received Gaul as his province he had had no training in the duties of a general officer except that gained in the Lusitanian campaign. There was no training for the larger operations of war known to the ancients. The management of a campaign depended solely on the ability of the leader. The grasp of a military problem came purely from his personal equipment. Today, instruction is given to students of war in its broader phases, and precept is enforced by the example of great commanders. We hear of no such teaching among the ancients. Instruction there was, and perfect of its kind; but it went not beyond the tactical and logistic requirements of an army. Strategy was still unknown as a teachable science. It must not be assumed that to be an adept in the book-lore of strategy will make a great captain. Character counts for more than half. The personal equation is the one that tells. But character coupled to a well-trained intellect are essential to produce the greatest results. Today only the highly-trained officer is efficient; it was less so in ancient days, but intellect then won as it does now and always will.

Caesar was his own pedagogue in war. He taught himself his trade in Gaul. He accomplished this self-training by dint of many errors. In the Civil War, Caesar committed fewer, and these were generally from over-anxiety to get at his work. His operations, all things considered, were well-nigh faultless.

We have already considered the strategic plan of the Gallic War and incidentally that of the Civil War. Let us recapitulate the latter. In this war Caesar wisely chose Italy, the centre point of the empire for which he was contending, as his first objective. This accords with his uniform habit of selecting for attack the most important point. He never adopted indirect means. His blows were always aimed at the key-point. In sixty days from crossing the Rubicon he had, by his directness and the moral ascendant which followed his vigorous initiative, acquired possession of the peninsula.

Once seated in Italy, Caesar found the enemy on three sides of him,—in Spain, Greece, Africa. He had gained a central position from which to operate. If he could hold himself in Rome, he could attack each of his enemy's divisions in turn. To hold Rome and carry on an offensive, demanded two things, legions and speed. In the former, counting out essential detachments, he was weaker than his adversary; in the latter he proved himself far superior.

We have assumed that Caesar's better plan was at once to move on Greece, where Pompey stood with his main force. This was of a part with Caesar's common habit of aiming directly at his enemy's army. We are forced to guess at Caesar's reasons for doing otherwise,—the *Commentaries* are not specific. They tell us that Pompey had command of the sea and that Caesar feared that it would consume much time to gather a fleet; that meanwhile not only would he be forced to inactivity, but that Pompey's veteran legions might "confirm Spain in his interest," gather large levies, and, more dangerous still, invade Gaul from Spain, and arouse an enemy in his rear. Caesar knew Pompey and gauged his temperament correctly. He could more safely rely on Pompey's keeping quiet in Epirus than on Pompey's lieutenants doing the same in Iberia. This reasoning does not convince us; but action under it was crowned with success; it may, therefore, be deemed to have been sufficient.

The Spanish campaign and the siege of Massilia, however rapid, took long enough to bring Caesar back to Italy at an inopportune season. But Caesar could never wait. Driven by exhaustless energy, he crossed the Adriatic to Epirus with half his army, because he had not transports for the whole. That he would have been wiser to march through Illyricum seems clear. It was his own province. From the Padus through Illyricum to Epirus was almost as short a march as to Brundisium, and the bulk of his army had rendezvoused on that river. Reaching Epirus with limited forces, Caesar with energy and unequalled good fortune held his ground until, after the lapse of five months, he was joined by Mark Antony. How Caesar would have fared with an abler opponent in his front is a matter of conjecture. He owed his safety to Pompey's laxness. Why Antony was not ordered to march by Illyricum when his presence was so essential in Epirus is explainable only in that Caesar and he both hoped from day to day that chance would afford him the opportunity to cross the Adriatic.

The operation at Dyrrachium resulted in a marked defeat for Caesar, directly due to his undertaking an operation which could succeed only by virtue of a miracle or an accident. He was able to rescue himself from disaster because he was Caesar and had Pompey opposed to him. Having saved his army from this danger, he skilfully manoeuvred to join Domitius, which done, with an audacity worthy of a Frederick, he attacked and beat Pompey at Pharsalus. All this is so splendid, the errors are so completely swallowed up in the well-deserved success, that criticism is put to the blush.

Upon this decisive victory followed Caesar's overhasty and uncalculating pursuit of Pompey with a bare corporal's guard to Alexandria; his political mistake in mixing himself up in petty Egyptian affairs when the world was still at stake; his being blockaded in Alexandria by a horde of barbarians, whom three of his old Gallic legions might have overwhelmed; his holding himself by pure stubbornness until released by Mithridates; his two months' dalliance with Cleopatra while his enemies were daily gaining strength. Add to these delays the essential campaign in Pontus, and there was again a year consumed, during which the Pompeian party had acquired control of Africa. However much we may admire the skill exhibited in the details of the Alexandrian campaign, as well as the courage to see it through to a successful issue, it is clear that Caesar for the moment lost sight of the broad plan of his mighty game which had the world for a theatre of operations. This error was the origin of the bitter struggle which it cost to reduce the Pompeians to terms in the succeeding years.

Again, when Caesar was compelled to take up arms to bring Africa into subjection, his hyper-activity drove him to ship over to that continent at one of the worst seasons of the year,—and this without giving a rendezvous to his fleet; by which neglect the same untoward situation was brought about on the African coast which had happened a year before on the Epirotic. The man who held in his grasp the resources of the Roman state was reduced for months to a petty defensive scarcely befitting a legate, until he could gather forces sufficient to go over to the offensive; and during all this time he was in a danger which an able opponent might have rendered fatal. It was Caesar's luck which placed Scipio in command instead of Cato. To this situation and the difficulty of procuring corn must be traced the narrowness of his movements. At the same time his danger showed up his fertility in resources in a wonderful measure. Having again recruited up his forces to a proper standard, we are led to look for an immediate and vigorous offensive. But we are disappointed. Though opposed by a less good army, and by trivial generals, Caesar hazarded nothing. For the moment all his audacity disappeared. He played the game which Hannibal was forced to play when he was facing thrice his numbers of superior troops under consummate leaders; and he appears to small advantage when contrasted with the Carthaginian. But when the opportunity for which he had long manoeuvred had come, and Scipio had been brought to battle on advantageous terms, Caesar, or rather Caesar's army, made short work of him in the brilliant victory at Thapsus.

Then came the Spanish campaign, to crush out the relics of the Pompeian party. The clever manoeuvres on the Baetis, followed by the hard-won Battle of Munda and the ensuing sieges, again took more than half a year. We know less about these movements than we could wish. What we do know shows Caesar up in brilliant colours.

It is clear that the Civil War might have been carried through in half the time it actually consumed had Caesar been more judicious. But he started with only a moiety of his army for Epirus at a bad season; he committed precisely the same error in opening the African war; the Alexandrian and Pontus campaigns came in between the other and more important ones and prevented the prosecution of the latter in due season. These events had depended upon Caesar's own volition. Had he marched to Epirus overland before the fall of 49, had he in the spring of 48 gone with a respectable force to Africa, this year would probably have seen the end of the Pompeian coalition. That despite these mistakes he was victorious in each campaign in so comparatively short a time he owes to his extraordinary ability, his simply astonishing good fortune, and the weakness of his opponents. It is, perhaps, hypercritical to suggest errors in a record which history can scarcely equal. And yet the errors are glaring; they are such as Hannibal was never guilty of; such as cannot be traced to Alexander.

Speaking broadly, the Civil War was a war of conquest as much as the Gallic. Caesar was content with no less than sole control of Rome. In accomplishing this end his political and military management were, as always, admirable. He was constantly on the offensive. Except as the result of an overeager movement, he was never put on the defence. His constant endeavour, as in the Gallic War, was to surprise his opponents before they were ready. It may be claimed as a valid reason why he did not march overland against Pompey, that the latter, being master of the sea, would have ascertained his movements and prepared for them. It may be claimed that it was to take the enemy unawares that Caesar moved on Pompey in Epirus in the winter season. It may be claimed that to surprise the aristocrats was the object of the winter movement on Africa. For as a rule Caesar was careful to put his troops into winter-quarters. But to allow these claims does not palliate the lack of preparation.

Caesar's scouting system was always good. In the Civil War he could more readily gather information of his enemy's plans than in Gaul. He was in countries where he had many adherents, sometimes the bulk of the population, in his favour. Deserters were more frequent from the enemy. Pompey had similar advantages in a lesser degree. The tide of desertion was apt to set in Caesar's favour. Caesar used his light cavalry for scouting purposes to better advantage and was generally more active in collecting information than his opponents.

Though Caesar was always numerically the weaker, his troops were of a higher grade in discipline and *morale*. He had not many auxiliary troops. He felt that his *legionaries* were stronger without them. He kept enough for an efficient skirmishing line, but did not care for the hordes of them which were usual at his day.

In the Civil War Caesar kept his troops well concentrated. He rarely made detachments from his army except those necessary for foraging. In the first Spanish campaign he left three legions in Massilia and took six to Spain; four remained in Sicily, one in Sardinia, and the rest in Italy. With less than these he could not hold the territory he had already conquered. While Caesar concentrated his own, his constant endeavour was to make his opponents divide their forces or to keep them from concentrating, so as to beat them in detail.

His objectives were well chosen. They were generally the forces of his enemy. In 49 it was Brundisium, where Pompey was in force, seeking to leave Italy. Being the chief seaport, it had the advantage of protecting Rome if he drove Pompey across to Epirus. Later objectives were the passes of the Pyrenees, to open his route to Spain; Ilerda, where Afranius and Petreius lay in force; Dyrrachium, to rob Pompey of his base of supplies; Pharsalus, or in other words, the army of the enemy; Alexandria, to which place he thought Pompey had fled; the upper Delta, where Ptolemy was in force; Zela in Asia Minor, where he could strike Pharnaces without delay; Ruspina, as a secondary base near the enemy; Ucita and Thapsus, the enemy's *dépôts*; Ulia, Corduba and Attegua, important cities held by the enemy in force; and Munda, where he could force a decisive battle upon Cnaeus; each and every objective he chose was a thrust at the heart of his adversary, Caesar never looked askance at his work. His look, thought and act went to the very centre. *Veni, vidi, vici* might well have been his motto, instead of being applied to one campaign.

Caesar was frequently in distress for rations. In victualling he was less apt than Alexander, less careful than Hannibal. Over-anxiety to get into the field lay at the root of the evil; but, though often with difficulty and risk, Caesar always managed to keep his men in food. In offensive campaigns the enemy is apt to control the supplies. Caesar was fairly careful in victualling, but his movements were not wont to be controlled by the question of rations unless famine stood at the door. He was ready to take his chances of subsisting on the country or of capturing his enemy's supplies. Not infrequently he made a mistake. On the whole he was a good provider.

As in Gaul so in the Civil War, Caesar preferred combat in the open field; but he was at times compelled to sit down before fortified places and to waste time in besieging them. According to the custom of the time, he drew up near the enemy in the open in nearly all his battles. He had none of the sublime audacity of Frederick or Alexander; he was cautious not to be lured into an attack on entrenchments or difficult positions; but he was not slow to accept equal battle.

Caesar's manoeuvring and blockades were on a large scale. The object of his manoeuvring was for battle, to compromise the enemy or to reach his magazines. In the Civil War this was more frequent than in Gaul. Caesar had gained self-confidence. The earliest example of able manoeuvring was at Ilerda. A good example was the operation at Zeta.

In adversity Caesar was strong and elastic. He never weakened in *morale*; he was never disastrously defeated. After Dyrrachium he marched away rather like a victor than a badly beaten man. He showed no sign of loss of self-confidence; he cheered his legions by explaining away their defeat; he raised their courage by sundry small operations like the one at Gomphi, until they again felt that they could cope with the Pompeians even if outnumbered two to one. This ability to cope with adversity is more than any other a mark of Caesar's genius. No one ever exhibited it as Hannibal did; but it was a distinct characteristic of Caesar.

The tactics of Caesar in the Civil War was substantially the same as in Gaul, somewhat altered to conform to the fact that he had Roman soldiers in his front. His attacks were less summary than on the Gallic barbarians. At Ilerda the *cohorts* fought five hours with the spear before, they took to the sword.

In battle, flank movements were common. The general effort of each commander was to rupture the enemy's line or break down one of its flanks. The tactics of Caesar was simple. There are few examples in his battles of splendid tactical formations like Epaminondas' oblique order at Leuctra or Mantinaea, Alexander's wedge at Arbela, or Hannibal's withdrawing salient at Cannae. Caesar's one instance of battlefield manoeuvring was at Ruspina. This was good, but not on an extensive scale. Why he did not profit by the tactical lessons of other captains is not clear. He did not appear to think the grand-tactics of battle available for his purposes. Nearly all his engagements were in simple parallel order, coupled with prudent forethought against unusual danger, as in the creation of a fourth line at Pharsalus. What one admires in other captains as original grand-tactical combinations are absent in the case of Caesar. The more usual combinations we do find. The *orbis*—or square—we saw used at Zeta with excellent effect. At Ilerda we saw Caesar march in order of battle a much longer distance than usual, showing exceptional steadiness in his formation and discipline. In marching by the flank in two or three lines, peculiar heed was given to the flank which was toward the enemy; it was so formed that it could readily come to a front against a sudden attack.

Caesar's ordinary formation was in three lines; but the accomplishment of the fourth line at Pharsalus is peculiarly noteworthy. Scarce another instance exists in which so great an effect has been produced by so small a body of men used at the right time in the right way. The Fifth legion at Ucita was a sort of fourth line; the same legion at Thapsus acted in a similar capacity against elephants; and we notice at Ucita that Caesar had two lines in his left and three in his right wing, or with the Fifth legion really four. It was a species of a strengthened left wing, though not for the usual purpose of such a reinforced wing.

In formation for battle Caesar's line of ten to twelve legions was generally divided into a centre and two wings, each of these under a legate. He had not enough legates to place one in command of each legion. One or other wing opened the battle. This duty was most frequently performed by the Tenth legion, whose post was wont to be on the right. Caesar was always with the opening wing and gave the signal. From this there sometimes arose a sort of oblique order, because the wing which opened the battle pressed forward faster than the rest of the lines, much in the same way as in Alexander's battles; but this was not an oblique order in the same sense as the formations at Mantinaea or Leuthen.

The Romans were never able in the use of mounted men. Pompey's cavalry at Pharsalus was massed in one heavy body on one wing and should have gained the victory; but it was badly organized and commanded. Caesar's small corps was employed to better advantage. Caesar's Gallic and German horse—of which at times he had large bodies—was, in its way, efficient. Occasionally as many as four thousand men rode in one column. There had been an improvement in the Roman cavalry since the Punic Wars, principally due to the employment for that arm of the natives of countries which made a specialty of cavalry. But on the whole, Caesar's cavalry was defective. It did not act the legitimate part of cavalry. It was often mixed with foot. Nothing in Caesar's battles even faintly approaches the magnificent use of cavalry by Alexander or Hannibal.

A general is often gauged by his opponents. Pompey had long ranked as a great soldier; but he had ceased from war; he was resting on his laurels. He had never been noted for initiative, and the political intrigues of many years had unfitted him for the field. Caesar had just emerged from an eight years' war in perfect training. His political scheming had gone hand in hand with war and had not weakened his soldier's habit. Add to each man's equipment his own peculiar qualities and Caesar could scarcely help winning in the contest, if he had means at all equal to those of his adversary. There needs no proof of Caesar's ability to cope with the difficulties which lay before him; and that Pompey looked quietly on at Caesar's conquest of Spain is proof enough of the latter's hebetude. Caesar had had the best training, actual war under, in this instance, the best master,—himself. His experience was bred of the errors he had made and intelligently profited by. Not that he now ceased to commit errors. Dyrrachium was a blunder of the first water. Caesar needed a back-set to teach him caution. He got it at Dyrrachium; he at once adopted a more rational scheme, and won.

From the beginning Caesar grew in every department of the art of war. His ability in strategy, tactics, fortification, sieges, logistics, was more marked at the end of his career than at any other period. It is a question as to whether his aggressiveness did not decrease towards the end of his campaigns. It would have been strange had it not done so. To Caesar's personality his soldiers owed all they knew and all they were. They some-times lacked the spirit of discipline, but they were remarkable for tough-ness, force, adaptiveness, patience in every matter of difficulty and self-denial, endurance and courage in battle, attachment to and confidence in their general. Caesar's legionaries were an equal honour to Caesar and to Rome. They were a standing reproach to Roman rottenness. Pompey's men could not compare with them in any sense, and this was because Pompey had created his soldiers and Caesar had created his.

Pompey had never shown the highest order of ability, but it will not do to underrate him. He had at small outlay won his salute as Imperator; he had yet more easily come by his title of Magnus. Still some of Pompey's work was excellent, when he actually set to work and good luck ran in his favour. In what has been said it has not been intended to convey the idea that Pompey was not still a good, perhaps a great soldier, though he fell short of being a marvellous one. It is in comparison only to Caesar that he pales. Had a lesser man opposed him, Pompey might have shown in higher degree the qualities he may fairly be credited with possessing. But Caesar overshadowed him to a degree which made him not only seem but be less than himself. He dwindled because he met a moral force which bore him under. Cae-sar, on the contrary, was and always will be simply Caesar,—symbol of all that is greatest as a captain and a ruler.

Scipio lacked both energy and ability in any marked degree. He was merely a military hack. Solely as Pompey's father-in-law it was that he came by his command.

Cato, who was really the superior of all the Pompeians, refused the supreme command in favour of Scipio, made no use of his unquestioned powers, and avoided disaster by committing suicide.

Labienus showed much energy, but his skill was weakened by hatred of Caesar. He was a fair sample of the excellent lieutenant, but poor captain. He had been a worthy and able soldier under Caesar; against Caesar he sank to a less than second-rate position. In every encounter with his ancient chief he lost his head.

Both of the young Pompeys showed at first some promise. But when taxed, Sextus dropped back to a low grade of skill. Cnaeus exhibited more but not marked ability. Neither was a dangerous opponent. The rest of the generals opposed to Caesar were distinctly of a low order.

Caesar's abilities stand out in singular contrast to all of these. Tried by the ability of his opponents, which is a tempting theme, but neither a fair test nor a fruitful subject, Caesar ranks lower than Alexander, vastly lower than Hannibal. But as one of the marks of the great captain is to utilize the errors of opponents who lack high qualities, a thing which he always did, the soldier Caesar cannot be placed on a level other than theirs. His wonderful power of mind and will produced a marked influence on everything he touched. Everyone relied on him, all looked to him as the centre of motion. As has been before said, the test of greatness in a campaign may be applied by seeking the general who is the mainspring of the movement, the motive power which keeps the rest at work. This in all his campaigns was Caesar. It was not what his enemies did, but what Caesar did, which furnished the keynote of all that happened.

Caesar was generous in rewards, praise and largesses to his soldiers. He was ever ready to distinguish the brave and thus incite others to imitate them. He had the rare capacity of winning his men's devotion to himself, both as a soldier and as a man; and this without losing his power or descending from the dignity of his position. He dressed and equipped his legions well, distinguished many by giving them weapons ornamented with gold and silver, took pride in seeing his men well-mounted and handsomely attired. Though his soldiers were dubbed "scented dandies," they yet knew how to fight. In this they were like their leader. Beware of underrating dandies. Some of the stoutest hearts and clearest heads have lurked under a foppish dress.

Caesar never lacked a pleasant word for his men, remembered the face of anyone who had done a gallant deed, and when not in the presence of the enemy encouraged amusements, in which he not infrequently personally joined. After the disaster to Sabinus and Cotta, Caesar allowed his beard and hair to grow and vowed he would not cut them till his soldiers had revenged their comrades' death. This to us trivial act had its meaning to Caesar's legionaries. Such things wrought up the feeling of his soldiers to a worship almost fanatical. However lax when danger was not near, in the vicinity of the enemy Caesar demanded discipline of the strictest. He required the most unheard-of exertions and sacrifices; he allowed no rest, day nor night; season or weather had no recognition. Every man must be ready at all times for duty. A willingness to do and suffer all this Caesar comprehended in the name soldier. It was his use of "citizens" instead of "comrades" that broke up the mutiny of the Tenth legion. He was generous in overlooking smaller faults, but severe beyond measure in punishing larger ones. He was the more requiring of a man the higher he stood in office. His severest punishment was dismissal, as in the case of the *tribunes* and *centurions* of the Tenth legion when it came to Africa. In the Roman state this was political and social excommunication. Caesar's officers were capable of more under his command than under any other conditions. Witness Labienus in Gaul and Labienus afterwards. This was owing not only to his gigantic personality but to the fact that he was ready and able at all times to do thrice the work that anyone else could do. No one in the army laboured so hard as Caesar. All this makes it stranger that Caesar's men more than once escaped from his control in a manner which showed a limit to their discipline. Of this Thapsus was the most noted example. The same may be said of their occasional demoralization, as at Dyrrachium.

Caesar's career as a soldier shows to a marked degree how great in war is the factor of personal character. Caesar's art was not a thing he had learned from or could impart to others. It was the product of his vast intellect and bore the seal of his splendid moral force.

CAESAR AS *PONTIFEX MAXIMUS*

CHAPTER 45

Alexander, Hannibal, Caesar

Alexander had the most beauty;-we think of him as the Homeric youth; of Hannibal and Caesar as in sober maturity of years. In all his qualities, Caesar is the most splendid man of antiquity; as a soldier he equals the others. Alexander's ambition and Caesar's was coupled to self; Hannibal's pure. Caesar the man was kindly; Caesar the soldier ruthless. In capacity for work all were equal. Alexander's will was fiery; Hannibal's discreet; Caesar's calculating. In battle Alexander was possessed of divine fury; Hannibal was cool but bold; Caesar had not their initiative. In influence over men Hannibal was supreme. Caesar was an orator; Alexander and Hannibal spoke simply and to the point. As statesmen, Alexander built on a mistaken foundation; Hannibal's work was doomed to fail; Caesar's is everlasting. For performance with slender means and against great odds Hannibal stands the highest. Alexander had luck, but used it; Hannibal had no luck; Fortune smiled on Caesar as on no other man. The strategy of each was the same. In extent of conquest Alexander was the most distinguished; in speed, Caesar; in endurance, Hannibal. Alexander was the cavalry-leader; in tactics Caesar was below the others; in sieges, Hannibal. As men Alexander and Hannibal stir us with the touch of nature, as Caesar does not. Caesar evokes our admiration; Alexander and Hannibal our sympathy.

In beauty of person and stateliness of presence the king of Macedon was more distinguished than the Carthaginian general or the Roman imperator. Few of the heroes of history appeal to us in the physical sense so distinctly as Alexander; and, adding youth to splendid achievement and royal bearing, the conqueror of the Great King stands out the most lustrous of mortals. In bodily strength and endurance Hannibal was his equal; Caesar, while gifted with unsurpassed nervous force, and physically able, does not wear the Homeric garb with the right of Alexander. Nor had he the youth of warlike glory of the son of Hamilcar. When our thoughts call up Caesar or Hannibal, we are apt to see in our mind's eye the mature man, superb in his power of intellect and character; Alexander stands before us clad in a blaze of divine strength and youthful fervour. All Alexander's portrait-busts are those of the hero who subdued the world and died before he passed his youth; those of Caesar and the sole authentic one of Hannibal show us the man of middle age, all the more powerful, perhaps, but less the demi-god than the son of Philip.

If we take him as statesman, jurist, author, thinker, soldier, Caesar has no peer in antiquity. If we take him merely as the soldier, he stands beside the others. There are things which can be neither weighed nor measured. In intellectual activity and moral force these captains varied as their temperaments varied. In uprightness of purpose and purity of life neither Alexander nor Caesar in any sense approached Hannibal,—the unselfish, model patriot, whose ambition was solely for his country, whose appetites were always curbed, whose life was one long and earnest effort, whom pleasures could not seduce, nor position warp, nor flattery turn.

Alexander was rash in temper and succumbed all too often to his love of wine. His ambition was a dream of personal greatness coupled to the hope of Hellenizing the world; and around this he cast the atmosphere of his all-pervading intellect, his boundless ability to conjure up mighty projects, his fabulous power of compassing the impossible. Caesar was by nature cool and calculating. He neither resisted nor succumbed to temptation. To him there was no temptation; what he craved he took. It was his boundless egotism which made him Caesar. His ambition was Rome; but Rome was not Rome without Caesar as its guiding star. With many of the noblest personal qualities, which he manifested at every turn, Caesar had not a glint of patriotism in its finest sense. All that he did or aspired to do was coupled to self. He could not serve Rome, as Hannibal sought to serve Carthage, though he himself was swallowed up. Generous and kindly by nature, he yet has to his charge holocausts which stop one's heartbeats. Caesar, the conqueror, knew not Caesar, the man. If he felt a qualm at the treacherous butchery of nearly half a million souls in a few hours, no one ever knew it. Alexander was warm-hearted but hasty; generous at one moment, violent at another. Hannibal had that gentle fibre whose human kindness to fallen foemen overcame his hatred of their race. Caesar was gracious in his dealings with persons, ruthless to insensibility in his treatment of peoples.

Intellect and moral force alone do not suffice to make a great man. Work is at the root of all that man has done or will ever do. In his capacity for work Alexander drew on a body and mind which never knew fatigue. If in any respect Alexander came near to being the demigod he loved to be thought, it was in his superhuman ability to labour. No professional athlete was his superior in arms or games; no philosopher had a clearer grasp of any new or knotty problem; no soldier was ever so truly instinct with the *gaudium certaminis* as he; no one ever performed so much in so short a life. Hannibal, in his youth, was much like Alexander; but maturity early sat on Hannibal's brow; eternal youth ever shone from Alexander's visage. Caesar we only know in youth as the dandy who was noted for bold political acts; in manhood as the sublime orator, and as the statesman who overrode all with whom he came in contact; in middle age as the magnificent soldier, but the soldier whose boldness was not Alexander's nor his caution Hannibal's; in old age as the legislator, the governor, the creator of what today we look upon as the foundation of our civilization.

The will-power of Alexander was that of a man who brooked not restraint; whose fiery purpose respected neither bosom friend nor ancient servitor; who would destroy even himself in seeking to compass his chosen end. Hannibal's will never outran an inborn discretion which subordinated even Hannibal. We do not know what Alexander might have become at the age of Hannibal's greatest power; we do know what Hannibal was at the age of Alexander's greatest performance. Alexander did his brilliant work in the twenties, Hannibal in the thirties and forties. Caesar was well on in middle life before he wore the purple *paludamentum*. When he won his most splendid battle on the field of Pharsalus, he had by two years passed fifty; his best work followed this. His will-power was of a different kind. What he set out to do, he did, with the courage of Alexander, the persistency of Hannibal; but he could yield here a little, insist there a little, cajole, command, weave his way into opposition or tear its fabric into shreds, without for a moment losing sight of his once conceived, never forgotten purpose.

The courage of each was unsurpassed. So soon as battle was engaged, Alexander was possessed of a divine fury scarcely sobered by his divine intelligence. In the death struggle of legion and *phalanx*

Hannibal never for a moment lost his quiet power of seeing and doing the proper thing; never failed to take advantage of the least error of his opponent, nor to force the fighting at the critical moment. In the execution of his projects he was obstinately bold; deliberate when doubtful, rapid at the instant when a blow would tell. Caesar's courage as a soldier lay rather in the power to push a strategic advantage than in the longing to meet and annihilate the enemy. Alexander and Hannibal, like Frederick, never counted numbers; unless forced into action, Caesar sought to get the chances on his side before he fought.

Alexander's influence over others as a man, was marked; as a king, was supreme. He would have been the chief of any assembly had he not been king; but his royal character added to his manly force. Hannibal had no equal in his power over men. He who could hold together a motley array of diverse tribes, with clashing instincts and aspirations, weld them into an army and, though outnumbered many times by superior troops, could with it keep his clutch on the throat of Rome for half a generation, has no peer. By just what method he did it we do not know; but the bare fact suffices. Caesar won his influence much as Napoleon did. His gigantic grasp, his fluent tongue, his plausible method, his suggestive mind, his appearance of reasonably yielding to those whom he desired to control, carried every point. He was truly Caesar Imperator, embodiment of all which should be *czar* and emperor,—which, alas, so rarely is.

Caesar was by nature and training an orator. His style was direct, convincing; his manner animated; he held his audience. Alexander and Hannibal were both intellectual and cultured; neither had studied rhetoric as an art; but each had the power of saying the right thing at the right moment and in such fashion as to sway his hearers and to compass his ends. None of these great men dealt in mere words. What they said proceeded from the glowing thoughts within. Who thinks clearly speaks clearly. None of these men spoke without due effect. Whoso listened was convinced, persuaded, or silenced. Alexander spoke as the master; Hannibal as the diplomat, with peace or war in either hand; Caesar, however powerful, never lost his plausibility. No man ever conjured right to his side, ever made the worse appear the better reason, more surely than he.

That Alexander's statesmanlike projects left a permanent trace of Hellenism on every country he over-ran is praise enough. Hannibal was sagacious and farsighted. Had he not been endowed with the craft of a Talleyrand as well as the purity of a Washington, he could never have come so close to upheaving the foundations of the Roman republic. But as a statesman Caesar's work was the more enduring, as it had the better basis. He built on what was left of the solid Roman character; his corner-stones were well laid; his superstructure lasted for generations; the inner meaning of his work has modified all human endeavours towards civilization from his own age to ours. Alexander wrought like a giant, but on a mistaken plan. Traces of his work still stand, like the pyramids of Gizeh. Hannibal' s work could not last; the Carthaginians were bound by the rule of progress to disappear from the world's economy. Baal could not endure; no Punic structure but must perish. Caesar had a groundwork prepared for him by twenty generations of rational, honest thinkers, who builded even better than they knew. On this his perspicacity and wisdom erected what will ever be the pattern of growth in statecraft. That the Roman Empire did not last was due to other causes. The fabric wrought by Caesar the statesman can never perish.

Apart from other work—as a soldier simply—no performance with slender means can equal Hannibal's. Alexander started worse handicapped than Hannibal, but circum-stances favoured him and, once he had attacked his problem, his material resources grew as he advanced into the bowels of the land. Hannibal's resources dwindled from the first; he was forced to create everything he had. He made bricks without straw; he himself forged every weapon with which he slew a Roman. We shall never see such soldier's art again. Caesar's re-sources were ample. He could have drawn on more than he put to use. Vast as was the result of his achievements as a soldier, there is no part of his work which can be fairly compared to the record of Hannibal. To win is not the test of military skill.

Alexander had a way of courting Fortune so that she always smiled on him. One's fancy readily ascribes her fidelity to his fascinating influence; in truth, it was that he never neglected a chance the fickle goddess offered. The smallest favour he on the instant put to use. He never called on Hercules until his own shoulder was at the wheel. How could Fortune be fickle with such an ardent wooer? To Han-nibal the youth, Fortune was kind; on Hannibal, past his youth, she turned her back, and never again smiled. And yet this noble soldier wrought as persistently as if he had basked in her favours from morn to sunset. No man ever tempted Fortune as did Caesar. He was suc-cessful beyond any in his devotion to women; he obtained before he asked. So with Fortune. She who forsook watchful Hannibal never turned from reckless Caesar. Always at hand and kinder the more Caesar neglected what she requires in all others, she saved him a thousand times when his schemes deserved to come to naught. History furnishes no instance of a great man being so beholden to her whom he rarely sought to court. Foolhardiness which in others Fortune would leave to the punishment which ought to follow, in Caesar she would favour. He could not overtax her patience. And knowing that Caesar was happy in his conquests of women, we must allow that his greatest was the easy conquest of this wont-to-be hard-won goddess.

Though Alexander was outnumbered as no one else, he fought only barbarians and semi-civilized armies; he attacked an effete monarchy without cohesion, a structure already, toppling. Caesar fought barbarians first and then troops of his own kindred, though not so well equipped or commanded. The barbarians Caesar showed less aptness in handling than Alexander or Hannibal; in the Civil War he had stancher forces to oppose him than Alexander. Hannibal fought barbarians in Spain, and in Italy troops far better than his own, the stoutest then on foot, under leaders who had been taught by himself and who had assimilated his method. Marcellus and Nero and Scipio learned Hannibal's lessons by heart as the Archduke Charles and Blücher and Wellington had mastered the art of Napoleon. Hannibal was overtaxed as no captain in the history of war has ever been and held his own a moment. The more we compare Hannibal with any other soldier, the brighter the effulgence of his genius.

The art of each of these captains was based on a rare combination of intellect and moral force; and in the case of each the third element, opportunity, was not wanting. Each had a method; he saw distinctly the point at which he aimed, and he drove his shaft straight and unerringly into the target,—and through it. Each was careful of his base; each saw and sought the enemy's weak spot; each kept his army well in hand. Alexander and Hannibal were better providers than Caesar, whose army, from his over-anxiety to grapple with his problem, was often on the point of starvation. Alexander won by bold strokes, the brilliancy of which can be found on no other historic page. Hannibal won by a careful study of the when and where to strike; his blow when delivered never failed to cripple the enemy. Caesar was less bold than Alexander; in a way he was more cautious than Hannibal; but with his caution was mixed a precipitancy which should in many cases have wrecked his schemes. Alexander's first glance told him where to strike, and the blow fell with lightning speed and force. Hannibal was deliberate; he lured his enemy into a false position and annihilated him. Caesar, while never failing to grasp the whole, and to act on a method fully abreast of the problem, was so lax in many of the parts that to succeed required the intervention of a luck which often comes like a *deus ex machinâ*. Alexander would not steal a victory; Hannibal was the master of stratagem; Caesar was by turns Quixotically bold and a very Fabius for lack of tactical enterprise. Yet *finis coronat opus*; Caesar won, and he stands beside Alexander and Hannibal.

The element of speed in accomplishing a task is a test not to be overlooked. Caesar took eight years to conquer Gaul; Alexander in eight years had conquered a vast territory of neighbouring barbarians, had ground Hellas under his heel, had restored to the Ægean cities their independence, and had overrun Asia to the Jaxertes and India to the Hyphasis. In the Civil War, Caesar was second in extent and rapidity of conquest only to Alexander. Hannibal must be tried by another standard. In five years he subdued half of Spain, crossed the Alps to Italy and, though reaching the Po with but twenty-six thousand men, throttled the gigantic power of Rome,—a city which could levy three quarters of a million men. This record for speed against odds excels that of Alexander and Caesar. And when we take up the question of endurance,—the man who, forsaken by his own people and cast on his own sole resources, could hold Rome at bay and on the verge of dissolution for fifteen years has not, cannot have a peer.

Alexander had no confidant but Hephaestion. Hannibal never had a confidant. Caesar had many friends to whom he confided his schemes in part; the whole he kept strictly to himself. Caesar trusted men so far as he could use them. But though on the surface plausible, frank and open as few men ever are, no one knew Caesar's ulterior purpose. What he aimed at as the result of all he did, no one divined. He was an adept at concealing his intentions under a veil of candour. It befits Alexander's sunny character to have a Hephaestion; it befits Hannibal's vast and trying task as well as his patient isolation that he should alone hold the key to his purpose. It befits Caesar's versatility and self-reliance that he should use many friends to aid his kaleidoscopic plans. But under all a well-kept counsel added to his chances of success. Hannibal is said to have worn masks to conceal his person; Caesar's face was always masked when it came to his inner motives.

Alexander's strategy was gigantic in conception; the theatre of his campaigns was the world. Hannibal's strategy differed from Alexander's as the problems of each differed; but it was equally skilful and bold; in a certain sense keener if not so vast. Caesar's strategic push was always noteworthy. His apprehension of the strategy of the Gallic problem was as fine as his judgment of what was required by the conditions which faced him as he stood on the bank of the Rubicon. It could not be better.

As a cavalry leader Alexander cannot be equalled. No one ever repeated charges with the same body of horse on the same place in the enemy's line as he did at the Hydaspes. No one ever trained such squadrons; the "Companions" stand unrivalled in history. Next to him, but with a distinct interval, came Hannibal with his Numidians. Alexander's Companions won with naked blade in hand; the Numidians by clever tactics. Caesar never knew the uses of cavalry in this sense. His Gallic and German horse were each excellent; but they cannot be mentioned beside the others.

Alexander's tactics was audacious and clean-cut. He thrust home on the instant, and blow succeeded blow until his enemy was a wreck. Hannibal studied his tactical problem with deliberation; he thrust not till by skilful feints he had found the weak side of his adversary's defence. But when he thrust, his blade never failed to find an opening. Caesar's tactics was not strong. He had neither the audacity nor persistence of Alexander; he had none of the originality of Hannibal. His battles were not won because of his own perfect plan, but because of the weak behaviour of the enemy. As a tactician Caesar is far below Alexander; still farther below Hannibal. Alexander was boldness personified; Hannibal was careful in plan, strong in execution; Caesar was neither. When Caesar was forced to fight—as at the Sabis, or at Munda—he fought nobly; but he never fought as if he liked the task. Pharsalus is the only battle boldly planned and boldly carried through; and this was won by Pompey's laxness as much as by Caesar's courage and good judgment.

In personal bearing, Alexander was, as he strove to be, an Achilles. Hannibal's gallantry in youth is testified to by Livy, but we forget it; we look on him as the thoughtful soldier, running no unnecessary risks, calculating his chances closely and then striking a blow marvellous for its effect. Caesar never appeals to us as the *beau sabreur*; he is the intellectual captain. In the few instances in which his personal conduct was called upon he was acting in self-defence. He never led his men, as Alexander did at the city of the Malli, from sheer exuberance of courage. Caesar won by brain tissue backed by strong moral force. He was not Homeric in his heroism.

In the history of sieges. Tyre and Alesia stand side by side. Hannibal never did such work. Saguntum, though fine, is on a lower level.

Alexander's opponents were far below him in capacity; Caesar's rank higher. Vercingetorix was able; Pompey had been great, but his powers had waned. Neither Alexander nor Caesar faced such men as Marcellus and Nero, Fabius and Scipio, or such troops as the burgess-legion. Tried by this standard Hannibal is the pattern of patterns.

In marches Alexander holds the record for great distances; his pursuit of Darius is hard to equal. Hannibal is unmatched for craft and skilful eluding of the enemy. Some of Caesar's marches are remarkable. The march from Gergovia to the Æduan army and back—fifty miles in twenty-four hours, with a force of fifteen thousand foot—is only equalled by the Spartan march to Marathon. Alexander's passage of the Hindu-Koosh is like Hannibal's crossing of the Alps. Caesar was never called on to do such work. Alexander was cautious on the march; Hannibal still more so. It was from Hannibal that the Romans learned to march an army. Caesar began by being careless; but surprises taught him caution; he ended by conducting his marches in the ablest manner.

Alexander demanded of his men the severest exertions, without regard to season or circumstances, but took excellent care of them whether at work or rest. Hannibal was never out of bread, though living most of the time on the enemy's country. On occasion, as in crossing the Alps or the Arnus marshes, he called on his men for labour untold. Caesar was not always a good provider; the African campaign was largely a tramp for victual. He was more apt to put his men in winter-quarters than Alexander or Hannibal.

In exerting influence over his men, each of these captains exhibited the highest power. That each was the hardest worked man in the army was apparent to all; each could do every part of a soldier's duty in a manner no man in his command could approach. Justice, generosity and high character made them the example all strove to imitate. Each inculcated a spirit of emulation among his men; each rewarded gallantry and good service as they deserved.

As simple man, Hannibal far outranks the others in his purity of life and his elevated patriotism. Alexander had two sides—the one lovable, admirable; the other lamentable in its want of self-control. Caesar the man lacks the one touch of nature. One can truthfully say a thousand admirable things of him. Quite apart from his greatness,—his reasonableness, his warm friendships, his generosity, the fine qualities of his mind, the many noble traits to which all testify, commend him to our admiration, to our regard. And yet there is to Caesar, as there is to Napoleon, an artificiality which one never can forget. He wears an armour we cannot penetrate. We say much to praise him, but the epithets lack an inward meaning. Alexander, in his love for Hephaestion, in his violence to Clitus, was a man. Hannibal, in his hatred of Rome, in his self-immolation at the altar of Carthage, was a man. Gustavus, the Christian king, falling at the head of his squadrons at Lützen, and Frederick, the monarch of iron, writing poor French verses as a relief from his defeat, are both full of human nature. Caesar and Napoleon impress us as characters in history. Each calls out a thrill of admiration; neither calls out a thrill of human sympathy.

Tried solely by the standards of the soldier, these equal captains, if one may pronounce between them, stand: Hannibal the peerless; Alexander the Homeric; Caesar the unvanquished.

Taken in all his characters, Caesar is the greatest man in antiquity.

CHAPTER 46

The Art of War of the Roman Empire

Augustus formed from the relics of the legions of the civil wars a new standing army some three hundred thousand strong, which was distributed mostly on the frontiers. The empire rested on the army; but Augustus' method was good. The praetorian guard gradually increased, acquired great power and used it illy. Later on, when there was a good ruler there was a good army; under weak emperors, the army was bad. On the whole the material degenerated; service was avoided, even by mayhem; barbarians filled the ranks. The use of the sword decreased in favour of jactile weapons; engines were employed in line of battle; elephants and trained wild beasts were used. Intervals decreased so that the legion again became a phalanx. Tactics reached a high point, but the soul of the army was not there. Baggage and non-combatants reached Oriental proportions. Pay and largesses were enormous. Camps were more strongly fortified. Fortification and sieges were expert. Theory was developed; practice retrograded. Standing armies called out regular fleets. Declining soldierly spirit was supplemented by petty defensive means. There were many and able generals during the first five centuries of our era; but there was no growth in the art of war.

From the history of the army of Julius Caesar we have seen that it was the genius of the captain and not the personal qualities of the rank and file which won his splendid victories. When Caesar Augustus became sole ruler of Rome, military matters were not long in being put on a new footing. The ancient army of the republic had been a burgess-militia, and it is only necessary to recall the events of the Second Punic War to show that, rather than the ability of any one leader,

313

it was the steadfastness of the Senate and army—for the army was the people—that saved Rome from annihilation by Hannibal.

During the civil broils of Rome, professional soldiers and mercenaries had gradually crept in until they formed the bulk of the rank and file; and these had prepared the way for the standing army which was now to form a part of the equipment of the empire, in peace and war alike.

Augustus went to work in a systematic way. From the forty-five legions and fifteen thousand cavalry remaining over from the civil wars, the slaves, freedmen and all of that ilk were discharged. Some one hundred and twenty thousand volunteers and veterans were settled in twenty-eight colonies on the lands in Italy donated to them. The remainder, mostly Roman citizens, were consolidated into twenty-five legions and a number of bodies of auxiliaries. These new legions and the cavalry attached to them were quartered in permanent camps, principally on the Rhine, Danube and Euphrates, to hold head against the inroads of foreign hordes. These troops were thus removed from the temptations of too great proximity of the capital or larger cities. Auxiliaries were raised in large numbers for service in their respective provinces.

For the protection of Italy there were raised ten praetorian *cohorts*, of one thousand men each. This was the famous body-guard of the emperor. Three of these *cohorts* formed the garrison of Rome; the seven others those of the principal near-by cities. The sum total of all this standing force has been estimated at three hundred thousand men.

The soldier's oath had in early days been to the republic; from the time of Marius down it had been taken individually to the general who was raising legions to hold his province or to make war upon the neighbouring nations; now that the emperor was the state, it ran:

"In the name of the emperor I swear unconditionally to obey him, never to leave the ensign, nor spare my life for emperor and state."

The term of service varied from twelve to twenty years, and every third year a careful levy was held to fill the service gaps. The excessive privileges which the soldiers had enjoyed during the civil wars and gradually claimed as a condition of military life, were restricted, and a special fund, under the emperor's sole control, was created from which to pay, clothe and ration the troops.

Thus was the power of the Roman emperor as firmly-grounded on the army as the power of the republic had been grounded on the *burgess*-soldier; and while the exceptional personal qualities of Augustus made this reorganization a benefit to Rome, the army, under later and less worthy rulers, became a curse. The ten *praetorian cohorts* were all drawn in to Rome by his successor, and from thence on remained there, and by their corruption and tyranny grew to be the terror of the land. Nearly the entire first century of our era was made unquiet by the antagonism between people and army.

During the second century, from Nerva to Marcus Aurelius, the army was held in better leash. But luxury and lax political morals had been doing their work in people and army alike. Both were degenerating. The citizens avoided military service to such a degree that the habit of self-mayhem became common. The succeeding period of threatened invasions by Germans and Parthians again obliged the emperors to resort to raising mercenaries,—and these among the barbarians, a necessary but dangerous practice.

The third century saw the power of Rome fallen practically into the hands of the praetorian guards, who made and unmade emperors at will. Though their abuses were some-what reformed by Septimius Severus, the gulf between people and army had grown apace. The army was largely German,—the Roman Republic was fast drifting to its fall.

The ancient arms and equipment of the legionary were not changed until the second century, though the use of the sword was steadily decreasing in favour of the spear. As the material of the arms-bearing class decreased, the latter weapon grew lighter. As the discipline and character of the rank and file waned, so whatever intervals between *cohorts* were still left decreased, and in the third century, under Caracalla and Alexander Severus, an organization like the Grecian *phalanx* was adopted, though but temporarily. The general tendency was to make all weapons lighter, for the man himself had ceased to be the well-trained, strong and able citizen of old. The legions were no longer expected to close with the foe, and the men carried additional jactile weapons, rather than those of hand-to-hand conflict.

Cavalry was still as of old heavy, with man and horse in armour; or light, using only darts for weapons.

Artillery began to accompany the legions. This it will be remembered was no new thing. Alexander in the prime of his power had employed field artillery; in their decline the Greeks had employed it in line of battle to protect their foot. The same thing now occurred with the Romans. At first this purported to be only for use on the walls of the permanent camps. But later, in the third century, the *onager* or smaller *ballista* was transported on a two-ox cart, and the hand-ballista on a one-horse wagon. Each was served by eleven men.

They could cast stones and darts three to four hundred paces. They were placed in line of battle, between the legions, to save these from too sudden or close contact with the enemy.

Elephants again appeared, and trained wild beasts and dogs were occasionally used against the enemy. These artificial aids exhibit the declining value of the legions.

The strength of the legions grew to be somewhat greater, at the normal from six to seven thousand men. Armies rarely numbered more than eight or ten legions.

Flags replaced other ensigns, sometimes cut into dragon-shape; and the bust or likeness of the emperor took the place of the eagle. To the old military horns was added a peculiar flute.

A number of changes, owing largely to the new enemies encountered as well as the less good material of the legions, gradually took place. The third line of battle was given up so as to strengthen the first, and each line had five *cohorts*. The first *cohort* was doubled in number, was often as high as twelve hundred strong, and was composed of the best men. It was not infrequently divided into halves so as to be placed on the right and left of the first line, or the fifth *cohort* was made equally strong, so that a powerful body was on each extremity of the first line. The *cohorts* of the second line stood behind the intervals of the first so long as they existed, and these at a time not well settled appear to have been diminished by half. This was the Hadrian formation. The entire question of intervals and of the space occupied by the men is a puzzling one. Tribunes now commanded *cohorts*; legates legions; the praetorians were led by *praetorian praefects*, the army by imperial or consular legates. The staff-officers were *quaestors* and *procurators*.

Trajan introduced still another system. The ten *cohorts* of the legion were placed in one line. The first had nine hundred and sixty chosen men in ten centuries and two hundred and forty cavalry. The others had four hundred and eighty men in six centuries. Arrian says the men stood in eight, Vegetius in six ranks. The front ranks were of the heavier and older *legionaries*; the rear ranks of the younger and lighter. Each man occupied three feet in width, and the ranks were six feet apart from back to breast. Light troops stood behind the legionaries. The *cohorts* stood in order from one to ten with very small, next to no, intervals, and these were filled by horizontal-fire engines. Behind the line were engines of high trajectory which could fire above the line. Behind the flanks were special troops, such as the praetorians, and cavalry and bowmen were on the flanks.

This formation had its advantages against barbarian nations, such as the Dacians, Parthians and Germans. It suited either the offensive or defensive, any kind of ground, and could be used against cavalry or infantry. It had certain features of the old class ordering of the legion. Hadrian and Trajan were specially apt at utilizing the legion thus formed. It seems to have been an attempt to reconcile the useful side of the class organization of old *burgess* times with the necessarily growing *phalangial* idea.

Armies appear to have drilled, manoeuvred and marched much as of old. The tactics of the parade-ground often reached a high point. But that old instinct for war which enabled a Roman consul to raise his army of citizens and leave Rome in one day was not present.

The hollow square for marches, on open plains and against sudden attacks, remained common. It was a safe defensive formation. The wedge or hollow wedge was successfully put to use. An instance of this was seen at Treviri, 70 A. D.

Josephus narrates how Vespasian and Titus disposed their armies. In the former's march from Syria to Galilee in 67 A. D., the column was as follows: the light troops (bowmen and slingers) sustained by a small body of heavy foot and some horsemen, in the van; following them the mechanics (*fabri*) like our pioneers, to repair bridges and roads; then the officers' baggage with cavalry, the emperor and staff, the military engines; then the bulk of the army,—the legions in a column of sixes; next the army-train. Last came the mercenaries, mixed with legionaries and cavalry to steady them.

Up to the third century the Roman armies marched rapidly; the speed and distances then decreased markedly, owing in part to the less good material, in part to the greater amount of baggage and enginery.

An army was marshalled for battle in much the same manner as a legion, and occasionally the position of the legions was determined by lot. When the army was in one line, the light troops and enginery opened the action. The heavy foot then advanced, and the light troops retired through them,—as there were no intervals, by the even-number men stepping for the moment behind the odd. The front ranks of *legionaries* closed and couched their spears, though these were not formidable, and the rear ranks fired above their heads. The light troops and engines which were in the rear aided the front lines by their fire. The mounted archers moved from point to point and the cavalry operated on the wings.

The farther the Roman army grew away from its old self-reliance the more it was sought to supplement this by enginery and defensive tactics of various useless sorts. The assault with naked weapon was now rarely seen. Distance weapons were preferred. Instead of the Roman soldier being more than a match for the barbarian so soon as he closed with his man, the reverse was now the case. The bulky German could laugh in earnest at the Roman *legionary*. Under able emperors this was not so apparent; but before the end of the third century the old-fashioned Roman organization, bravery and reliability had vanished, as had happened in Greece five hundred years before.

In the same measure as the evidences of the ancient Roman gallantry in war, there disappeared from the legions the sense of discipline, order and good conduct. Caesar Augustus had somewhat re-established the old Roman military virtues; but it was only for a time. The pay of the troops rose as their value decreased, and largesses became enormous. Under Domitian the foot soldier is said to have received four gold pieces (about twelve dollars) a month, the *centurion* eight, the mounted man or *praetorian* twelve; and the deductions for arms, equipment and rations were given up. This seems excessive, in view of the value of gold. Allowances were increased to a luxurious extent and the trains and non-combatants correspondingly increased, until they reached Oriental proportions, and of the nimbleness of the Roman army there remained but a tradition. Occasionally a vigorous emperor or an energetic general improved these conditions, but only during his period of control. The tendency was downward.

Augustus had brought back military gymnastics and drill; and under Vespasian, Titus and Antoninus these were encouraged; but in the third century they again disappeared. The drill-marches which Augustus compelled the legions to make three times a month, with baggage—sometimes doubled—and over all kinds of country, were forgotten; the army manoeuvres which were then conducted on as large a scale as today in Germany or France became onerous and were dropped; and the splendid public works, especially military roads, were no longer built. The troops mutinied against such labours.

So far as military science and study were concerned, they were less practical and more pedantic. Though the empire produced numberless writers on military matters, there were none to approach Polybius or Caesar. They admirably wrote up details, but they failed to give the soul of the matter.

So far as the moral tone of the army was concerned, it could not be worse. If the ancient *burgess-legion* of the Second Punic War was the type of all that is excellent from a military standpoint, so it may be said that the army of the later empire represented all that was vicious. It was a monster whose work was to destroy the structure of the empire, even, as its predecessor had been the creator of the power and greatness of Rome. The army may be said to have been held together solely by a system of fearful punishments and unreasoning rewards.

Up to the era of Gratian, toward the end of the fourth century, the daily camp was still the rule and was made to conform to the ground with much skill, the ditch and wall being deeper and higher. The permanent camps were like regular fortresses, and enginery was much more abundant on the parapets. A system of such permanent camps was some-times constructed as a military frontier, like Hadrian's wall from the Tyne to the Solway, or Trajan's wall from the Danube to the Euxine. On the whole, while no works exceeded in ability Caesar's wonderful defences, fortification grew in skill as troops grew in worthlessness. Terraces and rams increased in size. Titus built four huge terraces opposite Jerusalem, and Vespasian had a ram which weighed one hundred tons and required fifteen hundred men to set it in motion and one hundred and fifty pairs of oxen or three hundred pairs of mules to transport it. Mines were cleverly designed and executed. The subterranean war at Jerusalem in 70 A. D. was remarkable. Double tortoises for assaulting walls and the use of inflammables in ballistics are to be noted. The number of engines accompanying an army was huge. Titus had, says Josephus, before Jerusalem, three hundred catapults and forty *ballistas*. This would be called a very large artillery force for an army of equal size today.

In a certain sense, during this period, the art of war was not on the decline but rather on the increase. The theoretical was more highly developed, the practical simplicity was less. The ancient Roman habit of winning by hard knocks had given way to a system which protected the soldiers who were no longer ready to expose life and limb for the public weal. The gain in theoretical knowledge was but a cloak to cover the loss of the old military virtues.

Standing armies soon called for regular fleets. Augustus had two,— at Ravenna and Misenum,—in the Adriatic and Tyrrhenian seas respectively. A third was later placed on the coast of Gaul. Flotillas were on the Rhine, Danube and other rivers. The type of vessel was Illyrian, and it had from one to five rows of oars. Many light boats for reconnoitring and scouting and dispatch-bearing were in use. The material of the fleets was of the worst. Slaves and criminals made up the crews. The tactics remained as of old, so far as it could be utilized.

The changes in organization of the last two centuries of the Roman empire have no interest. They all tended to the same end,—to sustain a declining soldierly spirit by petty defensive inventions in tactics, ballistics and fortification. The old offensive tone of Rome had disappeared. The Roman soldier no longer felt that if he could but get at the enemy with sword and shield, he was more than a match for him. Everything tended to invite an attack by the enemy, and to an attempt to destroy him before he reached the line of battle.

To recapitulate, chronologically, the changes by which the old *quincuncial* legion of brave *burgesses* became the one line phalanx of unsoldierly mercenaries: Marius, a century before the Christian era, changed the class-rating of citizen-soldiers to one of mere physical capacity, and began to introduce a lessening of the intervals. Caesar fully matured Marius' plan, deployed his men for battle so that the front line, and perhaps the second, had no intervals, and changed the *cohort* from a body in three lines, with light troops and cavalry pertaining to it, into a body of heavy foot in one line eight or ten men deep. His legion was habitually set up in three lines. In the first century a. d. the ten legionary *cohorts* were set up in two lines, five in each, with whatever intervals there existed filled with ballistic machines. In the second and third centuries the *cohorts* were gradually marshalled in one line without intervals, and the spears were lengthened. In the fourth and fifth centuries the legion became absolutely a *phalanx* and a very poor one. As we remember, the courageous and enterprising Roman citizens of the early republic had adapted the old Dorian *phalanx* to their own ideas of a *quincuncial* form; the gradual decline of the imperial army had, by converse causes, brought it back, not to the *phalanx* of Miltiades, Epaminondas and Alexander, but to the phalanx of the degenerate Greece of the second century B. C. This was a noteworthy but a perfectly natural series of events.

It must not be forgotten that, during the five first centuries of the Christian era, there were many able generals, both among the Romans and their barbarian opponents; and that there was a skilful adaptation of means to end. But there is nothing in the way of improvement to the art of war which claims our notice. The fact that Augustus, Arminius, Civilis the Batavian, Tiberius, Drusus, Germanicus, Vespasian, Titus, Trajan, Marcus Aurelius, Diocletian, Constantine, Julian, Theodosius, Stilicho, Aëtius, Ricimer, Odoaker, Alaric, Attila, Belisarius commanded huge armies, conducted far-reaching campaigns, displayed military talents of a high order, does not concern us here. Many of the lesser lights of war at the inception of its story are of more consequence because in what they did we first discover some principle which had its bearing on subsequent events. It is not wars, but the art of war whose history we are tracing. And if in a subsequent volume we devote but a passing notice to the entire period from the fall of the Roman empire to the invention of gunpowder, we shall not interrupt the sequence of events which have brought the art of war from its crude beginnings in the age of Cyrus to its wonderful development in our own nineteenth century.

TRIUMPHAL CAR

APPENDIX A

CASUALTIES IN SOME ANCIENT BATTLES.

Battle of	Date B. C.	Number Engaged.	Nationality.	Number Killed.	Percentage.	Usual Per cent.[1]	Killed and Wounded.	Percentage.	Usual Per cent.[1]	Loss of Enemy.	Remarks.
Marathon	490	11,000	Greeks	192	1¾	5	2,100	19½	13	6,400	
Platæa	479	*38,700	"	1,300	3⅓	4	15,000	13½	13	257,000	* Hoplites, who alone fought.
Chæronæa	338	50,000	"	2,000	4	4	18,000	36	13		
Thebes	335	33,000	Macedonians	500	1½	4	5,500	17	13	6,000	
Granicus	334	3,000	Macedonian Cavalry	85	3	2	935	31	16	*19,000	* Mostly massacre of Greek Phalanx; 1,000 Persian horsemen fell.
Issus	333	30,000	Macedonians	450	1½	4½	5,000	16½	13	*100,000	* The usual massacre.
Arbela	331	47,000	"	500	1	4	5,500	12	13	*40,000	* The usual massacre. Diodorus says 90,000; Arrian says 300,000.
Megalopolis	330	40,000	"	3,500	8¾	4½					
"	330	20,000	Spartans	5,300	26½	5					
Jaxartes	329	6,000	Macedonians	160	2⅔	7	1,160	19½	20	1,000	
Hydaspes	326	14,000	"	930	6⅔	5	10,200	73	13	*12,000	* Arrian says 23,000.
Heraclea	280	25,000	Epirots	*4,000	16	5	–	–	–	–	* Dionysius says 13,000 loss.
"	280	20,000	Romans	*7,000	35	5	–	–	–	–	" " 15,000 "
Asculum	279	70,000	Greeks and Italians	*3,550	5	4	–	–	–	–	" " " "
"	279	70,000	Romans and Italians	*6,000	8½	4	–	–	–	–	" " " "
At Rhone	218	500	Numidian Cavalry	200	40	2					
"	218	300	Roman Cavalry	140	46⅔	2					
Geronium	217	50,000	Carthaginians	6,000	12	4					
"	217	50,000	Romans	5,000	10	4					
Cannæ	216	42,000	Carth. and Gauls	6,000	14⅓	4½	–	–	–	*40,000	* Some authors say 70,000.
" (Camp)	216	11,000	Romans	2,000	18	5					
Nola, 2d	215	20,000	"	1,000	5	5	–	–	–	5,000	
Beneventum	214	20,000	"	2,000	10	5	–	–	–	15,000	Usual massacre.
Nola, 3d	214	20,000	"	400	2	5	–	–	–	2,000	
Asculum, 2d	209	20,000	"	2,700	13½	5					
" 2d day	209	17,000	"	3,000	17⅔	5	–	–	–	8,000	
Grumentum	207	40,000	"	500	1¼	4½	–	–	–	8,000	
Metaurus	207	40,000	"	8,000	20	4½	–	–	–	35,000	Usual massacre
Crotona	204	20,000	"	1,200	6	5					
Magos' Battle	203	20,000	Carthaginians	5,000	25	5					
" "	203	40,000	Romans	2,300	5¾	4½					
Zama	202	43,000	"	*2,000	4⅔	4½	–	–	–	20,000	* Clearly understated.
Aduatuca	53	5,000	"	350	7	7½	4,450	89	13		
Gergovia	52	16,000	"	746	4⅔	5					
Ilerda	49	5,000	"	71	1⅓	7	671	1½	20	200	
Pharsalus	48	22,000	"	230	1	5	–	–	–	15,000	Usual massacre.
Thapsus	47	40,000	"	50		4½	–	–	–	10,000	" "
Munda	45	58,000	"	1,000	1¾	4	1,500	2½	13	30,000	" "

[1] For armies of this size in a very stubbornly contested battle.

SOME ANCIENT MARCHES.

By whom Made.	Where Made.	Date B.C.	Number and Kind of Troops.	Distance Miles.	Time of March.	Distance Miles per Day.	Remarks.
Spartans	Sparta to Marathon	490	2,000 Infantry	150	3 days......	50	
Ten Thousand Greeks	Myriandrus to Thapsacus	401	10,000 "	230	12 " ...	19	
" "	Retreat	400	6,000	4,000	215 "	18½	
Macedonians	Drill Marches	c. 350	All arms			30	Mountain road.
"	Pelium to Thebes	335	33,000 all arms	300	14 days...	21½	
"	Pella to Sestos	334	35,000 "	350	20 "	17½	
"	Phoenicia to Thapsacus	331	50,000 "	300+	11 "	19+	
"	Pursuit at Arbela	"	5,000	70	1 night and day	70	
"	Uxians to Persian Gates	"	15,000	113	5 days...	22½	
"	Persian Gates to Araxes	"	4,000 Cavalry	40	1 night...	40	Bad mountain road.
"	Ecbatana to Rhagae	330	30,000 all arms	220+	11 days...	20	Hot, midsummer tropical weather.
"	Pursuit of Darius	"	3,000+Cavalry	400	11 "	36½	Hot, sandy road, part desert.
"	"	"	3,000 "	175	4 "	44	" " " "
"	"	"	500 "	47	1 night......	47	Desert. The end of thirty-six hours continuous marching ; of eleven days at nearly forty miles a day.
"	Hecatompylos to Aria	"	23,000 all arms	500+	20 days.....	25	
"	To Artacoana	"	6,000+ "	75	2 "	37½	Ptolemy's march.
"	Capture of Bessus	329	6,000 "	150	4 "	37½	
"	Jaxartes to Maracanda	"	15,000 "	170	3½ "	44	
"	Desert of Sandar	325	20,000+ "	57	1 day...	57	Desert.
Romans	Lilybaeum to Ariminum	218	20,000 "	650	40 days...	16	
"	Canusium to the Sena and back	207	7,000	500	14 "	38½	
"	Vesoutio to Axona	57	60,000	145	15 "	9	
"	Samarobriva to relief of Cicero	54	8,000	110	5 "	22	13 marching days : 1 day of battle.
"	Gergovia to Aelian army and back	52	16,000	50	24 hours...	50	
"	Corfinium to Brundisium	49	25,000	290	17 days...	17	Winter roads.
"	Apparagium to Dyrrachium	48	21,000	45	26 hours...	41¼	
"	Z-ta raid	46	15,000	36	16 "	48	

LEONAUR

ALSO FROM LEONAUR
AVAILABLE IN SOFTCOVER OR HARDCOVER WITH DUST JACKET

AFGHANISTAN: THE BELEAGUERED BRIGADE by G. R. Gleig—An Account of Sale's Brigade During the First Afghan War.

IN THE RANKS OF THE C. I. V by Erskine Childers—With the City Imperial Volunteer Battery (Honourable Artillery Company) in the Second Boer War.

THE BENGAL NATIVE ARMY by F. G. Cardew—An Invaluable Reference Resource.

THE 7TH (QUEEN'S OWN) HUSSARS: Volume 4—1688-1914 by C. R. B. Barrett—Uniforms, Equipment, Weapons, Traditions, the Services of Notable Officers and Men & the Appendices to All Volumes—Volume 4: 1688-1914.

THE SWORD OF THE CROWN by Eric W. Sheppard—A History of the British Army to 1914.

THE 7TH (QUEEN'S OWN) HUSSARS: Volume 3—1818-1914 by C. R. B. Barrett—On Campaign During the Canadian Rebellion, the Indian Mutiny, the Sudan, Matabeleland, Mashonaland and the Boer War Volume 3: 1818-1914.

THE KHARTOUM CAMPAIGN by Bennet Burleigh—A Special Correspondent's View of the Reconquest of the Sudan by British and Egyptian Forces under Kitchener—1898.

EL PUCHERO by Richard McSherry—The Letters of a Surgeon of Volunteers During Scott's Campaign of the American-Mexican War 1847-1848.

RIFLEMAN SAHIB by E. Maude—The Recollections of an Officer of the Bombay Rifles During the Southern Mahratta Campaign, Second Sikh War, Persian Campaign and Indian Mutiny.

THE KING'S HUSSAR by Edwin Mole—The Recollections of a 14th (King's) Hussar During the Victorian Era.

JOHN COMPANY'S CAVALRYMAN by William Johnson—The Experiences of a British Soldier in the Crimea, the Persian Campaign and the Indian Mutiny.

COLENSO & DURNFORD'S ZULU WAR by Frances E. Colenso & Edward Durnford—The first and possibly the most important history of the Zulu War.

U. S. DRAGOON by Samuel E. Chamberlain—Experiences in the Mexican War 1846-48 and on the South Western Frontier.

LEONAUR

ALSO FROM LEONAUR
AVAILABLE IN SOFTCOVER OR HARDCOVER WITH DUST JACKET

ZULU:1879 by D.C.F. Moodie & the Leonaur Editors—The Anglo-Zulu War of 1879 from contemporary sources: First Hand Accounts, Interviews, Dispatches, Official Documents & Newspaper Reports.

THE RED DRAGOON by W.J. Adams—With the 7th Dragoon Guards in the Cape of Good Hope against the Boers & the Kaffir tribes during the 'war of the axe' 1843-48'.

THE RECOLLECTIONS OF SKINNER OF SKINNER'S HORSE by James Skinner—James Skinner and his 'Yellow Boys' Irregular cavalry in the wars of India between the British, Mahratta, Rajput, Mogul, Sikh & Pindarree Forces.

A CAVALRY OFFICER DURING THE SEPOY REVOLT by A. R. D. Mackenzie—Experiences with the 3rd Bengal Light Cavalry, the Guides and Sikh Irregular Cavalry from the outbreak to Delhi and Lucknow.

A NORFOLK SOLDIER IN THE FIRST SIKH WAR by J W Baldwin—Experiences of a private of H.M. 9th Regiment of Foot in the battles for the Punjab, India 1845-6.

TOMMY ATKINS' WAR STORIES: 14 FIRST HAND ACCOUNTS—Fourteen first hand accounts from the ranks of the British Army during Queen Victoria's Empire.

THE WATERLOO LETTERS by H. T. Siborne—Accounts of the Battle by British Officers for its Foremost Historian.

NEY: GENERAL OF CAVALRY VOLUME 1—1769-1799 by Antoine Bulos—The Early Career of a Marshal of the First Empire.

NEY: MARSHAL OF FRANCE VOLUME 2—1799-1805 by Antoine Bulos—The Early Career of a Marshal of the First Empire.

AIDE-DE-CAMP TO NAPOLEON by Philippe-Paul de Ségur—For anyone interested in the Napoleonic Wars this book, written by one who was intimate with the strategies and machinations of the Emperor, will be essential reading.

TWILIGHT OF EMPIRE by Sir Thomas Ussher & Sir George Cockburn—Two accounts of Napoleon's Journeys in Exile to Elba and St. Helena: Narrative of Events by Sir Thomas Ussher & Napoleon's Last Voyage: Extract of a diary by Sir George Cockburn.

PRIVATE WHEELER by William Wheeler—The letters of a soldier of the 51st Light Infantry during the Peninsular War & at Waterloo.

LEONAUR

ALSO FROM LEONAUR
AVAILABLE IN SOFTCOVER OR HARDCOVER WITH DUST JACKET

OFFICERS & GENTLEMEN *by Peter Hawker & William Graham*—Two Accounts of British Officers During the Peninsula War: Officer of Light Dragoons by Peter Hawker & Campaign in Portugal and Spain by William Graham .

THE WALCHEREN EXPEDITION *by Anonymous*—The Experiences of a British Officer of the 81st Regt. During the Campaign in the Low Countries of 1809.

LADIES OF WATERLOO *by Charlotte A. Eaton, Magdalene de Lancey & Juana Smith*—The Experiences of Three Women During the Campaign of 1815: Waterloo Days by Charlotte A. Eaton, A Week at Waterloo by Magdalene de Lancey & Juana's Story by Juana Smith.

JOURNAL OF AN OFFICER IN THE KING'S GERMAN LEGION *by John Frederick Hering*—Recollections of Campaigning During the Napoleonic Wars.

JOURNAL OF AN ARMY SURGEON IN THE PENINSULAR WAR *by Charles Boutflower*—The Recollections of a British Army Medical Man on Campaign During the Napoleonic Wars.

ON CAMPAIGN WITH MOORE AND WELLINGTON *by Anthony Hamilton*—The Experiences of a Soldier of the 43rd Regiment During the Peninsular War.

THE ROAD TO AUSTERLITZ *by R. G. Burton*—Napoleon's Campaign of 1805.

SOLDIERS OF NAPOLEON *by A. J. Doisy De Villargennes & Arthur Chuquet*—The Experiences of the Men of the French First Empire: Under the Eagles by A. J. Doisy De Villargennes & Voices of 1812 by Arthur Chuquet .

INVASION OF FRANCE, 1814 *by F. W. O. Maycock*—The Final Battles of the Napoleonic First Empire.

LEIPZIG—A CONFLICT OF TITANS *by Frederic Shoberl*—A Personal Experience of the 'Battle of the Nations' During the Napoleonic Wars, October 14th-19th, 1813.

SLASHERS *by Charles Cadell*—The Campaigns of the 28th Regiment of Foot During the Napoleonic Wars by a Serving Officer.

BATTLE IMPERIAL *by Charles William Vane*—The Campaigns in Germany & France for the Defeat of Napoleon 1813-1814.

SWIFT & BOLD *by Gibbes Rigaud*—The 60th Rifles During the Peninsula War.

LEONAUR

ALSO FROM LEONAUR
AVAILABLE IN SOFTCOVER OR HARDCOVER WITH DUST JACKET

COLBORNE: A SINGULAR TALENT FOR WAR *by John Colborne*—The Napoleonic Wars Career of One of Wellington's Most Highly Valued Officers in Egypt, Holland, Italy, the Peninsula and at Waterloo.

NAPOLEON'S RUSSIAN CAMPAIGN *by Philippe Henri de Segur*—The Invasion, Battles and Retreat by an Aide-de-Camp on the Emperor's Staff.

WITH THE LIGHT DIVISION *by John H. Cooke*—The Experiences of an Officer of the 43rd Light Infantry in the Peninsula and South of France During the Napoleonic Wars.

WELLINGTON AND THE PYRENEES CAMPAIGN VOLUME I: FROM VITORIA TO THE BIDASSOA *by F. C. Beatson*—The final phase of the campaign in the Iberian Peninsula.

WELLINGTON AND THE INVASION OF FRANCE VOLUME II: THE BIDASSOA TO THE BATTLE OF THE NIVELLE *by F. C. Beatson*—The final phase of the campaign in the Iberian Peninsula.

WELLINGTON AND THE FALL OF FRANCE VOLUME III: THE GAVES AND THE BATTLE OF ORTHEZ *by F. C. Beatson*—The final phase of the campaign in the Iberian Peninsula.

NAPOLEON'S IMPERIAL GUARD: FROM MARENGO TO WATERLOO *by J. T. Headley*—The story of Napoleon's Imperial Guard and the men who commanded them.

BATTLES & SIEGES OF THE PENINSULAR WAR *by W. H. Fitchett*—Corunna, Busaco, Albuera, Ciudad Rodrigo, Badajos, Salamanca, San Sebastian & Others.

SERGEANT GUILLEMARD: THE MAN WHO SHOT NELSON? *by Robert Guillemard*—A Soldier of the Infantry of the French Army of Napoleon on Campaign Throughout Europe.

WITH THE GUARDS ACROSS THE PYRENEES *by Robert Batty*—The Experiences of a British Officer of Wellington's Army During the Battles for the Fall of Napoleonic France, 1813 .

A STAFF OFFICER IN THE PENINSULA *by E. W. Buckham*—An Officer of the British Staff Corps Cavalry During the Peninsula Campaign of the Napoleonic Wars.

THE LEIPZIG CAMPAIGN: 1813—NAPOLEON AND THE "BATTLE OF THE NATIONS" *by F. N. Maude*—Colonel Maude's analysis of Napoleon's campaign of 1813 around Leipzig.

LEONAUR

ALSO FROM LEONAUR
AVAILABLE IN SOFTCOVER OR HARDCOVER WITH DUST JACKET

THE RELUCTANT REBEL by *William G. Stevenson*—A young Kentuckian's experiences in the Confederate Infantry & Cavalry during the American Civil War..

BOOTS AND SADDLES by *Elizabeth B. Custer*—The experiences of General Custer's Wife on the Western Plains.

FANNIE BEERS' CIVIL WAR by *Fannie A. Beers*—A Confederate Lady's Experiences of Nursing During the Campaigns & Battles of the American Civil War.

LADY SALE'S AFGHANISTAN by *Florentia Sale*—An Indomitable Victorian Lady's Account of the Retreat from Kabul During the First Afghan War.

THE TWO WARS OF MRS DUBERLY by *Frances Isabella Duberly*—An Intrepid Victorian Lady's Experience of the Crimea and Indian Mutiny.

THE REBELLIOUS DUCHESS by *Paul F. S. Dermoncourt*—The Adventures of the Duchess of Berri and Her Attempt to Overthrow French Monarchy.

LADIES OF WATERLOO by *Charlotte A. Eaton, Magdalene de Lancey & Juana Smith*—The Experiences of Three Women During the Campaign of 1815: Waterloo Days by Charlotte A. Eaton, A Week at Waterloo by Magdalene de Lancey & Juana's Story by Juana Smith.

TWO YEARS BEFORE THE MAST by *Richard Henry Dana. Jr.*—The account of one young man's experiences serving on board a sailing brig—the Penelope—bound for California, between the years1834-36.

A SAILOR OF KING GEORGE by *Frederick Hoffman*—From Midshipman to Captain—Recollections of War at Sea in the Napoleonic Age 1793-1815.

LORDS OF THE SEA by *A. T. Mahan*—Great Captains of the Royal Navy During the Age of Sail.

COGGESHALL'S VOYAGES: VOLUME 1 by *George Coggeshall*—The Recollections of an American Schooner Captain.

COGGESHALL'S VOYAGES: VOLUME 2 by *George Coggeshall*—The Recollections of an American Schooner Captain.

TWILIGHT OF EMPIRE by *Sir Thomas Ussher & Sir George Cockburn*—Two accounts of Napoleon's Journeys in Exile to Elba and St. Helena: Narrative of Events by Sir Thomas Ussher & Napoleon's Last Voyage: Extract of a diary by Sir George Cockburn.

www.ingramcontent.com/pod-product-compliance
Lightning Source LLC
Chambersburg PA
CBHW030931150426
42812CB00064B/2761/J